D1052898

KING RICHARD

KING RICHARD

NIXON AND WATERGATE
An American Tragedy

Michael Dobbs

 ALFRED A. KNOPF | NEW YORK | 2021

THIS IS A BORZOI BOOK
PUBLISHED BY ALFRED A. KNOPF

Copyright © 2021 by Michael Dobbs

All rights reserved. Published in the United States by Alfred A. Knopf,
a division of Penguin Random House LLC, New York, and distributed in Canada
by Penguin Random House Canada Limited, Toronto.

www.aaknopf.com

Knopf, Borzoi Books, and the colophon
are registered trademarks of Penguin Random House LLC.

Library of Congress Cataloging-in-Publication Data
Names: Dobbs, Michael, [date] author.
Title: King Richard : Nixon and Watergate—an American tragedy / Michael Dobbs.
Description: First edition. | New York : Alfred A. Knopf, 2021. |
"THIS IS BORZOI BOOK PUBLISHED BY ALFRED A. KNOPF" |
Includes bibliographical references and index.
Identifiers: LCCN 2020028534 (print) | LCCN 2020028535 (ebook) |
ISBN 9780385350099 (hardcover) | ISBN 9780385350105 (epub)
Subjects: LCSH: Nixon, Richard M. (Richard Milhous), 1913–1994. |
Watergate Affair, 1972–1974. | United States—Politics and government—1969–1974.
Classification: LCC E860 .D643 2021 (print) | LCC E860 (ebook) | DDC 973.924092—dc23
LC record available at https://lccn.loc.gov/2020028534
LC ebook record available at https://lccn.loc.gov/2020028535

Jacket photograph by Don Carl Steffen / Gamma-Rapho / Getty Images
Jacket design by Tyler Comrie

Manufactured in the United States of America
First Edition

For my brothers:

Geoffrey, Peter, and Christopher

CONTENTS

DRAMATIS PERSONAE

FAMILY
Richard Nixon.............................. President of the United States
Pat Nixon..................................... His wife
Tricia and Julie........................... His daughters
Rose Mary Woods .... His secretary
Manolo Sanchez........................... His valet
King Timahoe .... His dog
Charles "Bebe" Rebozo .... His friend
Robert Abplanalp .... His friend

WHITE HOUSE
H. R. "Bob" Haldeman................ Chief of staff
John Ehrlichman .... Domestic policy adviser
Charles "Chuck" Colson............. Special counsel
Henry Kissinger........................... National security adviser
Alexander Haig............................ Deputy national security adviser
Ronald Ziegler .... Press spokesman
John Dean..................................... White House counsel
Maureen Dean .... His wife
John "Jack" Caulfield................... Aide to Dean
Alexander Butterfield................... Deputy to Haldeman
Lawrence Higby........................... Aide to Haldeman
Gordon Strachan .... Aide to Haldeman
Spiro Agnew................................. Vice president of the United States
William Rogers .... Secretary of state
Steve Bull .... Aide to Nixon

Howard Hunt .... Security consultant/plumber
Ray Price .... Speechwriter
William Safire .... Speechwriter
Patrick Buchanan .... Speechwriter

COMMITTEE TO RE-ELECT THE PRESIDENT
John Mitchell .... Director
Martha Mitchell .... His wife
Jeb Magruder .... Deputy director
Gail Magruder .... His wife
Maurice Stans .... Finance chairman
Gordon Liddy .... Leader of Watergate break-in team
James McCord .... Security consultant
Frederick LaRue .... Aide to Mitchell
Robert Reisner .... Aide to Magruder
Paul O'Brien .... Counsel
Anthony Ulasewicz .... Private detective

INVESTIGATORS
John Sirica .... Chief judge of U.S. District Court
Patrick Gray .... Acting FBI director
Mark Felt .... Deputy FBI director
Richard Kleindienst .... Attorney general
Henry Petersen .... Assistant attorney general
Elliot Richardson .... Succeeded Kleindienst as
attorney general
Earl Silbert .... Watergate prosecutor
Seymour Glanzer .... Watergate prosecutor
Sam Ervin .... Chairman, Senate Watergate
Select Committee
Howard Baker .... Deputy chairman
Sam Dash .... Majority counsel
Scott Armstrong .... Democratic staffer
Donald Sanders .... Republican staffer
Matthew Byrne .... Judge in Ellsberg trial

LAWYERS

Charles Shaffer .... Lawyer for Dean
Robert McCandless .... Lawyer for Dean
William Bittman .... Lawyer for Hunt
Richard Moore .... Lawyer for Nixon
Chapman Rose .... Lawyer for Nixon
Len Garment .... Lawyer for Nixon

REPORTERS

Carl Bernstein .... *Washington Post* reporter
Bob Woodward .... *Washington Post* reporter
Helen Thomas .... UPI reporter, friend of
                        Martha Mitchell
Theodore White .... Author, *The Making of the President*
Robert Jackson .... *Los Angeles Times* reporter
R. W. "Johnny" Apple .... *New York Times* reporter

OTHERS

Le Duc Tho .... North Vietnamese negotiator
Nguyen Van Thieu .... South Vietnamese president
Daniel Ellsberg .... Leaker of Pentagon Papers
Robinson Risner .... Prisoner of war
Jeremiah Denton .... Prisoner of war
Anna Chennault .... Republican "Dragon Lady";
                        Watergate resident

PROLOGUE

πρόλογος—prólogos

introduction to a play or novel

———————————

It doesn't have an on-and-off switch.

—ALEXANDER BUTTERFIELD
to President Nixon, February 16, 1971

I t had been "one helluva show." The Grieg piano concerto, in particular, had been a revelation. Van Cliburn was superb: no one could match his virtuosity. Of course, most of the Republican high rollers who feasted on colonial roast duckling and plantation pineapple in their tuxedos and long dresses—"clowns," in Richard Nixon's estimation—"did not know what the hell was going on." But the president had thoroughly enjoyed both the music and the political symbolism of the evening.

His arrival at the Kennedy Center had been heralded with "ruffles and flourishes" from sixteen military trumpeters in full Ruritanian regalia. The orchestras at each of the three inaugural concerts had blared out "Hail to the Chief" as he entered the presidential box, as per an "action memo" from his chief of staff, H. R. "Bob" Haldeman. Best of all, he had succeeded in "sticking it to Washington" by excluding the dreary, politically correct National Symphony Orchestra from the festivities. Instead, he had brought the outspokenly conservative Eugene Ormandy down from Philadelphia to conduct the rousing finale to a wonderful event.

The clanging church bells and simulated cannons of Tchaikovsky's *1812 Overture* were still reverberating in Nixon's ears as he said good night to the evening's guest of honor, Mamie Eisenhower, at the front door of the White House. He took the mirror-paneled elevator to the residence on the second floor and then headed left through a succession of grand hallways lined with books and paintings to his private den in the far corner of the mansion. This was the Lincoln Sitting Room, the smallest room in the White House and his personal favorite. The cozy Victorian parlor was the place where he did his best thinking and writing, scribbling his ideas onto yellow legal pads to the booming strains of *Victory at Sea*. He settled into his plush Louis XV–style armchair, a birthday present from his wife Pat, resting his feet on the matching ottoman. A black-and-white print of the Lincoln family hung on the wall above his head, next to the window, which provided a perfect picture frame for the floodlit Washington Monument.

Snug in his sanctuary, Nixon gazed into a crackling fire set by his personal valet, Manuel "Manolo" Sanchez. He was still dressed in the tuxedo he had worn to the Kennedy Center, offset by black bow tie and gleaming presidential cuff links. His hair, dark brown with splotches of gray, was carefully brushed back, a sartorial choice that emphasized his receding hairline and protruding widow's peak. His already thick jowls had filled out even more during his first four years in office. Combined with his darting eyes, they gave him a tortured look, as if he were perpetually brooding over past slights and disappointments. The upturned, slightly twisted nose, on the other hand, suggested a bumbling American everyman, like Walter Matthau in a goofy Hollywood comedy. Assembled together, it was a face that was neither handsome nor ugly, distinguished nor plebeian. But it was certainly memorable.

It was already past midnight, but the thirty-seventh president of the United States had no desire to sleep. In less than twelve hours, at noon, he would be appearing on the steps of the Capitol to deliver his second inaugural address. He was still tinkering obsessively with the text. "As I stand in this place so hallowed by history, I think of others who have stood here before me," read one of his last-minute tweaks. Another note reflected his determination to scale back the Great Society that his Democratic predecessor, Lyndon Johnson, had devoted so much energy to constructing: "our goal for government—to take less *from* people so that people can do *more* for *themselves*."

Nixon read through the speech once more, fountain pen in hand, marking the passages he wished to emphasize in dark blue ink. He underlined some phrases and scratched in a few additions, until the text resembled a heavily annotated sheet of music. He had issued strict instructions that the speech not go "a word over 1200 words." As with

*Nixon at work on his yellow legal pad in his favorite room
in the White House, the Lincoln Sitting Room. His conversations on
the telephone by his left shoulder were recorded automatically.*

so many of his peremptory commands, the order had gone unfulfilled,
largely due to his own contradictory impulses. He had planned to emulate Abraham Lincoln—who had used just 701 words for his second
inaugural address, one of the most memorable in American history—
but there was too much he wanted to say. In the end, he had settled for
a speech of 1,800 words, still reasonably short by modern-day presidential standards. He calculated that it would take sixteen minutes to
deliver, including applause.

———————

As he prepared to take the oath of office for the second time, the son of the struggling Quaker grocer had many reasons to celebrate, despite his perpetually restless nature. He had been reelected by the largest margin of popular votes of any president in the nearly two-hundred-year history of the Republic. He had won the grudging respect of the foreign policy crowd—that despised band of elitist snobs—for the geostrategic brilliance of his opening to China. Most gratifying of all, he was on the cusp of concluding a peace agreement with the Communist government of North Vietnam, heralding an end to a war that had cost the lives of fifty-eight thousand Americans and countless Vietnamese. Four years previously, in his first inaugural address, he had described the "title of peacemaker" as "the greatest honor history can bestow." The road to peace had been long and bloody, but the prize was finally within his grasp. The initialing of the peace accords was set for January 23, just three days away, in Paris.

Of course, the Nixon haters were still out in force. They had seized on the bizarre scandal spawned by the attempted bugging of Democratic Party headquarters in the Watergate office building back in June 1972—"a third-rate burglary attempt," the White House spokesman Ron Ziegler had termed it—to cast a shadow over his smashing reelection victory. There had been sensational stories in the press alleging a link between the White House and the hapless band of Cubans caught in the act of breaking in to the Watergate. But the trail seemed to be petering out. The burglars were refusing to provide the names of the mysterious higher-ups who had set the plot in motion. Important witnesses had developed amnesia. Even *The Washington Post,* which had covered the scandal most aggressively from the beginning, was running out of leads to pursue. A special inaugural section of the newspaper titled "The Nixon Years" did not contain a single mention of the dreaded word "Watergate."

Unable to sleep, and excited by the prospect of four more years in the White House, Nixon was eager to share the moment with "the son I never had." He lifted the receiver of the telephone on the polished mahogany coffee table beside him and was instantly connected to an operator.

"Mr. Colson, please."

The political operative known around Washington for his boast that "I would walk over my own grandmother" to ensure Nixon's reelection came on the line less than a minute later, at 1:04 a.m.

"Yes, sir, Mr. President." Despite the late hour, Chuck Colson managed to sound chipper and eager to please. He had evidently been waiting for the call.

"Well, how'd you like the evening?"

Nixon cut off his aide before he could answer the question. He wanted Colson to know that he had practiced the Grieg piano piece as a sophomore in high school, back in California, at a time when he had been "quite advanced in music." He had never heard it performed better. In the hands of a less skillful conductor, the orchestra could easily have overwhelmed the piano. But Ormandy was superb. He was a fantastic musician and a fantastic man. Word had reached the president that the Hungarian-born maestro had told dissident members of his orchestra—"goddamn left-wingers"—to go to hell when they asked to be excused from the concert as a protest against the Vietnam War.

"Marvelous, that's marvelous," enthused Colson.

Formally, Colson had the title of special counsel, but this concealed his true function in the White House, which was to serve as Nixon's chief political adviser and confidant. The self-described "hatchet man" was accustomed to such late-night calls, which he considered a form of "handholding." One of his responsibilities was to help Nixon deal with his chronic insomnia and talk himself to sleep. A few months earlier, he had received a 1:00 a.m. call from Camp David, the president's weekend retreat. Nixon had just returned from Moscow. It was obvious he had been drinking, in addition to taking sleeping pills to fight jet lag. He slurred his words so badly that he was practically incomprehensible. In the middle of the telephone conversation, he passed out. Worried that the president might have injured himself or could even be dead, Colson tried desperately to get back through to Camp David. He could not make a call on his own phone, because the party on the other end—Nixon—had not hung up. Rushing out into the night, he woke up a neighbor and managed to reach Manolo Sanchez, who went to investigate. After a few minutes, the valet reported back: the commander in chief was snoring peacefully.

This time, Colson had no difficulty understanding his boss. Both men viewed the inaugural festivities as an opportunity to promote a new conservative majority in the country that had cleaved off great chunks of the old Democratic coalition. They had already made inroads into the Democratic power base in the Old South by appealing to white voters alarmed by the gains of the civil rights movement. Colson had now set his sights on the labor unions, allied traditionally with the Democrats. He wanted to bring pro-Nixon union leaders to the front of the presidential reviewing stand on Pennsylvania Avenue one by one so they could stand alongside the president as he took the salute at the parade. It would be a visible demonstration of a seismic shift in American politics. Soon, the Democrats would be left with just the blacks, the poor, the intellectuals, and a "lavender shirt mob" composed of "homos and queers."

Nixon could see the value of giving the defectors their moment in front of the television cameras. Those two and a half hours on the reviewing stand could be mined for "a hell of a lot of gold." But he was worried about being caught chatting with a supporter when he should be saluting the flags carried aloft by the marching bands.

"You see, I've got to stop every two minutes to put my hand on my heart as the flag goes by," he reminded Colson, his deep baritone voice tinged with irritation. He wanted to make sure that actual conversation was kept to a minimum. Wives must definitely be excluded.

Colson reassured him. "We won't do too much of it, but I think a little bit of it would be a nice touch . . . I believe that the New Majority is there, Mr. President. I really do."

The conversation turned to Nixon's controversial decision to launch a massive bombing campaign against North Vietnam over Christmas. For eleven tension-filled days, waves of American B-52s supported by thousands of tactical aircraft had pounded North Vietnamese ports and airfields and power plants, as well as air defenses around Hanoi. The North Vietnamese had earlier agreed to release all American prisoners of war and permit the anti-Communist South Vietnamese leader, Nguyen Van Thieu, to remain at least temporarily in office. They refused to make further substantive concessions but did allow some token modifications to the peace agreement that were sufficient for Nixon to claim he had achieved his goal of negotiating a "peace with honor." His toughness had been vindicated. The huge sacrifices of the last four years, including a further twenty-one thousand American lives, had been justified. That, at least, was how Nixon saw it.

It had not been easy. Even his national security adviser, Henry Kissinger, had wavered toward the end beneath a firestorm of criticism of the bombing from Congress and the media. Had Nixon given in to the critics, "the goddamn war" would have continued for months if not years, and thousands more Americans would have been killed. There was one outstanding problem: that "son of a bitch Thieu" was threatening to boycott the signing ceremony in Paris because he mistrusted Communist promises of an end to hostilities. But Nixon believed that his South Vietnamese ally would cave when threatened with a cutoff in American aid. Thieu was not about to "commit suicide."

"We go ahead and make our deal," he told Colson. "We sink Thieu and everybody says, 'Thank God [Nixon] was a tough son of a bitch on both sides.' The hell with them."

"That's right," Colson chimed in. "We accomplished our objectives."

Once "peace with honor" was achieved, Nixon continued, it would be Colson's job to stick it to the antiwar people, both on Capitol Hill and in the country. "We just pour it right to 'em."

It was the kind of assignment the hatchet man relished. A bespectacled former marine captain with a mischievous grin, Colson shared the president's disdain for the "East Coast elite," even though he was himself the product of a top New England prep school. He liked to boast that he had turned down a full scholarship to Harvard, choosing instead to attend slightly less prestigious Brown University, where he became a champion debater and leader of the Young Republicans. He was proud of his reputation for political ruthlessness, summed up by the Teddy Roosevelt quotation he kept in the den of his house: "When you've got 'em by the balls, their hearts and minds will follow." The president knew he could rely on Colson to carry out his orders without question—unlike some other aides, who would prevaricate when asked to do something that seemed impractical or illegal. He had put Colson in charge of "dirty tricks," such as tracking down photographs of Edward

Kennedy dancing with starlets or harassing the leakers of secret government documents. He praised his forty-two-year-old assistant for having "the balls of a brass monkey." For Nixon, Colson was "Mr. Can-Do."

Although the hour was late, Nixon wanted to give his most appreciative audience a preview of his inaugural address. He flicked through the large-font, double-spaced copy he had been marking up and began reading his favorite portions aloud.

"The stuff on the world is good. I mean, it's very strong," the president enthused. "*The time has passed when America will make every other nation's conflict our own or make other nations' future our responsibility or presume to tell the people of other nations how to manage their own affairs* . . . Get the point?"

"Yes, sir. Yes, sir."

"*Abroad and at home, the time has come to turn away from the condescending policies of paternalism, of Washington knows best.*"

"Oh, great."

"This is the key line. *Let us measure what we will do for others by what they will do for themselves.*"

"Mmmmm. Beautiful." Colson emitted a moan of pleasure down the phone line.

The president rushed on toward his peroration.

"*Let each of us remember that America was built not by government but by people, not by welfare but by work, not by shirking responsibility but seeking responsibility.*"

"Oh, Jesus!"

"*In the challenges we face together, let each of us ask not just how can government help, but how can I help.*"

"Magnificent. Just magnificent, Mr. President. That is the Nixon legacy, in my humble judgment." The era of the 1960s, when Americans looked to government to solve all their problems, was definitively over.

The two men turned to the practical question of building support for Nixon's Vietnam policy in the weeks that followed. Colson confidently expected the furor over the Christmas bombing to be forgotten as soon as the peace agreement was signed. He rattled off a stream of opinion polls to bolster his argument that the antiwar crowd was out on a "big limb" that was about to get "sawed off."

"The important thing to remember, Mr. President, is that the country does not buy a lot of the crap that they're fed. Obviously the American people have an uncomfortable sense about the bombings and wish they had not taken place. But sixty-seven [percent] do not believe that we deliberately bombed hospitals or civilian targets."

"Good God," Nixon exploded. "When you think of what Eisenhower did in World War II. I mean, he decimated cities."

"So did Truman."

"Why did Truman drop the atomic bomb? Not because he wanted to demolish cities. Because he wanted to end the war. Why did Eisenhower bomb the shit out of the cities of North Korea?"

"That's right."

"And that's what ended the war, you know."

Colson could not wait to "slash the bejusus" out of the Nixon critics and the "jackasses" in Congress who had proposed holding up funding for the war.

"It's treasonable," Nixon exclaimed.

"Totally treasonable," Colson agreed. "We'll cut the bastards right to the bone."

In the meantime, he had a nugget of good news to relay. His campaign against *The Washington Post* for its aggressive coverage of Watergate was showing gratifying results. He had orchestrated challenges to the renewal of the parent company's lucrative television licenses in Florida. Its stock price had plummeted by more than 25 percent in the last two weeks alone. Nervous investors were demanding the firing of the editor, Ben Bradlee. Colson had made clear that the price for calling off his attack dogs was "a complete change of management." To show good faith, the *Post* would be required to publish "a few obviously friendly editorials on how well the President is handling the Vietnam War" and put "the Watergate case back inside the paper where it belongs instead of blasting it across the front pages."

Colson was delighted to inform Nixon that the economy was doing great and everybody's fortunes were up except those of the *Post*.

"Oddly enough, their stock has dropped three more points since I told you last. It's now $28."

"That's too damn bad," the president replied sarcastically.

"Isn't that a shame? It was $38 in December and had record earnings, and it's dropped ten points."

"Keep 'em busy," Nixon instructed.

It was nearly 2:00 a.m., finally time to go to bed. The president had to be up early the next morning for the Inauguration Day ceremonies. He said good night to his special counsel and hung up the phone. Two floors below, in a locked cabinet in the West Wing basement, a Uher 4000 reel-to-reel tape recorder stopped whirring.

The tape recorders in room WT-1 were activated by an ingenious system of electronic signals that did not require the pushing of buttons. The Secret Service logged the president's movements around the White House. Aides could determine his location from panels of twinkling bulbs hanging above their desks, similar to the device used in English country homes to summon servants. The First Family Locator system powered up individual tape recorders, depending on the room Nixon had just entered. The Uher machine hooked up to the telephone in the Lincoln Sitting Room—extension 586—had switched itself on automatically after Nixon returned to the residence from the Kennedy Center. When he picked up the receiver to call Colson, the voltage on the line dropped. This was the signal to start recording. Placing the phone on its cradle produced a small spike in the voltage that turned off the recorder.

The taping system in other parts of the complex depended on a combination of locator devices and voice activation. The president had to be physically present in the Oval Office or his hideaway retreat in the Executive Office Building next door for the designated tape machine to power up. The recorder switched itself on whenever Nixon, or one of his aides or visitors, began to speak. It switched itself off after fifteen seconds of silence.

When first elected president, Nixon had recoiled from the very idea of a recording system. Informed that his predecessor, Lyndon Johnson, had routinely taped many of his telephone calls, he ordered that the equipment be removed, along with other LBJ gadgets, such as a triple-screen television monitoring system. But after two years in office, his thoughts turned increasingly to his own place in history. He appreciated Winston Churchill's dictum that "history will be kind to me for I intend to write it myself." Writing the kind of memoir he had in mind—one that would meticulously chronicle his accomplishments, settle scores with his enemies, and put uppity subordinates like Kissinger in their place—required the keeping of an authoritative record. Naturally, this record would be under his complete control. He alone would determine right of access. Apart from a very few trusted aides, no one else would even be aware of its existence.

Initially, he had included a note taker in important meetings, particularly with a foreign leader. The "anecdotalist" was also responsible for including some "color," such as subtle changes of tone or facial expression, what Nixon called "the intangibles." But it was difficult to find people with sufficient literary flair and high enough security clearance who were also completely trustworthy. The introvert president felt that the "scribbling intruders inhibited discussion." He tried to dictate his own notes as soon as a meeting was over but was unable to set aside the necessary time. Another experiment involved stationing an aide outside the room to interview the people he had met. But this was also unsatisfactory, because it produced a skewed account of the conversation, from the point of view of Nixon's interlocutors rather than the president himself. Eventually, at the beginning of 1971, Nixon reverted to the idea he had earlier rejected: taping his meetings and telephone conversations.

He discussed the possibilities with Bob Haldeman, who quickly identified a problem. "You'll never remember to turn it on except when you don't want it. When you do want it, you're always going to be shouting—afterwards, when it's too late—that no one turned it on." That was a tactful way of putting it. Privately he considered the president "far too inept with machinery ever to make a success of a switch system." Pat Nixon liked to joke that her husband had "almost killed himself" as a young man attempting to roller-skate. He was especially inept with tape recorders. He had trouble operating the Dictaphone that he used to record his private thoughts because he could not get the buttons straight. Any system that depended on Nixon to start and stop the recording was likely to fail, in Haldeman's view. The solution, they both agreed, was devices that would switch themselves on whenever Nixon engaged in conversation. They instructed Haldeman's assistant, Alexander Butterfield, to make the necessary arrangements.

To ensure maximum discretion, Butterfield turned to the technical security division of the Secret Service, the agency charged with protecting the president. The supervisor, Alfred Wong, immediately raised objections. His people were responsible for sweeping the White House to eliminate electronic eavesdropping devices, not installing new bugs, even officially sanctioned ones. They were not audio specialists. Wong mistrusted the "suede-shoe operators-hucksters" in the recording industry who boasted that they could guarantee high fidelity under any conditions. He foresaw a host of "environmental problems," such as what might happen if the Secret Service installed a microphone in a table lamp in the Oval Office and the interior decorator wanted to take the lamp out. In that case, "we would have to wrestle him to the ground and get the table lamp back." This was definitely "not a simple job of mixing a few martinis and hoping you can put a microphone in an olive," he told Butterfield.

Butterfield was adamant. The president wanted a taping system. It was up to the Secret Service to create one "as expeditiously as possible." Wong dropped his objections.

The first microphones and recording devices were installed over the long weekend of February 12–15, 1971, while Nixon was away in Florida, relaxing in the sun. Because there was insufficient time to design a state-of-the-art system, Wong instructed his men to use standard electronic equipment lying around their storage rooms. They spent the weekend drilling holes in the presidential desk in the Oval Office and feeding cables through the walls and floorboards. To test the microphones, they took turns sitting behind the presidential desk and holding conversations in different parts of the room. After experimenting with various options, they ended up concealing five microphones in the desk and another two behind lighting sconces on the opposite wall next to the fireplace. The microphones were connected, via mixers and switching devices, to a pair of Sony TC-800B reel-to-reel recorders in a disused telephone cabinet in the basement below. Wong's men secured the steel closet with an iron bar and pick-resistant locks to prevent unauthorized access.

Butterfield demonstrated the Oval Office taping system to Nixon after the president got back from Florida. He explained that the recording devices were linked into the presidential locator board and were activated automatically, by voice. "It doesn't have an on-and-off switch," he informed Nixon proudly.

It was the absence of an on-off switch, not the practice of secret recording, that made Nixon unique. Every American president from FDR onward had made some use of magnetic recording devices first popularized in Germany in the mid-1930s. Angry about being mis-quoted by *The New York Times,* Roosevelt began to record his presiden-tial news conferences in August 1940 after deciding to run for reelection to an unprecedented third term. Technicians installed a single micro-phone in a lamp shade on his Oval Office desk, linked to a "continu-ous film recording machine"—originally developed for the movie industry—that they hid in the basement below. The president activated the bulky machine from a control box in his desk drawer. He stopped using it after he won the election. Truman and Eisenhower both experi-mented with recording press conferences and scraps of private conver-sations but soon abandoned the practice. The first president to tape himself extensively was John F. Kennedy, who made a copious record of the anguished debates with his advisers during the Cuban missile crisis. Kennedy's successor, LBJ, routinely recorded his telephone con-versations, accumulating more than eight hundred hours of material he intended to use for his memoirs.

Like his predecessors, Nixon assumed that the tapes were his private property. After being shown the newly installed microphones in the Oval Office, he again demanded assurances that no one be allowed to listen to the recordings without his authorization. Butterfield assured him that "only five people" on the Secret Service staff were even aware of the existence of the tapes. "They only change the spools. They cannot monitor it."

"Mum's the whole word," Nixon told Butterfield later that morning. He would not be transcribed without permission. There might be times when he would ask Butterfield to transcribe a specific conversation to "correct the record," but the recordings and any transcripts were for him alone.

In accordance with Nixon's wishes, the taping system was expanded over the next fifteen months to include the Cabinet Room, his hide-away office in the Executive Office Building, and his weekend retreat at Camp David in the mountains of Maryland. Taps were also placed on the telephones he used most frequently. With the exception of the recording devices in the Cabinet Room, which were controlled by Butterfield, there were no on-off switches.

The taping system had become so much a part of the daily White House routine that Nixon no longer gave any thought to the fact that he was recording himself. At times, he even forgot which rooms—apart from the Oval Office—were bugged and which were not.

HUBRIS

ὕβρις—húbris

excessive pride, presumption, or arrogance

———————

Hubris became the mark of the Nixon man because hubris was the quality that Nixon admired most.

—CHARLES COLSON

T he Secret Service caught up with Richard Nixon as he emerged from the elevator on the ground floor of the White House, two floors below the private residence. He had come to work a little earlier than usual in order to meet with Henry Kissinger. The national security adviser was about to leave for Paris for a final negotiating session with the North Vietnamese. If all went well, he would initial an agreement to end a war that had lasted almost two decades. As was often the case in the hours leading up to a climactic point in his presidency, Nixon was on edge. He was already worrying about minor details of scheduling and presentation, determined to ensure that his moment of triumph not be sullied.

He walked along the long, red-carpeted corridor, striding past the portraits of former First Ladies and the Map Room, where Franklin D. Roosevelt had charted the course of World War II. A Secret Service man scampered in front of him, opening the twin sets of glass doors that led to the colonnade adjoining the Rose Garden. But instead of heading to the Oval Office, Nixon descended another flight of stairs to the West Wing basement. He strode across West Executive Avenue, the closed-off street that separated the West Wing of the White House from the monstrous neo-Baroque pile of the Executive Office Building. A grand outdoor staircase of twenty-six stone steps, framed by multiple pillars and balconies, brought Nixon to the hideaway office that he used for what he called his "brainwork."

*(Above) Nixon crosses West Executive Avenue from the West Wing
to his private office in the Executive Office Building, or EOB.
(Below) Aerial view of the White House Mansion, the Rose Garden,
the Oval Office, and the West Wing taken from the presidential helicopter
as it landed on the South Lawn. The EOB, where Nixon had
his hideaway, can be seen in the background.*

For decades, the EOB had served as the unloved adjunct of the White House, a place of exile for bureaucrats who were not sufficiently close to the president to command an office in the West Wing. Dubbed "the ugliest building in America" by Mark Twain, it had been built in the aftermath of the Civil War to house a rapidly expanding federal bureaucracy. But it had acquired a sudden prestige as a result of Nixon's decision to use the Oval Office primarily for ceremonial purposes. Obsessed with privacy and solitude, he was determined to escape the hothouse atmosphere of the West Wing and the prying eyes of aides and journalists who were still camped out in the lobby at the beginning of his presidency.

After reviewing various possibilities, he settled on an airy first-floor suite known as EOB 175, with twenty-foot-high ceilings and a patio overlooking the White House. He decorated his study with a selection of gavels from his time presiding over the Senate as vice president, dozens of miniature elephants, the symbol of the Republican Party, footballs, and a prized hole-in-one golf card. A collection of political cartoons celebrating his various election victories, beginning with his trouncing of the "soft on Communism" congressman Jerry Voorhis in California in 1946, adorned the walls of the staff office next door. Hidden behind the bathroom and kitchen, in the mysteriously named room 175½, was a telephone equipment closet used to house a battery of tape recorders connected to microphones drilled into the desk in Nixon's office. The placement of the microphones made it difficult, sometimes impossible, to pick up conversations in other parts of the room.

Prior to moving in, Nixon had demanded that his study be equipped with "a big comfortable chair similar to the one I now have in the Lincoln Sitting Room." His wife, Pat, arranged for a much-loved lounge chair and matching ottoman to be brought down from his Fifth Avenue apartment in New York, where he had worked as a lawyer before assuming the presidency. He also requested "a pretty good bookshelf" where he could place books by the authors he most revered, such as Winston Churchill, Abraham Lincoln, and Charles de Gaulle. For relaxation, he turned to biographies of Theodore Roosevelt, political thrillers by writers like Allen Drury, and the World War II novels of Herman Wouk, which he kept on his desk.

Nixon permitted his alter ego, Colson, to move in to a neighboring suite but kept other top aides, including Haldeman, Kissinger, and his press secretary, Ron Ziegler, a safe distance away in the West Wing. They would come only when summoned.

A bodyguard logged the arrival of "Searchlight"—Nixon's Secret Service code name—in the Executive Office Building at 7:56 a.m. on Monday, January 22. It was the first full working day of his second presidential term. As he stepped into his private office, he was greeted by his valet, Manolo. After ten years in Nixon's service, Manolo had become accustomed to his routines. Breakfast usually consisted of cold wheat germ cereal, orange juice, coffee, and glass of skim milk, served in his bedroom. After breakfast, Nixon typically ran in place for a few minutes to get his adrenaline going. He had already picked out what he was going to wear the night before, a dark suit, white shirt, and sober tie. On this particular morning, he delayed washing up until arriving in his EOB suite. The voice-activated Sony TC-800B tape machine began rolling as he issued a gruff instruction to Manolo to fetch his bathrobe.

Kissinger poked his head around the heavy oak doors twenty minutes later. Nixon had been sitting in his armchair dictating a letter to the evangelist Billy Graham about the Sunday church service in the White

Nixon with Kissinger in his hideaway office in the Executive Office Building. A paging device for summoning aides is visible beside the telephone on the president's desk, at bottom right, alongside one of Nixon's miniature elephants.

House. He gestured to Kissinger to pull up a chair opposite him. "All set for your trip?" he asked. Kissinger assured him that the peace treaty would be initialed by Tuesday evening, in time for Nixon's planned television broadcast. He had been shuttling back and forth between Washington and Paris for three and a half years. The first few meetings with the North Vietnamese had taken place in complete secrecy, surrounded by the kind of mystery and intrigue including disguises, false identities, and lies about his schedule that Kissinger relished. It was only after Nixon publicly revealed the existence of a back channel to Hanoi in January 1972 that reporters finally caught up with the man they came to call "Super K."

After Kissinger left the room, Nixon noticed with irritation that a key phrase was missing from the draft TV speech. He wanted to tell the American people that "peace with honor" had finally been achieved. But the speechwriters had omitted the phrase, perhaps because those same three words had been used by Neville Chamberlain to describe his ill-fated negotiations with Adolf Hitler at Munich, prior to World War II. Nixon, by contrast, associated the phrase with one of his political heroes, Woodrow Wilson, and the end of World War I. He reached Kissinger as he was being driven to Andrews Air Force Base in a White House limousine. The national security adviser assured him that the missing words would be restored. "It must be a typing thing."

The president was still fuming over the protests that had been organized to coincide with his second inaugural, particularly a peace rally at the National Cathedral attended by members of the Kennedy family. He shared his contempt for the antiwar crowd in a telephone call with Kissinger's former deputy, Alexander Haig, now back at the Pentagon as vice chief of staff of the army. Nixon relished the thought that his political enemies "must be gnashing their goddamn teeth" over the peace agreement.

"They will, of course, say that we didn't get anything out of it," said Nixon, referring to the criticism of the Christmas bombing campaign. "We didn't get anything out of waiting since October, we could have gotten it then, it wasn't worth fighting for four years, it isn't going to last, it's a bad peace, and so forth. I don't think that's going to wash with most people. Whaddya think?"

The newly promoted four-star general had recently emerged as the voice of the hard-liners on the National Security Council. He had opposed a framework peace deal negotiated by Kissinger back in October that would have ended the war on terms very similar to those embraced by Nixon three months later. He was happy to assure his commander in chief that he had been right to take a tough line with Hanoi.

"I don't think it washes at all."

"They were really a pitiful bunch during the inauguration, squealing around," the president continued. "They are going to commit suicide, some of these bastards, you know. Really, physically, when they don't have something to hate. Isn't that it?"

"That's exactly it."

"They're really so frustrated. They hate the country. They hate themselves. And that's what it's really about. It isn't just war. It's everything."

The time had come for his daily meeting with his chief of staff, a stream of consciousness affair guaranteed to produce a stream of "action memos," ranging from the vital to the trivial, that coursed through the many tributaries of the administration. Nixon reached out to a discreet white box, about the size of a cigarette pack, next to the telephone on his desk. Four push buttons were mounted on top. He pressed the first button, marked "H," once, causing a loud bell to ring in Haldeman's office down the corridor from the Oval Office. This was the signal for the former advertising executive to drop whatever he was doing and hurry into his master's presence. There was no way of accidentally missing the bell, which was programmed to keep on ringing until either Haldeman or his secretary physically turned it off. The chief of staff appeared in EOB 175 a few minutes later.

With his closely cropped hair, lean physique, sober ties, and crisp white shirt, Harry Robbins "Bob" Haldeman looked like an advertisement for a management training school. Around the White House, he was known as "the Prussian"—a reference to his German ancestry but, even more significantly, to his reputation as a disciplinarian. "From now on, Haldeman is the Lord High Executioner," Nixon had told his cabinet at the beginning of his presidency. "Don't come whining to me when he tells you to do something. He will do it because I asked him to, and you are to carry it out." Naturally averse to personal confrontation, Nixon had selected Haldeman as his instrument for dealing with the outside world. In addition to chopping off heads, his role was to serve as a shock absorber for the president's temper tantrums and keep him focused on the job of running the country. He was at once his enforcer, his nanny, and his therapist.

They had been together for nearly two decades. After graduating from the University of California, Los Angeles, and doing a stint in the navy, Haldeman had risen through the ranks of the J. Walter Thompson advertising agency. His portfolio of clients ranged from Walt Disney to the toilet bowl cleaner Sani-Flush. He worked as an advance man for Nixon during his vice presidential campaign in 1956. For the 1960 presidential campaign that pitted Nixon against Jack Kennedy, Haldeman was promoted to campaign tour manager. For an entire year, the two men were virtually inseparable, a process repeated two years later, when Nixon ran unsuccessfully for governor of California. Nixon spent more time with Haldeman than anyone else. They complemented each other's strengths and weaknesses. The visionary Nixon was incapable of running a campaign or large organization; Haldeman was the quintessential marketing man with no political ambitions of his own. Together, they merged into a formidable leader. In the opinion of John Ehrlichman, another UCLA alum brought into the White House by Haldeman, it was "hard to tell where Richard Nixon left off and H. R. Haldeman began." Sometimes, when Nixon wanted to disguise his authorship of a reprimand, he would simply issue it in Haldeman's name. As Haldeman put it, "Every president needs an S.O.B.—and I'm Nixon's."

Entrusted with building a White House staff after Nixon won the presidency in 1968, Haldeman sought out carbon copies of himself. Many of the people he recruited were university friends like Ehrlichman, who was put in charge of domestic policy, or associates from the advertising world like Ron Ziegler, who became press secretary. They were all clean-cut young men, conservative in outlook but more focused on execution than ideology. Many had gone through the election campaign ordeal as Haldeman-trained advance men. They were expected to be "nameless and faceless, as unobtrusive as possible, always concerned for the candidate, never thinking of their own comfort." Their job was to ensure that cars were parked in the right sequence for motorcades, camera angles perfectly aligned, microphones properly positioned, and high school bands appropriately thanked. They were permitted to share a joke at the end of a long day, as long as they preserved a united front to the outside world. Haldeman had various sarcastic nicknames for the president, including Leader of the Free World, Milhous (Nixon's middle name), and Thelma's Husband, after Pat Nixon's discarded first name. Ehrlichman referred to Nixon as the Mad Monk. But these were all inside jokes, never to be shared with others. Loyalty and cool efficiency were the qualities Haldeman prized most.

Haldeman's greatest strength in managing the frequently irascible Nixon was inexhaustible patience. He had the ability to sit with his boss for hours, listening to his monologues and diatribes. He was always available, responding to the president's telephone calls in the middle of the night without betraying a hint of irritation. There was often little ostensible purpose to these conversations. Haldeman understood that the president simply needed to ruminate, particularly when faced with a big decision. Haldeman called this process "circling like the dog." Just as a dog paces round and round when he is trying to settle down, so too Nixon would go off on obscure tangents before eventually deciding on a course of action. It was Haldeman's job to gently hold the leash, to allow Nixon to be Nixon without inflicting too much damage on either the country or himself. On occasion, this meant ignoring Nixon's instructions, or at least delaying implementation, until the president had moved on to some other obsession.

Haldeman's approach differed markedly from that of Chuck Colson, who believed that Nixon's orders should be carried out without hesitation. This was part of Colson's appeal to Nixon. "Colson—he'll do anything," Nixon liked to brag. "He'll walk right through doors." Colson's willingness to fulfill Nixon's every wish extended to trivial matters like organizing an impromptu expedition to the Kennedy Center to attend the final moments of a military concert. "You could have put the president's life in jeopardy," Haldeman shouted, when he heard about the unauthorized addition to Nixon's schedule. "Just tell him he can't go, that's all. He rattles his cage all the time. You can't let him out."

After many years of observing Nixon, Haldeman had concluded that his boss was "the strangest man I ever met." To take a minor example, Nixon was obsessed with organizing his time efficiently. He boasted about his ability to "add hours to the day by not sleeping." He once calculated that he could save a few seconds by shortening his official

signature from "Richard M. Nixon" to plain "Richard Nixon." Whenever possible, he would simply write "RN." In compliance with this
theory, senior staff members were all identified by single initials. Haldeman became "H," Ehrlichman "E," Kissinger "K." All these time-saving
devices were offset by Nixon's passion for minutiae. The president spent
many hours discussing which pictures would hang where in the West
Wing, how he should be greeted on entering a room, when his dog
would be given a bath, and so on. Haldeman became accustomed to
receiving bizarre directives like "no more soup at dinners" (after Nixon
spilled soup down his shirt at a state dinner) and even "no more landing
at airports" (after an airport arrival ceremony went awry).

While Haldeman was more aware than anyone of Nixon's idiosyncrasies, he considered him "head and shoulders" above "the run of
ordinary mortals." A remarkable memory enabled Nixon to dredge up
arcane details of events and slights that everyone else had forgotten. This
was combined with a facility for absorbing new information extremely
quickly. The only person in Haldeman's experience comparable to Nixon
in personal drive and scope of imagination was Walt Disney. Both men
were plagued by "incredible self-doubt" and burned up people around
them, but both were "exceptional" in their own way. Both were tough
on their subordinates. During their entire sixteen years together, Nixon
had never treated Haldeman as a friend, only as an employee. There had
been only one family dinner together with their wives, back in 1962.
Haldeman spent so much time with Nixon that he had almost become a
stranger to his own family. Sitting down next to the president, his hand
hovered over his own legal pad, ready for instructions.

The first order of the day was for a misleading "leak" to *The Washington Post* and Dan Rather of CBS. Nixon's number one enemies in the
press should be informed that the Vietnam peace settlement would be
initialed in Paris on Friday rather than Tuesday as already agreed with
Kissinger. The purpose was simple: Throw "the bastards" off balance.

Next, Nixon began obsessing over minor hitches in the inaugural
ceremonies. At one event, he had been annoyed to see a member of
the presidential press pool stationed between him and the TV cameras. "In next four years, never again have press in front of P," Haldeman recorded dutifully, underlining the word "never." Switching topics,
Nixon instructed his chief of staff to find "an impresario" for White

House entertainment, which should include "more country music." He then began fretting over the public perception that he was somehow isolated from criticism. He told Haldeman to get the word out that he read three national newspapers a day, in addition to scanning the regional coverage. Shifting back to the inaugural events, he wanted to ensure that the antiwar protester who ran toward the presidential limousine on Pennsylvania Avenue was properly charged. He could be released later—as a well-publicized act of presidential clemency. Changing gears yet again, he announced that "a humor man" should be added to his speech-writing staff, as part of his efforts to lighten up.

After more than two hours of these and similar ruminations, Nixon allowed Haldeman to escape. He called for Manolo and requested a bowl of consommé. Normally, his lunch consisted of cottage cheese and a slice of pineapple, but he had eaten much more than usual at the inaugural lunches and dinners. He was proud of keeping his weight down to 173 pounds, precisely what it had been at the age of forty, twenty years earlier. He made "a fetish" out of self-discipline. "It's important to live like a Spartan," he told a journalist. "The worst thing you can do in this job is to relax, to let up." After wolfing down the clear broth, he withdrew into his "thinking time."

From Nixon's point of view, the two and a half hours after lunch were the most essential of the day. His aides knew he was to be left undisturbed during this downtime. Sometimes, he would relax on his lounge chair, reading a history book or biography of one of his political heroes while scribbling notes on a yellow pad. Sometimes, he would listen to booming classical music from the tape deck behind him. And sometimes, he would stretch out on the long settee opposite his desk and nod off to sleep. He claimed he was following the example of LBJ, who recommended a snooze in the middle of the day as a means of cramming two workdays into one. But the truth was that Nixon needed to nap during the day because he slept so irregularly at night. His sleep patterns had been mixed up for years, and he rarely got enough rest.

Nixon cherished his moments of solitude. He drew strength from the years he had spent in the wilderness between his defeat by Jack Kennedy in 1960 and his election as president in 1968. He tried to model himself on General de Gaulle, who retreated to his home in Colombey-les-Deux-Églises after stepping down as head of France's provisional government in 1946. In his well-thumbed copy of de Gaulle's memoir *The Edge of the Sword*, Nixon underlined the sentence "Great men of action . . . have without exception possessed in a very high degree the faculty of withdrawing into themselves."

One of the principal lessons that Nixon drew from de Gaulle was the importance of creating a mystique around his office. "Thinking about schedule, he feels that he should be more aloof, inaccessible, mysterious," Haldeman recorded at one of their daily meetings, early in his presidency, pointing to de Gaulle as an example. "Read de Gaulle on the mystery of power, the power of mystery," Nixon told his aides on another occasion. "He understood that better than anybody." As instructed, they looked up the relevant passage in *The Edge of the Sword*. "There can be no power without mystery. There must be a 'something' which others cannot altogether fathom, which puzzles them, stirs them, and rivets their attention . . . Nothing more enhances authority than silence."

Nixon's problem was that he was almost entirely lacking in the personal charisma that distinguished wartime leaders like de Gaulle and Churchill or even some of his own contemporaries, such as Jack Kennedy. He both envied and resented JFK for his seemingly effortless grace and hold over the popular imagination. By contrast, nothing came easily to the poor boy from Yorba Linda, California, who had clawed his way to the top of the political pile through sheer determination. At Duke University, he had been given the nicknames Gloomy Gus and Iron Butt for the countless hours he spent holed up in the law library while other students were out enjoying themselves. It was the same with politics. With Nixon, everything had to be studied and practiced. Dealing with other people was particularly painful. As he once observed, he was "an introvert in an extrovert profession."

An avid reader of history books and biographies, Nixon had been a student of greatness all his adult life. At moments of crisis, he would compare his woes with those of former presidents. At the height of the Vietnam War, when the White House was circled by heavy trucks to hold back demonstrators, he comforted himself with the thought that Abraham Lincoln had endured much worse. He reminded his aides that

Lincoln had to deal with an insane wife who lost two of her brothers fighting for the Confederacy, a rebellious cabinet, and a secretary of war who refused to speak to him. At one point, Nixon recalled, Lincoln ordered cannons to be lined up on the streets of New York to shoot draft resisters. "All of those things added up make our situation look pretty simple," he concluded.

Many of Nixon's historical analogies dealt with rejection and redemption. He saw himself as an outsider engaged in an endless war with a political establishment determined to destroy him. The leaders he most admired were those who had followed a similar trajectory. He quoted with approval the opinion of his friend the former Texas governor John Connally that "Lincoln was the great figure of the 19th century and Churchill and de Gaulle were the two great figures of the 20th century. The big thing about all of them is their comeback from defeat, not their conduct of the wars." Aides noted that Nixon was most impressive when he was up against a wall fighting for his survival, looking for creative ways out of seemingly impossible situations. Victory had the curious effect of depriving him of his energy and drive.

By his own account, he had gained little personal satisfaction from his landslide defeat of George McGovern in the 1972 election. He had won every state in the Union, with the exception of Massachusetts, capturing more than 60 percent of the popular vote. He had the support of every key population group identified by the exit polls with the exception of blacks and Democrats. Some of these groups, such as Catholics and members of labor unions, had never before been in the Republican column. He had achieved his goal of building a "New Majority," but felt curiously deflated now that he had secured his victory. He was a passive bystander to the excited celebrations taking place around him. He would long remain "at a loss to explain the melancholy that settled over me on that victorious night."

The following day, he assigned Haldeman the task of demanding the resignations of every single member of his staff. He planned to get rid of many of them, keeping only those who had proven their energy and loyalty. He had just finished reading a biography of Benjamin Disraeli, the Victorian-era British prime minister. While serving as leader of the opposition, Disraeli had talked dismissively about the "exhausted volcanos" sitting opposite him on the government benches in the House of Commons. For Nixon, Disraeli's phrase summed up the perils faced by politicians who had been in office too long and run out of new ideas. "We must avoid the exhausted volcano syndrome," he told his aides. "We must recharge ourselves."

He worried incessantly about how he would be perceived in the pantheon of American presidents. On a flight back to Washington from his Florida home at Key Biscayne just prior to the election, he scribbled a private note to himself that he squirreled away in a drawer of his desk in EOB 175:

Presidents noted for:
FDR-Charm.
Truman-Gutsy.
Ike-Smile, prestige.
Kennedy-Charm.
LBJ-Vitality.
RN-?

As he began his second term as president, Nixon wanted above all to be remembered as a peacemaker. He dreamed of the "big plays," like the opening to Communist China or détente with the Soviets or ending the Vietnam War. "*Being* president is nothing compared to what you can *do* as president," he told his aides. Like Teddy Roosevelt, he yearned to be "the man in the arena." He believed that his best days were yet to come. On his sixtieth birthday, January 9, 1973, he made a list of "older men" who achieved their greatest victories late in life. The list included de Gaulle, Eisenhower, Churchill, Adenauer, and Chou En-lai. "No one is finished until he quits," Nixon jotted down on his legal pad. "Age— not as much time. Don't spin your wheels. Blessed with good health. Live every day as if last." He might be running out of time, but he was still younger than all the political giants on his list at the height of their political power. He still had another four years to change the world.

Nixon emerged from his thinking time in a foul mood. Among the materials stacked neatly on his writing table was the latest edition of

Time magazine. It included an interview with a former CIA official named Howard Hunt who had run undercover operations against Nixon's political enemies. Hunt had been dragged into the Watergate scandal when his EOB telephone number and easily deciphered initials had been found in the address book of one of the burglars the day after the break-in. Along with his Cuban subordinates, he had recently pleaded guilty to conspiracy, burglary, and eavesdropping in federal court in Washington. The interview contained dark hints that Hunt was prepared to reveal who ordered the bugging of Democratic Party headquarters unless he and his friends were properly looked after. Hunt had already received nearly $200,000 from his "friends" in the administration, supposedly to cover his defense costs. The secret cash payments had come out of unused campaign funds and been delivered through intermediaries. It now seemed Hunt wanted more money. He was also, not very subtly, pushing for a presidential pardon.

"I protect the people I deal with," Hunt told the *Time* magazine reporter, referring to his long career with the CIA, which included planning the failed Bay of Pigs operation against Fidel Castro in 1961. "A team out on an unorthodox mission expects resupply, it expects concern and attention. The team should never get the feeling that they're abandoned. End of story."

Most damaging to Nixon was an unsourced claim in the article implicating two of his closest associates in the bungled bugging operation. One of the men named by *Time* was Colson, who knew Hunt through the alumni network of Brown University and had hired him to work at the White House. The other was Nixon's old law partner John Mitchell, who had served as attorney general and later as head of the Committee to Re-elect the President. The official abbreviation was CRP, but it was more popularly known as CREEP. "It's got to be done," Hunt had allegedly told the burglars as they were preparing to break in to the Watergate complex. "My friend Colson wants it. Mitchell wants it." If either Colson or Mitchell could be shown to be involved, the scandal would move a big step closer to the president himself.

The *Time* story enraged Nixon. Even today, there is no credible evidence that he ordered the Watergate break-in, or knew about it in advance. Most people who investigated the matter, including many of Nixon's otherwise harsh critics, concluded that he had no prior knowledge. On the other hand, there is little doubt that he set in motion the chain of events that resulted in the bugging of Democratic Party head-quarters by waging an all-out war against his political enemies. His own tapes would demonstrate that he led the conspiracy to obstruct the FBI's investigation into the crime, assisted by Colson, Mitchell, Haldeman, and others. His relationship with Colson, his surrogate son and alter ego, was particularly complicated. Many years later, Colson acknowledged that he helped to bring out "the dark side of Nixon," but "it was always close to the surface. He was a gut fighter . . . His first reaction was to fight back."

Time had been very friendly to Nixon during his political ascent, put-ting him on the cover numerous times and praising his anti-Communist rhetoric. The magazine was generally regarded as a conservative pub-lication, with its finger on the pulse of mainstream America. But the once symbiotic, mutually beneficial relationship between ambitious politician and influential media outlet had frayed to breaking point in recent years. Sensitive to even mildly critical coverage, Nixon had rejected attempts by *Time* editors and reporters to gain favorable access. He now regarded the magazine as part of the liberal media conspiracy against him. It could no longer be relied upon for sympathetic, or even objective, reporting. Next to *The Washington Post, Time* had been most aggressive in covering the Watergate story. They had particularly good sources in the FBI.

Nixon discussed the *Time* story with Colson, whom he had sum-moned from the office next door. Colson denied any prior knowledge of the Watergate bugging and threatened to sue the magazine for libel: he claimed that the article had been written with "malice aforethought." With Colson sitting beside him, Nixon then called Press Secretary Ron Ziegler. Speaking in clipped, angry tones, he was barely able to contain his rage.

"In view of *Time* using that story on Mitchell and Colson, anybody, *anybody* in the White House who talks to *anybody* from *Time,* his res-ignation must be on my desk within one minute. Is that clear?"

"Yes, sir."

"You get that order around as fast as you can. You tell the NSC crowd: no calls at all are to be taken or returned from *Time* magazine unless I approve them in the future. Is that clear?"

"Yes, sir."

Slamming down the phone, Nixon called back one minute later to say that his order applied to the entire foreign policy bureaucracy as well as the economic affairs apparatus, supervised by John Ehrlichman.

"Of course, it's particularly important to get this to the NSC crowd. And I want you to call Haig and tell him I expect him to enforce it at the Pentagon."

"Okay."

"You are to hit Ehrlichman hard on it. He is to take that whole god-damn domestic council—all the left-wingers in there—and shut their damn mouths."

"Yes, sir."

Nixon had barely finished dealing with the fallout from the *Time* article when he began picking up rumors that President Johnson might be dead. He had been looking forward to sharing news of a Vietnam peace settlement with the president who had been hounded from office by the antiwar movement. Although they represented different political philosophies—Nixon was determined to wind down the Great Society welfare programs launched by Johnson—he felt a kinship with his pre-decessor over Vietnam. He recalled with horror the "awful, mindless chant" of the antiwar protesters, "Hey, hey, LBJ, how many kids did you kill today?" Johnson's mistake, in Nixon's view, was to attempt to buy off his youthful critics. The "hatefulness" of their attacks on Johnson's Vietnam policy, Nixon wrote later, "frustrated him, then it disillusioned him, and finally it destroyed him."

It took several calls from Haldeman to establish that Johnson had suf-fered a fatal heart attack at his ranch in central Texas. He had died in an ambulance plane on his way to a hospital in San Antonio. Nixon's main concern, on hearing of Johnson's death, was to head off any attempt to organize a memorial service for LBJ at the National Cathedral. In Nixon's mind, the cathedral and its dean, Francis Sayre, were synony-mous with the antiwar crowd. The fact that Sayre was a grandson of a former president—Woodrow Wilson—and had even been born in the White House himself merely added insult to injury. Nixon regarded the dean as a sanctimonious "ass." Prior to staging an antiwar rally to coincide with the inaugural, Sayre had personally led a "peace march" to the White House to denounce the Christmas bombing of North Vietnam. When Harry Truman died a few days later, Nixon had refused to attend a commemorative service at the Gothic-style cathedral, high on a hill overlooking Washington. He preferred to sulk by himself three miles away at the White House rather than sit through one of Sayre's moralizing sermons.

"Regardless of what all these babbling idiots say," he lectured Haldeman, referring to members of his own staff who were urging him to be "presidential," "there is not to be anything at that cathedral. I will not go, even if it's the only thing. Is that clear?"

Haldeman assured him the Johnson family was unlikely to select the cathedral as the site of a memorial service, but Nixon would not drop the subject.

"I just hope that—Christ, Bob, on this one—the Johnsons will be savvy enough not to let that goddamn cathedral get into it . . . If Ziegler or one of our other little boys get a question about this, they're to stand damn firm. 'The president will not go to the cathedral.' I want that said. You understand?"

"Yes, sir."

Nixon's voice rose to a shout. "Draw the line, goddamn it!"

"Draw the line," Haldeman echoed dutifully. "The son of a bitch runs the place."

"I'm not going to the cathedral. That's all there is to it. I mean, he's in the pale as far as I'm concerned."

"He's opposed to the national policy."

"That's right. He's opposed to Johnson; he's opposed to me. To hell with him!"

The president had been planning a television address attacking Johnson's welfare programs and calling on Americans to learn the virtues of self-reliance. It occurred to him that this was hardly in "goddamn good taste," given the circumstances. He did not want to "kick the hell out of the Great Society" only hours after paying tribute to its creator. Instead, he mused, the mourning period for Johnson might be an opportunity for him to escape to Florida for some rest.

With his appreciation for history, and particularly his own place in it, Nixon quickly picked up on a piece of presidential trivia his aides had missed. "This is the first time in forty years there hasn't been a former president," he told Colson later that night. The deaths, in rapid succession, of Eisenhower, Truman, and now Johnson meant that Nixon was the only living person who had served as leader of the free world.

Colson, as always, was suitably impressed. "My God, I hadn't thought of that."

Henry Kissinger with his briefing books en route to Paris peace talks,
January 22, 1973

enry Kissinger learned about LBJ's death on his arrival at Orly
airport. He was struck by the symbolism of "this hulking, imperious, vulnerable, expansive, aspiring man, so full of life," coming
to his end at the same time as "the war that had broken his heart." After
a few hours' sleep, he prepared for his final negotiating session with the
men who had been waging war, first against the French, then against
the Americans, for more than a quarter of a century. It would take place
beneath the crystal chandeliers of the iconic Majestic Hotel, just steps

away from the Arc de Triomphe. The place where George Gershwin composed "An American in Paris" and Nazi generals plotted the assassination of Hitler was a pleasant contrast with the cramped apartments on the outskirts of the city, where he had held his early secret meetings with Le Duc Tho. "Very narrow space between us," Kissinger remembered. "No food—no lunches, no drink. Four to five hours discussion at a time. Their strategy was to break our spirit, show us that they were in no hurry." But that was behind him now as he sought to wrap up an agreement that would bring the last American combat troops home from Vietnam.

It was 9:35 a.m. Paris time, still the middle of the night in Washington, because of the six-hour time difference. Kissinger went around the room shaking hands before turning his full attention to the gray-haired man in the somber Mao suit. One of the founders of the Vietnamese Communist Party, Tho had spent ten years in French colonial prisons. He had devoted his entire adult life to waging guerrilla war. Behind his back, Kissinger nicknamed him Ducky as a way to make fun of his dour Marxist-Leninist persona. Ducky had lectured Kissinger frequently on the evils of American imperialism and the "heroic struggle" of the Vietnamese people. Today, however, he was on his best behavior.

"I changed a few pages in your Vietnamese text last night, Mr. Special Advisor," Kissinger kidded his old sparring partner. "But it only concerned North Vietnamese troops. You won't notice until you get back home."

Tho laughed politely at the joke. Over the previous two days and nights, his aides had laboriously checked every detail in the draft, binding agreed texts with ribbons and sealing wax to prevent any unauthorized alterations. Humor was a standard Kissinger negotiating tool, a way of establishing a personal bond with an ideological adversary. In this case, he was also gently poking fun at North Vietnamese suspicions of American good faith and their paranoid obsession with security.

Permitting Communist troops to remain in South Vietnam following a full American withdrawal had been a crucial part of a hard-fought compromise that had opened the way to a final peace settlement. In return, Ducky dropped a long-standing demand for a coalition government in Saigon to replace the "puppet" Thieu administration. The Thieu government and Communist Vietcong would continue to administer areas they already controlled. There would be a cease-fire followed, within sixty days, by the withdrawal of all remaining U.S. troops and liberation of prisoners of war.

Kissinger had sent repeated signals to Hanoi, through both Moscow and Beijing, that the United States would not stand permanently in the way of a Communist victory. In contacts with Soviet and Chinese officials, he talked about the need for a "decent interval" of one or two years between a full U.S. withdrawal from Vietnam and the reunification of the peninsula under Communist rule. During his first trip to Beijing, in July 1971, he explicitly conceded that the Thieu government might be toppled in the aftermath of a U.S. pullout. "If the government is as unpopular as you seem to think," he told the Chinese prime minister, Zhou En-lai, "then the quicker our forces are withdrawn, the quicker it will be overthrown. And if it is overthrown after we have withdrawn, we will not intervene."

Kissinger and Tho had been on the verge of a deal back in October 1972, when Ducky agreed to a transitional period for South Vietnam, leading eventually to free elections and the return of American POWs. Determined to flatter his boss, Kissinger compared the breakthrough to Nixon's visit to China and détente with the Soviet Union. "Well, Mr. President," he told Nixon, "it looks like we've got three out of three!" To celebrate the occasion, Nixon invited his aides to join him for a steak dinner in his EOB office. "The P told Manolo to bring the good wine, his '57 Lafite-Rothschild, or whatever it is, to be served to everyone," Haldeman recorded in his diary. "Usually it's just served to the P and the rest of us have some California Beaulieu vineyard stuff."

The celebration was premature. When Thieu learned about the latest twist in the negotiations, he exploded. Allowing a Communist troop presence in the South—even disguised as Vietcong irregulars—would end up destroying his government. Thieu insisted there could be no cease-fire without a full North Vietnamese withdrawal. "Have you ever seen any peace accord in the history of the world in which the invaders had been permitted to stay in the territories they had invaded?" he asked Haig, who was sent to Saigon to placate him. For Thieu, the proposed peace accord was tantamount to "committing suicide."

With the U.S. presidential election only a few days away, Nixon could not afford a public confrontation with a loyal American ally. More than

twenty thousand Americans had been killed in Vietnam since he took
over as president in January 1969, in addition to the thirty-six thousand
who had died under LBJ. Any suggestion that their lives had been sacrificed in vain would undermine Nixon's claim to be delivering "peace
with honor." From Nixon's point of view, it was vital that any break with
Thieu be postponed until after he had "crushed" McGovern and the
Democrats. He could not risk the charge of betrayal.

Nixon assigned Kissinger the task of keeping everything "confused
and fuzzed up" until after the election. Ordered to "bamboozle the
bastards," the national security adviser assured reporters that any last-
minute glitches could be quickly ironed out. He held a televised press
conference on October 26 to proclaim, "We believe peace is at hand."
Delivered in a thick, sententious German accent, it was a phrase that
would soon return to haunt him. When he presented Ducky with the
full list of Thieu's demands, including a complete withdrawal of North
Vietnamese troops, it became clear that the gulf between Hanoi and
Saigon was insuperable. As everyone dug back in to their entrenched
positions, Kissinger began to speak of both sides with hatred. The Communists in Hanoi were "tawdry, filthy shits" who "make the Russians
look good." Thieu was an "unmitigated, selfish, psychopathic son of a
bitch." In short, they were all crazy. "When you meet with two groups
of Vietnamese the same day, you might as well run an insane asylum,"
he complained.

For Nixon, the way out of the impasse was another round of bombings of the North, more intense than anything that had gone before.
He ordered every available B-52, the heaviest bomber in the American
arsenal, to join the fight. Knowing that Nixon was a football fan, the air
force code-named the raids Linebacker II. For eleven days in succession excepting only Christmas Day, wave after wave of B-52s, supported
by hundreds of tactical aircraft, pounded railroads, bridges, airfields,
ammunition dumps, power plants, and SAM sites in the Hanoi area.
Kissinger described the policy as "total brutality." Each wave of B-52s
was the equivalent of "a 4,000-plane raid in World War II." Many of
the same targets were hit multiple times, until there was nothing left to
destroy. The North Vietnamese reported 1,624 civilian casualties; losses
on the American side included fifteen B-52s, at $15 million apiece, and
a further 90 killed or captured pilots. The raids were the culmination of

an eight-year air war that had showered more American ordnance on North Vietnam than all the bombs dropped in all the theaters of World War II combined.

The "Christmas bombing" did little to change the basic outlines of the peace agreement that Kissinger had previously negotiated with Ducky. The few, largely symbolic, modifications to the original document made no difference to the overall balance of forces. But Nixon had shown that he was prepared to go "the extra mile" on behalf of his South Vietnamese ally. By his demonstration of massive American airpower, he could claim that he had bombed the Communists back to the negotiating table. He had also won vital breathing space for the government in Saigon. "Call it cosmetics or whatever you want," Nixon had told Haig back in October. South Vietnam had to be given "a chance to survive. Not to survive forever, but they've got to survive a reasonable time. And if they don't, everybody will say, well, goddamn it, we did our part."

Both Kissinger and Le Duc Tho did their best to maintain a friendly, lighthearted tone at their final meeting. Kissinger joked that he hoped Tho would take him on a guided tour of the Ho Chi Minh trail. Ducky referred only obliquely to the destruction wrought by the B-52s in discussing the logistical problems posed by a proposed Kissinger visit to Hanoi. Damage to the airport runway in Hanoi would make it difficult for his plane to land.

"We must have been aiming at a different airport because we never hit the airport we want," joked Kissinger.

"I thought you could land by parachute," said Ducky.

The last point that needed to be settled was the question of U.S. economic assistance to North Vietnam as an incentive for respecting the peace agreement. After a final round of haggling with Tho, Kissinger agreed to an aid package of up to $4.75 billion. In the spirit of the occasion, he could not resist adding, "I give you my shirt, too." A few minutes later, the two negotiators went through the pile of documents on the table, initialing each one by one. They then walked outside into the Parisian drizzle for a celebratory photograph. Nixon had repeatedly instructed Kissinger not to smile when photographed with Tho. But on this occasion, each man grinned broadly as he clasped the other's right hand. To outside appearances, they were the best of friends.

———

Back in Washington, the trial of the Watergate burglars was about to
resume in the U.S. District Courthouse, a mile down Pennsylvania Avenue from the White House. After nine days of hearings, Judge John J.
Sirica was making little progress in establishing the truth. The questions
that had intrigued Americans for months—who ordered the bugging
of the Democratic Party headquarters and why—remained unresolved.
The judge was sure of one thing only: the defendants, and at least some
of the government witnesses, were hiding things from him.

It was a strange and perplexing case that had begun with a routine
discovery by an alert night watchman at the recently completed Watergate office building. The ten-story office block was part of a complex of
five buildings designed by a futuristic Italian architect on a triangular
swath of land on the Potomac River adjacent to the Kennedy Center.
The Democratic headquarters occupied the entire sixth floor with a
balcony that looked northward, away from the river, across a dreary
six-lane road. The residential buildings, by contrast, were distinguished
by their swirling shapes and curving concrete balconies with spectacular views across the water. From the river, the complex resembled a
giant cruise liner, a self-contained world with its own swimming pools,
restaurants, post office, bakery, florist, and hairdresser. "A city within
a city," the developers boasted. The vaguely nautical architecture and
upmarket clientele caused Washington wags to refer to the Watergate
as "the ship of fools." *The Washington Post* described the complex as "a
glittering Potomac Titanic with no icebergs or steerage class."

Criticized as out of keeping with Washington's predominantly neo-
classical architecture, the Watergate had quickly become one of the
most sought-after addresses in the city, particularly for Republicans.
Bob Haldeman had rented an apartment while waiting for his home in
Georgetown to be redecorated. Other residents included several Nixon
cabinet members and his secretary, Rose Mary Woods. The head of the
president's reelection committee, John Mitchell, and his wife, Martha,
owned a lavish duplex with a marble entryway that spanned the seventh
and eighth floors of Watergate East. The beehived, alcoholic Martha
was hailed as a "media-age Marie Antoinette" for her tart observa-

*Government exhibit in Watergate case showing the Watergate office building
sandwiched between Watergate West (bottom center) and Watergate East.
The Democratic Party offices were on the sixth floor of the office building
with a balcony, opposite the Howard Johnson motel (bottom left).
The Watergate Hotel is behind the office building. The Kennedy Center
and the Lincoln Memorial are visible in the background.*

tions on American politics delivered in a distinctive southern drawl. In
Watergate social terms, however, she ranked below the "Dragon Lady,"
Anna Chennault, who occupied the penthouse suite six floors above.
The Chinese-born widow of the commander of the Flying Tigers fighter
group from World War II was lauded in the press as "a figure of glamor
and mystery," the Republican "hostess with the mostest." A diminutive,
intimidating beauty, she employed a personal chef to prepare thirteen-
course dinners for the Washington elite. As a Nixon fund-raiser, she
refused to accept political donations for less than $500, considering
them a "waste of time."

Back in the Watergate office building, the security guard Frank Wills reported for duty at midnight on Saturday, June 17, 1972, for what was known as the graveyard shift. Soon after starting on his rounds, he noticed that a piece of duct tape had been placed across the latch to a door leading to an underground parking garage. Because the tape was preventing the door from locking, he dutifully removed it. Feeling hungry, he went in search of some take-out food from the Howard Johnson motel across the street. After leisurely finishing his burger and fries, he rechecked the door to the parking area. To his surprise, he discovered that the latch had been re-taped during the hour he had been away. Whoever applied the tape the first time was evidently still in the building and planning to exit via the garage. At 1:47 a.m., Wills called the police to report a suspected burglary in progress.

Three plainclothes police officers arrived five minutes later in an unmarked patrol car. As members of the so-called bum squad, they had been on the lookout for drug dealers in Georgetown when they were diverted to the Watergate. They all had long hair and were dressed in windbreakers and surplus army jackets. A trail of taped latches led them through back stairwells to the Democratic Party offices on the sixth floor. When they entered the office suite, guns drawn, they found five middle-aged men in suits and ties crouching behind desks and cubicle partitions. The burglars put up no resistance, instead raising their hands, which were covered with blue surgical gloves. "Five of the easiest lockups I have ever had," one of the cops later remarked.

A search of the burglars' belongings revealed a walkie-talkie, two Minolta cameras, lock picks, pen-size Mace canisters, an assortment of electronic bugging devices, miniature radio transmitters, and wads of crisp $100 bills, many of them numbered sequentially. The arrested men all gave false names, but fingerprints revealed their true identities. Four of them were Miami-based Cuban exiles who had been involved in a variety of anti-Castro activities, including the abortive Bay of Pigs invasion in 1961. The fifth was a "security consultant" named James McCord who had earlier worked for the Central Intelligence Agency as an anti-bugging specialist. Further investigation established that McCord was "chief of security" for Nixon's reelection committee. He had even been a bodyguard for Martha Mitchell. McCord reported to a former FBI agent, G. Gordon Liddy, who was responsible for the committee's "counterintelligence operations." Liddy had also recruited

Howard Hunt, whose name and White House telephone number were found in the address books of the Cubans.

And there the trail ended—at least for the time being. Months of investigation by the FBI had failed to uncover a White House link to the burglars higher than Liddy and Hunt, who were arrested and then released on bail in September 1972. But there were unconfirmed reports in the press that the defendants were receiving financial support and help with their legal bills in exchange for keeping quiet. The government also possessed evidence that Liddy had received $235,000 in campaign funds for his counterintelligence activities. It seemed to stretch credulity that nobody higher up in the campaign had any knowledge of how these funds were spent. Judge Sirica did not accept the prosecutors' contention that Liddy was a rogue operator. He was a believer in the maxim "Follow the money."

On the second day of the trial, Hunt changed his not-guilty pleas to guilty. This excused him from giving evidence in the case or even appearing in court prior to sentencing. The Cubans quickly followed the example set by Hunt, their onetime CIA superior for the Bay of Pigs operation, and also pleaded guilty. Suspecting a cover-up, the judge took the unusual step of questioning the four Cubans directly after sending the jury out of the room. They denied ever working for the CIA. They had agreed to take part in the Watergate operation after Hunt assured them it would help advance the cause of freedom in Cuba. "I will do anything to protect this country against any Communist conspiracy," declared one of the defendants, Eugenio Martinez. Precisely how breaking in to the Watergate would forestall a "Communist conspiracy" the Cubans did not know. Exasperated, Sirica inquired about the source of the freshly printed $100 bills found in their wallets. "A blank envelope" that arrived through the mail came the reply.

"I'm sorry, I don't believe you," snapped the judge.

The son of an Italian immigrant, Sirica had been involved in Republican politics for much of his life. He had the reputation of being a tough law-and-order judge, nicknamed Maximum John by reporters for his harsh sentencing practices. Despite being reversed on appeal more often than any other judge, he had no qualms about stretching his legal powers to the limit when he thought that defendants were getting away with something. As the chief judge of the U.S. District Court, he had assigned himself the Watergate case, fully aware of the "political over-tones." He reasoned that it would be hard to accuse him of political bias if the facts of the case, as developed in the trial, proved embarrassing to the Republican Party.

Five feet six inches tall, he still looked like the professional welter-weight boxer he had been in his youth. His pugilistic face and swept-back black hair made him appear younger than his sixty-eight years. Seated on a high dais beneath the emblem of an outstretched eagle, Sirica had a commanding view of the wood-paneled courtroom. A panic button hidden beneath his desk enabled him to summon mar-shals in case of an emergency. To his immediate right was the witness stand, flanked by an American flag and the jury box. In front of him were the defense and prosecution tables. A hundred or so spectators were crammed on benches at the back of the courtroom, mainly jour-nalists who covered the trial on a daily basis. During breaks in the proceedings, the reporters surged through the double doors facing the judge, pushing each other aside as they sprinted down the corridor in search of pay phones.

Following the guilty pleas of Hunt and the Cubans, only two defen-dants remained in the courtroom. One was "the smart-alecky, cocky Liddy who seemed only to be amused by the fact that he might be going to jail for breaking the law." The newly mustachioed lawyer took pride in his willingness to undergo extreme hardship in service of a higher cause. His loyalty to Nixon and the Republican Party was mingled with a defiant, contrarian nature. He had trained himself to endure pain by holding his finger in a candle flame until it burned. Growing up in Hoboken, New Jersey, in the 1930s, he had idolized Adolf Hitler. Lis-tening to Hitler's speeches over the radio, he felt an "electric current" surge through his body communicating "a sheer animal confidence and power of will" that Liddy sought to emulate. He revised his views about the Führer following America's entry into the war but remained fascinated by Nazi Germany. He took a special delight in shocking lib-erals. Building on his reputation as a gun-toting prosecutor in Pough-keepsie, New York, he ran for Congress on the slogan "Gordon Liddy doesn't bail them out—he puts them in." While he failed to wrest the Republican nomination away from the incumbent, he was a master at self-publicity.

Gordon Liddy, with newly grown mustache, leaves U.S. District Court in Washington after being charged with the Watergate break-in on September 25, 1972.

As the case officer for the bugging operation, Liddy had monitored events from room 214 of the Watergate Hotel, together with Hunt. He was in three-way communication by radio with the burglars on the sixth floor of the office building and another Cuban stationed in an observation post in room 723 of the Howard Johnson motel across the street. The first sign that something had gone terribly wrong came when the observation post reported some "guys wearing hippie clothes" on the terrace outside the Democratic Party office. "Four or five guys," continued the transmission. "One's got on a cowboy hat. One's got on a sweatshirt. It looks like . . . guns! They've got guns. It's trouble." Liddy barely had time to order his men to abort the operation when a crackly voice murmured, *"They've got us."* Liddy and Hunt fled the Watergate complex just as police cars were pulling up, sirens blazing. "Some people got caught," Liddy told his wife when he got home. "I'll probably be going to jail."

Seated next to Liddy at the defense table was James McCord, who had led the break-in team that fateful night. Stocky and balding, McCord was as reserved as Liddy was flamboyant. His ramrod military bearing and gaunt, hollow cheeks suggested a man struggling with competing calls of duty, loyalty, and conscience. He had served in the U.S. Army Air Corps in World War II, held the reserve rank of lieutenant colonel, and attended church regularly. He viewed himself as a superpatriot. He had resisted suggestions from his defense lawyers to depict the break-in as a clandestine CIA operation. The "CIA defense" might have provided a plausible reason for the bugging of Democratic Party headquarters, but McCord refused to shift the blame onto his former employer. He had worked for "the Company" for nineteen years as a security officer and was not about to betray it now. Back in December, he had sent an anonymous letter to his White House handler, warning that "every tree in the forest will fall" if the agency was made to take responsibility for the Watergate operation. "It will be a scorched desert," he wrote, before switching metaphors. "The whole matter is at the precipe [*sic*] now."

How close to the precipice the world would soon find out.

As Henry Kissinger was flying back to Washington from Paris that Tuesday morning, Jeb Stuart Magruder strode confidently to the witness stand in Judge Sirica's courtroom. The deputy campaign director of the Committee to Re-elect the President had been summoned to testify in the trial of *United States v. Liddy et al.* As instructed by the bailiff, he raised his right hand and repeated the oath. "I swear that the evidence I shall give shall be the truth, the whole truth and nothing but the truth, so help me God."

The prosecutor, Earl Silbert, led the witness through a series of prepared questions. Looking younger than his thirty-eight years, Magruder made a good impression on the judge and jury. He "was as smooth as silk," Sirica recalled later. "He did not appear flustered or nervous. He is a handsome man, well dressed, well spoken. If you wanted a model of the respectable, responsible, honest, young executive, Magruder would be perfect." The former cosmetics salesman exuded an earnest Boy Scout's demeanor. He wore a little American flag in the lapel of his conservative business suit.

Magruder acknowledged asking Liddy to conduct an "intelligence-gathering" operation to head off any potential trouble at the Republican National Convention in San Diego while insisting he do nothing "embarrassing or illegal." After Liddy reported that 250,000 demonstrators were planning to show up in San Diego, the location of the convention was switched to Miami Beach. Asked about their personal relationship, Magruder conceded that there had been some friction. Their "management philosophies" were very different. Magruder was a team player; Liddy preferred working on his own. Magruder testified that he had 250 full-time employees working under him, plus another 2,000 or so volunteers, and was responsible for a $35 million budget. The implication was that he could not possibly keep track of everything his subordinates were doing.

Silbert asked the witness if he had given Liddy "any assignment concerning the Democratic National Committee."

"No," Magruder replied.

Had he received "intelligence information" or a "report of any kind" from Liddy concerning the Democratic headquarters in the Watergate building?

"No."

Had he ever authorized McCord to "establish a listening post and wiretap telephone conversations at the Democratic National Committee?"

"No, sir."

Had he known about any illegal acts by McCord and the other Watergate burglars prior to their arrest on June 17, 1972?

"No, sir."

"That is all."

Without being aware of it, the judge and jury had just witnessed a federal crime being committed right under their noses. By lying about his role in the Watergate break-in after swearing to tell the truth, Magruder had committed perjury, punishable by up to five years in prison. In reality, he had served as Liddy's direct superior in the Watergate chain of command.

The cherubic-looking man perjuring himself in front of Judge Sirica was a recognizable Washington type, the political aide dedicated above all else to self-advancement. He was a protégé of Bob Haldeman, who recruited him to serve as White House deputy director of communications following an undistinguished stint on the Nixon for president campaign in California. Even though Magruder had studied ethics at Williams College in Massachusetts, he seemed to lack firm moral principles of his own. His White House colleagues regarded him as a weak man easily swayed by others. He had majored in political science, but his real talent was marketing, particularly marketing himself. The presidential speechwriter William Safire called him "the Game Plan Man . . . He would reduce ideas and general orders to specific and often mechanistic Game Plans, with assignments, follow-ups, and analyses of results. He was eager, harried, confident, optimistic, and usually over his head." If Haldeman created the machine that connected Nixon to the vast government bureaucracy, Magruder was the cog that kept everything running more or less smoothly.

As the campaign season approached, Haldeman decided he needed someone to keep an eye on the Nixon reelection effort, which operated separately from the administration. He arranged for Magruder to become deputy director of CREEP under John Mitchell, working out of a plush new office on the opposite side of Pennsylvania Avenue to the White House. Gordon Liddy showed up a few months later to fill the job of general counsel. Liddy struck Magruder as "a cocky little bantam rooster who liked to brag about his James Bond–ish exploits." An exercise fanatic, he had a disconcerting habit of dropping to the floor and without notice performing a hundred push-ups. He boasted about his method for killing people with a pencil: Hold the eraser end in your hand and ram the finely sharpened tip into your victim's neck, just above the Adam's apple. Not too long after their first meeting, Magruder made the mistake of resting his hand on Liddy's shoulder as he critiqued a legal brief drafted by his subordinate. Liddy did not appreciate the gesture. "Jeb," he growled, "if you don't take your arm off my shoulder, I'm going to tear it off and beat you to death with it."

In the fight against the hippies and the Communists, Liddy firmly believed that the ends justified the means. He was deeply offended by the counterculture of the 1960s. "To permit the thought, spirit, life-style, and ideas of the '60s movement to achieve power" in the United States, he later wrote, was as offensive to him as "the thought of surrender to a career Japanese soldier in 1945." Images of "rioting, burning cities," "attempts to close down the nation's capital by mob violence," and Jane Fonda visiting Hanoi haunted his dreams. Convinced that the United States "was at war internally as well as externally," he had no qualms about breaking the law himself. "Spies in the enemy camp and electronic surveillance were nothing new in American politics," but Liddy intended to go "far beyond that." Faced with "a wartime emergency," he was ready to risk "blowing the entire system."

A Haldeman aide, Gordon Strachan, put the matter more simply when Magruder suggested that Liddy perhaps be reassigned. "Liddy's a Hitler," Strachan joked, "but at least he's our Hitler." Magruder understood that in addition to his legal responsibilities Liddy would be in charge of "dirty tricks," reporting back to the White House.

Eager to please his White House bosses, the "Game Plan Man" accepted a scaled-down version of an intelligence-gathering plan first presented by Liddy in January 1972. The most outrageous elements of Operation Gemstone—including a proposal to hire prostitutes to compromise Democratic Party leaders—had been stripped out of the plan on Mitchell's insistence. The budget was cut from $1 million to a quarter of a million. Whatever doubts Magruder felt about Liddy were swept aside by Haldeman's demands for actionable intelligence against the Democrats. Magruder had also received a call from Colson urging him to take action on Liddy's project. "Why don't you get off your duff over there, Jeb, and do something instead of having these people running around getting up plans," Nixon's hatchet man barked, according to his own later recollection of the conversation. Under pressure on multiple fronts, the weak-willed Magruder flew to Florida to present the latest version of the Gemstone proposal to Mitchell, who was on vacation in Key Biscayne. According to Magruder, the head of the Committee to Re-elect the President signed off on "Gemstone III" after a perfunctory twenty-minute discussion on March 30. Without anyone giving much thought to the possible consequences, Liddy's wild ideas had become part of the bureaucratic paper flow.

The new plan provided for "an initial entry" into Democratic Party offices in the Watergate. This occurred on the night of May 28. Liddy's men succeeded in planting bugs in two of the street-side offices that could easily be monitored from the Howard Johnson motel across the street. Liddy spent the following week transcribing the private telephone conversations of Democratic Party officials on special Gem-stone stationery marked "Exploitation May Compromise Source." The intelligence "product" was deeply disappointing. One of the bugs, for which Liddy had paid $30,000, malfunctioned completely. The most compromising information involved Democratic aides arranging dates and sexual liaisons for themselves. A second break-in was planned for June 17 to improve the quality of the intelligence.

The arrest of the five Watergate burglars cemented the contempt that Magruder and Liddy felt for each other. As Magruder saw it, the would-be "James Bond had been exposed as a bumbling clown." In the imme-diate aftermath of the fiasco, Liddy appeared deflated, even depressed, but quickly regained his bounce. He regarded Magruder as a wimp and a coward. When they crossed paths in the corridor outside Judge Sirica's courtroom, Liddy greeted his former superior with a conspira-torial grin and ostentatious salute in full view of the assembled journal-ists. This alarmed Magruder, who was doing his utmost to minimize his ties with the noxious, fatally compromised Liddy.

As Magruder gave his testimony, Liddy rocked back and forth on his chair at the defense table, whispering to his neighbor, McCord. Liddy's sarcastic commentary could not be heard by the judge or jury, but it was obvious to McCord that Magruder was perjuring himself. Magruder was obliged to pass the defendants on his way out of the courtroom. Sensing his discomfort, Liddy flashed another big smile and very obvi-ous wink.

Chuck Colson had long marveled at Nixon's political and physical resil-ience, his ability to come back "tougher and stronger" from every gru-eling experience. But as he sat with the president awaiting Kissinger's return from Paris, he could not help noticing how tired he looked. The day-to-day pressures of Vietnam and Watergate were taking their toll. They were visible in the lengthening creases on his face, "the dark shad-ows under his eyes," "the melancholy of his voice," and the "specks of gray" that had recently appeared in his hair. It seemed to Colson that Nixon was "aging right before my eyes."

The two co-conspirators treated themselves to a couple of Dubon-

Nixon's customary lunch of cottage cheese and canned pineapple,
photographed on his last day in office, August 8, 1974.

nets on the rocks in Nixon's hideaway office before being served the
standard lunch of cottage cheese atop a slice of canned Dole pineapple. "How rough it's been," the president mused, staring into his drink.
"No telling how long this peace agreement will last—a year, two years
maybe, who knows. But we kept our word, we'll get our prisoners home
and well, the South Vietnamese—at least those poor devils will have
a fighting chance." He looked forward to being able to ram the peace
agreement down the throats of his critics. "Kick them right in the balls,"
he instructed.

Nixon was still stewing over the latest affronts from *Time*. Rather
than put him on the cover to mark his second inaugural, the news-
weekly had chosen to give top billing to the erotic film *Last Tango in
Paris,* which was about to open in New York after scandalizing Europe.
Featuring Marlon Brando and Maria Schneider, the X-rated movie featured "frontal nudity, four-letter words, masturbation, even sodomy."
Hailed by some as a groundbreaking opus by the master Italian director
Bernardo Bertolucci, *Last Tango* had been denounced by conservatives
as a crude commercial offshoot of the counterculture of the 1960s. In
the opinion of one critic, it was a piece of "talented debauchery that
often makes you want to vomit." The puritan Nixon was predictably

outraged. It did not take much prompting from Colson to reignite his loathing for his once favorite newsmagazine. He was so angry that he picked up the phone to remind Ron Ziegler to cut off all contact with "the bastards at *Time* . . . for the next four years I'm in office.

"Under no circumstances whatever is any call to be returned to *Time* magazine and nobody is to see them," he instructed yet again. "Is that totally, absolutely understood and clear?" Without waiting for the press secretary's reply, he slammed down the phone.

Later that afternoon, Nixon and Colson briefly turned their attention to another story from the front pages of the morning newspapers, occupying second billing beneath the banner headlines about Johnson's death. By a vote of 7 to 2, the Supreme Court had overturned state laws restricting a woman's right to obtain an abortion during her first three months of pregnancy. The case was known as *Roe v. Wade.* Jane Roe was the fictional name given to the plaintiff who had filed one of the original lawsuits; Henry Wade was a district attorney from Dallas, Texas, who had sought to uphold a state law making abortion illegal except to save a woman's life. Nixon was conflicted about the outcome. On the one hand, easier access to abortions would break up the family and encourage permissiveness. Girls did not have to worry about getting pregnant anymore: They could simply go to a doctor and get an abortion for $5. On the other hand, there were times when abortions were "necessary."

He cited the first example that came to mind. "When you have a black and a white."

"Or a rape," Colson interjected.

"Or rape. You know what I mean. There are times."

Talk about the Supreme Court decision was interrupted by the sudden appearance of Henry Kissinger, who had just arrived from Andrews Air Force Base. In the space of thirty-two hours, the national security adviser had flown twice across the Atlantic, wrapped up a peace agreement with the North Vietnamese Communists, and met three times with the South Vietnamese foreign minister. After mounting a desperate rearguard action, the Saigon delegates had finally bowed to the inevitable. Everything was finally in place for the formal signing ceremony in Paris in four days. Sidelined by Kissinger during the secret negotiations, Secretary of State William Rogers would sign the document on behalf of the United States, together with the representatives of North Vietnam, South Vietnam, and the Vietcong.

"Congratulations," Nixon told Kissinger magnanimously. "You were right and I was wrong. You kept saying that Thieu would cave."

The president had spent much of the last two days debating the appropriate backdrop for his long-awaited announcement of an end to America's war in Vietnam. One option, reserved for special occasions, was an address to Congress. Another was a simple televised address from the White House. In the end, Nixon rejected the Congress option. He did not want to give congressional critics of the war more television time or compete with LBJ's forthcoming lying in state in the Rotunda. "The more I think about it, the announcement is so powerful it doesn't need any damn backdrop," he informed Ziegler. "I could do it in the men's room."

As important as the choice of venue was the small American flag emblem that Nixon inserted into his lapel. It was a gesture born out of a mixture of patriotism and cussedness. He had recently seen a movie called *The Man* that featured a manipulative secretary of state with an American flag pin attempting to oust the nation's first black president. Haldeman reported that the same device had been used to identify bad-guy Republicans in *The Candidate,* a political satire starring Robert Redford. Appalled, Nixon announced that he intended "to wear the flag, come hell or high water, from now on." He encouraged the staff to follow his example.

At 10:01 p.m., Nixon addressed the nation live from the Oval Office. Nearly a hundred million Americans tuned in to hear the president announce that an agreement had been initialed to "bring peace with honor in Vietnam and Southeast Asia." He delivered the ten-minute speech in the solemn news anchor voice he reserved for special occasions, stressing phrases like "the right *kind* of peace" and "let us be *proud.*" His even, well-modulated tones were difficult for impersonators to imitate, so they focused on other idiosyncrasies, such as the brooding eyes and flapping jowls. At the end of the address, he paid tribute to LBJ for enduring "the vilification of those who sought to portray him as a man of war" when his true goal was "a lasting peace."

After bidding good night to the television audience, the president met his wife and daughters in the third-floor Solarium. He was particularly pleased by a comment from his daughter Julie, who had watched the address on CBS, one of his media bêtes noires. According to Julie, the CBS commentators—Dan Rather, Marvin Kalb, and Eric Sevareid— all looked "sick" with envy at the successful outcome of the long diplomatic battle. This was confirmation to Nixon that he had "really stuck 'em in the groin."

Half an hour later, he was urging Colson to go on the attack, in a telephone call from the Lincoln Sitting Room. "I just hope to Christ that our bomb throwers are out." He was particularly stung by criticism that his peace agreement was unlikely to last. "Did the Treaty of Versailles last? What about the Metternich treaty?" he asked angrily, referring to the treaties that ended World War I and the Napoleonic Wars. "What lasts?" Nixon made clear he would resist appeals from some members of his staff to reach out to his political enemies. If he was sent any more memos proposing national reconciliation, he would "flush 'em down the goddamn john." On the other hand, he was glad that he had mentioned Johnson in the speech, a bipartisan gesture that had been widely praised, even though LBJ never did "a goddamn thing for me, as you know."

"It was a beautiful touch, Mr. President," Colson agreed. "Really what you did was to bring credit to yourself by giving him credit. Because he stood against the same critics."

Henry Kissinger, too, was effusive in his praise for "a real gem" of a speech. "The overwhelming reaction is ecstasy," he told the president in a late-night telephone call. "It just kills the bloody liberals . . . You've wrapped it all up on terms that every one of them thought was impossible."

Kissinger had often sat with Nixon in the Lincoln Sitting Room. He imagined the scene: the president "solitary and withdrawn, deep in his brown stuffed chair with his legs on a settee in front of him, a small reading light breaking the darkness, and a wood fire throwing shadows across the room." Classical music, perhaps Tchaikovsky, was playing softly in the background. "He was talking to me, but he was really addressing himself," he wrote later.

On occasions like this, Kissinger understood that it was his job to tell the boss what he wanted to hear, tapping into both his sense of history and his sense of grievance. *"Meez-ster Preh—zee-dent."* He rolled the elongated syllables around in his throat, his ponderous tone paired perfectly with his German accent. "Vot you have accomplished runs counter to vot zeh intellectual establishment of zis country has been preaching for thirty years. Your success is almost more painful to zem dan . . ."

"They've got to change, goddamn it. The intellectual establishment is important to this country."

"But zey don't *vont* to change."

"Then let's build a new establishment."

Together, Nixon and Kissinger had pulled off some of the most stunning coups in American foreign policy since World War II. As the president's secret emissary to Beijing, Kissinger had paved the way for the dramatic opening to Communist China that had defined Nixon's first term in office. They had then played the "China card" to put pressure on Moscow to sign a nuclear arms limitation agreement. For all the criticism they had endured over Vietnam, they had ultimately found a way to extricate America from a horrific misadventure that Nixon had inherited from his two Democratic predecessors. They were partners, but also rivals. While Nixon respected Kissinger's exceptional negotiating skills and brilliant mind, he could not abide sharing the credit for all these diplomatic breakthroughs. Kissinger should never be allowed to forget his subordinate status. His job was to implement policy, not to determine what the policy should be. The title of peacemaker should deservedly go to Nixon himself, not to Kissinger.

The president suspected his assistant of being behind a series of articles and press leaks that boosted Kissinger at Nixon's expense. Influential commentators had somehow got the idea that Kissinger was the adult in the room restraining a trigger-happy commander in chief. As he shuttled between world capitals, the national security adviser had become a personality in his own right. His jet-setting image was enhanced by paparazzi images of him arm in arm with well-known actresses like Candice Bergen, Raquel Welch, and Jill St. John. But Kissinger's Rolodex did not only include beautiful women. In the name of promoting a bipartisan foreign policy, he reached out to Democrats, academics, and journalists, many of whom were fixtures on Nixon's enemies list. It seemed to Nixon that Henry could never resist a request for a meeting or a press contact that would cast him in a positive light.

The president had been particularly irritated by an interview his aide had given to an Italian journalist, Oriana Fallaci, who asked him to explain the reasons for his "incredible movie-star status" and popularity. Rather than deflect the question, Kissinger appeared to revel in his stardom. "Being alone has always been part of my style," he was quoted as saying. "Americans like the cowboy who leads the wagon train by riding ahead alone on his horse." The image of the slightly pudgy professor riding into Moscow or Beijing on a white steed was greeted with a mixture of hilarity and outrage by his White House colleagues. As far as anyone knew, he had never mounted a horse in his life. More important, the role of lonely hero facing down America's enemies was one that Nixon reserved for himself. As John Ehrlichman commented acerbically, "If there was a Lone Ranger handling foreign affairs, the President would have cast Henry, I suspect, as Tonto." Although Kissinger insisted he had been misquoted, the damage was done.

"Make the point to Henry that he doesn't make the decisions," a furious Nixon instructed Haldeman. "Henry should stop having interviews alone."

But still the leaks and flattering profiles of Kissinger continued. The more praise that was showered on Henry, the madder Nixon became. When *Time* magazine revealed in mid-December that Nixon and Kissinger would share its coveted "Man of the Year" title, the president became almost "white-lipped in anger." He told Haldeman to instruct the White House switchboard to block telephone calls from *Time* to Kissinger, an order the chief of staff declined to implement. He was even more angry when he read a James Reston column in *The New York Times* on December 31 that alluded to a split between the president and his national security adviser. If Kissinger resigned, Reston reported, he would be free to "write the whole story of the Paris talks and why they broke down, and this would probably be highly embarrassing to Mr. Nixon." Given Reston's reputation as the éminence grise of Washington reporters, Nixon assumed that the story had been planted by Kissinger himself.

"I will not tolerate insubordination," he shouted at Colson down the phone from Camp David. "You tell Henry he's to talk to no one, period! I mean no one. And tell him not to call me. I will accept no calls from him."

On Nixon's instructions, Colson ordered the Secret Service to make a log of Kissinger's phone calls. The logs quickly revealed a call that Kissinger made to another columnist, Joseph Kraft, on January 2 at a time when he claimed that he "wasn't talking to anyone." Two days later, Kraft published a blistering piece criticizing "the murder-bombing" of Hanoi. "Dr. Kissinger remains perhaps the only instrument for effective foreign policy available to President Nixon," Kraft concluded. "But he has been compromised and everybody in town knows it. Unless he gets a new mandate from the President—the kind of mandate he can only get by being made Secretary of State—he should probably resign in the next year."

"I'll be goddamned," exclaimed Nixon, after reading the Kraft article and learning about his earlier phone conversation with Kissinger. "That's unbelievable."

When Colson explained that it was only possible to track Kissinger's outgoing office calls, not the incoming, Nixon demanded that his home phone also be monitored. "The FBI is to keep the log on his phone. All we want to know is who the hell he calls."

Privately, Nixon had decided that he would soon part ways with his grandstanding national security adviser. After the "lonesome cowboy" interview he told Colson that he was counting the days until Henry returned to academia. "It's not good for a man to stay too long in that position," he confided. "Time for him to get back to other things." Kissinger, too, understood that his usefulness to Nixon would dwindle rapidly once Vietnam was wrapped up. As the second term of the Nixon presidency began, he was thinking about accepting an offer of a visiting professorship at Oxford. He complained to his friends about being "stabbed in the back" by the "public relations geniuses" at the White House.

Nixon's concerns about Kissinger went beyond the daily newspaper headlines. Even more important to him was the judgment of history. His decision to install a White House taping system had been motivated in large part by their rivalry. He wanted to be able to demonstrate that he, not Henry, was the author of the most important foreign policy initiatives of his presidency. That meant compiling—and controlling—the primary source documentation.

The president was aware that Henry was keeping his own record of meetings and telephone conversations that could one day compete with the record that Nixon was assembling. Kissinger aides listened in to his phone calls and took shorthand notes, pressing a mute button on their extensions known as a "dead key" to avoid interfering with the conversation. White House wags were soon referring to the Kissinger archive as the "Dead Key Scrolls." As Nixon's suspicions of Kissinger grew, he instructed Haldeman to "physically move" the secret scrolls into the president's own files. It was yet another order that the chief of staff chose not to fulfill. He wanted to avoid an open rift with Henry.

Interspersed with the denunciations of Kissinger for suspected disloyalty were expressions of solicitude for the psychological strain under which he was operating. For insights into Henry's "suicidal complex," Nixon recommended that Haldeman read a book by his former doctor, Arnold Hutschnecker, called *The Will to Live*. Nixon had found the book helpful back in 1951 at a time when Hutschnecker was treating him for insomnia and stress. An Austrian-born internist and psychotherapist, Hutschnecker had made a specialty out of studying the mental stability of political leaders. For him, the issue was not curing neuroses—many of his prominent patients were neurotic in some fashion—but putting them to good use. He believed that outstanding leaders were driven by "inner aggression," which he defined as an obsessive need to prove oneself, frequently resulting from "childhood experiences of inferiority and helplessness." Such men should be helped to find a way to channel the "lust for power" in a positive rather than negative direction. The willingness to talk to a psychiatrist was an important first step.

Nixon "wants to be sure that I make extensive memoranda about K's mental processes and so on for his files," Haldeman recorded on December 8. Playing amateur psychiatrist, John Ehrlichman speculated that Kissinger "wants subconsciously to flee rather than fight," and was maneuvering to blame the president for the possible failure of the Vietnam peace talks. Nixon urged his aides to boost the morale of the temperamental national security adviser until a peace agreement had been concluded.

Shying away from face-to-face rows, Nixon avoided confronting Kissinger with his suspicions directly, assigning unpleasant tasks to Colson or Haldeman. For his part, Kissinger was always at his most obsequious when meeting or talking with the president. His tone of voice would change from matter of fact to subservient when he received a phone call from Nixon. He learned how to ape the speech patterns of his boss, throwing in cusswords and epithets calculated to please him. He was the only White House staff member who could match Nixon's ability to dredge up obscure historical references and parallels. As they agonized over China and Russia, they would veer off into discussing whether the United States should have formed an alliance with Germany at the end of World War II to counter the rising Soviet menace. This followed on from their long-running debate about the merits of various Wehrmacht generals, a subject that fascinated Nixon, having read Churchill's multivolume history of the war.

At the heart of their odd-couple relationship were two very different personalities. Nixon was a loner who defined himself in relation to his many enemies. "Never forget, the press is the enemy," he lectured Kissinger after the temporary breakdown in the Vietnam peace negotiations. "The establishment is the enemy. The professors are the enemy. Write that on a blackboard a hundred times and never forget it." A longtime practitioner of the politics of division, he fed off other people's hatred. Kissinger, by contrast, was one of the world's most accomplished networkers. As a refugee to the United States, he had a natural desire to assimilate and fit in. He worked hard at wooing and winning over the very elites that Nixon despised. This did not prevent him from assuring Nixon that he "needed no instruction at all" about the nature of the enemy, particularly concerning "professors." The Harvard professor of government was adept at talking to different audiences out of different sides of his mouth.

They were both outsiders, but outsiders of a different kind. Kissinger was a Jew whose family had been driven out of Germany by the Nazis. Nixon was the son of a pious Quaker mother and a struggling California grocer. Kissinger was driven by a desire for approval, Nixon by a yearning for revenge. Kissinger used self-deprecating humor to make fun of his interloper status; Nixon lashed out at the elites who attempted to exclude him. Kissinger detected a sensitive soul beneath the president's tough-guy facade. He wrote later that he was "touched" by the "vulnerability of a man who lived out a Walter Mitty dream of toughness that did not come naturally." He saw in Nixon a "strange mixture of calculation, deviousness, idealism, tenderness, tawdriness, courage, and daring" that "evoked a feeling of protectiveness among those closest to him—all of whom he more or less manipulated, setting one against the other." It took one insecure, exceptionally complicated outsider to understand the dreams and neuroses of the other.

Vietnam had been a draining experience for both men. The war had poisoned American politics, causing rifts not only between left and right, young and old, but within the White House itself. It had created a climate of paranoia that fed on itself, with aides suspecting each other of leaking damaging information to the press. When *The New York Times* began publishing a classified history of the war known as the Pentagon Papers in June 1971, Kissinger exploded. "This will totally destroy American credibility forever," he raged. "No foreign government will ever trust us again." The president needed little persuading that draconian action was necessary. According to Haldeman, "Henry got Nixon cranked up, and then they started cranking each other up until they were both in a frenzy." This in turn inspired the creation of a "special investigations unit" to track down leakers of government documents. The team set up shop in a warren of offices on the ground floor of the Executive Office Building known as Room 16. Because they were charged with plugging leaks, unit members jokingly affixed a sign to the entryway that read simply, "Plumbers." Gordon Liddy and Howard Hunt were among the first recruits.

A former Kissinger aide named Daniel Ellsberg had already come under suspicion as the man who supplied the Pentagon Papers to the *Times.* Ellsberg had helped run the CIA rural pacification program in South Vietnam but had returned home disillusioned. His top secret security clearances enabled him to obtain an assignment from the Rand Corporation to assemble an official history of the war. He went into hiding after the FBI showed up to interview him, turning up later on the CBS evening news to accuse the U.S. government of responsibility for millions of deaths in Vietnam. As a suspected leaker, Ellsberg became an early target of the White House Plumbers. In one of their first forays into illegal activity, they broke in to the office of his psychiatrist in

National Guard troops resting in the corridors of the
Executive Office Building while on standby during Vietnam War protests
in May 1970 to prevent demonstrators from attacking the White House.

Beverly Hills in an attempt to gather incriminating material. The seeds of Watergate were sown.

The domestic and foreign policy dramas quickly became intertwined. The toxic legacy of Vietnam bled into Nixon's handling of the Watergate scandal and vice versa. Massive antiwar protests spawned a bunker mentality inside the White House—an atmosphere of "Us against Them," in the phrase of Howard Hunt—that led directly to Watergate. Distracted by Vietnam, Nixon paid little attention to the gathering legal storm during the weeks that followed his reelection. By the time he began to focus on the events unfolding in Judge Sirica's courtroom, his ability to influence them was already much diminished.

Nixon reluctantly acknowledged that the Vietnam negotiations had turned Kissinger into "the hottest property in the world." He sensed an opportunity for a public relations campaign that would "give no quarter whatever to the doves." The results, however, were deeply disappointing. Why was the administration's "big gun" failing to emphasize the message "peace with honor"? Why was no one building up

RN the way that JFK had been built up by acolytes like Ted Sorensen and Arthur Schlesinger? Why did Kissinger mention the commander in chief only three times in his most recent press briefing when he mentioned him fourteen times back in December when everything was falling apart? Why no references to the president as a "profile in courage"?

"Henry kept saying we'd kill the critics," Nixon grumbled to Haldeman. "We haven't done that at all."

But still there was light beckoning him on through the darkness. At the end of January, the Gallup public opinion poll recorded a 68 percent approval rating for Nixon, the highest of his presidency, a fourteen-point gain in two weeks. Three out of four Americans endorsed his handling of Vietnam. The "silent majority"—the hard hats, the people of supposedly "limited intelligence," the voters out in the boondocks—had stood with him and become even more numerous. Perhaps, just perhaps, he could escape the political bunker in which he had been trapped for the last four years. If all else failed, he would certainly be vindicated by history—assisted, of course, by his tapes.

F ive hours after Nixon addressed the nation on Vietnam, the deputy director of the Federal Bureau of Investigation stood by the pillar next to space D32 of a dreary underground parking garage waiting for his reporter friend. Mark Felt was privy to the inner secrets of the Watergate inquiry. His name was stamped on the top of the distribution list for every single document assembled in the case, a collection that now ran to twenty-five volumes, each containing between two hundred and three hundred pages. By year-end calculations, 343 agents had expended 21,658 man-hours interviewing 2,321 persons, following up on 2,670 leads. All this documentation had ended up on Felt's desk on the fifth floor of the Justice Department, six blocks down Pennsylvania Avenue from the White House. Most of it was marked "CONFIDENTIAL."

It was a cold night, about forty degrees, and even chillier three stories belowground on the bottom floor of the parking garage in the Washington suburb of Arlington, directly across the Potomac from the Watergate complex. Felt had selected the spot for his meetings with the *Washington Post* reporter Bob Woodward because it was reasonably convenient to his home. It also offered multiple escape routes if they were disturbed. But that seemed unlikely at two in the morning. The bland twelve-story office building on top of the garage was closed and the surrounding area almost completely deserted. A thirty-one-year bureau veteran, Felt had learned his spy tradecraft during World War II, when he was assigned to follow suspected Nazi agents.

Felt now led two very different lives. By day, he was the smooth, superefficient G-man (government man), writing obsequious notes to his boss, the acting FBI director, L. Patrick Gray III. "Morale outstanding, never higher," ran a typical missive. A stern disciplinarian, Felt did not hesitate to order a leak investigation when he suspected a subordinate of disclosing unauthorized information to the media. By night, he was a whistle-blower, fulminating about the "dirty tricks" of the Nixon White House and fretting about threats to the U.S. Constitution. A master bureaucratic schemer, he saw himself as the rightful heir to J. Edgar Hoover, the legendary founder of the FBI, who had died in May 1972. In pursuit of his ambition, Felt was ready to go to extreme lengths to discredit the interloper Gray. Even for someone trained to compartmentalize his activities, it was a strange and stressful existence.

He had first met Woodward, quite by chance, in the White House in the winter of 1970, long before Watergate. Hoover had asked Felt to investigate a rumored "ring of homosexuals at the highest levels of the White House" that was alleged to include both Haldeman and Ehrlichman. Felt found no evidence to support the accusations and recommended the case be closed. He had handled the matter discreetly, winning the confidence of Nixon and his aides. During one of many visits to the West Wing, he ran into Woodward, then a U.S. Navy lieutenant, in the basement reception area outside the Situation Room. Felt was waiting to meet a senior official; Woodward was delivering some documents from the Pentagon. Despite the huge difference in age and seniority, they struck up a conversation. The debonair, highly experienced Felt became an informal mentor to Woodward. After Woodward left the navy and joined the *Post* as a junior reporter in 1971, Felt remained a valued source.

Felt had helped Woodward with some of his early reporting on Watergate, notably a June 20, 1972, scoop that linked the burglars to the White House consultant Howard Hunt. On that occasion, Woodward had simply telephoned Felt at the Justice Department. Felt had replied to Woodward's questions but was clearly very nervous. He demanded an elaborate protocol for future contacts. Instead of talking on the phone, they would meet in inconspicuous places in the dead of night.

To make sure he was not being followed, Woodward had to take at least two different cabs to a meeting and walk part of the way. It was all very cloak-and-dagger. Any information that Felt provided to Woodward would be "on deep background," meaning it could be used as guidance but Felt could not be quoted. The phrase "deep background" inspired *Post* editors to refer to Woodward's secret source as "Deep Throat" after the title of a new pornographic movie.

Their first clandestine meeting in the underground parking garage at 1401 Wilson Boulevard had occurred on October 9. Deep Throat arrived first. Even though he claimed to have given up smoking in 1943, Felt was puffing at a cigarette when Woodward showed up at 2:00 a.m. The principal message he wanted to convey was that Watergate was much more than just "a third-rate burglary," to use Ron Ziegler's phrase. FBI investigators were uncovering a vast "offensive security" operation directed against political opponents involving dozens of people reporting to senior Nixon aides. The following day, the *Post* splashed a story across its front page written by Woodward and his colleague Carl Bernstein that was headlined "FBI Finds Nixon Aides Sabotaged Democrats." The most ambitious attempt yet by a news organization to pull together the multiple tentacles of Watergate was sourced to "information in FBI and Department of Justice files." How the two reporters came to know what was in these files was left to the readers' imagination.

Felt was frustrated by the narrowness of the FBI investigation, which focused on the Watergate break-in itself. Justice Department prosecutors had refused to examine other dirty tricks and violations of campaign finance laws for their connections to Watergate. To make matters worse, White House lawyers had been allowed to closely monitor the investigation. They insisted on being present whenever anyone from the FBI interviewed someone from the administration. Some witnesses were understandably reluctant to share information when they knew their jobs were on the line.

As Felt saw it, news outlets like the *Post* served as a kind of heavy artillery, clearing the way for FBI ground troops to advance. A newspaper article could "apply public pressure on the White House to come clean." At a minimum, it would certainly speed up the investigation by providing leads for other institutions to pursue. If Congress and the courts became involved, the FBI would be obliged to follow suit.

Felt had observed firsthand how J. Edgar Hoover had skillfully used leaks to trusted journalists as a weapon in his ruthless turf battles with other parts of the vast federal bureaucracy. For Hoover, the power and prestige of the FBI were virtually synonymous with his own power and prestige. What served one also served the other.

Nicknamed the White Rat by his colleagues for his mane of silver hair and mastery of bureaucratic intrigue, Felt had learned from the master. As with Hoover, it was difficult to distinguish personal ambition from patriotism in the way he conducted himself. By leaking sensitive information to Woodward and other journalists, he was making a White House cover-up more difficult. But he was also taking revenge against the people who had blocked his promotion to FBI director following Hoover's death. The succession struggle was not yet over. Gray had been appointed only "acting director." Although he had previously served as an assistant attorney general and had a reputation of being a Nixon loyalist, he did not have his own power base at the bureau. Agents called him "Three-day Gray" because of the long weekends he spent at his home in Connecticut. If Felt played his cards right, it was quite possible he could prevent Gray from being confirmed in the position. In this case, the way would be open for Felt to grab the top job for himself.

But first he had to coach his young protégé in the basics of cracking a criminal conspiracy. At one of his first meetings with Woodward in the parking garage, on October 27, he reprimanded him for prematurely naming Haldeman as a target of a grand jury investigation. The story had turned out to contain some errors that allowed the White House to attack the *Post* for lousy reporting. "Shit, what a royal screw-up," Felt complained. It was necessary to proceed slowly and deliberately, particularly when going after someone as high up as Haldeman. "You build convincingly from the outer edges in, you get ten times the evidence you need against the Hunts and Liddys. They feel hopelessly finished. They may not talk right away, but the grip is on them. Then you move up and do the same thing at the next level. If you shoot too high and miss, then everyone feels more secure. Lawyers work this way. I'm sure smart reporters must too."

The FBI was still far from resolving the mystery of who ordered the break-in by the time Deep Throat met again with Woodward at parking space D32 at 2:00 a.m. on January 24. Felt and other senior investigators were convinced Colson and Mitchell were "involved up to their ears," based on their ties to Liddy and Hunt. Assembling the necessary proof was another matter. The evidence was circumstantial at best. The White House was doing an excellent job of keeping everything under wraps.

"If the FBI couldn't prove it, I don't think *The Washington Post* can," Felt told Woodward. Nixon's men would deny everything and attack the out-of-control media. To illustrate the point, he placed his gloved hands on the hood of one of the parked cars, acting the part of the White House spokesman standing behind a rostrum. "From this podium, I'm prepared to denounce such questions about gentle Colson and noble Mitchell as innuendo, character assassination, and shoddy journalism." Woodward burst out laughing as the pretend Ziegler attacked the "small Georgetown coterie of self-appointed guardians of public mistrust who seek the destruction of the public's will."

At this point, they both heard a noise. As Woodward later recalled in *All the President's Men,* "Deep Throat ducked behind a car. Woodward walked up the ramp guardedly. A very convincing old drunk was leaning against the wall, shivering. Woodward made sure he was real, then gave him a $10 bill and told him to find a hotel room."

The interruption put an end to their levity. Felt became thoughtful. It all came down to whether anyone with knowledge of the actual chain of command was willing to talk. "Liddy and McCord should realize that no one can help them because it will be too obvious. Any congressional investigation is going to have a big problem unless they get someone from the inside to crack. Without that, you come up with lots of money and plans for dirty tricks but no firsthand account or detailing of what happened at the top."

Woodward left the parking garage with empty hands. He did not have enough for a story implicating Mitchell and Colson. Not yet, anyway.

H istory is full of surprising twists and turns unfolding in obscure places hidden from public view at the time but destined to become notorious. One such twist occurred the day after Woodward's most recent secret meeting with Deep Throat in the underground parking garage. The location was a picturesque spot on the Potomac River four miles upstream from the Watergate. The Virginia side of the river has been preserved as parkland, overlooking the monuments of downtown Washington, the cliffs of Georgetown, and a series of dramatic gorges and waterfalls. During the Civil War, the river marked the front line between north and south. From the roof of the White House, President Lincoln could observe the twinkling fires of Confederate army camps on the opposite bank of the river, in Virginia.

On the morning of January 25, James McCord drove along the George Washington Memorial Parkway for a meeting with his White House contact. They met, as usual, at an overlook on the northbound side of the parkway. Jack Caulfield, a retired New York policeman, reported to the White House counsel, John Dean, who had been running the damage containment efforts on Watergate. Dean was worried that the head of the Watergate break-in team had wandered "off the reservation" and was resisting direction from the White House. He was alarmed by the "scorched desert" letter that McCord had written to Caulfield warning of horrendous consequences if the cover-up continued. It was Caulfield's job to get his man back onto the reservation through a carefully calibrated mix of threats, promises, and material inducements. The two men had known each other for many years, but McCord was proving very stubborn.

The original goal had been to get McCord to follow Howard Hunt's example and plead guilty in the Watergate trial, avoiding the need to testify. In return for his cooperation, he would be promised a presidential pardon, probably by Christmas, terms similar to those already dangled in front of Hunt. Caulfield arranged for McCord to go to a pay phone in a parking lot near his home to receive a telephone call from the White House. "Plead guilty," an unknown voice had informed him. "You will get executive clemency. Your family will be taken care of and when you get out, you will be rehabilitated and a job will be found for you."

During an initial meeting with Caulfield at the Potomac overlook, on the evening of January 12, McCord made clear he was not interested in an eventual pardon. He had already spent six horrible days in the District of Columbia jail after his arrest at the Watergate with the other burglars. He wanted his freedom right away. They met again, two days later, at the same place. This time, they scrambled down from the parking area to the tree-lined riverbank. McCord had been upset to open *The Washington Post* that very morning and read a flattering profile of Jeb Magruder. It bore the headline "Jeb Stuart Magruder: No Rebel Despite the Name," a reference to the dashing Confederate cavalry general J. E. B. Stuart, after whom Magruder had been named. Photographs of Jeb's wife, Gail, and their three children, all in matching clothes, were splashed across the front page of the Style section. The article described how Magruder had moved on from CREEP to run the presidential inaugural committee, a "total marketing project," in his words. It painted a picture of a successful young executive surrounded by an adoring family. "Jeb Stuart Magruder is 38 and even on his worst day, after suffering the most sleepless of nights, he could pass for, well, 25," the article began. "There is a look of perpetual innocence on his boy-next-door face with the brown eyes and apple cheeks."

Even though they were never in direct contact, McCord had learned about Magruder's involvement in Watergate through Liddy. He could not abide the thought that he would soon be sent to prison for his role in the break-in while the man who authorized the operation continued to enjoy a happy home life and public esteem. The whole situation was terribly unfair. McCord warned Caulfield that he might make his own "statement" laying out the true facts if Magruder continued to deny any connection to Watergate. In his opinion, if one person went to jail, "all who are involved must go."

Caulfield emphasized the momentous choice facing McCord. "The president's ability to govern is at stake," he told his old friend. "The government may fall. Everybody else is on track but you. You are not following the game plan. Get closer to your attorney."

By the time of their final meeting, on January 25, McCord had heard Magruder commit perjury in open court. He joined Caulfield for a two-hour car ride. They drove northward up the parkway in the direction of Caulfield's rural Virginia home, before returning to Washington. Caulfield again accused McCord of "fouling up the game plan" and urged him to accept the offer of an eventual pardon in exchange for keeping quiet. Angry with Magruder and his White House superiors, McCord refused to back down. He told Caulfield he would speak publicly when the time was right.

Horrified, Caulfield warned McCord that the administration would certainly defend itself. "Jim, I have worked with these people. I know them to be as tough-minded as you and I. When you make your statement, don't underestimate them."

"I have had a good life," replied McCord. "My will is made out."

I t took just ninety minutes for the jury in the Watergate bugging trial to find Gordon Liddy and James McCord guilty on all charges. Sequestered inside the court building for the past three weeks, the jurors wanted desperately to go home. Wary about aggressively challenging the White House on the basis of inconclusive evidence, Justice Department prosecutors had depicted Liddy as the "mastermind, the boss, the money man" of the operation. They maintained that Liddy had gone far beyond the parameters established by his superiors for "legitimate intelligence gathering activities." He had diverted Nixon reelection funds for his own purposes, splurging on extravagant hotels and restaurants. No higher-ups were involved: the conspiracy ended at Liddy's level. McCord, meanwhile, had been motivated by financial considerations alone. He had obeyed Liddy's instructions because he needed the money.

Mistrusting this explanation for Watergate, Sirica postponed sentencing to a later date. He had the power to send Liddy to prison for up to thirty-five years and fine him $40,000. As the leader of the break-in team, McCord could be jailed for up to forty-five years and fined up to $60,000.

U.S. marshals appeared behind both men after Sirica refused to hold a bail hearing. From the courtroom on the second floor, the two convicted defendants were escorted to holding cells in the basement. A few hours later, they were taken to a larger room where they were ordered to strip. Along with other prisoners, they stood naked in two lines, waiting for a marshal to summon them forward.

"Arms up," barked the marshal, as each man approached.

The prisoner exposed his armpits to show that there was nothing hidden in the cavity.

"Lift your stick."

The prisoner raised his penis.

"Balls."

The said objects were displayed to the satisfaction of his jailer.

"Turn around and spread 'em."

Bending over, the prisoner separated his buttocks to allow his anus to be inspected.

It was a humiliating procedure, particularly for McCord, who prided himself on being a respectable family man motivated throughout by love of country. He was a lieutenant colonel in the Air Force Reserve and had received a Distinguished Service Award from the CIA for "outstanding performance." Together with his wife, Sarah, he was a pillar of the Rockville United Methodist Church, organizing a "social fellowship" for retirees. They had helped raise funds for a special school attended by their mentally impaired daughter. At least externally, it was hard to imagine a more upstanding leader of the community than the quiet, balding man with a military bearing who now stood with his buttocks exposed to a federal marshal.

After receiving the order to put their clothes back on, the prisoners were handcuffed and chained together at the waist. Marshals escorted them to a bus specially outfitted with heavy steel mesh covering the windows and an even more impenetrable steel barrier separating them from the driver's area. From the federal courthouse on Pennsylvania Avenue, they were taken on a fifteen-minute drive to a squalid redbrick building beside the putrid Anacostia River. As the gates swung open, they entered "a courtyard befouled with pigeon droppings that had accumulated for a century." In Liddy's later recollection, "furtive cats hunting the ever present rats and mice darted aside as the bus emptied." The lone two white men in the chain gang waited bemused as a prisoner greeted a returning convict. "Hey, Leroy! Movafucks gotcha 'gan, huh?"

"Yeah, bum beef, man," the old-timer acknowledged.

They had arrived at the D.C. jail, a 104-year-old facility that had become notorious for riots, overcrowding, and casual brutality on the part of both guards and inmates. Just a few weeks before, the inmates had seized eleven guards as hostages to protest intolerable conditions. It was freezing cold in winter, stifling hot in summer. Rats and roaches crawled over prisoners as they slept on soiled mattresses. Many toilets consisted of a hole in the floor. Violent rapes were commonplace. "This is an act of rebellion against the system," an inmate informed a reporter who attempted to mediate. "This is an act for respect and for us to be treated as men and not as animals in animal-like cages." The rebellion was defused, but the "animal-like cages" remained. By the time Liddy and McCord were admitted, the public defenders' office had filed a lawsuit alleging that their clients were being subjected to "cruel and unusual punishment."

Once again, the two new inmates were made to undress for a strip search. They were then "deloused" with a chemical spray and issued ill-fitting prison garb. A trusty—a senior prisoner delegated to perform menial bureaucratic tasks by the guards—interviewed them both as part of the intake process. Quite apart from the obvious racial differences, they seemed a very unusual pair. Liddy took a perverse pleasure in claiming a wage rate of $100 an hour and twenty years of formal education, including a doctorate in law. The trusty gave him a disbelieving look as he laboriously typed out the answers. Finally, the penny dropped.

"You Watergate?"

"Right."

"You Liddy?"

"Right again."

"You really know Nixon?"

"Yup."

The cellblock consisted of four rows of cages bounded by a brick wall on one side and steel walls on the remaining three sides. Each cage measured six feet by eight feet, just enough room for a bunk bed, metal desk, and seat welded to the wall. There was a slot in the metal door wide enough to insert a food tray from the catwalk that ran the length of the gallery. According to Liddy, the overall effect was of living in a corner of "a huge cavern through which shouts, screams, screeches, and moans echoed and reechoed into an unintelligible roar." Loudspeakers blared music from a local African American radio station all day and much of the night. The cacophony brought to mind "a stadium crowd following a touchdown in some hellish arena from the imagination of Dante."

"Is it always this noisy?" Liddy asked McCord after they were led to their cell at the end of the first tier.

"It quiets down about two o'clock in the morning. Breakfast is about 4:30, then everyone goes back to sleep until about eight. Then they turn on the radios and televisions."

The two Watergate convicts reacted to their prison experience in profoundly different ways. McCord sank deeper into a depression. He complained repeatedly about Magruder and the newspaper article about his happy home life and beautiful family. He was angry with Sirica, describing the judge as "mentally unstable." Liddy began to tire of his companion's increasingly bitter tirades and feigned sleep in order to avoid conversation. His own attitude was one of uncompromising defiance. Subjected to racial taunts by the other inmates, he responded by singing, at the top of his lungs, "the anthem of the nation whose psychotic obsession with race sent millions of those believed inferior to their graves."

"Die Fahne hoch!" he belted out in German, as enthusiastically as any Nazi stormtrooper. *"Die Reihen fest geschlossen."* It seemed unlikely that anyone else in the cellblock understood the words of the "Horst Wessel Song"—"Raise the flag! The ranks are tightly closed"—but Liddy was confident they "got the message."

On February 3, Liddy and McCord were returned to Sirica's courtroom for their bail hearing. The feisty little magistrate was in an unforgiving mood. Although he had swallowed Magruder's perjury without asking any questions, he had "great doubts" that other witnesses had told the truth and was not prepared to act the part of a "nincompoop." "I am still not satisfied that all the pertinent facts that might be available—I say *might* be available—have been produced before an American jury." He expressed the hope that a planned Senate investigation "would try to get to the bottom of what happened in this case."

The judge set bail for Liddy and McCord at $100,000 each, pending final sentencing on March 23. Because neither man had the funds to secure his provisional freedom, both were sent back to prison. The remaining five defendants had all pleaded guilty. Privately, Sirica hoped, the prospect of lengthy jail sentences would cause one or more of them to "reconsider their defiant stance."

As an antidote to his Watergate troubles, Richard Nixon yearned to connect with "real Americans." At a breakfast meeting with his cabinet on February 8, he talked about the family of Colonel William Nolde, the last of 57,597 Americans to be killed in Vietnam. Nolde had been hit by enemy artillery fire just hours before the cease-fire came into effect. After Nolde's funeral at Arlington National Cemetery, his widow and five children had met the president at the White House, leaving a powerful impression. "She carried herself like a queen," Nixon recalled. Equally memorable was Nolde's seventeen-year-old son. A lanky boy with a scraggly beard, mustache, and long hair, he looked like a typical student rebel, the type TV networks loved to highlight in their reports. But he wore a large American flag in his lapel.

"If he had not been a member of the Nolde family, I don't know if the Secret Service would have let him in," Nixon joked. "But he was a great kid. Really proud of his dad."

He choked up when he described how the sixteen-year-old daughter had stepped forward to greet him. She had blond hair and blue eyes. "You might expect her to be crying, but she was not crying. She said to me, 'Mr. President, can I kiss you?'"

For the next fifteen seconds, Nixon was unable to speak. "Well, anyway," he murmured. There was another long pause, until he said, "I guess that's what it's all about." After an agonized silence, he walked quickly out of the State Dining Room.

That evening, Nixon flew to California on Air Force One, newly rebranded the *Spirit of '76,* after America's upcoming bicentennial. He was accompanied by his wife Pat, daughter Julie, and son-in-law David Eisenhower, a lieutenant in the U.S. Navy. It was the maiden flight for a new Boeing 707 replacing the now outdated plane that had flown the body of the murdered John Kennedy back from Dallas. The cabin configuration was similar to its predecessor, except that there was now much more room in the lounge area behind the president's cabin. The space was reserved for senior staff. Junior staffers relegated to the back of the plane with the Secret Service complained of cramped seats that would no longer recline. Word reached Nixon through Julie that they blamed the imperious Haldeman for the new arrangement.

Richard Nixon had been planning a California vacation for some time, but now felt a particularly urgent need to escape the toxic political climate of Washington. By a vote of 77–0, the U.S. Senate had just approved a resolution to establish a "select committee" to conduct an investigation into Watergate and other "illegal, improper, and unethical" political campaign activities. The committee consisted of seven senators, four Democrats and three Republicans, with full subpoena powers to demand documents and summon witnesses. The investigation would begin as soon as a staff could be assembled. Hearings would be held in public.

With its whitewashed walls, red-tile roofs, thick wood-pegged doors, and shady cloisters, Nixon's vacation home at San Clemente resembled a Mexican hacienda. It was situated high on a cliff, looking down on one of the best surfer beaches in Southern California. The bedrooms and living areas were built around a light-filled patio lined with flower beds. Palm and eucalyptus trees shielded a swimming pool from the house and the beach. From the gazebo, Nixon and his guests could enjoy evening cocktails as they watched the spectacular sunset over the Pacific Ocean. Best of all, from the president's point of view, was a cozy den on the second floor where he could shut himself away with his books and music. It was so restful that he named the place La Casa Pacifica, the "peaceful house."

He had purchased the fourteen-room house on thirty acres of land for $1.4 million in 1969 with the idea that he would eventually retire there. A millionaire friend, Robert Abplanalp, who had made his for-

Aerial view of Nixon's La Casa Pacifica estate in San Clemente, California, a Mexican-style hacienda built around a courtyard.

tune from aerosol sprays, helped out with a loan. In order to repay the debt, Nixon subdivided the property. He kept six acres and sold the remainder to an investment company controlled by Abplanalp and his Florida real estate buddy Charles "Bebe" Rebozo. That left Nixon with the villa and the gorgeous clifftop views (for which he ended up paying around $350,000). His friends owned the surrounding buffer zone that provided both privacy and security for the president and his family. A group of businessmen calling themselves the 76 Club chipped in $85,000 for a three-hole golf course. The complicated financial transaction reflected the fact that Nixon was not a rich man. He had managed to save some money as a lawyer in New York prior to his election as president but was dependent on others for what had become a lavish lifestyle.

San Clemente was more than just a private residence, of course. Under Haldeman's supervision, more than $9 million in taxpayer money had been spent to transform the estate into the "Western White House." A helipad was installed on the grounds of the neighboring Coast Guard station, along with offices for the president, his staff, the Secret Service, and communications specialists. The improvements included $156,000 worth of landscaping, $33,000 in fire protection equipment, and an $1,800 flagpole. For an administration obsessed with the hated "eastern establishment," it was important to demonstrate that the country did not have to be run from Washington, D.C. The essential business of the executive branch could be carried out equally well in California or in Florida. Indeed, there were some advantages to operating outside the media glare. Nixon was reluctant to expose foreign leaders to the "hostile atmosphere" of the capital. "In San Clemente, we can control the damn place," he had told Alexander Haig a few days before.

Always restless and on the move, Nixon ended up spending large chunks of time outside Washington. His speechwriter William Safire found it ironic that "a man who had spent most of his adult life struggling to get to the White House" derived so little satisfaction from living there. During his first presidential term, Nixon had notched up 195 days in San Clemente and 157 days in the "Florida White House" at Key Biscayne. Another favorite "escape hatch" was Camp David. Nixon would frequently helicopter up to the presidential retreat in rural Maryland two or even three times a week from the South Lawn of the White House. During the four-week period immediately following his reelection victory, he had withdrawn to Camp David for a total of eighteen days, isolating himself from most of his aides and advisers as he made plans for the second term.

Although Nixon was now more than two thousand miles from the White House, his workday routine remained very similar. The morning after his arrival, he summoned Haldeman to his office at the Coast Guard station. They reviewed the daily news summary together, a ritual they had been performing for years. Nixon was delighted with his long-ignored secretary of state, William Rogers, for blasting the antiwar critics on Capitol Hill. "Infinitely more effective than Kissinger," he told Haldeman. He then veered off into a riff against wasting time with foreign dignitaries, particularly at embassy luncheons and arrival ceremonies. "No arrivals now for anyone who has already had one," he instructed his chief of staff. This was followed by boasts about his skill in delivering off-the-cuff speeches without ever referring to his notes. A way should be found of letting the public know that he had never read a toast at a White House dinner—or even one of those useless foreign leader arrival greetings that never made the evening news.

Then it was on to Watergate and the need for a strategy to deal with the newly formed Senate select committee. If the Democrats wanted to play rough, he would too. Searching for a diversionary counterattack, he suggested that the Senate committee also investigate Democratic Party leaders. He instructed Haldeman to put out word that the Democrats had supported peace protests, funded with "foreign or Communist money," that later turned violent. Talk about how "we ran a clean campaign compared to their campaign of libel and slander." Look into wiretapping allegations against the Kennedys. "We should play a hard game on this whole thing," Nixon ordered.

The beautifully landscaped hacienda on the edge of the Pacific Ocean was fifty miles but a world away from the parched citrus grove where Richard Milhous Nixon was born on January 9, 1913. His father, Frank, had built a cottage on the edge of a small town called Yorba Linda from a kit he had purchased through a mail catalog. The tiny house was exposed to the winds that blew across the basin from the Santa Ana Mountains to the east. The land was hard and arid, full of coyotes and rattlesnakes. There was dust everywhere. Frank planted lemon trees in the dry soil, but they did not yield much fruit. A stubborn man who resisted advice from others, he had no knack for farming. He took his frustration out on his family, yelling at his children when they misbehaved.

Richard's mother, Hannah, came from a family of persecuted Irish Quakers who settled in the North American colony of William Penn, dedicated to religious freedom, in 1729. In many respects, she was the opposite of her husband. He wore his emotions on his sleeve; she was icy and controlled. He used belts and sticks to discipline his boys; she preferred the silent treatment. He was a dreamer; she was severely practical. "Two more temperamentally different people can hardly be imagined," Richard recalled later. "In her whole life, I never heard her say to me, or to anyone else, 'I love you.'" Even so, Hannah made clear that she expected great things of her boys by naming them after the early kings of England: Harold, Richard, and Arthur.

There were three King Richards in English medieval history, reigning centuries apart. As president, Nixon was most frequently compared to Richard III (1483–1485). Whatever his merits as a ruler, the last of the Plantagenet kings is now chiefly remembered for Shakespeare's portrayal of a blood-soaked tyrant willing to do anything to gain and hold on to power. Nixon's critics saw a parallel between the scheming hunchback of Shakespearean tragedy and the socially awkward American politician embroiled in illegal foreign and domestic wars. Later on, they would point to another Shakespeare hero, Richard II (1377–1399), who was forced to abdicate his throne after being accused of misgovernment by his nobles.

The monarch that Hannah Nixon had in mind as a model for her second son, however, was neither Richard II nor Richard III, but Richard I (1189–1199). Known as "Richard the Lionheart," the original Richard spent much of his reign waging crusades in the Holy Land. Criticized by some historians for his single-minded pursuit of military glory at the expense of the public good, the Crusader King was the epitome of medieval chivalry as far as Hannah was concerned. She was quick to admonish an elementary school teacher who made the mistake of calling her son Dick. "I named him Richard," she corrected.

The matriarch of the family was Hannah's mother, Almira Milhous, who had moved to California in 1897, following the railroad and the economic boom. She and her husband, Franklin, purchased a plot of land in the Quaker town of Whittier. Although Almira adhered to the old Quaker practices of silent prayer and plain speech—as in "Where art thee going today?"—she soon discovered that the California Quakers were much more evangelical and Bible-thumping than their eastern forebears. The family was soon caught up in the religious revivals that swept through the state at the turn of the century. The young Richard

grew up in "a religious environment that was at once unusually strict
and unusually tolerant." He went to church four times on Sunday and
never went to bed at night without reading a few verses from the Bible.
At the same time he was brought up to regard religion and prayer as
private matters entirely separate from politics. He developed a lifelong
aversion to mentioning God in his public speeches.

As the representative of an old Quaker family, Almira looked down
on the rough-hewn Frank Nixon, who converted to Quakerism from
Methodism after his marriage to Hannah. But she took "a special interest" in the studious Richard, particularly after Frank gave up on his
lemon grove in Yorba Linda and moved the family to Whittier, closer
to his Milhous in-laws. Having failed at farming, Frank opened a gas
station and grocery store on a deserted stretch of highway outside town.
Richard walked two miles each way every day to school in Whittier.
On his thirteenth birthday, Almira gave him a $5 bill and a framed pic-
ture of Lincoln, her favorite president, which he hung over his bed. It

Nixon and his brothers in Yorba Linda around 1923.
(From left) Donald, aged seven, in tire; Richard, nine; Harold, twelve;
and Arthur, four. Both Harold and Arthur later died of tuberculosis.
Like Richard, they were named after famous English kings.

became one of his most treasured possessions. Underneath the portrait, Almira inscribed a quotation from Henry Longfellow that summed up the philosophy of life she sought to instill in her favorite grandson:

> *Lives of great men oft remind us*
> *We can make our lives sublime,*
> *And departing, leave behind us*
> *Footprints on the sands of time.*

Richard's life was far from "sublime" at the time he received this birthday present. His younger brother Arthur had died from tuberculosis five months earlier. For weeks after Arthur's funeral, there was "not a day that I did not think about him and cry," Richard later wrote. "For the first time I had learned what death was like and what it meant." Frank blamed his son's death on "divine displeasure" and vowed to never again open his store on Sunday. His newfound religiosity did not help his oldest son, Harold, who contracted the same illness as Arthur. Hannah took Harold to live in the mountains of Arizona, where the air was drier and cleaner than in Whittier. For almost three years, she boiled his sheets and plates, disposed of his sputum cups, and looked after three other consumptive patients to make ends meet. But it was all to no avail. After becoming so thin that "it was painful to look at him," the spirited, gregarious Harold passed away in 1933, a few weeks after Richard turned twenty.

Richard, meanwhile, had been getting up at four in the morning to help his father in the grocery store. After driving into Los Angeles to pick up produce, he would set up the vegetable counter, peeling rotten leaves off old lettuces and sprinkling them with water to make them look fresh. He loathed the whole routine but did his best to conceal his straitened circumstances. "He didn't want anybody to see him go get vegetables, so he got up real early and then got back real quick," remembered a cousin. The young Nixon blamed the family tragedy at least in part on the stubbornness of his father, who had refused to check the family cow in Yorba Linda for tuberculosis. But rather than criticize his father, "he sank into a deep, impenetrable silence," according to Hannah. "From that time on, it seemed that Richard was trying to be three sons in one, striving ever harder than before to make up to his father and me for our loss," she recalled later. "Unconsciously, too, I think that Richard may have felt a kind of guilt that Harold and Arthur were dead and that he was alive."

A bequest from his Milhous grandfather enabled Nixon to attend Whittier College. Founded by Quakers on a hill above the town, it resembled liberal arts colleges out east, complete with Grecian columns, ivy-covered buildings, and a football gridiron. By this time, Richard had become "Dick" to everyone except his mother. He was a star of the debate team, enthusiastic amateur actor, and intense, if clumsy, football player. Lacking natural athletic ability, he stood out through sheer persistence. Knocked down by a brutal tackle, he would immediately pick himself up again. His indestructibility made him a team mascot, even if he did not get to play very much. "Put Nixon in! Put Nixon in!" the crowd would roar in the dying moments of a game when Whittier was safely ahead. From his coach, Wallace "Chief" Newman, Nixon learned a lesson in never quitting. "You know who a good loser is?" the coach asked his players. "It's somebody who hates to lose and who gets back and fights again."

At least in public, Dick learned to control the temper he had inherited from his father. He once lost a student debate after becoming angry with his opponent. To prevent himself blurting out something inappropriate, he doubled down on debate preparation. He was always looking for "the ace in the hole" that would destroy the arguments of the other side and leave them flustered and off balance. The trick was to sound as if he were speaking extemporaneously even if he had carefully rehearsed his lines. "To be a good debater, you've got to be able to get mad on your feet without losing your head," he advised his teammates.

From his time at Whittier College he also gained valuable insights into the art of tapping into social grievances. Excluded from an elite student society known as the Franklins, he helped found a rival club designed to appeal to the underclass. They called themselves the Orthogonians, from the Greek word for "right angle." The implication was that they were "straight and square," unlike their stuffy, aristocratic rivals. They adopted the motto "Beans, Brains, Brawn, and Bowels" and had themselves photographed in open-necked shirts to distinguish themselves from the tuxedo-wearing Franklins. "They were the haves and we

were the have-nots," was how Nixon later explained it. Dominated by
the student athletes, the Orthogonians provided Dick with his political
base when he ran successfully for student government president in his
senior year. Displaying an early populist instinct, he campaigned on
a platform of allowing dancing on campus, even though he had little
interest in dancing himself.

It was also at Whittier that Dick developed his first serious relationship with a brainy, dark-haired girl named Ola Florence Welch. They
had dated in high school but became an established couple in college.
It was widely assumed that they would get married after graduating.
Ola's friends were puzzled by the friendship. She was outgoing; he
was reserved. She was tender; he was combative. She was a Democrat
who worshipped FDR; he was a Republican who preached the need
for self-reliance. They argued frequently, about politics and everything
else. "His face would cloud and he'd make a conscious effort to restrain
himself," she remembered later. "He'd be harsh and I'd cry. Then we'd
make up." When asked to explain what she saw in him, she mentioned
his exceptional intelligence. To the daughter of a small-town police
chief, the ambitious, book-loving Quaker boy represented intellectual
sophistication. "I considered myself provincial and him worldly," she
said later, long after they had broken up. At the same time, there was
something about him she could never quite figure out. "Sometimes I
think I never really knew him, and I was as close to him as anyone."
To Ola Welch, like many of his old California friends, Dick Nixon was
ultimately "a mystery." They drifted apart after he was accepted to Duke
University Law School in North Carolina in 1934. Four years later, he
began dating a "vivacious" Irish girl, Pat Ryan, who shared his love for
movies and football. They married in June 1940.

Later, people who knew Nixon well speculated that he had suffered
some deep hidden hurt in his childhood, perhaps at the hands of his
irascible father or his emotionally distant mother, that accounted for
the dark side of his character. Without going into details, Nixon himself
would attribute at least part of his success as a politician to miserable
experiences growing up. "What starts the process, really, are laughs and
slights and snubs when you are a kid," he told an associate many years
later. "But if you are reasonably intelligent and if your anger is deep

enough and strong enough, you learn that you can change those attitudes by excellence, personal gut performance while those who have everything are sitting on their fat butts."

Another clue to understanding the awkward young man from Yorba Linda lay in the Longfellow verse. Driven by a sense of resentment and insecurity, he was determined from an early age to leave some "footprints on the sands of time," whatever the obstacles, whatever the cost.

A ll presidents need outlets from the enormous pressures of office. Many have hobbies or other forms of recreation. For FDR, it was stamp collecting and mixing martinis for his cronies. Harry Truman liked to gamble for very small stakes. Eisenhower played golf. Kennedy sought relief in the company of beautiful young women. LBJ loved to drive around his Texas ranch and yank his beagles by the ears. Nixon was the exception. He tried his hand at golf but gave it up because it took too much time. He had an eye for pretty girls, but he was not a philanderer. If he had a hobby, it was the presidency itself. He relaxed by reading books about his predecessors, talking shop with Haldeman and Colson, and immersing himself in the minutiae of White House protocol.

He approached the topic of relaxation with the same grim determination that he applied to every other subject. In a March 1971 memorandum describing his "personal habits," he noted that he rarely spent more than five minutes on breakfast and five minutes on lunch. He recoiled at the idea of the "social lunch," the "social dinner," and the "social cocktail hour" as occasions "where there is a great deal of talk and many promises but very little follow-through." "Four to five hours on the golf course," including the traveling back and forth, was a luxury he could not afford. He lacked the patience to become a fisherman, although he enjoyed "being on a boat and watching other people catch fish." While acknowledging that a president needed to "recharge his batteries," he believed this could be accomplished most efficiently through an hour's worth of bowling, a walk on the beach, or a ride on a boat in the Florida Keys. He cited with approval the opinion of his friend Bebe Rebozo, who observed that he would often come to Florida "looking very tired" and be fully restored within one day. "I can recharge my batteries very fast," Nixon boasted. "A few dips in the saltwater, sitting in the sun, brings me back completely." One of the purposes of the frequent trips to sunny climes was to acquire a tan, which made him feel and look better, offsetting his naturally pale skin. He maintained the tan by spending two to three minutes under a collapsible sunlamp that an aide carried around in a briefcase for easy access. Too many sunlamp sessions turned him an unnatural orange color, so they had to be restricted.

Key to Nixon's relaxation strategy was the soothing personality of the self-made millionaire who had acquired his nickname, Bebe, from an older brother struggling to pronounce "baby." The son of a Cuban cigar maker who moved to Miami when he was eight, Rebozo was the man who helped Nixon unwind. They met first on a fishing trip in 1951. Then a senator, Nixon spent most of the trip working on his papers and barely spoke. The fun-loving Bebe did not know quite what to make of his dour new acquaintance. "He doesn't drink whiskey, he doesn't chase women, he doesn't even play golf," he complained. But he also recognized "a kind of genius" in Nixon and learned to adapt to his long silences. "Shhh," he admonished another Florida businessman who attempted to engage in small talk with an obviously reluctant Nixon on one of their boat trips. "He's meditating." White House aides joked that Rebozo was "the perfect companion for a man who likes solitude, because being with Bebe can be almost as good as being alone." Despite his generally accepted status as Nixon's closest friend, Bebe always respected the distance separating him from the man he addressed as "Mr. President."

He helped Nixon with several of his real estate deals like the purchase of his properties in Key Biscayne and San Clemente. Other favors included funding the construction of the White House bowling alley and using campaign funds to help buy a pair of earrings for Pat Nixon. But these financial transactions do not explain the essence of their relationship. According to the president's speechwriter William

Nixon and his friend Bebe Rebozo on the beach in Key Biscayne
with Nixon's Irish setter, King Timahoe. Rebozo lived next door to Nixon
and helped him buy his properties.

Safire, the quality that Nixon appreciated most in Bebe was that he "brooded well." He was able to listen to Nixon's "long, somber, resentful thoughts" for hours on end and regurgitate them back in slightly different form to please his friend. He reinforced Nixon's prejudices, particularly about the hated press, and was unfailingly loyal and discreet. Put simply, he "worshipped Nixon and hated his enemies." Virtually the same age as the president, he became a surrogate brother, "the man who could be 'there' without having to be addressed, noticed, or otherwise attended to."

"Old Bebe is a great guy to have around," Nixon had told Lyndon

Johnson just a few weeks before, in their final telephone conversation before LBJ's death. "He cheers people up. He never brings up any unpleasant subjects."

Among the many services that Bebe had performed for the Nixons was to introduce them to Manolo and Fina Sanchez, a Spanish-born couple who had moved to Cuba and immigrated to the United States from there. Manolo had worked as driver and handyman for the Nixon family in California and New York, while Fina did the cooking. They had proved so helpful and discreet that the Nixons brought them to the White House as personal assistants, installing them in a small apartment on the third floor of the mansion. Nixon had repaid their loyalty by sponsoring their applications to become American citizens. At the height of the antiwar demonstrations, unable to sleep, he had even taken Manolo on an impromptu 5:00 a.m. tour of the Lincoln Memorial, where they met with stunned protesters. From there, they had proceeded to the House of Representatives, where Nixon insisted that his valet deliver a speech from the Speaker's rostrum. (In his broken English, Manolo said he was proud to be a U.S. citizen.) "The weirdest day so far," Haldeman later recorded.

Another Bebe virtue, from Nixon's point of view, was that he always came when summoned. A longtime divorcé, he was ready to drop whatever he was doing and cross the country on a few hours' notice to be with the president. When Nixon asked him to fly to San Clemente for the weekend from Florida, he agreed instantly. He knew the drill: lounging by the pool, a drive along the coast, dinner at a local restaurant, privately screened movies in the evening. It was Rebozo's job to select the movie, according to Julie Nixon. If the movie turned out to be "a lemon," as frequently happened, Bebe would drop off to sleep, but Nixon would stick it out until the end. "Wait," he would tell family members tempted to call it a night. "Wait, it'll get better."

On Sunday morning, February 11, the Nixons drove a few miles up the coast, to Capistrano Beach, for a service at Palisades United Methodist Church. "He who would be great must be humble," the preacher sermonized. "He who would lead the people must be a servant." This was followed by a hair-raising two-hour drive in the pouring rain along the highways and back roads of Southern California with Bebe at the wheel, Nixon beside him, and Pat, Julie, and Julie's husband, David

Eisenhower, crammed into the backseat. At least it was hair-raising for the White House aides who attempted to keep up with them in a chase car.

"At times the rain came down in torrents and Bebe didn't even slow up," complained the presidential aide Steve Bull in an "Eyes Only" memo to Haldeman that bore the ominous title "Bebe Rebozo's Driving." He reported that Bebe drove "in excess of 70 miles an hour" in poor visibility through rain squalls and high winds. The Secret Service had given Bebe "special pointers on driving" and training in a test vehicle, but his performance behind the wheel remained erratic. Bull shuddered to think what might happen if a child darted in front of the car or it slid on a spot of oil. Even a minor accident would result "in a major story" and expose both the president and Bebe to harsh criticism. While Nixon's desire for "a bit of privacy with his friend" was understandable, it would be best if he was driven by an agent in future and for Rebozo "to act as a passenger in the vehicle."

It was not just Bebe's driving that was the problem. By making a detour through the canyons leading up into the Santa Ana Mountains, he risked taking the president out of normal communications range. On a recent trip to Florida, a helicopter had to be dispatched with an emergency communications link after the pair "drove off someplace into the boondocks," Bull noted. He had a nightmare vision of the president "stopping at a gas station and using a pay phone had it been necessary for him to make a decision such as launching nuclear missiles."

That evening, the Nixons and Bebe watched the 1946 movie *Undercurrent,* a noirish thriller starring Katharine Hepburn about an industrialist who murders his wife. After the unsanctioned escape into the mountains, Haldeman-approved presidential routine had been reestablished.

While Nixon was careening around mountain canyons with Bebe Rebozo, Bob Haldeman was focused on the political and legal perils facing the presidency. The chief of staff had summoned top Nixon aides to California to discuss the upcoming Senate Watergate investigation. They met in his villa at the Rancho La Costa, a luxury resort thirty miles down the coast from San Clemente used to accommodate the overflow from the Western White House. Complete with health spa, golf course, tennis courts, and equestrian ranch, the sprawling fifty-six-hundred-acre estate had become a favored vacation spot for Frank Sinatra, Bob Hope, and other members of the Hollywood elite. Haldeman and his men could take off their dark suits and somber ties, put on brightly colored golf pants and polo shirts, and relax in the sun in the knowledge that they were now in safe "Nixon country."

The key participant in the meeting was the thirty-four-year-old White House counsel, John Wesley Dean III, who was responsible for containing the legal fallout from Watergate. Smart and handsome, Dean impressed his superiors with his cool competence and seemingly photographic memory. The son of a mid-level executive at the Firestone Tire and Rubber Company, he had attended a military academy and served in the Justice Department under John Mitchell. He was flashier than most of the conservative young men recruited by Haldeman to serve in the senior levels of the Nixon White House. He wore expensive suits, drove a maroon Porsche 911 to work, and was openly ambitious. Three years after divorcing his first wife, a senator's daughter, he tired of the frenetic bachelor lifestyle and remarried. His new wife was a former airline hostess named Maureen, a glamorous blonde always impeccably dressed and groomed. They owned an expensive town house in Alexandria, Virginia, sailed their boat on the Chesapeake Bay on weekends, and took vacations in the Mediterranean and the Philippines. Life was good.

As the president's trusted lawyer, Dean became the go-to person for keeping tabs on the FBI investigation into Watergate and orchestrating the cover-up. He persuaded Justice Department officials to provide him with copies of FBI interviews of Watergate suspects. He coached Jeb Magruder in his perjured testimony, first to the grand jury and later in Judge Sirica's courtroom. He also dealt with the escalating demands of Howard Hunt and the other Watergate burglars for financial support and eventual presidential pardons. Prior to dealing with Watergate, he had been responsible for tracking anti-Nixon demonstrations and compiling lists of the president's enemies.

"Dean's doing a hell of a good job," Haldeman told Nixon admiringly in November 1972. "He's a damn good lawyer . . . Thank God we've got him there." In Haldeman's opinion, Dean was more effective than any of their allies at the Justice Department. He had worn himself out on behalf of the president.

"Poor John," said Nixon sympathetically.

Haldeman and Dean were joined in La Costa by John Ehrlichman, Nixon's domestic policy adviser, and a White House consigliere by the name of Richard Moore, a trusted friend to Mitchell. Together, they developed a "game plan" for dealing with the Senate inquiry: "total cooperation" in public and "maximum obstruction" in private. They would make it "as difficult as possible" for the senators to gather evidence and hear testimony. As Dean later recalled, "A behind-the-scenes media effort would be made to make the Senate inquiry appear very partisan. The ultimate goal would be to discredit the hearings and reduce their impact by attempting to show that the Democrats have engaged in the same type of activities."

Exhibit A in the "they did it to us first" defense was the alleged bugging of Nixon's plane by the FBI during the final days of the 1968 campaign. This had become a mantra to justify any wrongdoing by his people. Nixon had originally heard the story from J. Edgar Hoover, who said the bugging was carried out at the personal request of President Johnson. Dean proposed a simple trade. Nixon would keep mum about the bugging of his plane if the Democrats dropped their Watergate investigation. For the gambit to work, however, it was first necessary to assemble "hard evidence" showing the bugging of Nixon's plane.

This proved impossible. The wiretap allegation was not completely without foundation, but the story was much murkier and more complicated than Nixon made out. It originated with a compromising conversation between the Republican Dragon Lady, Anna Chennault, and the South Vietnamese ambassador in Washington that was captured on an FBI intercept three days before the November 5 election. In a telephone call from her Watergate penthouse, Chennault urged the South Vietnamese to reject Johnson's latest cease-fire proposals. The intercept disclosed that she had just spoken to "her boss" in New Mexico who told her to pass the message on to Saigon: "Hold on, we are gonna win." The Saigon government followed the Dragon Lady's advice and rebuffed an invitation to peace talks in the expectation of securing a better deal from Nixon. As it turned out, Nixon defeated Johnson's preferred can-

*Nixon shares elevator with LBJ while touring the White House
in December 1968 prior to his first inaugural.*

didate, Vice President Hubert Humphrey, by less than 1 percent of the
popular vote.

LBJ suspected the Nixon campaign of sabotaging his peace initiative
in order to gain a last-minute advantage in the closely fought race. "This
is treason," he fumed. The question then became how to demonstrate a
link between the Nixon campaign and the Dragon Lady. The embassy
intercept pointed to Nixon's vice presidential running mate, Spiro
Agnew, as the possible go-between. Informed that Agnew had made a
campaign stop in Albuquerque, New Mexico, on November 2, Johnson
ordered the FBI to find out whom he had called from his plane. The
bureau reported that Agnew had spoken with Secretary of State Dean
Rusk about the status of the Vietnam peace talks. He, or someone acting
on his behalf, had then called Nixon-Agnew campaign headquarters in
Washington. The jigsaw pieces seemed to fit together.

Nixon's version of events was wrong on several essential points. It
was not his plane that had been monitored, but Agnew's. The monitoring was conducted on the basis of telephone company records,
not wiretaps, and it occurred after the event. The FBI complied with

Johnson's request to place Chennault under surveillance as a potential national security threat. Agents logged her comings and goings from her Watergate penthouse and tracked her movements around Washington. Her telephone calls with the South Vietnamese ambassador were wiretapped at the embassy end of the conversation, not her end. All this became grist for daily, sometimes twice daily, reports to Johnson, who kept a secret file on "The Lady."

Johnson had been furious to learn, shortly before his death on January 22, that Nixon was planning to dredge up the alleged bugging of his plane as part of his response to Watergate. He warned the White House, through intermediaries, that he was ready to reveal his competing version of events. He never did find out the identity of the Dragon Lady's mysterious "boss in New Mexico." It might not have been Agnew at all but a code name for someone else. In her 1980 memoir, *The Education of Anna*, Chennault identified John Mitchell as the likely conduit. She wrote that Mitchell used cryptic codes and other espionage techniques to set her up as a secret "back channel" between Nixon and the South Vietnamese during the run-up to the election. "Big John" was in charge of the Nixon election campaign, having earned his trust as a senior partner in their Manhattan law firm. There is little doubt that both Mitchell and Chennault were acting in accordance with Nixon's wishes. Among Haldeman's notes from this period is a comment by Nixon on the Johnson peace initiative: "Any other way to monkey wrench it?"

Nixon's hopes for an armistice with the Democrats were undermined by LBJ's refusal to play along. Even though Johnson was now dead, there was always the possibility that his aides could go public with the treason charge. This worried Nixon, but he refused to drop the subject. He remained convinced that his plane had been bugged on Johnson's orders. "Bullshit," he declared, when informed that the FBI was unable to confirm the wiretap claim. Through Haldeman, he ordered a full "FBI investigation against those who tapped Nixon and Agnew in 1968," with lie detector tests for anyone who might have been involved.

In addition to the bugging allegation, Nixon dredged up other material for "a counteroffensive" against the Democrats. "We need to get our people to put out the story on the foreign or Communist money that was used in support of demonstrations against the President in

1972," Haldeman instructed Dean on February 10. "We should tie all 1972 demonstrations to McGovern and thus to the Democrats as part of the peace movement." It was important to establish "to what extent the Democrats were responsible for the demonstrations that led to violence or disruption."

At the end of the La Costa meeting, John Ehrlichman raised a troubling issue: Would the Watergate defendants remain silent through the Senate hearings? The men who had planted bugs in the Democratic Party headquarters at the Watergate had been involved in other illegal acts, including breaking in to the Beverly Hills office of Daniel Ellsberg's psychiatrist. They guarded some of the Nixon administration's most incriminating secrets. If one of them broke ranks, other dirty tricks could be exposed, potentially even more embarrassing to the president than Watergate.

Faced with this "bottom line question" from Ehrlichman, Dean was obliged to concede that the demands for "hush money" were becoming overwhelming. He had already blown through a secret White House campaign fund of $350,000, originally earmarked for political polling, to cover the legal bills and living expenses of the seven Watergate defendants. The pressure was particularly intense from the former CIA operative Howard Hunt, whose wife, Dorothy, had been killed in a plane crash in December. Hunt had two school-age children, who would need someone to look after them if he was sent to prison, plus another two away in college. He was also responsible for channeling funds to the four Cubans he had recruited to join the operation. "What we've been getting has been coming in very minor dribs and drabs," he complained to Colson back in November. "Surely your cheapest commodity available is money." Since Dorothy's death, he had been sending threatening messages to his White House contacts, reminding them that "loyalty is a two-way street."

The four Nixon aides batted around ideas on how to raise the necessary funds. Someone suggested approaching Mitchell, who, they suspected, had signed off on the Watergate break-in as executive director of CREEP. The former attorney general was now back in New York at his old law firm, where he had made a fortune in municipal bonds. He was again earning big money and had plenty of rich friends. Because Moore had been to school with Mitchell and had worked for him at the

Justice Department, he was given the task of feeling out his old friend. But the gruff, pipe-smoking Mitchell was tired of doing favors for the Nixon White House.

"Tell them to get lost," was his reply when Moore reached him a few days later.

C huck Colson had become a political liability for Richard Nixon, now back in Washington after a long weekend in California. The special counsel's name was cropping up ever more frequently in the press in Watergate-related stories. His recruitment of his fellow Brown University alum Howard Hunt represented a direct link between the White House and the Watergate burglars. Other Nixon aides were skeptical of Colson's denial of advance knowledge of Watergate. Haldeman had learned about the telephone call that Nixon's "hatchet man" had made to Magruder in February 1972, urging him to approve Liddy's intelligence-gathering project. That, by itself, did not prove that Colson was aware of the plot to plant bugs in Democratic Party headquarters but could be embarrassing if any of the burglars decided to talk. As Haldeman explained to Nixon, "If Liddy decides to pull the cork, Colson could be in some real soup." It was quite likely that Colson had already perjured himself in interviews with the FBI, along with Magruder and Mitchell.

The president was reluctant to sacrifice his political soul mate. Fortunately, there was a way out of the difficulty. Colson would give up his special counsel position and high-ceilinged office next to the president's EOB hideaway but would not go very far. By returning to his old law firm on the other side of Pennsylvania Avenue, he would still be available for late-night chats in the Lincoln Sitting Room. He would head an informal "Kitchen Cabinet" and use his impeccable White House connections to make big bucks as an attorney. As a parting gift, Nixon asked Colson to make a prestigious trip to Moscow to push the Kremlin on the emigration of Soviet Jews.

Colson visited Nixon in the Oval Office, two days after the president's return from San Clemente, for a formal leave-taking. He knew that "the machismo cult we so fervently worshipped in the White House" prohibited any display of mawkishness. Even so, he felt "close to tears" as he said goodbye to his political mentor. He had experienced Nixon in many different guises, from cold and calculating to caring and compassionate. Examples of the president's vengeful pettiness were legion, but this was also a man who "held up his own mother as a saint and could never bring himself to point out to a secretary her misspellings." Colson had seen Nixon "redictate a letter to eliminate a troublesome word, rather than embarrass the secretary."

Nixon was focused not on Soviet Jewry but on the forthcoming Senate Watergate hearings. Colson advised him to invoke "executive privilege." White House aides should refuse to testify before the committee, except on the narrowest of grounds. Nixon agreed, although he wanted to avoid being accused of "stonewalling." He kept returning to the Alger Hiss case, the springboard for his own career. As a young congressman on the House Un-American Activities Committee, Nixon had taken the lead in exposing a prewar Soviet spy ring. His key informant was a washed-up reporter for *Time* magazine, Whittaker Chambers, who named Hiss as a fellow agent. At the time Chambers made his accusation, Hiss was one of the top people in the State Department. He had accompanied President Roosevelt to Yalta for his summit meeting with Stalin and overseen the founding of the United Nations. Smooth and sophisticated, with impeccable social connections, Hiss was the epitome of the elites Nixon despised. The elegantly dressed diplomat denied ever meeting the dissolute-looking journalist. Through dogged detective work, Nixon and his investigators were able to prove that they had in fact known each other, thereby undermining Hiss's entire line of defense. Because the statute of limitations had expired on the crime of espionage, Hiss was charged instead with perjury and sentenced, in 1950, to five years in prison.

Nixon's battles with the ultra-respectable Hiss made him a household name and led directly to his selection as Eisenhower's vice presidential running mate in 1952. What should have been a simple espionage case became a clash of cultures and social classes: the outsider with a chip on his shoulder versus the suave, self-satisfied insider. Hiss made the fatal mistake of trying to demean his opponent by pointing out the difference in their social backgrounds. Asked by Nixon to name his alma mater, he replied, "Johns Hopkins and Harvard," before adding condescendingly, "And I believe your college is Whittier?" According to a Nixon associate, this was the moment when the battle between the two men became very personal. Nixon was also upset by the way the establishment rallied around Hiss and sought to defend him. His victory over Hiss, and President Truman as his protector, was an object lesson in the hardscrabble game of politics.

"The administration was doubly guilty," Nixon lectured Colson. "First, [Hiss] was guilty. But second, what really creamed them was the charge that the administration was trying to cover it up . . . It was the cover-up that hurt, not the fact that Hiss was guilty. Get my point?"

Colson did not entirely get the point. Watergate was "dumb," but no one got hurt. Compared with espionage, it was a minor affair, "a burglary without weapons," in Nixon's phrase.

"My God, it isn't like the Hiss trial," Colson protested.

Nixon tried again.

"My point isn't that Hiss was a traitor. It was the cover-up."

"Yeah."

"The cover-up is the problem. That's where we've got to cut our losses."

The difference this time around, of course, was that Nixon was no longer the investigator but the man under investigation.

The two men turned their attention to whom to blame for Watergate. The obvious candidates were Mitchell and Magruder, Liddy's superiors at CREEP. Nixon was in awe of Mitchell and his "great stone face." His old law partner would certainly deny everything. He would never agree to go to prison on behalf of the administration. Magruder presented a different problem. He had almost certainly "perjured himself" but was not an ideal witch for sacrificial burning. He had worked for Haldeman at the White House before transferring to the Committee to Re-elect the President. Any trail that led to Magruder would inevitably drag in the chief of staff. It was left to Colson to finish this uncomfortable

Chuck Colson (left) recruited his friend Howard Hunt (right)
as a member of the Plumbers team to plug government leaks.

thought. "Bob is so much an extension of you. I mean, his everyday work."

And then there were the vulnerabilities posed by the seven Watergate defendants. The four Cubans were unlikely to be a problem because they knew very little. That left Liddy, Hunt, and McCord. The weak link was probably Hunt. The former CIA operative had written to Colson bemoaning his abandonment by the White House. "There is a limit to the endurance of any man trapped in a hostile situation, and mine was reached on December 8," he wrote, referring to the plane disaster that had killed his wife. In reply, Colson had sent word to his old friend through his attorney holding out the possibility of a presidential pardon after a few months in prison.

"I don't think he'll crack, but who knows?" said Colson. "How do you know what goes through the minds of anybody in a situation like this?"

"Right."

"God only knows."

Nixon was still steamed up about leaks to the media. *The Washington Post* had reported that very morning that information from national security wiretaps had been regularly routed to Hunt and Liddy while they worked at the White House. Neither man was authorized to receive the highly classified data. The story bore the bylines of Woodward and Bernstein, whose Watergate reporting had bothered the president for months. It was a constant drip, drip, drip.

"Where are they getting these stories, Chuck?" he demanded.

"The bureau."

In Colson's opinion, every embarrassing story about Watergate could ultimately be traced back to the FBI.

"When Hoover was there, it didn't leak," said Nixon wistfully.

"Oh, hell no! They were scared stiff."

Nixon had dreamed of cleaning house at the FBI ever since becoming president. His once strong relationship with Hoover had deteriorated after the legendary G-man refused to go along with some of his requests for wiretaps. Nixon felt that his old friend was becoming "senile" and losing his grip. He wanted to appoint a new director who would carry out his wishes without question but was afraid of antagonizing the vindictive Hoover. There was always the risk he would "pull down the temple" by releasing the damaging files he kept on politicians, Nixon included. That situation could now be corrected.

The man Nixon had in mind for the mission was L. Patrick Gray III, the government lawyer who had been serving as acting FBI director since Hoover's death in May 1972. As a young submarine commander, Gray had patrolled the Pacific during World War II. Long since retired from the navy, he had retained his military bearing and sense of duty. He still asked his barber to cut his hair to "military length—maybe a little tighter." He had handled logistics for Nixon's first presidential campaign, against Jack Kennedy in 1960, and was proud of his reputation as a Nixon loyalist. In the aftermath of Watergate, he had kept John Dean informed about the progress of the investigation. His principal character flaw, from Nixon's point of view, was that he was "a little bit on the stupid side." But stupidity was not necessarily a disqualification for high office if combined with unthinking fealty to the commander in chief.

Before naming Gray to head the FBI on a permanent basis, Nixon summoned him to an early morning meeting in the Oval Office on February 16 to double-check his suitability and fealty. He began by complaining about the leaks that were embarrassing the White House on an almost daily basis. Gray was defensive. He compared his war against FBI leakers to the military campaigns of ancient history.

"I've been wiping people out of there like the Assyrian [army] on the foe. I've wiped out a whole division."

Nixon was pretty sure where at least some of the leaks were coming from. A few months earlier, he had been stunned to learn that the deputy FBI director, Mark Felt, had been talking privately to *Time* magazine. The tip had come from a *Time* lawyer, who was good friends with the assistant attorney general, Henry Petersen. Haldeman speculated that Felt was leaking to other reporters as well, as part of a campaign to undermine Gray and become FBI director himself. Nixon was hesitant to move against Felt for fear he would "unload everything" if pushed out of the bureau.

Gray found it difficult to believe that his loyal, supremely competent deputy was capable of betrayal. As an old navy man, he was inclined to take his subordinates at their word. Felt had flatly denied leaking "anything to anyone" when Gray confronted him with the White House suspicions. Gray concluded that Felt had become a victim of internal bureau intrigue.

"These people over there are like little old ladies in tennis shoes," he told Nixon. "They've got some of the most vicious vendettas going on."

Nixon insisted that lie detector tests be administered to Felt and anyone else at the FBI suspected of disloyalty. For all of Hoover's faults, there had been no leaking from the bureau during his thirty-seven-year tenure at the helm.

"It wasn't because they loved him. They feared him. They've got to fear the man at the top."

The Germans had the right idea in World War II, Nixon told Gray, citing a more recent military campaign. If they went through a town and one of their soldiers was hit by a sniper, "they'd line up the whole goddamn town and say, 'Until you talk you're all getting shot.' I really think that's what has to be done. I mean I don't think you can be Mr. Nice Guy over there."

As for the relationship between president and FBI director, Nixon needed a trustworthy ally, someone willing to "do something" and then "deny on a stack of Bibles." He was looking for "a loyalist" who would "crack the whip" on behalf of the White House, even if he maintained a neutral stance in public. That meant appointing a friend to the position rather than "some asshole from the outside." Listing his other requirements, he said he wanted a director who was willing to tail "some jackass in the State Department, some assistant to the secretary" whom he suspected of being "a little off."

Gray assured the president that he need search no further.

"Yes, I am, Mr. President . . . a Nixon loyalist. You're goddamn right I am."

C huck Colson's exile from the White House coincided with the admission of John Dean into the president's innermost circle. As the political dangers from Watergate grew in scale and complexity, Nixon desperately needed a new confidant. Haldeman and Ehrlichman, the two "Germans," had too many other responsibilities and were not on top of every twist and turn in the saga. Colson was off the payroll. That left Dean, who had been orchestrating the response to Watergate as White House counsel and knew all the key players. As he acknowledged later, Dean had, in effect, become "the desk officer of the cover-up."

A mid-level staffer, Dean had met Nixon on only one occasion for a Watergate-related conversation prior to February 1973. This was on September 15, after the first indictments were handed down by the grand jury investigating the Watergate break-in. Over the next five months, Nixon had been preoccupied with his reelection campaign and the diplomatic endgame in Vietnam. He had devoted little attention to the scandal, which appeared to be well contained. But that all changed with the convictions of the Watergate burglars and the Senate's decision to open a full-scale investigation. From February 27 onward, Nixon met with Dean on an almost daily basis, sometimes twice a day. What had once been an unwelcome irritation quickly became an all-consuming obsession.

The first few sessions were devoted to getting acquainted. As he did with other close aides, Nixon engaged in long, rambling digressions about the "assholes" in his cabinet and the "boobs" on the Supreme Court. He frequently repeated himself. His Oval Office desk was always "neat and spotless," but "his thoughts and actions were far from organized," it seemed to Dean. The young attorney began to lose his instinctive awe of the president as Nixon fumbled in his pockets for writing utensils. "The required objects would often elude his grasp, leaving the President struggling, his arms crossed in front of himself. Finally he would pull out the fountain pen, bite off the top, and hold it in his teeth as he scrawled with some difficulty on the scrap of paper he clutched in the palm of one hand." Nixon's lack of coordination made him reassuringly human.

Dean had a knack for pleasing his boss. Knowing that the president was "famous for reliving the Hiss case," he read everything he could about the archetypal Cold War scandal that Nixon rode first to the Senate, then to the vice presidency, and finally to the presidency. He studied the relevant passages in Nixon's book, *Six Crises,* and the four-hour speech he had delivered to Congress excoriating Truman for his handling of the affair. He listened patiently to the familiar recital of campaign abuses committed by the Democrats, including the alleged bugging of Nixon's campaign plane in 1968. He agreed that Watergate was primarily a political vendetta. At the same time, he held out the promise of an end to the debilitating scandal. "I'm convinced we're going to make it the whole road and put this thing in the funny pages of the history books rather than anything serious," he told the president. "It's got to be that way."

"The talk with John Dean was very worthwhile," Nixon confided to his diary at the end of their first session on February 27. "He is an enormously capable man. Dean went through quite an amazing recitation as to how Johnson had used the FBI." After another, hour-long meeting the following day, he wrote that Dean showed "enormous strength, great intelligence, and great subtlety . . . I am glad that I am talking to Dean now rather than going through Haldeman or Ehrlichman. I think I have made a mistake in going through others, when there is a man with the capability of Dean I can talk to directly."

In a subsequent conversation with Haldeman, Nixon described Dean as "a gem" and "awfully smart." "God damn, there's judgment there," he gushed. "He thinks things through." The chief of staff praised Dean for acting as "nursemaid" to the seven Watergate defendants, "trying to keep these people on an even keel and not having someone break and go rattling on." Alluding to Dean's playboy reputation and recent marriage to a beautiful woman, Haldeman fantasized about his relaxation techniques after work.

"He's a character. I think he takes out all his frustrations in just pure, raw, animal, unadulterated sex."

"Is that right?" Nixon asked, even more impressed.

"I guess he just solves all of his hang-ups that way. And then he can nail all the rest of this with real finesse."

Appearances were deceiving. Dean's four-month-old marriage was already on the rocks, largely due to the tensions of his White House job. It was becoming more and more difficult to juggle the conflicting pressures from burglars demanding bribes and prosecutors demanding answers. There was a good chance he might end up in prison himself as the orchestrator of the cover-up. When he got home in the evening after frenetic days in the office, Dean anesthetized himself with "one drink after another," sinking into "a solemn, numb catatonia." He switched from purchasing fifths of scotch to half gallons to convince himself that he was consuming fewer bottles. "I asked Mo to cancel our social engagements," he wrote later. "We quarreled, our new marriage already under severe strain." Maureen felt abandoned, even suicidal. One night, she locked herself in the bathroom, saying she was going to slit her wrists. He smashed the door down to stop her.

At first, he had enjoyed the elevated status that came with rising influence. A government limousine picked him up in the morning from home and remained at his disposal throughout the day. He rode on Air Force One and made helicopter trips to Camp David. New partitions went up in his office down the corridor from EOB 175 to accommodate his expanding staff. "I redecorated for the sake of redecorating: new chairs, carpets, draperies. Workmen crowded in; we were expanding." He was rising high in a world where "success and failure could be seen in the size, décor and location of offices." The more frequently interior decorators, carpenters, and furniture movers visited his office, the higher he felt in the White House pecking order. For a thirty-four-year-old attorney with no outstanding legal accomplishments behind him, it was all enormously gratifying.

*An official White House portrait of John Dean in his newly decorated EOB office,
down the hallway from Nixon's hideaway, in March 1973.*

Inside, however, he was dying. He understood, better than any of
his colleagues, the "grave weaknesses" in the White House position.
After Howard Hunt began making his extortionate demands, he had
hauled his thick purple lawbooks down from the bookshelf to study
the passages on obstruction of justice. The maximum punishment for
attempting to "influence, obstruct, or impede the due administration of
justice," he read in Section 1503 of the U.S. criminal code, was five years'
imprisonment and a $5,000 fine. As he thought about the crimes he
had already committed, including the suborning of perjury, he began
to view himself as "a contemporary Raskolnikov, paranoid, schizoid,
wanting to get caught." At times he even welcomed the prospect of
going to jail as "the only way to end the lies that had ruined my private
life even as they had made me a superficial success."

For a time, he had been protected by his relative obscurity. His name
was rarely in the newspapers. But that changed dramatically with the

Senate confirmation hearings for Patrick Gray. Nixon's nominee for FBI director was in a tricky position. To secure the nomination, he had to show he was a "Nixon loyalist"; to get confirmed, he had to prove he was his own man. That meant walking a political tightrope between keeping his mouth shut and responding candidly to senators' questions. He got into immediate trouble when he acknowledged sharing FBI files on Watergate with the White House beginning in July 1972. He had kept John Dean informed about the progress of the investigation and allowed him to sit in on FBI interviews. To defuse the resulting storm of criticism, Gray agreed to allow senators to review the Watergate files as well. His testimony spawned headlines such as "Gray Says White House Got FBI Data on Watergate Investigation" and "Dean Monitored FBI Watergate Probe." Overnight, the previously anonymous White House counsel found himself "a public Watergate target."

Gray's disclosures infuriated Nixon. It seemed that the old navy man was not so dependable after all. "I know the type," the president told Dean. "He's a nice guy, loyal in his own way. But he's panting after the goddamn job and sucking up." When Democratic senators began questioning Gray's qualifications for leading the FBI, the White House failed to come to his defense. Rather than dump his own nominee, Nixon decided simply to abandon him. "Let him twist slowly, twist slowly in the wind," was how John Ehrlichman, an aspiring novelist with a gift for memorable phrases, described the new strategy to Dean. Ridiculed by everybody, the former submarine commander would "twist slowly" for another month, before his fate was sealed.

The haggard men marching along the faded red carpet at Clark Air Base in the Philippines were all dressed in identical slacks and gray shirts issued by their captors. Some were on crutches; some clutched little American flags; some fell on their knees and kissed the ground. A few bore marks from harsh beatings. They were all terribly thin, but all wore huge smiles.

It was the little things that impressed them most, the kind of detail people who have never been deprived of their freedom would find unremarkable. For some it was girls in miniskirts; for others it was men with long hair and beards. For Major Harold Kushner, a military doctor who had been captured by the Vietcong after his helicopter crashed five years earlier, it was the appearance of a U.S. Air Force general in full dress uniform. To the mangy, half-starved Kushner, the well-fed, well-exercised American officer "looked magnificent. He had a breadth, a thickness, we did not have. His hair was plump and moist. Our hair was like straw." The humble C-141 military transport plane with the American flag on its tail that flew the former prisoners out of North Vietnam was the most beautiful sight imaginable. A glass of Coke on crushed ice served with a pack of Wrigley's chewing gum never tasted so good.

Nixon had been worried that the homecoming of the prisoners of war might turn into a political embarrassment. It was difficult to predict how they would react to the sudden glare of the media spotlight after years of isolation. They might be bitter about the political leaders

who had ordered them to fight an unwinnable war against an impla-
cable enemy. They might wonder why it took so long to negotiate a
peace settlement. In fact, the overwhelming majority of the released
POWs had only positive things to say about their commander in chief.
They praised his much-criticized Christmas bombing campaign as a
decisive contribution to their liberation. To the men rotting inside the
grim prison they called the Hanoi Hilton, the thunderous roar of B-52
bombers overhead and explosions all around had sounded like the
long-awaited arrival of the U.S. cavalry.

On February 12, the day that the first batch of prisoners arrived at
Clark Air Base, Nixon received a telephone call from their senior officer. Lieutenant Colonel Robinson Risner was an ace fighter pilot who
had been shot down more than seven years earlier while on a mission
to destroy a North Vietnamese air defense site. He had spent more than
three years in solitary confinement, much of the time in total darkness,
in retaliation for organizing prohibited church services. Prior to serving in Vietnam, he had shot down eight enemy fighter planes in Korea.

"This is Colonel Risner, sir, reporting for duty," he told the president, when they were finally connected. He described his release as "the
greatest moment of my life."

In Nixon's eyes, the men proudly saluting the flag at Clark Air Base
were throwbacks to an earlier, simpler age. They seemed unaffected by
the bitter political debates that had divided the country during the first
four years of his presidency. As career officers and pilots, they were in
a different category from the millions of conscripts who had returned
disillusioned from Vietnam. They had been insulated from the violent
antiwar protests that had swept American campuses in the late 1960s.
Far from being swayed by Communist propaganda, they had become
even more patriotic as a result of their experiences in North Vietnamese
prisons. "Compare these fine men with those sniveling Ivy Leaguers,"
Nixon told his aides after speaking with Risner.

The president's sentiments were captured by a cartoon in *The Atlanta
Journal* titled "The Unemployed." The foreground depicted a long-
haired war protester squatting unhappily next to a discarded protest
banner proclaiming, "Peace at any price!" In the background, the artist drew POWs marching off a plane as joyous crowds waved placards

*Nixon liked the cartoon of returning POWs and unhappy demonstrators
so much that he asked for the original.*

reading, "Thank you, Mr. Nixon" and "God bless America." "Get original for RN," Nixon scrawled across his copy of the cartoon.

He instructed his aides to make a compendium of patriotic "one-liners" by returning POWs to ram down the throats of the media skeptics. He pored happily over the results, underlining his favorite quotations. "It's time we started raising flags instead of burning them" (Captain James A. Mulligan, U.S. Navy). "I was just fantastically impressed with the courage that President Nixon displayed in an election year, reopening the bombing war against North Vietnam" (Lieutenant Commander Paul Galanti, U.S. Navy). "I would like to thank President Nixon for bringing us home on our feet instead of our knees" (Lieutenant Colonel George McKnight, U.S. Air Force). "In a cell in Hanoi carved in the wall is 'God bless you Richard Nixon'" (Lieutenant Commander Frederick Purrington, U.S. Navy).

The effusiveness of the praise caused some reporters to wonder if the POWs were spouting lines prepared by military public affairs people. "Ridiculous," snapped a Pentagon spokesman. "It insults the POWs' intelligence to say that they could have been brainwashed during a three-hour lay-over in Clark Field when the North Vietnamese couldn't do it in seven years." The president loved that line so much that he made it his own and instructed Ziegler to repeat it as often as possible.

On March 12, Nixon had a ninety-minute meeting in the Oval Office with Risner and another former prisoner, Navy Captain Jeremiah Denton. After listening to their harrowing stories of torture at the hands of their North Vietnamese guards, he briefed them on events in the United States during the years of their captivity. The 1960s had been a "revolutionary decade," he told them. "America is quite a different country from what it was. Up until 1967, there was still a strong patriotism. Even the media refrained from attacking that. But then, in '67 to '68, it turned around 180 degrees." Nixon lamented "the loss of faith" among the "so-called better educated people of this country" and the turn toward isolationism. There was a growing feeling that "we should concentrate on problems here at home," rather than defend the principle of democracy overseas. A boost to American morale was desperately needed.

"This is one reason why we had to see this thing through," said Nixon, referring to the Christmas bombing. Had he "bugged out" at the end, the "frustration and recrimination" over nearly forty thousand dead American soldiers in Vietnam would have been impossible to manage. He recalled with pride how he had ordered "every B-52 that can fly" into action over Hanoi to put pressure on the North Vietnamese to return to the negotiating table. He wondered if the men in the "Hanoi Hilton" knew what was going on outside their prison cells.

"We were in no doubt about what was happening," replied Risner. "We were jumping up and down. We were cheering. People were crying."

Even as Nixon was celebrating his decision to unleash the B-52s over Hanoi three months earlier, he was agonizing over how to enforce the peace agreement. In his view, the best guarantee of peace was the economic reconstruction of North Vietnam. "That place is poor," he told Risner and Denton. "They have lost a million men." Nixon hoped to create American political leverage over Hanoi at the expense of Moscow and Beijing. He was prepared to provide millions of dollars of economic assistance to Hanoi in return for an end to the fighting. For this policy to work, he needed political cover from the POWs. It was "going to be tough," the president acknowledged. The North Vietnamese leaders were deeply suspicious of American intentions. They were unwilling to give up on their dreams of national reunification under Communist leadership.

Nixon's desire to build economic ties to Hanoi floundered in the face of repeated cease-fire violations. U.S. reconnaissance photographs showed military trucks almost "bumper-to-bumper" on the Ho Chi Minh trail in March and April. Convinced that the Communists were continuing to infiltrate troops and weapons into the South, Henry Kissinger urged the president to resume the bombing of the trail and the Vietcong sanctuaries in Laos and Cambodia. "We have to take them on fairly soon," he warned the president. "These bastards made it nearly impossible to negotiate a peace. Now they are making it nearly impossible to preserve the peace."

Nixon was not so sure. He was hesitant to act before the final batch of POWs was released from North Vietnamese jails. But even after all the prisoners were home, a host of other political and military considerations complicated his decision. The American people were tired of the war. It would be very difficult if not impossible to persuade Congress that further military action was justified once U.S. troops had completely withdrawn from Vietnam. Previous bombing campaigns had done little to halt, or even slow, the flow of military matériel from North to South. North Vietnamese soldiers simply disappeared into the forest on either side of the trail, repaired whatever damage had been inflicted, and resumed their movement south as soon as the American planes disappeared.

"[Bombing] isn't going to do much good," Nixon grumbled. "The air force never hits a goddamn thing, as you know, Henry, except when they put it over Hanoi."

In his 1982 memoir, *Years of Upheaval*, Kissinger painted a portrait of a president so distracted by Watergate that he was "simply unable to concentrate his energies and mind on Vietnam." In the past, Nixon had displayed a remarkable instinct for the jugular, working himself up to a fever pitch of emotion prior to taking decisive action. By contrast, the Nixon of March 1973 "approached the problem of [North Vietnamese cease-fire] violations in a curiously desultory fashion. He drifted. He did not home in on the decision in the single-minded, almost possessed, manner that was his hallmark." Nixon ordered bombing raids against the Ho Chi Minh trail one day only to cancel them the next. There were always "excuses for inaction."

Other advisers, including the normally hard-line General Haig, reacted skeptically to Kissinger's calls for another round of bombing. Stopping the drive toward Vietnamese reunification under Communist leadership had not been possible with half a million American troops in Vietnam. To believe it would be possible with zero troops was myopic. The best the United States could hope for was to delay the inevitable by building up the South Vietnamese army with generous supplies of military equipment and financial aid. The "decent interval" strategy remained in effect, even though it could never be spoken out loud.

If Kissinger was correct in arguing that Watergate was a huge distraction from Vietnam, it was also true that Vietnam had been a huge distraction from running the country. The war had damaged the foundations of the American body politic, the social compact between government and governed. It had caused ordinary Americans to question the competence, good faith, even honesty of their leaders. The crimes of Watergate could themselves be traced back to the paranoid atmosphere inside a White House that felt under siege from hippies and peaceniks. Nixon had spent the last four years painfully extricating America from Vietnam, at huge cost to both the country and his own psychic well-being. He had neither the desire nor the will nor the political support to jump back in.

It was a Saturday and the White House was very quiet. The president was in the Oval Office to receive the traditional gift of shamrocks from the Irish ambassador in honor of St. Patrick's Day. He stuffed a piece of the green plant into his buttonhole to complement his bright green tie. Later in the day, he put on an even more garish green bow tie with white spots he had borrowed from Freddie the elevator operator. Haldeman thought the ostentatious wearing of the green made his boss look "a trifle ridiculous," but refrained from saying anything.

One of the few staffers to show up for work was John Dean, who had dragged himself reluctantly into the office to finish some long overdue tasks. He was meant to be compiling a much anticipated "Dean report" in advance of the Senate hearings that would clear the president of any involvement in the break-in. He was agonizing over what to say. Nixon was demanding a technical impossibility: a report that had the appearance of "hanging it all out there" but did not create any further trouble. If Dean limited his report to the usual denials of White House involvement, he might be held personally responsible for the falsehoods. If he went into any detail, he would risk opening up dangerous new lines of investigation. It was a lose-lose proposition.

When Nixon learned that Dean was at his desk, he called him in for another long conversation. He was finishing his lunch when Dean entered the Oval Office in his casual weekend clothes. The president startled his young associate by offering him the use of Camp David to write his report. "Anytime you need to get away, remember that my Camp David place is very conducive to that kind of thoughtful work." He then asked Dean to run through "the vulnerabilities" in the White House defenses on Watergate. The legal counsel began ticking off names. Mitchell, Colson, Magruder of course. Perhaps Haldeman, as someone who had put pressure on Magruder to gather intelligence against the Democrats. He then added his own name.

"And I'd say Dean to a degree."

"You?" asked Nixon, taken aback. "Why?"

"Well, because I've been all over this thing like a blanket," Dean replied, referring to his coaching of witnesses and handling the burglars' demands for hush money.

Nixon preferred to focus on the original crime rather than the subsequent obstruction of justice. As far as he was concerned, Dean was innocent because he had no prior knowledge of the "goddamn thing." The biggest concern was Magruder and whether he would implicate people like Haldeman and Colson.

Dean agreed that Magruder was a potential threat.

"Jeb's a good man. But if Jeb ever sees himself sinking, he will reach out to grab everybody he can get hold of."

As Nixon saw it, the danger was that a minor player "starts pissing on Magruder," who then "starts pissing on who . . . even Haldeman."

"We can't do that," he said. "What you've got to do, to the extent you can, John, is to cut if off at the pass." The White House would stick to its earlier line that responsibility ended with Liddy and Hunt. It was too late to go down what Nixon called "the hangout road." Any attempt to find someone else to blame for Watergate would only deepen the crisis.

Dean raised another, even more unsettling, consideration. It turned out that Liddy and Hunt were even bigger "idiots" than previously known. Nine months prior to breaking in to the Watergate, they had used miniature cameras on loan from the CIA to spy on the offices of Ellsberg's psychiatrist in Beverly Hills. They had returned the equipment to the agency along with the film for processing. The CIA had retained copies of the photographs and handed them over to the Justice Department as part of the Watergate investigation. Dean told Nixon that one of the photographs showed "Gordon Liddy standing proud as punch" outside the psychiatrist's office. The nameplate of the psychiatrist, Dr. Lewis Fielding, was clearly visible in another photograph. At some point an astute investigator was likely to link Liddy and the White House Plumbers to the still unsolved burglary at Dr. Fielding's office. Once this happened, the trail would lead to John Ehrlichman, who had supervisory responsibility for the Plumbers. Nixon's domestic policy adviser had signed off on the "covert operation" against Ellsberg in retaliation for his leaking of the official Vietnam War history to *The New York Times*. He had been pushing Dean to persuade the CIA to retrieve the compromising materials from the Justice Department. The agency had rejected the request.

What "in the name of God" had caused Ehrlichman to get involved? Nixon demanded.

"This was part of an operation . . . uh . . . in connection with the Pentagon Papers," Dean mumbled. "They wanted to get Ellsberg's psychiatric records for some reason."

"Why?"

"I don't know."

"Jesus Christ."

This Watergate stuff was a lot more complicated than Nixon had ever imagined. It was like playing whack-a-mole. If you succeeded in suppressing one scandal, another was sure to raise its head.

After meeting with Dean in the Oval Office, Nixon weaved his way through the cars parked on West Executive Avenue to his hideaway study in the EOB. A more congenial task awaited him. He had an appointment with a man whose sense of history and foreign policy interests matched his own. A journalist turned historian, Theodore H. White had made his name as a *Time* correspondent in China. He had interviewed all the leading actors in the Chinese revolution, beginning with Mao Tse-tung, Chou En-lai, and Chiang Kai-shek. He knew the top American commanders in Asia, including Douglas MacArthur and Joseph Stilwell. More recently, he had become the foremost chronicler of American elections, with a series of books titled *The Making of the President*. The first of these books, about the 1960 campaign between Kennedy and Nixon, had earned him a Pulitzer Prize. He was now finishing his fourth campaign book, on the 1972 election. He had mastered the art of turning sin-depth political reporting into thrilling narrative history.

An ebullient man with wire-rimmed glasses, Teddy White tended to glamorize his subjects in bursts of purple prose that sometimes verged on hero worship. He had a particularly soft spot for Jack Kennedy. After JFK was assassinated, he wrote an article for *Life* magazine comparing his doomed presidency to Camelot, the mythical English court of King Arthur. The suggestion for the Camelot analogy had come from Kennedy's widow, Jackie, mesmerized by the Alan Lerner lyric, "*Don't let it be forgot, that once there was a spot, for one brief shining moment that was known as Camelot.*" White was happy to build upon the imagery. For Jackie, he wrote later, the Kennedy era represented "a magical moment in American history when gallant men danced with beautiful women, when great deeds were done, when artists, writers, and poets met at the White House, and the barbarians beyond the walls held back." It was the kind of over-the-top eulogy of the slain president that made Nixon want to vomit.

He was obsessed with Jack Kennedy. He had recently read, and heavily annotated, an extract from a new book by a British reporter, Henry Fairlie, critical of the Camelot mythmaking. One of the passages that caught his attention examined Kennedy's techniques for wooing the media elite. A *New York Times* columnist, Arthur Krock, described a skillful policy of news management based on the "social flattery of Washington reporters and commentators" by the president and his senior aides. Nixon underlined the quotation, along with Fairlie's observation that the admission of American political journalists to the Kennedy court undermined their credibility as neutral observers. "Z[iegler] note!" Nixon instructed his press chief. He was convinced that many of his problems came down to poor image building and a hostile press. It was all terribly unfair.

Nixon knew that he would not be able to seduce White the way Kennedy had seduced such supposedly objective reporters as Joseph Alsop and Ben Bradlee. But he could tap into his romantic view of American history and deference toward the presidency as an institution. At the very least, they would have a stimulating conversation about the state of the world. As an old Asia hand, White had welcomed Nixon's opening to China. He had a feeling for the shifting sands of big-time politics and the awkward compromises that statesmen were obliged to make to achieve their goals. This was an opportunity for Nixon to impress an influential commentator with his intellectual sophistication and grasp of international affairs.

Nixon steered White toward the settee opposite the presidential desk as Manolo served refreshments. He put his feet up on the coffee table as he talked about his favorite presidents, notably Theodore Roosevelt and Woodrow Wilson. White had never "spoken to a President who gave the impression of being more completely self-possessed or in command of his job." Nixon's mind moved easily from one topic to another, from the desegregation of schools to rising gasoline prices to his visits to Moscow and Beijing. "Mostly he talked the shop talk of power— power as Mao Tse-tung sees it, power as the Pentagon sees it, power as the President must use it," White later recalled. "The President, he felt, must single out a few problems of the thousands and thousands of immensely complicated affairs that clamor for his attention, and must concentrate on those. He must wall himself off from detail."

If Nixon was tormented by Watergate, he gave no sign of it. Whenever White made a move to leave, the president waved him back to the settee. He seemed at peace with himself. It was this "quality of serenity" that struck White most forcefully later, after he had an opportunity to read the jarring transcript of Nixon's conversation with Dean earlier in the day. "He had swept the morning dialogue with Dean from his mind: he was out there, far, far out there in history, talking as a President should. His serenity could not have been feigned." White did his best to put Nixon in a good mood, avoiding Watergate entirely. As he wrote later, the scandal "did not, at that moment, seem relevant."

At the end of their two-hour conversation, the reporter-historian reached one of the sweeping conclusions that were a hallmark of his literary style. Nixon's election landslide of November 1972 represented a fundamental break with the era of the welfare state built by FDR and LBJ. Americans had voted for Nixon because they wanted to place restraints on "the power and reach of the Federal state into daily life." Loved or hated, Nixon personified a popularly supported change in the nation's direction. "My judgment," White informed readers of *The Making of the President, 1972,* "would have cast Richard Nixon as one of the major Presidents of the twentieth century, in a rank just after Franklin

Roosevelt, on a level with Truman, Wilson, Eisenhower, Kennedy. Thus the view from Olympus, on March 17, 1973, as Nixon described his use of a President's power."

By White's own account, it would take just a few days for him to be "brought down from Olympus" and for his upbeat assessment of the Nixon presidency to shatter into tiny pieces.

CRISIS

κρίσις—krísis

a decisive turning point

———————

Once the toothpaste is out of the tube, it's
going to be very tough to get it back in.

—H. R. HALDEMAN
April 8, 1973

I n the make-believe world of E. Howard Hunt Jr., the sex was always steamy, the spy gadgets worked flawlessly, and everybody laughed at his witticisms. He had written more than forty novels, most of them espionage thrillers. The formula varied little. Hero lacking purpose uncovers satanic plot, often involving Soviet agents or thinly disguised surrogates. Rescues beautiful woman from clutches of evildoers and enjoys great sex with her. Visits expensive restaurants and quaffs vintage French wine while outwitting bad guys. Stretches legal boundaries, but always in service of higher cause. As one of Hunt's alter egos, the CIA agent Peter Ward, remarks in *On Hazardous Duty,* "We become lawless in a struggle for the rule of law." His characters, like many of the characters in the Watergate saga, viewed themselves as "semi-outlaws who risk their lives to put down the savagery of others." A typical Howard Hunt novel was littered with corpses, exotic hardware, and pithy dialogue. The sentences were short and direct, imitating the macho style of Ernest Hemingway. The hero wins out in the end.

At the time of the Watergate break-in, Hunt had been working on a new novel, *The Berlin Ending,* about a former CIA agent (turned bored architect) who stumbles on a Communist conspiracy to infiltrate the West German government. As Hunt became ever more enmeshed in his own legal troubles, his view of life darkened. Prior to her death in the plane crash, his wife, Dorothy, had urged him to abandon the standard happy ending to his novel. "The way you have it, the good guys win," she pointed out. "But Howard, you know it isn't always the way in real life. More often than not, the good guys lose—so why not end it that way?" Following Dorothy's advice, he decided to let the bad guys win for a change. The final piece of dialogue in the novel, between a spy named Apelbaum and the architect–CIA retiree, Thorpe, reflected his own anger at the Nixon White House for failing to "take care" of him and the other burglars:

> "All of us," said Apelbaum, "did what we thought was right. But Werber was always the Soviets' man. And they take care of their own. Believe me, I know."
> "Unlike CIA," Thorpe said thinly. "Damn them, too."

Hunt's own life as a secret agent was neither as glamorous nor as successful as the lives of his fictional characters. His CIA career had peaked (or cratered, depending on the point of view) in 1961 with the failed invasion of Cuba at the Bay of Pigs. Posing as a writer who had mysteriously come into an inheritance, Hunt had made an undercover visit to Havana to get a better sense of opposition to the Castro regime. He visited the military bases in Guatemala where the anti-Castro exiles were being trained by the CIA, meeting several of the men he would later recruit to break in to the Watergate. When the invasion failed, he was in Miami, plotting the installation of a new Cuban government. Like many of the CIA officers involved in planning the invasion, he was shunted aside after the debacle and given a series of demeaning office jobs. He told a reporter later that he retired from the agency in 1970 because it was "infested with Democrats." In truth, his career was going nowhere. A damning efficiency report dismissed him as "the sort of spy who would trip over his cape and fall on his sword."

Hunt's recruitment by Colson in July 1971 to join the White House plumber unit was a chance to redeem himself. The "debonair, smooth-talking, unobtrusive" Hunt seemed to be the "ideal candidate" for plugging the leaks of sensitive national security information that were so troubling to Nixon and Kissinger. "He knew foreign policy, but more important, was a conservative true believer, fanatically loyal," Colson wrote later. As a fellow Brown University graduate, the former CIA agent had the right social background for the job. His erudite look in a "sporty tweed jacket, just properly baggy," was also reassuring. *"What a relief,"* Colson thought, *"to get a professional in here to deal with such matters."* Colson recommended Hunt highly to Nixon, mentioning that he had "spent twenty years in the CIA overthrowing governments." "Hard as nails," he enthused. "A brilliant writer. He's written forty books under pseudonyms. He scrambles." In addition to being "kind of a tiger," Hunt had one other essential quality. "Ideologically, he already is convinced that this is a big conspiracy."

"How old is he?" Nixon wanted to know.

"Fifty," said Colson.

"That's all right. He can do it. He may still have the energy," said Nixon.

Hunt's performance failed to live up to the promise. One of his first assignments from Colson was to "prove" that President Kennedy had ordered the assassination of the South Vietnamese leader Ngo Dinh Diem back in 1963. "I know that the New Frontier was responsible for those murders," Colson told him. "Got any ideas?" In response, Hunt forged a couple of State Department cables to demonstrate Kennedy's involvement, with the intention of leaking them to a friendly journalist. The forgeries proved too clumsy for publication. Frightened that the forged documents might be traced back to him, Hunt threw the type-writer he had used to produce the cables into the Potomac.

The penetration of the offices of Daniel Ellsberg's psychiatrist was another flop. In addition to the miniature cameras, Hunt borrowed an array of disguises from a CIA friend, including a long brown-haired wig for Liddy and a mechanical device that forced the wearer to limp. The spy gear was so cumbersome that Liddy threw it away in disgust, along with some cheap walkie-talkies that would not work. Despite rifling through a lot of old files, the burglars came up with nothing on Ellsberg. Prior to leaving the office, they scattered some pills around to make it appear as if the burglary had been carried out by an addict desperate for drugs. A few days later, the Los Angeles Police Department arrested a local junkie who confessed to the crime in return for a suspended sentence.

By March 1973, Hunt was desperate. He had lost his wife of twenty-three years in a tragic accident, his legal bills were spiraling, and he was expecting no mercy from Judge Sirica. His bleeding ulcer had flared up, and he was being treated for severe depression. As the man who had recruited the Cubans on behalf of the White House Plumbers, he was the connection between the men arrested in the Watergate and the Nixon administration. Together with Liddy, he was directly responsible for the operation that had gone so disastrously wrong. He needed to put his affairs in order and find money to support his children before being sent to prison. With only days to go before the sentencing hearing on March 23, he made a list of his monetary demands. In return for keeping quiet, he wanted $60,000 in legal fees and $70,000 in lieu of two years' salary—$130,000 in all. The deadline was "close of business" on Wednesday, March 21.

To demonstrate his seriousness, Hunt put out word that he had embarked on a new literary venture. It would be not another novel this time but a work of nonfiction bearing the one-word title *Watergate*. Hunt had made "self-executing arrangements" for his literary agent to put the book up for auction if he was sent to jail without receiving the money he believed was due to him. He imagined that bidding would start at around half a million dollars.

One of the people Hunt approached as an intermediary to the White House was a lawyer named Paul O'Brien who had served as counsel to the Committee to Re-elect the President. Hunt told O'Brien that he should deliver his demand for $130,000 to John Dean personally. On the afternoon of March 19, O'Brien showed up at Dean's office in the EOB to report the blackmail threat.

"Why me?" Dean yelled. "Why the hell did he send the goddam message to *me*?"

O'Brien did not know. He merely repeated Hunt's warning: "You tell Dean I need the money by the close of business Wednesday." If he did not receive it, he would have some "seamy things" to reveal about what he did for John Ehrlichman as a White House Plumber.

Dean buried his face in his hands. He understood instantly the legal jeopardy to which he was being exposed. Although he had facilitated money transfers to the Watergate defendants in the past, this was the first time he himself had become a blackmail target. It was "a game-changing event," he wrote later. "Hunt was dragging me directly into his extortion loop. He must have learned that I was the one who had carried the money messages before, and now he figured he had a hold on me for more. I could see Hunt extorting me, milking me, for the rest of our lives."

Pacing around his spacious, newly redecorated office, he explained that he was "out of the money business" and planned to stay out. Both he and O'Brien had already exposed themselves to obstruction of justice charges as conduits for payoffs to the burglars.

"Hunt can shove it up his ass!" Dean shouted. "I am tired of being put in the middle. I am going to bust this goddamned thing up."

Dean had accepted an invitation to a farewell party for Chuck Colson that evening but could not face it. Instead, he went home and pulled out his bottle of Cutty Sark. He, too, was at the breaking point.

Well, sit down. Sit down," said the president as John Dean entered the Oval Office, waving him to a chair in front of his massive desk. He talked to the White House counsel between the sides of his polished shoes, which were resting on the mahogany surface of the desk. He began with an attempt at joviality. "Well, what's the Dean summary of the day about?"

Dean felt like "an actor on stage for a big performance, with a bad case of butterflies." Nixon had phoned him at home the previous night for an update on Watergate. He wanted to know "where all the bodies are." He was still pressing for a Dean report—"my conclusions are this, bing, bing, bing, bing"—that would exonerate everybody in the White House. What he had in mind was "a complete statement" that would, in reality, be "very incomplete." Not too much "chapter and verse." Just "Haldeman is not involved in this," "Mr. Colson did not do this," "Mr. So-and-So did not do this," "Mr. Blank did not do this, and da-da-da-da-da, right down the line."

Four minutes into the conversation, Dean summoned the courage to come to the point. He leaned forward on the edge of his chair. "I think there's no doubt about the seriousness of the problem we've got," he said. "We have a *cancer*." He paused to allow the word to sink in.

"A cancer within. Close to the presidency. That's growing. It's growing daily. It's compounding. It grows geometrically now because it compounds itself."

Nixon took his feet off the desk. He held his hands together, with his chin on his fingers, and stared at Dean intently.

"One, we're being blackmailed," Dean continued. "Two, people are going to start perjuring themselves very quickly that have not had to perjure themselves to protect other people . . . There's no assurance . . ."

Nixon finished the sentence for him. "That it won't bust."

"That it won't bust."

"True."

Dean thought he should explain "how it all started," even though the president seemed to know most of the details already. Dean had been present when Liddy presented his original million-dollar Operation Gemstone plan to John Mitchell back in January 1972. It was "the most incredible thing" he had ever heard, involving "black bag operations, kidnapping, providing prostitutes to weaken the opposition, bugging, mugging teams." Mitchell had sat there amazed, laughing and puffing at his pipe. Dean thought that Liddy's "absurd proposal" had died a natural death, but parts of it reemerged, phoenix-like from the ashes, with the Watergate break-in six months later.

Exactly how this had happened was difficult to establish. As Dean described the decision-making process, it sounded like a tragicomedy of misunderstood messages and misinterpreted signals. Haldeman was pushing for actionable intelligence on the Democrats. Magruder was under pressure from Colson to make a decision on the Liddy project. "Mitchell probably puffed on his pipe and said, 'Go ahead,' and never really reflected on what it was all about."

After the Watergate break-in, "all hell broke loose." Dean had operated under "a theory of containment," as ordered by Haldeman. The burglars "had to be taken care of." In addition to Watergate, they could be shown to be involved in other crimes, such as breaking in to the office of Ellsberg's psychiatrist. The financial arrangements were made via Mitchell, with the knowledge of Bob Haldeman and John Ehrlichman.

"That's the most troublesome thing," said Dean. "Bob is involved in that. John is involved in that. I am involved in that. Mitchell is involved in that. And that's an obstruction of justice."

"The fact that you're taking care of witnesses?" asked Nixon.

"That's right."

"How was Bob involved?" Nixon wanted to know.

Dean explained that Mitchell and CREEP had run out of money to pay the burglars. In order to replenish their funds, Dean asked Haldeman for permission to tap into $350,000 in a White House safe that had originally been earmarked for polling. "I had to go to Bob and say, 'Bob, they need some money over there.' He said, 'What for?' And so I had to tell him what it was for, because he wasn't about to just send money over there willy-nilly. And John was involved in those decisions. We decided that there was no price too high to pay to let this thing blow up in front of the election."

Not only had "blackmail" occurred, Dean informed the president, but it was continuing. Howard Hunt had threatened to bring "John Ehrlichman to his knees and put him in jail" for his role in the Ellsberg psychiatrist affair. He wanted $70,000 in "personal expenses," plus legal fees, in exchange for keeping quiet. The demands for money might never end. Dean and other White House aides were "amateurs" when it came to paying blackmail.

"This is the sort of thing Mafia people can do," said Dean. "Washing money, getting clean money. We don't know about these things because we are not, you know, criminals. We are not used to dealing in that business."

Dean was attempting to come up with arguments against going down the blackmail route. He mentioned that it was becoming increasingly difficult to find the funds to pay Hunt.

"How much money do you need?" Nixon interrupted.

Dean had not been expecting that question. He made a wild guess.

"I would say these people are going to cost, uh, a million dollars over the next two years."

Nixon's next statement surprised Dean even more.

"You could get a million dollars. You could get it in cash. I know where it could be gotten . . . The question is who the hell would handle that. Any ideas on that?"

Dean volunteered Mitchell's name. "And get some pros to help him."

Both men were thinking out loud. They careened from one scenario to another, gaming them all out. Dean was worried about possible leaks. The circle of people with incriminating information was becoming wider by the day. Family members. Lawyers, including "a no-good, publicity-seeking, son-of-a-bitch" attorney for the Cubans. Secretaries, always easy prey for prosecutors. "It's a domino situation," he fretted. "If it starts crumbling, fingers will be pointing." People around the White House were watching out for "their own behind" and signing up lawyers. They were asking the question, "How do I protect my ass?" Dean's comment made a strong impression on Nixon, who noted in his diary that night, "It will be each man for himself and one will not be afraid to rat on the other."

Every conceivable course of action had a downside for Nixon, opening the door to even more unpalatable consequences. Paying off "the jackasses" in jail would likely lead to further demands. Hunt, in particular, seemed to think he had an undertaking from Colson to be out of prison by Christmas. Pardoning convicted Watergate defendants before the 1974 congressional elections was out of the question. Brazening it out would require more coaching of witnesses and more lying to investigators, risking perjury charges. The alternative was for someone higher than Liddy—perhaps Mitchell or Magruder—to admit to ordering the break-in. Whoever stepped forward would face criminal charges and a likely prison sentence. They might start revealing more high crimes and misdemeanors. That route was also unthinkable.

Whatever they decided in the long term, something had to be done about Hunt in the short term. Paying him off would at least buy some time.

"Just looking at the immediate problem, don't you have to handle Hunt's financial situation damn soon?" Nixon concluded. "You've got to keep the cap on the bottle that much in order to have any options."

"That's right," said Dean.

The president wanted to know how the deed would be carried out. Dean explained that a Mitchell aide by the name of Frederick LaRue had performed that service in the past.

"I gather LaRue just leaves it in mailboxes and things like that . . . Someone phones Hunt and tells him to pick it up. As I say, we're a bunch of amateurs in that business."

Haldeman had walked into the room, summoned by a buzz from the president. He seconded the recommendation that they leave "that sort of thing" to Mitchell and LaRue.

Dean emphasized once again that money laundering was a job for professionals. Even cash was problematic. Banknotes came with serial numbers that could be traced.

"I understand," said Nixon.

"You have to go to Vegas with it or a bookmaker in New York City. I've learned all these things after the fact. We'll be in great shape for the next time round."

The three conspirators chortled nervously.

"Jesus!" said Haldeman, laughing. "We're so goddamned square we get caught on everything."

Dean left the meeting and went back to his office, feeling as if he had been "squeezed in a vise." His head throbbed from the mental effort of accompanying the president down the multiple legal and political rabbit holes they had explored. In accordance with Nixon's wishes, he phoned LaRue to relay Hunt's latest financial demands.

"Should I make the delivery?" the moneyman wanted to know.

Dean repeated what he had told the CREEP lawyer two days earlier. He was out of "the money business" for good. LaRue would have to decide for himself whether to pay Hunt. He, Dean, was just a message carrier. This was not good enough for LaRue, who said he needed someone to authorize the transaction.

"I suggest you call Mitchell," said Dean, determined to shift responsibility to someone else.

Shy and bald, his thoughts hidden behind a pair of thick glasses, Frederick Cheney LaRue was the quintessential backroom political operator. His generosity to the Republican Party had earned him the nickname Bubba from the good old boys in his native Mississippi. The family had made a fortune in the oil-drilling business that passed to Fred at the age of twenty-nine after he accidentally killed his father while out hunting. An early contributor to the Nixon presidential campaign of 1968, he implemented the candidate's "southern strategy," weaning white working-class votes away from the Democrats. He became a confidant of John Mitchell, who brought him to Washington after the election as an unpaid adviser to the president. For the 1972 election, LaRue moved over to CREEP, where he worked closely with Jeb Magruder. He had neither "the desire nor the talent for an out-front role," Magruder recalled later. "He was homely, had extremely poor eyesight, and was not a good public speaker. His talents were for a backstage role. Because he was likable, sincere, and politically astute, he was excellent in dealing with people and in negotiating internal problems."

LaRue was with Mitchell and Magruder for the critical meeting in Key Biscayne on March 30, 1972, that led to the Watergate break-in. It took place in the den of a vacation house loaned to Mitchell by Bebe Rebozo overlooking the bay. They had to keep out of the way of an angry Martha Mitchell, who complained about her husband's conducting business while on vacation. All three men were wearing slacks and polo shirts as they sat around a coffee table munching sandwiches prepared by the maid. Liddy's intelligence-gathering plan was the last of thirty or so "action memos" requiring a decision.

Each participant would remember the meeting differently. According to Magruder, Mitchell reluctantly signed off on the project, the cost of which had been reduced to $250,000. Mitchell, by contrast, flatly denied giving the go-ahead. He later claimed to have told Magruder, "We don't need this, I am tired of hearing it out, let's not discuss it any further." In LaRue's version of events, Mitchell postponed a decision on the Watergate bugging plan, saying, "We don't have to do anything on this now." Whatever the truth of these competing accounts, when Magruder returned to Washington, he instructed an aide to "call Liddy and tell him it's approved."

Hush money payments to the seven Watergate defendants began within two weeks of their arrests. LaRue served as the conduit from the burglars to Mitchell, who approved the payments for legal fees and family expenses. A private attorney to Nixon, Herbert Kalmbach, raised the necessary funds. A retired New York City policeman, Anthony Ulasewicz, made the deliveries. With his sagging jowls, slicked-back hair, and hangdog expression, Ulasewicz looked perfect for the role of private investigator turned bagman. His first order of business was to assign everyone false names. He called himself Mr. Rivers, LaRue became Mr. Baker, Howard Hunt was the Writer, and so on. Essential communications were handled by pay phone. The phones gobbled up so many quarters that Ulasewicz began carrying around a bus conductor's change machine. He distributed the payoffs, which he referred to as "the laundry," in wads of $100 bills left in airport lockers, telephone booths, and hotel lobbies. After disbursing nearly $220,000 through Ulasewicz, Kalmbach decided he could no longer participate in "an illegal activity." At a September 21 meeting with John Dean, the self-described "desk officer of the cover-up," LaRue agreed to take over the role of moneyman.

LaRue made his first payment of around $20,000 to Howard Hunt's lawyer, William Bittman, in the middle of October. He introduced himself to Bittman as "Baker, a friend of Mr. Rivers," and sent the money to his office by CREEP courier. After Hunt complained that it was insufficient, Dean arranged for LaRue to tap into the $350,000 in surplus campaign funds controlled by Haldeman. LaRue put on a pair of surgical gloves to avoid leaving his fingerprints on the money, which he kept in a filing cabinet in his apartment in the Watergate. Recipients included Hunt ($50,000 in December, $60,000 in January), Liddy's lawyer ($20,000), and a committee to aid the Cubans ($12,000).

Now, by the middle of March 1973, LaRue was again running out of funds. He, too, wanted to get out of the "money business." Faced with Hunt's latest financial demands, he made a unilateral decision to pay only the portion that could reasonably be described as "lawyer's fees," which he estimated at $75,000. In order to protect himself, he followed Dean's suggestion and consulted with Mitchell, his former boss at CREEP. Mitchell encouraged him to make the payment. LaRue then called Bittman, identifying himself once again as Mr. Baker.

"Will you be at home at 11:30 tonight?" he asked.

"Yes, I will."

"Will you deliver an envelope to Mr. Hunt?"

"Yes, I will."

"We'll leave it in your mailbox."

That evening, LaRue invited a few friends over to dinner at the Watergate. It was a cold night. He had just moved in to a new apartment and had trouble operating the fireplace. A malfunctioning exhaust fan filled the apartment with smoke, causing much embarrassment and hilarity. One of the guests was a man named Manyon M. Millican, the marketing director of a snowshoe company who served as director of canvassing for CREEP. In December and January, Millican had delivered plain manila envelopes stuffed with cash to Hunt's lawyer without knowing what was inside. Toward the end of the evening, LaRue handed his friend another manila envelope containing thick wads of $100 bills. After leaving the Watergate, the snowshoe man drove to Bittman's home in the horsey Maryland suburb of Potomac. He stuffed the envelope into the mailbox at the end of the driveway and drove away.

Hunt picked up the money the following day—March 22—from his lawyer. He was distressed to find there was only $75,000 in the envelope, $55,000 less than he had demanded. "Somehow this payment seemed to have all the finality of a Dear John letter," he wrote later. "I felt that since I had had to pull teeth to get this amount delivered, I could probably count on no further assistance." His sentencing by Judge Sirica was just one day away.

P rior to the Watergate break-in, John Mitchell was widely regarded as the president's de facto deputy. The mastermind of Nixon's narrow election victory in 1968 had served as attorney general before heading up the reelection effort. Although he was eight months younger than the president, he seemed like a father figure, a calming, judicious presence in a world full of young sycophants. He was the only close aide to Nixon who was remotely his peer. During the years of Nixon's political exile, they had been partners together in Mitchell's New York law firm. Nixon looked up to his gruff, rough-edged friend, a self-made man just like himself. Before becoming a lawyer, Mitchell had been a standout student athlete and commander of patrol torpedo boats in World War II. (His subordinates included Lieutenant John F. Kennedy.) As a top bond attorney, Mitchell moved easily around the backdoor intersections of commerce and politics, negotiating deals with a nod and a handshake. His granitelike features, concealed behind a swirl of pipe smoke, gave him an air of authority and mystery. "I've found the heavyweight," Nixon proclaimed excitedly in 1967 when Mitchell agreed to become his campaign manager.

Mitchell was well aware of his importance to Nixon. During the 1968 campaign, he boasted that he was the only man who could say no to the candidate. "I've made more money in the practice of law than Nixon," he told a group of Republican congressmen, "brought more clients into the firm, can hold my own in argument with him, and, as far as I'm

Attorney General John Mitchell with his wife, Martha, nicknamed
"the Mouth of the South" because of her outspoken comments to reporters.

concerned, I can deal with him as an equal." After the election, Nixon
had to persuade an initially reluctant Mitchell to move to Washington
to become his attorney general. He needed Mitchell more than Mitchell needed him. At cabinet meetings, the president would often glance
across the table, seeking the approval of the stone-faced Mitchell. They
communicated by subtle gestures. If Mitchell was unhappy with the way
a discussion was going, an aide recalled, "he would jiggle or puff on his
pipe with some vigor. Nixon would get the signal and switch subjects or
terminate that line of conversation. If Mitchell looked serene—and that
was really the only word for it—Nixon would go on."

For all his power and influence, Mitchell had an Achilles' heel in
the form of his exuberant wife, Martha. A former grade school teacher
from Arkansas who had transformed herself into a southern belle, Martha was as impulsive as Mitchell was circumspect. It was the attraction
of opposites. "John is the most intelligent man in the world," Martha
explained. "He's soft, warm, sweet and cuddly." For his part, Mitchell
seemed to find in Martha an outlet for all his repressed desires. She
horrified his buttoned-down friends with her outrageous behavior and
constant demands for attention. Mitchell, however, was amused by her

and "head over heels in love." When he traveled on business, he would telephone her prior to going to bed for long rounds of romantic pillow talk. "The two made an odd couple," his biographer, James Rosen, would later write. "He in pinstripes, pipe, and wingtips; she in bouffant wigs, costume jewelry, and stilettos." Their relationship brought to mind Katharine Hepburn's classic remark about Fred Astaire and Ginger Rogers: "He gave her class, she gave him sex appeal."

The move to Washington sent the already unstable Martha into a downward spiral. Ensconced in her luxurious duplex in Watergate East, she drank heavily. Media attention became another addiction. Society reporters viewed her as a welcome splash of color in an otherwise gray administration. She gave a reporter from *Women's Wear Daily* a peek inside her dressing room closets—one for evening wear, another for "short cocktail things," a third for handbags and a hundred pairs of shoes, and a fourth for fur coats. She attacked senators and Supreme Court justices as Communist stooges and compared the antiwar protests to the Russian Revolution. Her willingness to blurt out whatever was on her mind on national TV won her an enthusiastic following in Middle America. A November 1970 Gallup poll reported that the woman known as "the mouth of the South" had 76 percent nationwide name recognition. Nixon jokingly called her "the soothsayer" because of her propensity for dramatic predictions.

The political scandal surrounding the Watergate break-in caused Martha to become even more erratic. She had traveled to California with her husband for some campaign fund-raising events, staying on for a few days with their daughter after Mitchell returned to Washington to deal with the crisis. Learning that her former security man, James McCord, was one of the burglars, she wondered if he might have also bugged her private apartment in the Watergate. With the crazed wisdom of a Shakespeare fool, she prophesied, "This could land my husband in jail." Over the next few hours, she became increasingly abusive and hysterical, downing several bottles of gin and whiskey. Her new bodyguard was under instructions from Mitchell to ensure she did not call any reporters. She nevertheless locked herself into her bedroom and made a call to Helen Thomas of United Press International. Hearing her on the phone, the bodyguard broke open the door and ripped the telephone line out of the wall in the middle of the conversation. He later pinned Martha down while a doctor forcibly removed her pants and plunged a needle into her thigh to administer tranquilizers. Martha fought back, smashing a glass door with her hand. She was taken to the local hospital, where she received six stitches. When Thomas attempted to call her back, she was informed, "Mrs. Mitchell is indisposed and cannot talk."

"That little sweetheart," said Mitchell, when asked about the incident. "She gets a little upset about politics, but she loves me and I love her and that's what counts."

Mitchell arranged for friends to escort his wife back across the continent on a red-eye flight. Confined to a country club in upstate New York, Martha found a way to complete her interrupted phone call with the reporter two days later. "If you could see me, you wouldn't believe it," she told Thomas tearfully. "I'm black and blue. I'm a political prisoner." She threatened to leave Mitchell unless he quit his job with the Nixon campaign. "I love my husband very much but I'm not going to stand for all those dirty things that go on." Nixon aides privately spread the word that she was mentally disturbed.

Martha's antics were a major distraction for Mitchell. Nixon came to believe that "the Watergate thing would never have happened" without Martha. "We have had a slip-up due to the fact that Mitchell was so obsessed with the problems he had with Martha," Nixon noted in his diary a few days after the scandal first erupted. "We just didn't have the discipline we should have had, and that we would have had, had he been able to pay attention to business." He accepted Mitchell's resignation as director of CREEP on June 30, 1972, two weeks after the break-in. Nixon recognized that Mitchell was likely to become a political liability to him, but this was not the official reason given for his departure. Instead, the White House released a letter from Mitchell explaining that he needed to "devote more time" to his wife and family. It was a line that still seemed original to Nixon, in addition to alluding gently to the Martha drama. "Excellent," he said appreciatively. "Very subtle."

The precise nature of Mitchell's involvement in the plan to bug the Democratic National Committee would remain mysterious. The case against him rested chiefly on the testimony of a perjurer, Jeb Magruder. Mitchell never put anything in writing. It seems unlikely, however, that the pliant, paper-pushing deputy CREEP director acted entirely on his own initiative. At the very least, he required a green light from his boss to disburse funds to the burglars. Four days after the break-in, Nixon himself speculated that Mitchell might well have said something along the lines of "Don't tell me about it, but you go ahead and do what you want." After Magruder returned from his meeting with Mitchell in Key Biscayne in March 1972, he authorized campaign finance officials to make an initial $83,000 cash payment to Liddy. The payment request was sufficiently unusual for the finance chairman, Maurice Stans, to check with Mitchell to make sure everything was in order.

"What's it all about?" Stans asked.

"I don't know," Mitchell replied, according to Stans. "Magruder is in charge of the campaign and he directs the spending."

Stans asked Mitchell if the campaign should honor all future requests from Magruder for cash payments to Liddy.

"That's right."

Whether or not Mitchell formally approved the break-in, he was savvy enough to distance himself from the decision by delegating financial authority to his deputy. After the arrest of the burglars, he authorized a series of cash payments to keep them quiet.

As the Watergate scandal deepened in early 1973, and the president and his aides looked around for someone to blame, Mitchell seemed like an obvious candidate. At a meeting with Nixon on the morning of March 22, Dean suggested a strategy of "putting the wagons around the White House." By this he meant drawing a sharp line between the White House and the reelection committee. Anyone inside the stockade— including Haldeman, Ehrlichman, Dean, and above all the president himself—would be protected. The top officials at CREEP—Mitchell and Magruder—would be abandoned. Dean's proposal was endorsed enthusiastically by Haldeman and Ehrlichman. With luck, the whole nightmare might go away if a sufficiently impressive sacrifice was offered to the marauding Indians.

There were several problems with the "circling the wagons" idea. First, lines of responsibility were blurred. People like Hunt and Liddy had ties to both CREEP and the White House. It seemed unlikely that the political and legal fallout from the rapidly expanding scandal could be contained within the now disbanded Committee to Re-elect the President. Second, Nixon was not prepared for a confrontation with Mitchell. He believed that he owed his election in 1968 largely to Mitchell's "strength as a counselor and his skill as a manager." The thought of abandoning "one of my very few personal friends" was particularly painful. The furthest Nixon was willing to go at this stage was to summon the former CREEP director to the White House for a discussion of the options. Mitchell was back at his old law firm in New York. He flew down to Washington later that same day to meet with Haldeman, Ehrlichman, and Dean, followed by a session with the president in his EOB hideaway. As was often the case with Watergate, the conversation led nowhere. It quickly became clear that Mitchell was unwilling to fall on his sword. Instead, he proposed a limited waiver of executive privilege that would allow White House officials to testify behind closed doors to the Senate select committee.

"What words of wisdom do we have from this august body?" asked Nixon, when everyone assembled after lunch.

"Our brother Mitchell brought us some wisdom on executive privilege," said Ehrlichman sarcastically.

Once again, they discussed how they might placate the Senate with a Dean report admitting to some "dirty tricks" during the election campaign while exonerating Nixon and his closest aides.

"Let it hang out, so to speak?" asked Nixon.

"It's a limited hangout," said Haldeman.

"A modified limited hangout," corrected Ehrlichman, with his flair for the memorable phrase.

They began fantasizing about what the Dean report might say.

"We went down every alley," proposed Ehrlichman. Emboldened by the chortles that greeted this remark, he made a joke that was, simultaneously, a suggestion. He said out loud, in front of Mitchell, what he had been urging in private for months. "John [Mitchell] says that he's sorry he sent those burglars in there, and that helps a lot."

"That's right," said the president.

"You are very welcome, sir," said Mitchell. He removed the pipe from his mouth and made a little bow, to nervous titters.

Nixon waited until the others had left the room before addressing

Mitchell's personal situation. He did so in a roundabout fashion, mentioning a scandal that had shaken the Eisenhower administration when Nixon was vice president. By Watergate standards, it was a trivial affair. Eisenhower's powerful chief of staff, Sherman Adams, had accepted a vicuña coat, made from the fur of a llama-like animal living high in the Andes, and several other expensive gifts from a longtime friend. In exchange for these gifts, he was accused of making helpful inquiries on behalf of his friend with two government agencies. Although he denied any quid pro quo, it created an impression of impropriety. Eisenhower sent a message to Adams through Nixon that he should resign.

"It was a very, very cruel thing," Nixon reminisced. "I don't want it to happen with Watergate. I think [Adams] made a mistake, but he shouldn't have been sacked."

He made clear he was not going to abandon Mitchell the way Eisenhower had abandoned Adams. "I don't give a shit what happens," he said, referring to the upcoming Senate hearings. "I want you all to stonewall it, let them plead the Fifth Amendment, cover up, or anything else if it'll save it—save the plan. That's the whole point."

There was, however, an alternative scenario that Nixon asked Mitchell to consider. It was one that he had been discussing with Haldeman earlier that week. There was always the possibility that the wolves were going to gobble up Mitchell and Magruder whatever the White House did. In this case, it would be better for them to preempt the opposition attacks and sacrifice themselves for the greater good. Afraid to speak as plainly as Ehrlichman, Nixon resorted to a tortuous circumlocution, the implications of which were left unsaid.

"On the other hand, I would prefer, as I said to you, that you do it the other way. And I would particularly prefer to do it that other way if it's going to come out that way anyway."

Nixon later wrote that this was his "oblique way" of persuading Mitchell of the need for "a painful shift in our Watergate strategy, a strategy that so far had been a dismal and damaging failure." Despite the indirect manner in which the message was delivered, Mitchell could hardly fail to pick up the hint. He would make an excellent scapegoat.

———

Nixon had a very good reason for his reluctance to abandon Mitchell, quite apart from his loyalty toward a friend. For Eisenhower, getting rid of Adams had been a simple matter. The accusations of impropriety had begun and ended with the chief of staff. Because the president was in no way involved, the crisis was resolved as soon as Adams was removed. The Watergate scandal was very different. To use John Dean's analogy, it was a malignant tumor that had spread far and wide. From tiny cells, the cancer grew until it consumed, and ultimately destroyed, the Nixon presidency. It was impossible to eradicate the cancer by surgically targeting just a few of the diseased cells: Nixon himself had created the culture in which the cancer metastasized. "I do not believe that Nixon did order the break-in," Bob Haldeman observed many years later. "Nor that he even knew about it. But I do believe that he caused it."

The mindset that spawned Watergate can be traced back to Nixon's war with the establishment, a stew of personal resentments, and a no-holds-barred style of political campaigning. He was particularly aggrieved by his narrow loss to Jack Kennedy in the 1960 presidential election, which turned on a few thousand votes in Texas and Illinois. Nixon was in "no doubt" that substantial voter fraud had been committed. He blamed his defeat on the dirty tricks of "the most ruthless group of political operators ever mobilized for a presidential campaign" and the "slanted reporting" of brazenly pro-Kennedy journalists. He did not contest the results of the election for fear of being labeled a sore loser. Nevertheless, from that moment on, he wrote later, "I had the wisdom and wariness of someone who had been burned by the power of the Kennedys and their money and by the license they were given by the media. I vowed that I would never again enter an election at a disadvantage by being vulnerable to them—or anyone—on the level of political tactics."

Under any president, the White House functions as a machine for fulfilling the wishes of its occupant. Foremost among Nixon's needs was more intelligence about his political opponents. The demands for intelligence became imperatives for action. Some of these actions were legal, some illegal. Some were in response to specific presidential directives; some were dreamed up by underlings determined to please him. Nixon's desires were often shrouded in ambiguity, making it difficult to distinguish between a specific instruction and a vaguely expressed wish. The attempts to divine exactly what he wanted were reminiscent of the prelude to the murder of Archbishop Thomas Becket in medieval England. "Will no one rid me of this troublesome priest?" Henry II had asked in exasperation, after Becket opposed him once too often. The king spoke in a fit of anger, but four of his knights took his words literally and slayed the archbishop with their swords in Canterbury Cathedral. White House courtiers behaved in similar fashion. "We wanted to make the president happy," was the way Jeb Magruder put it. "We knew that the president wanted as much information as we could get. The more information we got, the happier he was."

Nixon made plain early that he had no objection in principle to wiretaps, however obtained. "I want, Bob, more use of wiretapping," he told Haldeman more than a year before the Watergate break-in as they discussed plans for the 1972 election campaign. Rebuffed by J. Edgar Hoover at the FBI, he was willing to resort to illegal methods to gather dirt on his likely opponents, beginning with Ted Kennedy and Ed Muskie. "Maybe we can get a real scandal on any one of the leading Democrats," he mused.

Nixon's campaign to get even with his political enemies moved into higher gear in June 1971 following the leaking of the Pentagon Papers, first to *The New York Times* and then *The Washington Post*. For weeks, he lashed out against anyone perceived to have crossed him, from disloyal officials to partisan reporters to Kennedy supporters of all descriptions. Even though the Vietnam War history mainly dealt with the actions of his predecessors, particularly LBJ, Nixon regarded the leak as a threat to good government. "We're up against an enemy, a conspiracy," he told Haldeman and Kissinger on July 1, the day after the Supreme Court upheld the right of newspapers to publish the leaked documents. "They're using any means. We are going to use any means." An eye for an eye, a leak for a leak was Nixon's philosophy. His enemies, at the *Times* and elsewhere, had "thrown the sword down." But they had made a fatal error. "Never strike a king unless you kill him. They struck and did not kill. And now we're going to kill them. That is what I will do, if it's the last thing I do in this office. I don't care what it costs. They're going to be killed."

He urged his aides to gather compromising information on the presumed leaker of the papers, Daniel Ellsberg, that could be used to smear him. "Convict the son of a bitch in the press," he told them. "That's how it's done." He also raged against the number of Jews and "Harvard people" in the government. "Most Jews are disloyal," he told Haldeman. He exempted Kissinger and several other members of his staff from this blanket critique but added, "Generally speaking, you can't trust the bastards. They turn on you." The fact that Ellsberg was Jewish only confirmed his suspicions.

Another target of Nixon's anger was the Brookings Institution. He had heard that classified government documents relating to LBJ's secret Vietnam diplomacy might be stored in a safe in the think tank on Massachusetts Avenue less than a mile from the White House. He wanted the files, thinking he could use them to "blackmail" the former president. "I want it implemented on a thievery basis," he instructed his aides. "Goddamn it, get in and get those files. Blow the safe and get it." Nixon's wishes were transmitted via Colson to the Plumbers and the ever-eager Gordon Liddy. Liddy devised a plan to firebomb the building at night "so as not to endanger lives needlessly." Hunt's Cuban collaborators would enter the Brookings offices disguised as firefighters, "hit the vault," and make their escape with the documents amid the general confusion. For the plan to proceed, it would be necessary to purchase "a used but late-model fire engine." To Liddy's disgust, his superiors objected to the expense. The scheme was dropped because "the White House wouldn't spring for a fire engine."

It is symptomatic of the dysfunction within the White House that a break-in Nixon explicitly ordered was shelved while one that he never authorized became a mortal threat to his presidency. Haldeman was proud of his highly disciplined staffing system and paper trail for implementing presidential instructions. But the system broke down when it came to waging war on Nixon's political enemies. In these cases, orders were issued verbally or in code. Sometimes his instructions were ignored; at other times they were exaggerated. People down the chain of command interpreted his wishes according to their own priorities or pressure from third parties. This is what appears to have happened with Watergate. Nixon's push for actionable intelligence on the Democrats was transmitted through Haldeman to Magruder (via Haldeman's aide Gordon Strachan) and from Magruder to Liddy. Another line of communication ran from Nixon to Colson to Hunt, back up to Colson, and down to Magruder and Liddy. A third ran upward from Liddy to Magruder to Mitchell. The result of these competing channels of authority was that a man described by Nixon as "a little nuts" was able to build his own fantasies around the supposed wishes of his superiors.

"I mean he just isn't well screwed on, is he?" Nixon said of Liddy, after learning of his activities in the Watergate.

"No, but he was under pressure, apparently, to get more information," replied Haldeman. "As he got more pressure, he pushed the people harder."

The arrests of the Watergate burglars on June 17, 1972, posed a painful dilemma for Nixon. The smart option, at this point, would have been to cut his losses and blame the bungled break-in on overzealous subordinates at the Committee to Re-elect the President. Such a move, however, would risk the exposure of other crimes and dirty tricks committed by the White House Plumbers. "The problem is that there are all kinds of other involvements," Haldeman informed the president on June 21. If the FBI, the press, and other investigators began "a fishing thing on this," they would soon "start picking up tracks." It would be difficult to control whatever they might discover. With presidential elections less than five months away, Nixon and his aides instinctively opted for a cover-up. The FBI would have to be "turned off."

Two days later, on June 23, Nixon made the fateful decision to instruct the CIA to tell the FBI to steer clear of the Watergate investigation because it was a "national security" matter. "They should call the FBI in and say . . . don't go further into this case, period!" he told Haldeman. "And that destroys the case." If the spooks balked, they should be reminded of Howard Hunt's involvement in the Bay of Pigs. The agency would not want to reopen "that scab" or be reminded of the "hanky-panky" with the Cubans. "Play it tough," Nixon instructed. "That's the way they play it, and that's the way we're going to play it." Unfortunately for Nixon, CIA officials refused to play the game by his rules. Instead of warning the FBI to back away from the investigation, they documented his demands in memos "for the file" that eventually became part of the public record.

With the CIA and FBI refusing to play ball, the president became even more entangled in the cover-up. He approved the decision to encourage Magruder to commit perjury to keep the investigation away from Mitchell and the White House. Once he was safely reelected, the Watergate defendants could be freed from jail, along with antiwar pro-testers. "We'll just basically pardon the whole kit and caboodle after the election," he told Colson on July 19. That night, he was haunted by a "strange dream" about Watergate. Who knew where the nightmare would end? "We are whistling in the dark," he confessed to Haldeman, "but I can't believe they can tie the thing to me."

By the beginning of August, Nixon was approving payoffs to Hunt and the other Watergate burglars.

"Hunt's happy," reported Haldeman, following initial payments of $83,000 to his wife and $25,000 to his lawyer.

"At considerable cost, I guess?" said Nixon.

"Yes."

"It's worth it."

"It's very expensive."

"That's what the money is for," said Nixon. "They have to be paid."

By authorizing the payments to the Watergate defendants, Nixon forgot his own injunction about the cover-up being more damaging than the original crime, a mantra he repeated constantly when refer-ring to the Alger Hiss case. During the nine months that followed the break-in, he presided over the construction of an edifice of lies, eva-sions, and half-truths incapable of sustaining serious challenge. The world was about to discover what would happen if one of the pillars supporting this ramshackle structure was suddenly removed.

J udge Sirica tried to act "as nonchalant as possible" as he entered
his wood-paneled courtroom at precisely 10:00 a.m. on Friday,
March 23. High on his dais next to the American flag, he looked
down at the seven convicted Watergate defendants, their attorneys, the
prosecutors, and dozens of journalists who had been covering the trial.
Every seat was occupied. Security was extra tight. Everyone entering
the courtroom had been obliged to pass through a metal detector.

After wishing everybody a pleasant good morning, the judge mentioned "a preliminary matter" he wished to address before proceed-
ing to sentencing. At this point, one of his clerks produced a sealed
envelope that he showed to the court. The clerk opened the envelope
with a little flourish and handed the contents to the judge. Seated at the
defense table, Gordon Liddy was reminded of the artificial suspense of
an Oscar ceremony. Next to him, James McCord sank down into his
chair, realizing what was about to happen.

McCord had tried to deliver his two-page, single-spaced letter to
Sirica in person on March 20, but the judge refused to accept it. Afraid
that the envelope might contain a bribe, he told McCord to hand it to
his probation officer. When Sirica finally read the letter in the presence
of a court reporter, he sensed immediately that it would "break this case
wide open." He ordered the letter resealed and kept in his safe until he
could read it in open court. For the next three nights, he barely slept,

"worrying about the letter leaking, worrying about how to handle it in court, and wondering what would happen next." He had been up since 3:30 that morning.

McCord's anger with the Nixon White House had been building for weeks. He regarded the trial as "a sham" and "a massive injustice." Blame for Watergate was being placed on underlings like himself while the men who ordered the break-in were getting off scot-free. He resented the smugness of a smooth operator like Magruder, who was lauded in the press for his management skills while his subordinates were branded as criminals. A deeply religious man, McCord felt different from the other defendants. He was neither a fanatic, like Liddy, nor an ideologue, like Hunt, nor an exile from his homeland, like the Cubans. His principal loyalties were to his family, his church, and his employer for nearly twenty years, the CIA. He had already experienced the horrors of the D.C. jail and loathed the idea of returning there. The night before his sentencing, he had received a call from his old White House contact Jack Caulfield offering him $100,000 in exchange for his silence. But it was too late to persuade him to change his mind. His letter was already in the hands of Judge Sirica, who now proceeded to read it in open court.

As a preamble, McCord wrote that his family had expressed fears for his life if he disclosed certain facts. Careers, livelihoods, and reputations were at stake. It took the judge several minutes to reach the nub of McCord's complaint, which was contained in four numbered points:

1. There was political pressure applied to the defendants to plead guilty and remain silent.

2. Perjury occurred during the trial in matters highly material to the very structure, orientation, and impact of the government's case . . .

3. Others involved in the Watergate operation were not identified during the trial when they could have been by those testifying.

4. The Watergate operation was not a CIA operation. The Cubans may have been misled by others into believing it was a CIA operation. I know for a fact that it was not.

As Sirica read aloud from his letter, McCord sensed an "electrified" air in the courtroom, as if "no one was breathing for fear of missing a comma or a phrase." The scrappy little judge was doing his best to maintain a poker face despite an "excruciating pain" in the middle of his chest. "It was nearly more than I could bear, but I couldn't quit before the end of the letter," he wrote later. He somehow made it to the end and called a recess. As he staggered to his chambers, he noticed the reporters rushing toward the double swing doors at the other end of the courtroom in search of pay phones. "The dam had broken."

Sirica lay down on a sofa. He thought of calling for a doctor, but the pain gradually subsided. He had been suffering from fatigue and nervous tension. After half an hour, he felt much better and was able to return to the courtroom.

First up for sentencing was Gordon Liddy. His attorney praised his FBI career and "life of public service," but Liddy himself remained defiant. "I have nothing to say," he replied when the judge asked him to describe any mitigating factors. It was obvious to Sirica that he was not going to cooperate. After describing his offenses as "sordid" and "despicable," he sentenced Liddy to twenty years in prison, reducible with good behavior to just over six years. Liddy viewed the punishment as "an unintended but welcome compliment from my enemy."

Next was Howard Hunt, who seemed a broken man. The former CIA agent and spy novelist looked pale and haggard as he stood before Sirica, his pin-striped suit hanging loosely from his shrunken shoulders. Unlike Liddy, he had decided his only option was to throw himself on the mercy of "Maximum John." His four young children were without a mother. They should not be deprived of their father as well. According to Hunt, the "real victims of the Watergate conspiracy" were the conspirators themselves and their families.

"Today I stand before the bar of justice alone, nearly friendless, ridiculed, disgraced, destroyed as a man," Hunt told the judge. "Since the Watergate case began, I have suffered agonies I never believed a man could endure and still survive."

Sirica was unimpressed. He announced "provisional" maximum sentences of thirty-five years for Hunt and forty years for the Cubans. The final sentences would depend on their cooperation with the Senate Watergate Committee. If they told investigators everything they knew, they would likely serve less time in prison. "Other factors will, of course, be considered, but I mention this one because it is one over which you have control," was how Sirica put it. He postponed sentencing McCord on condition that he cooperate fully with the investigation.

Consigned to the "hellhole" of the D.C. jail, Hunt experienced the same humiliating procedure endured by McCord and Liddy a few weeks before. *Undress. Raise your arms. Open your mouth. Extend your tongue. Raise your testicles. Spread your buttocks.* Taken to his cell, he was overwhelmed by a "sensory overload" of raucous yelling and TV sets blaring an Aretha Franklin concert. A "stench of urine and old vomit" filled his nostrils, he later recalled. "This thick, dirty air was sucked into my lungs, making me feel slimy inside and out." Queens patrolled the catwalk outside his cell, offering their services to other inmates. He thought of McCord's letter to Sirica, which made him feel betrayed but also eager to tell his side of the story. To pass the time, he killed cockroaches until "the futility of trying to eradicate a never-ending supply of roaches" became "all too evident." A few words etched into the wall by a former occupant encapsulated his despair: "If I was God, I'd quit!"

Down the hallway, Liddy took a perverse delight in continuing to fight. Returning to his cell, he noticed that someone had rifled through his belongings and stolen his hairbrush. This constituted a "breach of the most fundamental of prison taboos, the violation of my territory." He tracked down the thief and took his hairbrush back. A brawl ensued in which Liddy received a deep gash to his ear that required multiple stitches. He later discovered that his opponent had been wearing a spiky metal "fighting ring," secretly ordered from the prison workshop, on his ring finger. Liddy bought his own fighting ring in exchange for a carton of cigarettes. His "territory" was much shrunken from his days in the Nixon White House, but he was equally ready to defend it.

In the meantime, McCord had begun to name names. Encouraged by Sirica, he provided Senate investigators with an annotated version of the trial transcript showing precisely where Jeb Magruder had perjured himself. According to McCord, the deputy CREEP director had been "knowledgeable of, and involved in, the Watergate operation sequence prior to June 17, 1972." The McCord memo also named John Dean as a

White House official privy to the plan to bug Democratic Party head-quarters. After speaking with the investigators behind closed doors, McCord met with a reporter from *The Los Angeles Times*, Robert Jackson. He had come to know Jackson through his parent-teacher association and trusted his news judgment. Jackson would be his channel for sharing his Watergate testimony with the outside world.

The *Los Angeles Times* splashed Jackson's story across three columns at the top of the front page on Monday, March 26: "McCord Says Dean, Magruder Knew in Advance of Bugging. Claims Political Pressure, Lying on Watergate." Citing McCord's interview with Senate investigators, the paper reported that Magruder had committed perjury during the Watergate trial.

John Dean was at Camp David when he heard about the bombshell revelations in a telephone call from Ron Ziegler. He had gone to the presidential retreat in Maryland to hide from journalists and work on the "Dean report" Nixon had been demanding. His wife, Maureen, had accompanied him. Intended as an escape from the pressures of Watergate, the trip was turning into a nightmare. Dean spent much of his time on the phone with White House officials or lawyers, managing the fallout from the scandal. Haldeman called three or four times a day, demanding the latest details on the investigation to pass on to the president. The man never seemed to let up.

On top of everything else, Dean was suffering from writer's block. He had earlier claimed that writing the report would be like packaging a TV advertising spot. "Sir, I can give them a show," he had boasted to Nixon just a few days earlier. Selling the White House line was no more difficult than "selling Wheaties." The reality turned out to be very different. He made a stab of drafting his report in his crabbed handwriting on the yellow legal pads that were lying around everywhere. He outlined the main sections ("Pre–June 17," "Post–June 17") with subsections like "The Dean Investigation," "The Blackmail Problem," and "The Plumbers." But the more time he devoted to the task, the more hopeless it seemed. If he shifted the blame onto others, it would look as if he were protecting himself. But if he described his own activities in any detail, he would be confessing his management of the cover-up. Nixon and the others could use the report to make him the scapegoat.

Desperate for relief, he took Maureen for a ride on a golf cart in the woods through the patches of dirty snow. Six presidents, from FDR to Nixon, had wandered along these paths discussing the state of the world with visitors like Winston Churchill and Nikita Khrushchev. Dean was focused instead on the prospect of a lengthy prison sentence for obstruction of justice. "I'm thinking of getting myself a lawyer, some guy who really knows the criminal law, and having him tell me how serious my problem is," he told Maureen. Secretly, he fantasized about being spirited away in a helicopter to South America to live "in grand splendor as guests of some Latin businessmen" until the scandal was over.

Maureen asked about the report he was writing.

"It's an idea of Ehrlichman's to protect the president by giving him a report that says everything is okay and no one in the White House has any problems. It says everything is just hunky-dory."

"That's not true, though, is it?"

"No."

"Then, John, you shouldn't write that report. That's not very smart."

And then there was the Magruder problem. The now fatally compromised campaign aide had been trying to reach Dean for days, ever since the shocking news of the McCord letter to Sirica. Dean refused to take his calls. He had coached Magruder on his perjured testimony and had no desire to relive that episode. But the *Los Angeles Times* story made him change his mind. Dean needed evidence to support his claim that he had nothing to do with the bugging of the Democratic Party headquarters. He remembered that Colson had secretly recorded a telephone conversation with Howard Hunt acknowledging that he had not been involved in the Watergate break-in. Dean would now attempt a similar trick with Magruder.

"I want to get Jeb on record that I didn't have any advance knowledge," he explained. Maureen did not think secretly recording colleagues was "very nice." He assured her that "everybody at the White House tapes people." He mentioned Haldeman, Ehrlichman, Colson, "and probably two dozen more that I don't even know about." She laughed at his trembling hands as he set up his dictation machine on the coffee table of their cabin while she kept guard to make sure they were undisturbed. By holding the microphone close to the earpiece of the phone, he discovered he could make a serviceable recording. After a test call back to his office, he phoned Magruder, who answered immediately.

"Hi, Jeb," Dean began. "How are you doing?"

"I'm doing fine. How are you doing?"

"Pretty well, incredible."

Magruder was not "doing fine" at all. After the events of the weekend, he felt like "a basket case," staring at "the wreckage of my life." It now seemed probable that the truth would come out. There were too many contradictions and outright lies in his cover story for it to withstand serious examination. He did not share his fear of going to jail with Dean, however. Instead, he talked about that morning's *Los Angeles Times* story.

"God, we got splashed all over that one, let me tell you."

"Is that right?" said Dean, feigning ignorance.

"I haven't seen it yet but my friend called me. Said 'Christ, you take up the whole front page.'"

"Is that right?"

"Yes. You and I. Pictures, the whole works."

Dean turned the conversation to the break-in. He was determined to get Jeb on tape, confirming his lack of involvement. While he had been present for the two preliminary Gemstone meetings with Liddy and Mitchell, on January 27 and February 4, 1972, he had attempted "to turn the damn thing off." He assumed it had been shelved.

"I'm taking a bum rap, Jeb."

"Well I know that."

"That's the incredible thing."

Magruder comforted himself with the thought that McCord's testimony was only "hearsay." Whatever McCord told investigators was likely based on secondhand accounts he had heard from Liddy and Hunt "as they sat around drinking at the Watergate." His evidence

would not be admissible in court because he had not himself participated in any of the original discussions on Gemstone.

This was true but missed the point. McCord's statements were devastating not because of their direct legal value but because of the political
and psychological fallout. By publicly breaking ranks with his fellow
conspirators, McCord was putting pressure on everybody to strike their
own deals with the prosecutors. His letter to Sirica had already led to
the resumption of the dormant Watergate criminal investigation and
reconvening of the grand jury. More witnesses would certainly be called
and offered immunity in return for information. The "every man protecting his own ass" scenario that Dean had outlined to Nixon a few
days earlier was coming to pass.

Magruder was most concerned about a divergence between his perjured testimony and what Dean might say if questioned by investigators. He recalled the day in early September when Dean had helped
him rehearse his grand jury testimony and explain away incriminating entries in Magruder's desk diary. The diary, which was now in the
hands of prosecutors, recorded the two Gemstone meetings they had
both attended with Liddy in Mitchell's ceremonial Justice Department
office. To conceal their knowledge of Gemstone, they had worked on a
false version. Magruder would claim that the January 27 meeting had
been canceled and rescheduled for February 4. The session had been
entirely routine, called to discuss Liddy's new job as legal counsel to the
Committee to Re-elect the President and the law on campaign finance
spending. Back in the fall, during the early days of the Watergate investigation, everything had seemed so simple. To get Nixon reelected, they
had to lie. "We were not covering up a burglary, we were safeguarding
world peace," Magruder recalled later. "It was a rationalization we all
found easy to accept." He thought of himself as a "good soldier."

Magruder reminded Dean of the essential points of the cover story.
The January 27 meeting had never occurred. There had only ever been
one meeting, on February 4, and it had nothing to do with bugging.
"We just went over the general framework of [Liddy's] job and the new
law . . . That was the extent of it." He was almost pleading now. If Dean
refused to confirm his perjured testimony, the entire cover-up could
collapse.

Dean did not want to be maneuvered into a position where he would also have to lie under oath. As a lawyer, he understood the perjury trap much better than Magruder. He said only that he had no plans "to go out and talk in any forum." They would simply have to wait and see what happened. "All we can do is sit tight right now."

Dean had barely got off the phone with Magruder when Haldeman called for the second time that day from Florida, where the president was taking a long weekend. Dean made clear he planned to tell the truth if required to testify to the grand jury. To his surprise, Haldeman did not object to the idea of abandoning the top men in CREEP to their fate.

"We've been protecting Mitchell and Magruder too long. And it got us in this damn mess," the chief of staff said.

Later that day, Nixon issued a statement voicing "absolute and total confidence" in Dean. Asked about the *Los Angeles Times* report, Ziegler formally denied that Dean had "any prior knowledge" of the Watergate break-in. He refused to give a similar undertaking about Magruder, saying he was unable to speak for "those who are not on the White House staff."

The wagons were being drawn tighter and tighter around the White House. For the moment, Dean was still inside the stockade. It was clear to him that the president had "decided to cut Mitchell and Magruder loose." But a second, more disturbing thought occurred almost simultaneously to the young White House counsel: perhaps he, too, was expendable.

Nixon returned to Washington from Florida late on Monday evening. During the four days in the sun in Key Biscayne, his presidency had begun to unravel. The stunning developments in Judge Sirica's courtroom had brought the Watergate scandal to the doorstep of the White House. In the opinion of the *Washington Post* columnist Joseph Kraft, what had previously been "a sideshow" had turned into "a political bomb that could blow the Nixon administration apart." The "finger of guilt" was no longer pointing solely at senior Nixon aides like Mitchell and Haldeman. "The man in the middle" was now the president himself. According to James Reston of *The New York Times,* even Nixon supporters were now asking how "an Administration that has been so cautious, shrewd, and successful in dealing with world affairs could also be so reckless, awkward and even stupid in dealing with human affairs."

The crisis of confidence extended far beyond Watergate. Bad news was pouring in from all directions. A White House that had seemed so sure-footed just a few weeks previously was now under challenge on multiple fronts. The removal of price controls had caused inflation to spiral. Food prices were up by more than 5 percent in January and February alone, and more than 8 percent on the previous year. The dollar had fallen sharply. Banks were charging 7 percent interest rates. There was talk of gasoline rationing. The humorist Art Buchwald joked about the connection between rising prices and increasing public concern about Watergate. He invented a mythical Republican friend who had no

Nixon in the Rose Garden with his daughters, Julie (left) and Tricia,
on Father's Day 1969.

qualms about voting for Nixon when he "could still get a decent steak
for $1.50" but was "not going to put up with corruption in the White
House" when asked to "pay 59 cents for a can of tomatoes."

Nixon's two daughters, Tricia and Julie, had come home to support
their father in his moment of trial. He drew strength and calm from
having them around. Twenty-four-year-old Julie, in particular, was a
great comfort. Married to Eisenhower's grandson, she was the "favorite
Nixon" for many of his aides. "She is like her father without a dark side,"
wrote Nixon's speechwriter William Safire. "That is, she is loyal, alert,
considerate, virtuous, intelligent, and sensibly impulsive." Nixon had
come to rely on Julie as an intermediary with friends like Bebe Rebozo,
political supporters, relatives, and even his wife. She softened him and
made him human. If he was in the middle of a meeting and received a
telephone call from Julie, his voice would change instantly from imperious and irascible to loving and caring. In contrast to her older sister,
who seemed as brittle as a China doll, Julie charmed almost everyone
with her infectious gaiety and spontaneity.

As his political troubles mounted, Nixon closed himself off from the family, dining alone on a tray in his office. Prodded by their mother, Julie and Tricia attempted to break through his isolation and at least entice him to a family dinner. But it was difficult. He complained about being swamped with work. In addition to his Watergate worries, he was preparing a big speech marking the return of the last American prisoners from North Vietnam and the end of the war. On the other side of the country, he was attempting to negotiate an end to a monthlong confrontation with rebellious American Indians at Wounded Knee that had degenerated into open warfare.

Julie called her father in his EOB hideaway on Tuesday afternoon, interrupting a tense conversation with Haldeman on Watergate. The two men had spent much of the day attempting to find out what was happening in the reconvened grand jury. They feared that Howard Hunt was "ready to fold" after seeing James McCord escape an immediate prison sentence. It seemed that Magruder had also "crumbled at the seams." Dean reported that the former deputy director of CREEP had become "a little psycho" and was attempting to shovel responsibility for Watergate onto the White House. "Going to jail for Jeb will be very, very, very difficult," Haldeman noted. Most troubling of all, it seemed that the president himself was being dragged directly into the firing line. A recent recruit to the McCord defense team had been overheard saying, "We don't give a damn about McCord, we're after Richard Nixon."

As usual, Nixon took Julie's call without question. "Daddy!" she said excitedly as she came on the line. She was determined to tell him "something cheery" to take his mind off his political troubles. Work had just been completed on a new one-lane bowling alley under the North Portico of the White House funded by his friends Bebe Rebozo and Robert Abplanalp.

"I wanted you to know it's so beautiful."

Nixon found it difficult to match his daughter's enthusiasm on this occasion, even though bowling was one of his favorite forms of relaxation. He sounded tired and distracted.

"That's great, sweetie. Nice of you to call."

"It's the prettiest one I've ever seen."

"I'll have to come and see it some time."

Julie would not let up. She had more home improvements to report.

"And also we've got the new music machine up in the Solarium. It has a TV, and on top of the TV is a record player, and on top of that is a tape cassette. It's fabulous. You'll really enjoy it up there."

"That's great."

He replaced the receiver gently, pivoting seamlessly back to reviewing the latest Watergate developments with his chief of staff.

Nixon did not make it back to the residence for supper that evening but did take time off before going to bed to inspect the new bowling alley with Julie. The following evening, he joined Julie, Tricia, and Pat for a family dinner that lasted seven minutes before being interrupted by another telephone call from Haldeman.

It had been "a hell of a hard day," he confided to his family, but he had experienced even "harder ones" in the past. He mentioned specifically the bleak days of the Christmas bombing campaign against North Vietnam when he was being branded a war criminal by influential commentators and even Kissinger seemed to be wavering. "Let's face it," he told Haldeman later. "What could have been harder than that? Really? We *were* alone then."

Gail Magruder shrieked as she opened the shades to her bedroom on Tuesday morning. Just a few weeks previously, in its flattering profile of Jeb, *The Washington Post* had described her suburban Maryland home as straight out of "a Hollywood set." A brief glance outside shattered the idyllic image. The picture-perfect front lawn was occupied by a scrum of unruly reporters and photographers, their cameras aimed directly at the house. The friendly scribes from the *Post* had turned overnight into sharks circling their prey. The Vassar-educated Gail threw herself on the floor in her nightgown to avoid being photographed.

Because Jeb's car was parked in the driveway, he had no choice but to push through the crowd of reporters to go to work. He replied to their frenzied questions with a muttered "no comment." When he arrived in the office, he received a call from John Mitchell. Magruder's former boss at CREEP wanted to meet with him that afternoon in New York to discuss their legal situation.

Magruder made a list of his concerns on a legal pad on the plane ride north. He had always been preoccupied with status symbols, like the personalized number plates on his Mustang that he had enjoyed as director of Nixon's Inaugural Committee. When the Watergate scandal first broke, he had been distressed about being excluded from a party on the presidential yacht because of his ties to Liddy and the burglars. "Those bastards," he thought at the time. "They want me to perjure myself for them and they won't invite me on their lousy cruise." His worries now were more existential. Would he get help with his legal fees? Who would take care of his family if he was sent to prison? Was there any chance of a pardon?

Mitchell tried to reassure him. "Don't worry, Jeb," he promised. "We'll take care of you." But the former attorney general and head of CREEP was now a private citizen. For the assurances to have any meaning, they would have to be confirmed by the White House. Mitchell had been summoned to Washington the following day, March 28, for a meeting with Haldeman. He agreed to take Magruder with him.

K eeping Jeb happy" had been a Haldeman priority in the months after Watergate. Magruder was the weakest link in the messy chain of command that had failed to adequately supervise Gordon Liddy. The goal was to keep him "on the reservation" but also at a safe distance from the White House. Following his stint on the Inaugural Committee, Nixon aides tried to find another position prestigious enough to appeal to Magruder's vanity but harmless enough to avoid any public scrutiny. They headed off his attempt to become director of the 1976 bicentennial preparations prior to running for office in California, fearing it could turn into a "media disaster." Jobs like special representative to the Panama Canal Zone and director of the Bureau of Outdoor Recreation were considered and rejected. Jeb was eventually buried deep in the federal bureaucracy as a deputy undersecretary at the Commerce Department. He was permitted to keep his prized access to the White House tennis courts as part of the deal. "I won't tell if you won't tell," Haldeman's assistant Larry Higby wrote a colleague.

"The president and I consider you one of the administration's best people," Haldeman told Magruder after he and Mitchell were ushered into the chief of staff's West Wing office on the morning of Wednesday, March 28. "We want to help in every way we can." He emphasized, however, that he was speaking only as "a friend," not on behalf of the White House.

*Congressman Nixon examines film of Pumpkin Papers
with a magnifying glass during the Alger Hiss case in 1948.
He is accompanied by his aide Robert Stripling.*

Magruder was most concerned about his testimony before the grand jury. He explained that his entire story would unravel if Dean refused to support his version of the early meetings with Liddy. Haldeman grasped the point immediately. He had sat through endless lectures from Nixon recalling his triumph over the lying Alger Hiss, a case that had also turned on perjury. Hiss's defense collapsed after his accuser, Whittaker Chambers, produced 35 mm film of purloined State Department documents he had hidden in a hollowed-out pumpkin on his Maryland farm. Nixon was able to show that the "Pumpkin Papers" had been typed on a machine that previously belonged to Hiss, thereby demonstrating a direct connection with Chambers.

"This could be the little thing that does it," Haldeman noted on his legal pad, referring to the disagreement between Magruder and Dean. "The typewriter or pumpkin of this case." Rather than adjudicate the dispute himself, Haldeman ordered Dean to return from Camp David to "work things out" with Magruder and Mitchell. Dean could not hide up on the mountain forever.

The three of them—Magruder, Mitchell, and Dean—met that afternoon in a little cubbyhole down the hallway from Haldeman's corner office. Magruder did most of the talking, wringing his hands nervously as he pleaded with Dean to remember the meetings with Liddy the same way he did. He claimed that Dean had encouraged him to alter his diary to eliminate the most incriminating meeting.

Dean was angry with Magruder for treating him as "his partner in the cover-up." The way he saw it, there was a distinction between helping Magruder rehearse his testimony and supporting his story under oath. "True, I had helped him save himself by helping him to commit perjury," he later wrote. "But I had never agreed to lie for him. Now he was threatening me. I latched onto my anger for dear life."

When Magruder asked him how he would testify if called before the grand jury, Dean again prevaricated. "I'll cross that bridge when I come to it," he said.

"But you agreed you'd go along," protested Magruder.

"There's no sense debating this now, Jeb," Dean repeated. "No one has asked me to testify."

Dean felt much more sympathetic toward Mitchell. He viewed the gruff bond lawyer as a father figure. Unlike Magruder, Mitchell hid his personal turmoil behind a stony face, but Dean sensed what his one-time patron must be going through. One of Mitchell's closest friends, Fred LaRue, had passed on word that he was "on the verge of breaking," meaning that he was contemplating suicide. That very morning, *The New York Times* had published another story based on a panicked phone call from Martha Mitchell. "I fear for my husband," she told the newspaper. "I'm really scared. I have a definite reason. I can't tell you why. But they're not going to pin anything on him. I won't let them, and I don't give a damn who gets hurt." From overhearing Mitchell's telephone conversations, Martha had concluded that someone was trying to make him "the goat" in the Watergate scandal.

Whether or not he was at his breaking point, Mitchell certainly had no intention of cooperating with prosecutors. "I ain't going to jail," he told the others, placidly puffing his pipe. "You can make your own decisions." He urged Dean to "stiffen up" and refuse to testify. "If you were to go before the grand jury, you won't be believed because your story doesn't jibe with mine."

Dean wanted Mitchell to know that he had no personal knowledge of his role in the bugging of the Democratic Party offices in the Watergate and therefore could not testify against him. He could only speculate about what might have happened, based on secondhand information that had come his way. After shooting down Liddy's original Gemstone plan in early 1972, Mitchell and the Committee to Re-elect the President had come under a lot of pressure from the White House to agree to a stripped-down version. The intelligence-gathering plan had been "approved without anyone really understanding its full import."

"Your theory is not far from wrong," murmured Mitchell, according to Dean's later sworn testimony. "Only we thought it would be three or four times removed from the committee."

Dean felt sick. Mitchell had gone further than ever before toward acknowledging his role in approving the Watergate break-in. Believing that he could count on his young protégé, Mitchell had trusted Dean with his most dangerous secret. If Dean struck a deal with the prosecutors, as he was considering, he would have to betray his mentor. He could be either "a perjurer" or "a squealer." There was no other option. Never in his life had he felt "more squalid."

He went straight home without returning to his own office across the alleyway in the Executive Office Building. That evening, he briefed Haldeman by phone on the latest twists in the resumed grand jury investigation into Watergate. He mentioned, in passing, that he wanted to seek the advice of a criminal defense lawyer regarding his own possible testimony. He already had someone in mind, a man called Charlie Shaffer, who was reputed to be one of the best in the business. If engaged by Dean, Shaffer would be able to provide the White House with a much-needed source of expertise on criminal law.

"Good idea," said Haldeman.

When Haldeman phoned Nixon later that evening, the president agreed that Dean should retain a lawyer. He still had complete confidence in the White House counsel.

"Christ, I wouldn't think of undercutting him. Never. He's been a hero."

To the consternation of his aides, Nixon wanted to deliver his eleventh and final television address on the Vietnam War standing up rather than seated behind a desk. By speaking directly to the camera without any notes, he would strengthen his emotional bond with the "silent majority" of Americans. The commentators might sneer, but ordinary television viewers would appreciate his homespun sincerity and command of the most agonizing of all foreign policy issues. In announcing the withdrawal of the last American troops from Vietnam and the release of all the POWs, he wanted to project the image of a supremely confident commander in chief. Under siege politically because of the Watergate scandal, he would reach out over the heads of the media elite to the people who had stood by him in good times and bad.

It was a tactic Nixon had employed most successfully back in 1952 at a time when his political career was on the line while running for vice president on the Republican ticket under Eisenhower. Accused of abusing a political fund for personal expenses, he had defended his actions on nationwide television. It was the first American political speech to be televised live, with a then record audience of sixty million viewers. The speech was best remembered for Nixon's maudlin reference to his daughters' cocker spaniel, Checkers, a gift from a political supporter that he insisted on keeping "regardless of what they say about it." There was also mention of his wife's "respectable Republican cloth coat." The address owed much of its emotional appeal to his decision to dispense with notes and speak directly to the American people. In the peroration to his Checkers speech, the embattled politician rose from his desk to explain why he had decided to "bare his soul" in such a public way. His answer foreshadowed the rise of a new conservative populism built around the politics of patriotism and social identity rather than economic advantage and class division. "Because, you see, I love my country. And I think my country is in danger." Dismissed as "corny" and "demeaning" by influential columnists like Walter Lippmann, the speech triggered a wave of sympathy from ordinary Americans who saw Nixon as one of their own, defending the country from Communists and Communist sympathizers. The Republican National Committee was swamped with a million telegrams splitting 350 to 1 in Nixon's favor. His political fortunes turned around overnight.

Haldeman and other aides sensed the potential for disaster when Nixon proposed a similar high-wire act for his epitaph to America's disastrous engagement in Vietnam. They knew he was tired and under great strain. He risked ridicule if he fluffed his lines. Better to play it safe with a conventional address from behind his desk in the Oval Office. His image consultant, Bill Carruthers, was summoned to Washington from Hollywood to supervise the production team. "He feels there will be problems for the President if he decides to stand," a Haldeman aide reported on March 28. "He feels that it is too informal, that the period for him to have to stand is too long, that it will look theatrical, and should be reconsidered."

The president's doctors also detected signs of stress and anxiety, even as they marveled at Nixon's ability to conceal his inner turmoil from the outside world. That evening, he was visited by his osteopath, Kenneth Riland, who recorded in his diary, "I discussed his sleeping pills, and the Valium is working, but he still says he can't sleep, and I'm beginning to understand why." In addition to Valium, Riland prescribed a barbiturate marketed as Seconal that Nixon had been taking for more than a decade to help him get to sleep. According to Riland, the president was "continually looking for a new pill." Nixon also experimented with Dilantin, an antiseizure drug promoted by a businessman friend, Jack Dreyfus, as a miracle cure for a wide variety of ailments. Shortly before the inaugural, Nixon had confided to his aides that he had taken

Dilantin "for sleeping a few times and it didn't do a damn thing." But he continued to talk with Dreyfus about Dilantin and listen to friends tout its supposed benefits. During a one-hour meeting with Nixon in the Oval Office on March 3, the mutual fund pioneer had assured him there was "nothing to lose" from taking Dilantin. Dreyfus left him with a sample bottle containing a thousand pills. According to the U.S. Food and Drug Administration, common side effects of the nerve-dulling medication include slurred speech, particularly when combined with alcohol, decreased coordination, nervousness, and, ironically in Nixon's case, insomnia.

In the event, Nixon himself decided against another Checkers-type high-wire act. He estimated that he would need "four straight days" of preparation to ad-lib successfully. The challenge was akin to an actor's memorizing his script so completely that nobody paid attention to the artificiality of the delivery. He acknowledged that he was "too damn tired" and distracted by Watergate to pull off the trick. "I might just appear to be trying to remember too hard," he told Haldeman.

"That's not good," Haldeman agreed. "Then you're trying to prove a point that nobody is looking to you to prove anyway."

Nixon relied on Haldeman's years of experience in marketing and advertising to package a successful television appearance. On occasions like this, the chief of staff became the mentor and the president the pupil. Nixon looked to his aide for both technical advice and emotional support. He had spent many hours crafting the first draft of his address on his yellow legal pad. The text would be polished by professional speech writers, but he still needed guidance in the art of appearing to be at ease with himself.

"Don't try to push yourself to look up all the time," Haldeman advised. "People do more looking to see if you're worried or nervous or happy or relaxed or confident than they do listening precisely to what you're saying. The look of confidence is more important than the words of the speech."

Nixon was well aware of the problem. He was widely judged to have "lost" his first presidential debate with Jack Kennedy back in 1960 after refusing to accept any makeup. He had sweated profusely under the television lights, in contrast to his rival, who was the picture of suntanned relaxation. The technical details of making Nixon look good on the small screen were now entrusted to Carruthers. The former producer of the hit TV show *The Dating Game* was in charge of everything from lighting and makeup to wardrobe and backdrop design. Carruthers jettisoned the blue backdrop used for earlier television appearances and installed instead a gold-colored drape behind the velvet-covered presidential desk. He felt that a gold backdrop would evoke the majesty of the Oval Office and help bring out the best features of Nixon's face. He wanted to avoid the "floating in space" look that had dogged the president in the past.

At 9:01, on Thursday, March 29, Nixon looked up from his sheaf of papers and addressed the television audience. He was wearing a dark blue suit, as recommended by Carruthers, with a miniature American flag in his lapel. "Tonight, the day we have all worked and prayed for has finally come," he declared. "For the first time in twelve years, no American military forces are in Vietnam. All of our American POWs are on their way home." As usual, he could not resist a few digs at the "small minority" of Americans who "advocated peace at any price— even if the price would have been humiliation for the United States." He ended the twenty-minute address by quoting the former POW Robinson Risner, who credited his survival to his "faith in God" and his "faith in America."

The after-speech routine rarely varied. From the Oval Office, Nixon took the elevator back to the residence, where he was greeted by his family. Like many television viewers, they were focused more on the way he looked than what he actually said. His older daughter was unhappy with the gold backdrop, which, she thought, made her father look "very pale."

"Tricia told me that the picture was very bad," grumbled Nixon to Haldeman after retiring to the Lincoln Sitting Room. "That poor Carruthers is so stupid."

Haldeman attempted to reassure him. Tricia was "dead wrong." Nixon looked better than he had "in years." The problem was with the television set in the residence, which was improperly tuned. The gold backdrop was less tolerant of tuning errors than the standard blue backdrop. He had experimented with his own TV to see what would happen if the colors were not adjusted properly. "It was bad if you moved it out," he conceded. "If you had it set right, it was sensational."

Other aides and friends waited in line to phone in their congratulations. "Fantastic, beautiful," enthused Bebe Rebozo, always his most faithful cheerleader. "The whole damn thing was perfect. Couldn't have been better."

"A very strong speech," intoned Henry Kissinger. "Very well delivered."

Nixon was most proud of his closing remarks about the "American spirit." He recalled that Risner had broken down and cried in the Oval Office when he talked about the combination of patriotism and religious faith that had kept him alive in a North Vietnamese prison. If only all Americans had the same fortitude.

"That's the thing, Henry. People have got to have a little faith."

"It's the key element," the national security adviser agreed. "Without it, it's impossible to do anything."

To Nixon's dismay, faith in America's institutions had been gravely undermined, first by Vietnam and now by Watergate. The foreign policy crisis had morphed into a domestic crisis. With the return of the POWs, Vietnam had ceded its place on the front pages of the newspapers to Watergate. "Scarcely anyone in the media seemed to care about Vietnam anymore," Nixon would later complain. "Not now that the Vietnam news was good and the Watergate news was bad."

Almost instinctively, the embattled president sought relief from his problems by heading out of town. He would spend the next week at the Western White House in San Clemente, a continent away from the draining cycle of courtroom sensations, damning newspaper headlines, and seemingly endless scandal.

John Dean waited until the president was headed to California before meeting with his new attorney. As the *Spirit of '76* lifted off from Andrews Air Force Base on Friday afternoon, Dean drove out to the Maryland suburb of Rockville in his Porsche. Waiting to meet him in an anonymous apartment building was a tall, elegantly dressed man with silver hair. As a prosecutor in Robert Kennedy's Justice Department, Charles N. Shaffer had pursued some of the toughest targets in the country, including the Teamsters union president, Jimmy Hoffa. He had served on the Warren Commission investigating the assassination of President Kennedy before becoming a top criminal lawyer, celebrated for his hardball negotiating tactics. His private passion, when he was not harassing his fellow lawyers in court, was hunting with hounds. The grandson of an impoverished New York seamstress rode his horses with the aplomb of an English country gentleman.

Dean had wrestled for days with the dilemma of what to do if compelled to testify before the grand jury. In his conversations with Mitchell and Magruder, he had dismissed that possibility as hypothetical and refused to seriously discuss it. In fact, it was constantly on his mind and had suddenly come much closer. Prior to leaving for California, Nixon had released a statement instructing members of the White House staff to cooperate with investigators. Given the precariousness of his political position, he might have had no other choice, but the consequence, in Dean's view, was alarming. The decision would likely lead to "an open war pissing match between Magruder, Mitchell, Dean, and the White House."

Dean was angered to think that he was being set up to shoulder the blame for Watergate. By meeting with a defense lawyer, he was taking the first concrete step toward separating himself from the criminal conspiracy that had ensnared many of his colleagues. He and Shaffer spent a lot of time over the weekend discussing ways Dean could lessen his legal problems and avoid eventual imprisonment.

"John, you're in big trouble," said Shaffer, on the evening of Monday, April 2. "As far as I'm concerned, you're guilty as hell of conspiring to obstruct justice. You may like to think of yourself as just a little guy carrying out orders, but the counsel to the President is no little guy outside the White House. Technically, you're just as much a part of the conspiracy to cover up as Haldeman, Ehrlichman, Mitchell, and whoever."

Dean said he was ready to tell the Watergate prosecutors everything he knew in the hope of receiving some kind of immunity. If he did that, said Shaffer, he would likely be indicted. That was not at all how the game was played. Dean did not have to "run into machine guns." Shaffer was friendly with one of the prosecutors, a man named Seymour Glanzer. He proposed an informal meeting with Glanzer to see if he could strike a deal. By now, it was around midnight, but that did not prevent him from calling Glanzer at home.

"Seymour, you need to talk with me," he announced with relish. "You don't know how badly you need to talk to me."

Dean could not hear what Glanzer was saying, but he seemed to be protesting the lateness of the hour.

"Yeah, I know, you've got your problems in life and I've got mine, but I'm going to give you some more."

There was a further long silence as the prosecutor continued to complain.

"You heard me. Now listen, Brother Glanzer, I'm about forty-five minutes from your house. Put some coffee on, because I'm coming to see you." After instructing Dean to go home to bed, Shaffer ventured out into the night.

Glanzer lived in McLean, Virginia, on the opposite side of the Potomac to Maryland. When he opened his front door to the defense attorney, he was greeted by a bizarre apparition. Shaffer was dressed in full riding gear with jodhpurs and polished brown boots. He brandished a braided leather whip, known as a quirt, in his fist. The balding, out-of-shape prosecutor looked at him incredulously.

"I'm an equestrian," said Shaffer, by way of explanation. "I ride."

Shaffer proceeded to offer Glanzer a tantalizing preview of the benefits that could flow from recruiting Dean as a Watergate witness. The prosecutors had erred by focusing almost entirely on what Ron Ziegler described as "a third-rate burglary." Equally important was what happened *after* the break-in. Dean could help them nail "some pretty big people." In return for providing information about events in the White House, Dean wanted immunity from prosecution.

The prosecutors were not prepared to grant Dean immunity immediately. They were, however, eager to hear his story. Under the agreement Shaffer reached with Glanzer, anything Dean told the prosecutors would be off the record initially. No notes would be kept of the conversations. They would not even be allowed to report the meetings to their Justice Department supervisors. This was a key concession because it allowed Dean to control the upward flow of information. He knew, from his own experience, that anything the prosecutors shared with their superiors would be immediately reported to the White House. He did not want Haldeman and Ehrlichman to know what he was telling the prosecutors.

To Shaffer's surprise, Glanzer and his boss, Earl Silbert, did not seem very interested in the cover-up. Their priority was to find out who had ordered the bugging of the Democratic Party headquarters. They had concluded that someone higher than Liddy was involved, and suspected Magruder, Mitchell, Dean, and possibly Colson. To extract information from Dean, they pretended that the hitherto defiant Liddy had told them "everything he knows." This was false, but by this stage virtually everyone involved in the scandal was lying or concealing something. Watergate had become an intricate game of deception, played at many different levels by many different actors.

Shaffer visited Dean in his office in the Executive Office Building to brief him on his talks with the prosecutors. Dean was struck by the way in which his hard-nosed defense attorney was as awed by the mystique surrounding the presidency as the average American. Spotting an autographed photograph of Mitchell on Dean's desk, Shaffer fantasized about confronting the former attorney general in court. "I could smoke this guy out," he boasted, rubbing his hands in anticipation. "I'd love to cross-examine him and turn that old stone face into jelly."

Dean still felt squeamish about turning on his onetime mentor and colleagues like Haldeman and Ehrlichman. Just as he was getting comfortable with his aggressive new lawyer, he was restrained by a fit of conscience. Shaffer brushed his qualms aside.

"It's your ass or theirs. Whose do you want to save?"

"*Mine,* of course, but . . ."

"Do you think they're going to protect you when the shit hits the fan?"

Dean had no real response to that. He was also caught off guard by Shaffer's next question. Did he want to "keep lying and covering up"? Reluctantly, he agreed to meet with the prosecutors himself on condition that he inform Haldeman in advance. The meeting was set for Sunday, April 8, the day Nixon was scheduled to return from California.

T he ostensible reason for Nixon's trip to California, apart from his endless quest for relaxation, was a meeting with President Thieu of South Vietnam. In fact, he spent much of his time in San Clemente in agonized discussions on Watergate with Haldeman and Ehrlichman. The conversations typically went around in circles, with nothing being resolved. He worried about his aides turning on one other. "We can't have a situation of every man for himself," he told Haldeman. "They're all on the team. No one's going to flush anybody."

This was wishful thinking. Under the pressure of political scandal, a once superbly disciplined administration was falling apart. Everybody was blaming everyone else for the Watergate mess. The president was besieged by conflicting advice as his aides sought ways to protect themselves. Everybody had a different strategy to propose, depending on what they were trying to hide. Mitchell and Magruder had approved the Watergate break-in under pressure from the White House to gather political intelligence; Dean had masterminded the cover-up; Haldeman had authorized the payments of hush money; Ehrlichman had approved the operation against Daniel Ellsberg's psychiatrist; Colson was behind many of the Nixon administration's dirty tricks. Alliances formed, broke apart, and re-formed as the spotlight shifted from one aspect of the scandal to another.

For Dean, the "ultimate solution" was for Mitchell and Magruder to take responsibility for the bugging. Haldeman and Ehrlichman were inclined to agree with Dean as long as their own supporting roles remained concealed. Magruder was desperate to defend himself from the perjury charge leveled by McCord, even if this meant implicating people at the White House. Mitchell continued to deny everything. In his view, the basic problem lay with Dean, who had broken ranks with the rest of the administration. He had been warning for days that the White House counsel was showing "poor judgment." Mitchell wanted the president to prohibit Dean from testifying on grounds of executive privilege.

If Dean was obliged to give evidence and refused to support Magruder's perjured testimony, "he will unravel the whole thing," Mitchell told Haldeman by telephone from New York on April 2.

Haldeman largely dismissed Mitchell's concerns. Unlike Magruder, who was no longer coordinating his moves with the White House, Dean was at least checking in regularly. In the short term at least, Magruder seemed a bigger threat than Dean. Nobody knew what he was planning, or how he would behave if the prosecutors granted him immunity. Word reached Nixon through Colson that Magruder had got drunk in a bar in Bermuda, where he was on vacation, and had made "sweeping charges about everyone in the White House." Nixon instructed Haldeman to speak with Magruder, "tell him that this is all coming through on the jungle telegraph, full circle, and he's got to quit talking."

Dean lulled Nixon and Haldeman into a false sense of security during the week they were away in San Clemente by minimizing his own dealings with the prosecutors. He depicted his discussions with Shaffer as beneficial to his White House colleagues by clarifying their legal exposure. He assured Haldeman that he was simply exploring hypothetical possibilities. If compelled to appear before the grand jury, he would limit his testimony to the "pre-Watergate planning." He told Haldeman that the prosecutors were not interested in the post-break-in events, which they regarded as "a can of worms."

Dean was leading a bifurcated existence. In the morning and early afternoon, he was still the loyal White House staffer, briefing Haldeman on the latest Watergate developments in long phone calls to California. He insisted that he was acting in good faith and preferred to be indicted for contempt rather "than cause anyone a problem." If he found himself in "an impossible position," he would refuse to testify, citing the

Fifth Amendment against self-incrimination. In the late afternoon and evening, he was the turncoat, preparing the ground with Shaffer for his eventual betrayal of Nixon. For the moment, he still refused to talk about his conversations with the president, citing lawyer-client privilege. He nevertheless briefed Shaffer on White House involvement in the cover-up, including the provision of hush money to the defendants. He had one foot in both camps simultaneously.

Dean called Haldeman on the evening of Saturday, April 7, to let him know that the prosecutors had requested an in-person meeting. "Dean feels we're at the moment of truth and that he should go," Haldeman recorded in his diary. Ehrlichman urged him to wait a couple of days, but Dean pushed for an immediate decision. "He's obviously really uptight on it," Haldeman noted.

Dean raised the subject again with Haldeman the following morning. He reached the chief of staff just as the presidential party was boarding the *Spirit of '76* to fly back to Washington. Haldeman urged him to wait until they could discuss the matter in person at the White House. He did not explicitly forbid Dean to make contact with the enemy but used a graphic analogy to warn him to be careful.

"Just remember that once the toothpaste is out of the tube, it's going to be very tough to get it back in."

Dean's reply was ambiguous. "I understand," he said. Unbeknownst to Haldeman, his lawyer had already offered the prosecutors his "full cooperation and truthfulness in the grand jury and later at trial" as well as a summary, or "proffer," of his potential testimony. Negotiations on an immunity deal were to be preceded by an off-the-record "meeting with Mr. Dean to hear his account."

There was no more time to talk. The president's plane was about to take off. Dean again drove out to his lawyer's office in Rockville.

The prosecutors began squeezing the toothpaste out of the John Dean tube on the afternoon of Sunday, April 8. The two sides sat across the table from each other in Charlie Shaffer's conference room. Dean recounted the events that had led to the Watergate break-in. Ever the performer, Shaffer urged his client to cut out any "self-serving bullshit" and give the prosecutors "the ugly realities of life."

When Dean got to the part about the meetings at the Justice Department involving him, Liddy, Mitchell, and Magruder, Earl Silbert interrupted him. He repeated the same false claim he had previously made to Shaffer. "Liddy's been talking to us privately," he told Dean. "Your story is going to have to square with his. You understand?"

Dean was shaken. If Liddy was telling the prosecutors everything he knew, it was all over for the White House. Shaffer came to his rescue. Forget about Liddy, he told Dean, focus on your own story. After almost two hours, the phone rang. It was the White House operator patching in a call from Air Force One, in flight between California and Washington. As required, Dean had left a number where he could be reached, so it was easy to track him down. Haldeman's aide Larry Higby came on the line. Because radio communications between the plane and the ground could be intercepted by third parties, he spoke in code, using air force terminology.

"Be in Wisdom's office at sixteen hundred hours, for a meeting with Wisdom and Welcome."

Hanging up, Dean explained that he had been summoned to the White House for an urgent meeting with Ehrlichman (Wisdom) and Haldeman (Welcome). The prosecutors were awed by the state-of-the-art communications technology, a reminder of the resources available to the president. They agreed to take a break and resume the interview the following evening. The interruption came at an opportune time for Dean, before he was obliged to answer questions about the cover-up. He would now have more time to consider how to address the topic that posed the greatest threat to the president and his top advisers.

He reached the White House at the same time as the presidential helicopter touched down on the South Lawn from Andrews Air Force Base. Haldeman and Ehrlichman were relaxed and friendly. They evidently suspected nothing. They joked with each other about a report in *The New York Times* that morning that Colson had taken a voluntary lie detector test. The examiners had concluded that he was speaking "truthfully" when he denied any advance knowledge of the plot to bug the Democratic Party offices.

"Chuck's more than a match for any lie detector machine," said Ehrlichman.

Dean concealed his interview with the prosecutors earlier that afternoon. Instead, he said, he had agreed to a meeting the following day, Monday, to discuss his appearance before the grand jury. He thought it important to "appear cooperative." While his testimony would inevitably hurt Magruder, who had lied about his meetings with Liddy, Dean would not incriminate Mitchell, Haldeman, or Ehrlichman. They should not feel threatened. The real danger, Dean suggested, came not from him but from Magruder and Liddy. "If Liddy blows, he can hit us all. He knows about Ellsberg. He knows about the money. He knows about the whole cover-up."

For the first time, the two "Germans" displayed signs of alarm. It seemed to Dean that they were looking for ways to protect themselves. The bonhomie was just a facade. Ehrlichman, in particular, had developed a conveniently selective memory, denying any involvement in the cover-up. "You bastard," thought Dean. "You've been forgetting this stuff for several weeks." But he was careful not to betray his anger.

Ehrlichman relayed Dean's views to Nixon in a telephone conversation later that evening. "His feeling is that Liddy has pulled the plug on Magruder," he reported. "He says there's no love lost there." Magruder, meanwhile, was turning into a "loose cannon," an assessment Nixon endorsed. As for Mitchell, Dean thought he was "living in a dream world." The former attorney general acted as if the whole nightmare would go away if the White House denied everything. "He hasn't bothered to retain counsel, hasn't done much to prepare himself or anything."

Both Nixon and Ehrlichman agreed that Dean "ought to talk to these fellas"—meaning the prosecutors—on the assumption that his testimony would help exonerate the White House. But the president had an important caveat. Dean had to decline "to testify to anything afterward," meaning the cover-up, and be "damn careful" about protecting the right people.

"We don't want Mitchell, you know, popping off," said Nixon.

There was no respite for the president from Watergate after he returned to the White House from San Clemente. At their regular Monday morning meeting in the Oval Office, Haldeman attempted to raise his spirits with upbeat news nuggets. *The Washington Post* had just published a letter from a reader in Florida depicting the bugging of Democratic Party headquarters as "an invasion of privacy" rather than a serious violation of criminal law. It was difficult to understand why the Watergate conspirators risked serving longer prison terms than "traitors, murderers, rapists, etc."

While he agreed with the letter writer, Nixon was too distracted to pay much attention. "You know, I was thinking," he told Haldeman. There was an uncomfortable pause as he looked for the best way to raise a matter he had been pondering in California, staring at the Pacific Ocean. He eventually continued: "With regard to the recording when it goes on here—in this room—I feel uneasy about it. Not uneasy in terms of anybody else seeing it, because we'll control it, but uneasy because it's even done."

As the Sony tape machine continued to roll in the basement below, the two men discussed the pros and cons of various record-keeping methods. Haldeman mentioned the copious notes on his legal pad. He used the notes to dictate a diary every evening that he planned to turn into a book eventually. Because of his closeness to Nixon, his diary covered "an awful lot," but not everything. Other staffers wrote memos

*Nixon and Haldeman return to the White House from
the Executive Office Building, trailed by Secret Service agents.*

for the files describing their meetings with the president. They were of
"varying degrees of usefulness," Haldeman explained. "Some are good,
some are lousy, and some never get done."

Thinking out loud, Haldeman said the main value of the tapes was
to help Nixon refresh his memory if other records proved inadequate.
By listening to the recording of a particular meeting, he would be able
to establish exactly who said what. The problem was that there were
now "unbelievable hours of tape" piling up in burglarproof safes in a
Secret Service storage room on the ground floor of the Executive Office
Building. Nixon had made clear he did not trust anyone else to listen to
the tapes, with the possible exception of Haldeman. He did not want his
longtime secretary, Rose Mary Woods, to hear sometimes disparaging
comments about her. He would have to review much of the material
himself. The prospect of reliving endless hours of disjointed conversations filled the president with horror. Even poring over transcripts
would be painful.

"I'll talk to Kissinger and the rest of them, and I'll throw out a hell of a lot of things, but I'm never going to want to read all that crap. I never will."

For the moment, security was not a problem. Only two Secret Service men knew the combinations to the locked safes. An alarm on the door, connected to the White House Control Center, prevented unauthorized entry or tampering with the tapes. Nevertheless, it suddenly dawned on Nixon that a verbatim record of his every utterance might be a disservice to the historical muse. He had noticed, he told Haldeman, that a reporter who showed up with a tape recorder typically wrote "a lousy story." Reporters who made notes usually crafted "a much better story." Sometimes the best stories were written by those who relied on memory alone.

"A tape record is worst of all because that's a crutch you lean on totally, but note taking is bad too," Haldeman agreed, staring up from his ever-present legal pad. "If you take notes, it releases you from an obligation of concentration."

Nixon's mind appeared to be made up. "You get them all and destroy them," he told Haldeman, referring to the tapes. If he hired someone to help him write his memoirs one day, he did not want the tapes "to burden us down."

In their rambling, roundabout fashion, the two men had identified the fatal flaw at the heart of the taping project. By the beginning of April 1973, Nixon had accumulated more than three thousand hours of tape recordings. The audio quality of many of these recordings was poor, sometimes entirely obscured by the rattling of coffee cups or the movement of chairs. To avoid frequent changes of tape, the Secret Service had set the recording speed at 15/16 inches per second, the slowest possible level. Government archivists would later estimate that compiling an accurate transcript of one hour of Nixon tape required a hundred hours of work. At that rate, a lone individual would need almost 150 years to make sense of all the tapes. Nixon estimated that it would take him and Haldeman "months and months" to decide which tapes were worth preserving and which should be destroyed.

As often happened, after delivering his instruction to Haldeman, he immediately second-guessed himself. He remembered various moments in his presidency where the fullest possible historical record might prove useful. Haldeman reminded him that there was valuable material on the tapes on major foreign policy initiatives, such as the opening to China, the Vietnam War, and his trip to Moscow. He encouraged his boss to preserve the most important tapes and be more selective about recording future conversations. This might be more efficient than a system that turned itself on whenever the president walked into a room.

"Another thing you could do is just put a little switch on your desk and turn it on when you want to," Haldeman suggested. The problem with this idea was that Nixon was hopeless with any kind of technical gadget, even one operated by a simple switch.

After insisting he did not want to keep tapes of any Oval Office conversations on Watergate, Nixon saw some advantages in preserving a full historical record. The tapes would show that he had never discussed "the goddamn thing" with his advisers prior to June 1972. When he first heard that burglars wearing suits and surgical gloves had broken in to the Democratic Party headquarters, he thought it was some kind of joke.

"That's the honest to God truth," he said, chuckling. "I said *what in the hell* is this."

Haldeman gently pointed out that Nixon's enemies could always claim that Watergate-related discussions had taken place in rooms that were not wired for sound. It was impossible to prove a negative. Nevertheless, by the afternoon, Nixon had effectively postponed a firm decision on the subject.

"We had a long discussion about the monitoring facilities in his offices," Haldeman recorded in his diary later that night. "He wants them all taken out, but then he later changed his mind and said to leave them in on a switch basis. He's obviously concerned about having everything covered and wants to set up some kind of limited means of coverage."

After dismissing Haldeman, Nixon spent more than two hours talking with two former POWs, James Stockdale and John Flynn, in the Oval Office, about the social upheavals provoked by the Vietnam War. The nation, he told them, had lived through one of the most difficult periods in its history. "We survived," he concluded, not because of the "leader class," which had been "rather shameful in its performance,"

*Nixon bowling in the EOB in 1971. He liked bowling so much that he had
a new alley built in the White House mansion, paid for by his friend Bebe Rebozo.*

but because "the common people, God bless them," had refused to cut
and run. Obtaining an honorable peace settlement was crucial to preserving America's influence in the world. "That is why we had to see
it through," Nixon told his guests. "That is why you had to suffer."

For relaxation, Nixon went bowling for the second night in a row
in the new facility that had been built under the White House portico.
"A lot of fun," he told his daughter Julie. "This alley is a great, great
invention." Before going to bed, he made a Dictabelt note about his
conversations with Stockdale and Flynn, which he found as moving
and inspiring as his earlier ones with Risner and Denton. "I hope we
have tapes," he told himself. He told Haldeman a few days later that he
had decided to "keep the damn machine in." It was impossible to tell in
advance which conversations were "worth keeping."

Conceived as a means of recording the triumphs and tribulations of
his presidency, the taping system had grown into a monster that Nixon
could neither slay nor tame. He would just have to live with it.

While Nixon was enjoying his new bowling alley in the White House, Dean was again closeted with prosecutors in Rockville. Contrary to the impression they had given earlier, the prosecutors had become intensely interested in the cover-up phase of Watergate. The tension in Shaffer's office rose sharply when Dean mentioned the burglars' demands for "financial support." He described the frenzied debates about hush money involving Haldeman, Ehrlichman, and Mitchell. The conclusion was inescapable: The president's top aides had conspired to obstruct justice, a crime punishable by up to five years' imprisonment.

"That's enough, John," Shaffer interrupted, rising from his chair. He walked back and forth across the room before turning to face the prosecutors. "I want to stop here a minute to make sure you guys realize the dimensions of the case you are being handed," he told them. "You've just seen a little peek inside the tent. My man has already given you a start on an obstruction case against half the White House staff. When he finishes, you're going to have enough targets to fill the goddamn room."

John Dean had finally crossed his self-imposed Rubicon. Whatever his original intentions, the logic of his decision to talk to the prosecutors made it impossible to stop halfway. To be accepted as a cooperating witness and minimize his jail time, he could not limit himself to a partial confession. He knew that Magruder and others would soon be testifying to the grand jury. If his story conflicted with theirs, he was sure to be cross-examined relentlessly.

He remained with the prosecutors until well after midnight. He tried several times to call his wife to tell her he would be late, but she did not pick up. He called a neighbor who reported that the lights were on but no one was responding to knocks. Already edgy because of his double life, he became even more alarmed. Perhaps something had happened to Maureen. When he got home, he ran upstairs to the bedroom. He found her sitting in the middle of the bed. She looked as if she had been crying.

"What's wrong?" he asked.

"You!"

"What do you mean?"

"Just what I said. *You*," she said angrily. "I know what you're doing. You're out fooling around."

Dean tried to convince her that he had been meeting his lawyer and the prosecutors, but she refused to believe him. As his Watergate troubles mounted, the person he loved most had fallen into a deep depression and even talked of suicide. Now she was accusing him of betrayal, a charge that others close to him would soon be making. Sensing he was about to snap, he went back downstairs to the kitchen and poured himself another stiff drink.

S ometimes it was the small things that tripped up a Watergate con-
spirator. At the end of March, Jeb Magruder read in a newspaper
that his former assistant Robert Reisner had been summoned to
appear before the grand jury. Reisner had helped set up the January 27,
1972, meeting where Liddy had presented his intelligence-gathering
plan to Magruder, Mitchell, and Dean. In sworn testimony, Magruder
had claimed that the session was canceled at the last moment. Reisner,
however, refused to support Magruder's version. He had a very clear
memory of searching for an easel to be used by Liddy to display his
elaborate demonstration boards. This alarmed Magruder, who was facing multiple perjury charges. He called Reisner in a belated attempt to
smooth out differences in their stories.

"Forget about the easel. If this gets out of hand, they're going to impeach the president."

Reisner said he did not want to hurt anyone but was obliged to tell
the truth. For a respite from his legal woes and the reporters camped
out on his front lawn, Jeb took his wife to Bermuda, where they com-
peted in a mixed doubles tournament. Back in Washington, he went
over his version of events with a new defense attorney, Jim Sharp, who
refused to believe it. Like Dean, Magruder began to drink heavily, taking tranquilizers to get some rest. Finally, he could bear it no longer. On
April 10, he told Sharp "the truth about Watergate." The lawyer urged
him to strike the best deal he could with the prosecutors. Jeb agreed. He

felt an immediate sense of relief, as if he was "sane again" after months of madness.

The prosecutors took a tough line. They told Magruder's lawyers that he was negotiating from "a position of weakness": Everyone else was talking. They refused to grant him immunity from prosecution but were willing to consider a plea bargain. Jeb risked being charged with multiple prison terms of up to five years each. He thought about the pain this would inflict on Gail and the children, "whose interests I'd ignored for so long while I was worried about Mitchell and Nixon." For the first time in his life, he considered suicide.

On Friday, April 13, as the plea bargain talks dragged on, Magruder received a call from the White House. It was Larry Higby, known to his colleagues as Haldeman's Haldeman. Higby fulfilled the role of SOB for Haldeman that Haldeman performed for Nixon. He did not let on that he was taping the call in the hope of gathering evidence to exonerate his boss. Dispensing with his usual sunny greeting, he passed on a story that "really bugs the shit out of me." Ehrlichman was claiming that Magruder was attempting to shift the blame for Watergate onto the White House. Supposedly, Magruder had told reporters that Haldeman had ordered the break-in.

"Bullshit," Magruder said, almost incoherent with anger. "Jesus Christ! I mean it just makes me sick, Larry."

Higby caught Magruder at the peak of his despair. Magruder had lied to juries and investigators so many times that he faced cumulative prison sentences of more than a hundred years on perjury alone. It was impossible for him to "stonewall it" any longer.

"I'm probably going to jail, Larry, goddamn it," he moaned. "Our lives are ruined right now anyway. You know, most of ours. Mine is certainly. And so will many others before this is over."

Higby delicately raised the Haldeman question. Magruder said he had discussed the intelligence operation against the Democrats with a Haldeman aide, Gordon Strachan, but had never discussed the matter with Haldeman himself. The prosecutors were not interested in small fry like Strachan, Magruder went on. They were after the "big fish."

"Did Gordon ever relay to you any instructions from Haldeman?" Higby wanted to know.

"Nope."

What about the president?

"Shit no. Nothing at all."

Pressed further by Higby, Magruder said he had forwarded transcripts of the bugged conversations to the White House, but it was unlikely that Strachan had done anything with them because they were "all junk." The operation had been "a waste of time."

Higby became much more friendly now that he had Magruder on tape denying Haldeman's involvement in the bugging conspiracy. Dropping his earlier charge of betrayal, he called him Jebber and promised to visit him in prison. Magruder traced his problems back to the letter that McCord had written to Judge Sirica three weeks previously, which had given the prosecutors the upper hand. By breaking so dramatically with the other defendants, McCord had undermined the bargaining position of everyone else.

"I don't have any chips," Magruder complained. "They don't need us anymore. Hell, they've got everybody down there."

That evening, Jeb and Gail attended a fancy Washington dinner party. He checked with his lawyers throughout the evening on the progress of the plea bargain negotiations. Eventually, Sharp called to say that the prosecutors were offering a one-count felony indictment on a conspiracy charge. With parole, he would likely serve no more than twenty months in prison. In return, Magruder had to promise to be completely "truthful, candid, and cooperative, and testify as a prosecution witness before the grand jury and at trial." He accepted the deal immediately and returned to the party.

W hen he finally came to write his memoirs, Richard Nixon would look back on Saturday, April 14, as the moment when everything began to "fall apart." Prior to this hectic, event-filled weekend, he had comforted himself with the thought that he would be able to ride out the scandal engulfing his presidency. He had been through much worse during the Vietnam War, when the White House was besieged by vast crowds of demonstrators. If the economy did well, everybody would forget what all the fuss was about. Unlike Vietnam, which had divided America down the middle, tales of campaign bugging and other dirty tricks were mainly an obsession of the Washington political class. Ordinary Americans were sick and tired of Watergate. That, at least, was what Nixon was being told by his inner circle.

"The damnable part is that it has a catchy name, like Teapot Dome," said Chuck Colson, referring to a bribery scandal that had rocked the administration of Warren Harding fifty years earlier. Nobody remembered what Teapot Dome was about, "but they remember that name." It would be the same with Watergate.

For a few days after returning from San Clemente, Nixon stuck to the line that Watergate was a minor matter. "I've really got to tend to the business of the country," he told Colson. He would leave the grubby details of the "political crapping around" to his subordinates. His complacency was shattered by a report from Colson that Howard Hunt had decided to "tell all" to the grand jury at 2:00 p.m. on Monday, April 16.

At a minimum, Hunt would likely implicate Mitchell and Magruder in the decision to bug the Democratic Party offices. His involvement in the distribution of hush money meant that he was also an important witness to the cover-up. His rumored defection meant that the president had only two days to "crack the case" in advance of the persecutors.

Nixon summoned Haldeman and Ehrlichman to a crisis meeting in EOB 175 on Saturday morning to discuss how to get ahead of the expected revelations from Hunt. They agreed that Mitchell and Magruder could no longer avoid taking the blame for Watergate. Mitchell, in particular, should be made to understand that he was "morally and legally responsible." There was not a moment to lose.

"Once Hunt goes on, then that's the ball game," Ehrlichman warned.

"You've got to be out in front earlier," said Nixon.

Ehrlichman outlined two alternative "scenarios" for shaping public perception of the scandal, using the standard White House euphemism for a media spin operation. To make the competing scenarios more realistic, he couched them in terms of hypothetical lead paragraphs to a forthcoming newsmagazine story. One version of the story, said Ehrlichman, would credit the prosecutors with exposing a White House "cover-up." A friendlier version might read like this:

Events moved swiftly last week after the president was presented with a report indicating that, for the first time, suspicion of John Mitchell and Jeb Magruder as ringleaders in the Watergate break-in were substantiated by considerable evidence. The president dispatched so and so to see Mitchell—or something of that kind. These efforts resulted in Mitchell going to the U.S. attorney's office on Monday morning at nine o'clock and asking to testify before the grand jury. The charges of cover-up by the White House were materially dispelled by the diligent efforts of the president and his aides, moving on the evidence which came to their hands in the closing days of the previous week.

"I'd buy that," said Nixon.

The question now became, who would instruct Mitchell to sacrifice himself for the greater good? Nixon ruled himself out immediately. While he always welcomed a political fight, he shied away from personal confrontation. Breaking with his old friend and law partner was just too "goddamn painful." He ran through a list of candidates to assume the role of messenger. One possibility was Secretary of State William Rogers, a former attorney general himself with the appropriate seniority and gravitas. The problem was that the two men did not get along. The aristocratic, soft-spoken Rogers would be no match for the scrappy, foulmouthed Mitchell. Rogers might have many excellent qualities, but as Nixon pointed out, he was no street fighter. Mitchell would wind him around his little finger.

"Mitchell will say, 'you're out of your fucking mind,'" agreed Haldeman. Besides, Rogers had a poor grasp of the complexities of Watergate, because he had not been involved himself.

Nixon turned to Ehrlichman, who had assumed Dean's old role as principal Watergate desk officer. "John, go see Mitchell," he instructed. He reached back into the morality tales of his youth for a suitable analogy. The stirring story of an American soldier who had crossed enemy lines to deliver a message from President McKinley to a Cuban insurgent leader, General Calixto García, suddenly came to mind.

"The message to García has got to be carried," Nixon said firmly.

A former Eagle Scout, Ehrlichman embraced the daring mission. He had never much cared for Mitchell and had clashed with him at the Justice Department. The Nixon administration had split into warring factions, one clustered around the president and the White House, the other around Mitchell, Magruder, and the now defunct CREEP. He, Ehrlichman, would cross the lines to deliver a blunt message to the leader of the opposing camp. Or perhaps Mitchell would be summoned to meet with him. The parallels with McKinley and García were not exact but captured the spirit of the occasion. With the help of Nixon and Haldeman, he spun out a scenario for the coming showdown. His report to the president would show that the man he nicknamed the Big Enchilada was "as guilty as hell."

"I'd say, 'The jig is up, John. I've listened to, uh, Magruder, and he's about to blow. And that's the last straw.'"

"And, also, Hunt is going to testify," Nixon interrupted. "Monday, we understand."

"We have to recognize that you're not going to escape indictment. Far better that you should be indicted based on your conversation with the U.S. attorney than on an indictment by a grand jury of fifteen blacks and three whites."

"We're trying to protect you," suggested Nixon.

"You have the dignified opportunity to discuss this in the office of Earl Silbert instead of the District of Columbia jail," proposed Haldeman.

"And I'm here at the president's request to ask you to do just that," summed up Ehrlichman. "He has reviewed the facts now. He has no alternative, John."

"The president has said, 'Let the chips fall where they may,'" said Nixon. "We're not gonna cover for anybody."

In addition to staring down the obdurate Mitchell, Ehrlichman would have to deal with the pesky Magruder. Under the scenario discussed by the president and his two top aides, they would likely be going to jail together. Nixon proposed that Ehrlichman throw in "a couple of grace notes" and stress the president's "great affection" for Jeb and his family. He had been thinking only last night of his "poor little kids in school."

"Yeah, beautiful kids," echoed Haldeman.

"And his lovely wife and all the rest. It just breaks your heart. And say, 'This is a very painful message I've been asked to give you, but I must do it, and that's that.'"

Nixon was astute enough to recognize that there was a problem with the Mitchell-Magruder scenario. There were "eight or ten people" around the White House who had varying degrees of knowledge about Watergate or the subsequent cover-up. He toyed with the idea of also getting rid of Dean and possibly Ehrlichman and Haldeman. In the end, everyone was disposable except the president. It wasn't about "the man," of course. It was the "goddamn office" that had to be protected.

"Give 'em an hors d'oeuvre and maybe they won't come back for the main course," he said, referring to the jackals closing in on the White House.

For Nixon, this was a moment of truth comparable to his decision to send the B-52s over Hanoi back in December during the endgame to the Vietnam War. The solution to his mounting political problems was still unclear, but he knew, instinctively, that he had to take dramatic action to save his presidency. He instructed Haldeman to summon Mitchell-García from his Manhattan fortress.

"We have to prick the goddamn boil and take the heat," he explained, mixing a few more metaphors.

Mitchell agreed to take the first available flight from New York. He would arrive at the White House by the middle of Saturday afternoon. In the meantime, events began to speed up, like the final scenes of an elaborate Broadway farce. Over the course of the next few hours, all the principal Watergate actors would be revealed in embarrassing situations in varying stages of undress. Portions of this frantic activity took place in front of random onlookers ignorant of what was really going on. Nixon began the day with a visit to his dentist to resolve a painful toothache. He ended it at a black-tie White House correspondents' dinner packed with his political enemies. In between, he dropped in on a garden tour led by his wife to showcase the magnificent tulips and cherry blossoms on the South Lawn. He had to carry out his presidential duties in as dignified a manner as possible amid the chaos swirling around him.

The first of his antagonists to appear onstage was John Dean. The White House counsel had been in his EOB office all morning, down the hallway from Nixon. While the president talked to Haldeman and Ehrlichman, Dean met with his lawyer, Charlie Shaffer, who was on the way to a hunt. Shaffer paced around the room in his polished brown riding boots as they jointly examined the options available to Nixon. He had earlier proposed that "the leader of the free world" personally interrogate Mitchell and then inform the grand jury that he had cracked the case. Dean relayed the idea to Ehrlichman in a midnight phone call, who relayed it to Nixon.

"I won't even comment on that," the president scoffed.

With Shaffer's help, Dean now drew up a list of everyone connected to Nixon who could be in legal jeopardy. He divided the list into two parts, reflecting the periods before and after the June 17 break-in. It included anyone involved in either approving the bugging of Democratic Party headquarters or cover-up actions such as payment of hush money to the burglars. He then drew a large bracket next to the "Post" portion of the list and listed the potential criminal charges. Article 371:

conspiracy to commit an offense against the United States; five years in prison on each count, $10,000 fine. Article 1503: obstruction of justice; five years, $5,000 fine. After he jotted down a total of fifteen names, it occurred to him that many of them were trained attorneys. He placed asterisks before the names of the lawyers.

Pre:
*Mitchell
Magruder
*Strachan

Post:
H [Haldeman]
*E [Ehrlichman]
*JWD [Dean]
LaRue
Mardian? [Robert Mardian, a deputy to Mitchell]
*O'Brien
*Parkinson [Kenneth Parkinson, counsel to CREEP]
*Colson?
*Bittman?
*Kalmbach / Tony (?) [Ulasewicz]
Stans?

Shortly after drawing up this memorandum, Dean received a call from Ehrlichman requesting a meeting in his West Wing aerie, directly above the Oval Office. As the "desk officer of the cover-up" prepared to walk across to the White House from the EOB, he placed the note in an inside jacket pocket for easy access. He felt like "a gunslinger practicing his draw." He could have been Gary Cooper in the movie *High Noon.* The White House clocks had just struck twelve.

Ehrlichman was waiting for him with his feet up on the desk, just like the president. Haldeman was also there. After some preliminary banter, Dean produced his list with their initials prominently featured. He read the fifteen names out loud, along with the possible charges against them. Ehrlichman took his feet off the desk.

"John, I wonder if someone might be slipping something putrid into your diet," he protested. "I don't believe that damn list."

According to Dean, Ehrlichman had been involved in the destruction of evidence following the Watergate break-in. He had instructed Dean to "deep six" a bulky briefcase found in Howard Hunt's safe that contained some of his most explosive materials. These included his files on Daniel Ellsberg, the forged State Department cables on the Diem assassination, and dirt on Senator Edward Kennedy. When Dean asked Ehrlichman what he meant by "deep six," he explained that it was an old sailor's expression for tossing something into six fathoms (thirty-six feet) of water. "You drive across the [Potomac] river at night, don't you," Ehrlichman allegedly told Dean. "Well, when you cross over the river on your way home, just toss the briefcase into the river." Dean had declined to throw the briefcase into the river but came up with an alternative proposal that was accepted by Ehrlichman. They would give the documents to the acting FBI director, L. Patrick Gray, but tell the proud Nixon loyalist to keep them to himself. If challenged, they would be able to claim that everything in the safe had been handed over "to the FBI."

Haldeman was also vulnerable because of his connection to the $350,000 political campaign fund used to pay hush money to the burglars. Like Ehrlichman, he was disturbed to learn that the prosecutors had expanded their investigation to include post-break-in events as well.

"Keep that damn list to yourself," Haldeman told Dean.

Dean knew that he had "grabbed the attention" of Nixon's two top aides with his piece of paper but was also worried about how they might react. If they saw him as a direct threat, they might try to pin all the blame on him. The meeting broke up in a hurry without the usual farewells. He drove home across the Potomac to Old Town Alexandria and pulled out his bottle of scotch.

Haldeman had been having trouble tracking Magruder down all morning. They finally spoke on the phone at 1:30. Haldeman switched on the tape machine hidden in a drawer of his desk as Magruder filled him in on a five-hour meeting he had just completed with the prosecutors.

"I'm going to plead guilty and go to jail," he said. "There's no way I can hold anymore. I've got no defense now. They've got witnesses on witnesses on witnesses."

Had he rejected the deal, Magruder explained, he would be facing a possible sentence of up to 135 years in prison.

"What in the world is that for?" asked an alarmed Haldeman.

"Oh, about eight counts of perjury, a couple of counts of conspiracy and a couple of counts of obstruction of justice."

Magruder laughed almost giddily and then turned serious. His testimony would leave "Big John"—Mitchell—in a tough spot. It would also cause problems for Haldeman's aide Strachan, but "that's the way it has to be, I guess." He agreed to come in later that afternoon with his lawyers to explain everything in person. In the meantime, he had a veiled warning for his former patron. The cover-up had fallen apart.

"I really think, Bob, you should realize that the whole thing is going to go."

"What do you mean?"

"LaRue's going to go. They're all going to go. There isn't anybody now that's going to hold. Except Mitchell, I think . . . Everybody better be aware of it, so we don't continue to have more disasters on disasters."

Speaking for the benefit of the hidden recorder, Nixon's chief of staff insisted that he was unaware that Magruder had lied to investigators. This surprised Jeb, who had informed Haldeman about his perjury three months earlier. But he was in no mood to argue.

"I'm sorry things didn't work out, Bob."

John Mitchell arrived at the West Wing of the White House just as Haldeman was finishing his telephone conversation with Magruder. He was immediately escorted to Ehrlichman's office on the second floor. On previous visits, Ehrlichman had invited the former attorney general to relax on a sofa next to a coffee table. On this occasion, he steered him toward a chair by his desk. The change in seating arrangements made

Mitchell suspect he was being taped, an impression strengthened by Ehrlichman's fidgeting. In fact, Ehrlichman had turned on his recording device a minute before he arrived.

Instead of the hand-to-hand combat Ehrlichman had promised Nixon, the two men circled each other warily, probing for weaknesses. Ehrlichman noticed that his opponent had "a very, very bad tremor," much worse than before. Nevertheless, the older man proved to be the more skillful combatant. Whenever Ehrlichman attempted to land a blow, Mitchell would mention some wrongdoing by the White House or Ehrlichman himself. For all his earlier bravado, Ehrlichman spent most of the half-hour interview on the defensive.

"Obviously you're in a situation of jeopardy, and other people are, too," he began. Magruder had decided "to make a clean breast of things," and Watergate was "coming unstuck in a number of other areas" as well.

"I'd like to know about it," said Mitchell, playing the innocent.

Ehrlichman told him that the prosecutors were now focusing on "the aftermath," meaning "the obstruction of justice." He alluded to hush money payments authorized by Mitchell and other CREEP officials. Mitchell threw the accusation back at him. His men, he told his interrogator, had simply been "trying to keep the lid" on various White House–generated scandals until after the election. Watergate topped the list, but there were "other things going on over here that would have been even worse, I think, than the Watergate business." This was an unmistakable reference to Ehrlichman's authorization of the Ellsberg psychiatrist caper.

Twisting the blade a little further, Mitchell made the point that the burglars had been paid out of a "White House fund" controlled by Haldeman. The two men then proceeded to fence around the question of who should bear the blame for the overlapping scandals.

"Obviously you're the captain of your own boat on this," said Ehrlichman, resuming his offensive. "But the president wanted to have me tell you right now that he is extraordinarily troubled by the situation in which you find yourself, and therefore everybody finds themselves. This, uh, in no way affects his feeling for you in any regard."

Mitchell wanted to know what "Brother Dick" was planning to do next. Ehrlichman conceded that he had very few options. Mitchell had a couple of suggestions. First, the president should "take care of his own house in an appropriate way." Second, he should not "impinge upon anybody's rights," particularly their right to a fair trial. Here Mitchell was signaling that he had no intention of being pushed into the role of scapegoat. Responsibility for Watergate rested with the White House and the president himself.

"The fact of the matter is that I got euchred into this thing . . . by not paying attention to what these bastards were doing," he told Ehrlichman, referring to Liddy and the White House Plumbers. "The whole genesis of this thing was over here, as you're well aware."

"No, I didn't know that," protested Ehrlichman, for the benefit of his hidden tape machine.

Mitchell mentioned the aggressive intelligence-gathering program approved by Haldeman during the run-up to the 1972 presidential election campaign that had created the climate for Watergate. He pointed out that he had thrown Liddy out of his office after he made his original presentation, conveniently omitting later dealings via Magruder. He had never even set eyes on Howard Hunt. He had not known "a goddamn thing" about the "dirty tricks department" run by Colson.

"I really don't have a guilty conscience," Mitchell concluded, speaking slowly and deliberately to make his point. "I didn't authorize these bastards to go ahead."

For his final thrust, Ehrlichman gave Mitchell a preview of Magruder's likely testimony to the grand jury. Jeb was claiming that he had discussed the bugging of Democratic Party headquarters with Mitchell during their March 1972 meeting in Key Biscayne. He had supposedly presented Mitchell with a memorandum outlining potential targets of the intelligence operation, including the Watergate, along with the necessary funding.

"Are you serious?" Mitchell protested.

"Yes, sir," replied Ehrlichman. "And that you, by some designation, circles or checks or something, picked the targets and authorized the operation."

"That's about as far from the truth as it's possible to get."

There was little left to discuss. Far from confronting Mitchell with his guilt, Ehrlichman had been battled to a stalemate. Preserving the veneer of collegiality, he said he was expecting another visitor. "I'm running kind of a musical chairs game here today." Ehrlichman asked Mitchell if he would like to meet with the president, but Mitchell saw no point. "I don't want to embarrass him." Ehrlichman offered him the use of a government plane to return to New York, but Mitchell was willing to fly commercial. "American Airlines, first class," he specified.

Arriving back at LaGuardia Airport, Mitchell put a good face on his ordeal. He told a waiting television news crew that he was eager to appear before the Senate Watergate Committee. "I think everybody who's involved, or has been stated to be involved, will come forward." The presidency would not be harmed. In private, over tumblers of scotch, he ruminated on the line between loyalty and treachery. A few nights later, his speech slurred with alcohol, he confided to a friend his true feelings about Jeb Magruder, his former deputy at CREEP. "Who would have thought that All-American boy, with that nice wife and the great little kids, would turn out to be such a viper?"

Ehrlichman walked down one floor to the Oval Office as soon as he was done with Mitchell. Nixon had just returned from greeting the first contingent of 11,474 visitors who would traipse through the Rose Garden, just outside his French window, all weekend. He considered the White House grounds in springtime "one of the great sights of the world" and took a boyish delight in seeing the crocuses or mums come into bloom. The garden tour was a Pat Nixon innovation. Never before had so many visitors been allowed to wander around the grounds and admire the flower beds adjoining the Oval Office. The towering southern magnolia tree planted by President Andrew Jackson one and a half centuries earlier as a tribute to his wife was in flower. Banks of bright red tulips sparkled in the sunshine beneath the softer pale pink flowers of the crab-apple trees. The U.S. Marine Band, also known as the President's Own, played sprightly military marches. The lovely spring afternoon was at odds with the storm clouds gathering inside the West Wing.

"All finished?" asked Nixon as Ehrlichman assumed his customary seat, adjacent to the president's desk, opposite the chair occupied by Haldeman.

*Nixon returns to the Oval Office on April 14, 1973, after
helping Pat lead the biggest ever public tour of the White House gardens.
He is followed by Press Secretary Ron Ziegler.*

"Yes, sir," replied Ehrlichman. "All finished. He is an innocent man
in his heart, and in his mind, and he does not intend to move off that
position."

Ehrlichman explained that the meeting had not gone as planned.
He had treated the former attorney general "with kid gloves," but Mitchell had "lobbed mud balls at the White House at every opportunity." He
had, for example, made a "great point" about the $350,000 fund used to
pay off the burglars. He had insinuated that Nixon's aides were aware
of the plot to bug the Watergate and had pulled all the strings. As Ehrlichman described the encounter, Nixon grew angry.

"Throwing it off on the White House isn't going to help him one
damn bit."

"Unless he can peddle the theory that Colson and others were effectively running the committee through Magruder," said Ehrlichman.

"Did he include me in 'the others'?" Haldeman wanted to know.

"Yup."

"He's got an impossible problem with that," Haldeman protested.

"It's bad if he gets up there and says that," said Nixon. "It's a hell of a problem for us."

"It's a problem for us, no question. But there's no way he can prove it."

The three men turned their attention to Dean's list of White House officials, led by Haldeman and Ehrlichman, who could be implicated in the cover-up. Haldeman dismissed the list as a panicky, worst-case scenario. "That shows you the somewhat unclear state of some of John Dean's analytical thinking," he scoffed.

The uplifting chords of the marine band wafted through the thick bulletproof windows, interfering with the conversation. The fanfares and marches provided an ironic commentary to the sordid matters being discussed inside the Oval Office. "Seems like we always have a drum on the lawn when these things are going on," commented Ehrlichman sourly. He recalled that the band had been playing on an earlier occasion when they confronted a cabinet member accused of fraud.

The meeting adjourned just before four to allow Ehrlichman to meet with Magruder, with Nixon blaming Mitchell for the entire Watergate mess. "He let it all happen himself," he said. There was a long, agonized pause as he tapped his desk to the rhythm of the music. "You know he'll never, never go to prison."

Another anguished silence ensued as the president ruminated on the troubles facing his friend. "What do you think about that?" he finally asked Haldeman. "Does a trial of the former attorney general of the United States bug you? This goddamn case!"

Nixon walked across West Executive Avenue to his EOB office, an oasis of calm away from the noisy intruders. He called Pat just before five to say that he would not be coming home for supper as planned because he had more work to do. "They're still piling through in their thousands," she informed him. Ehrlichman appeared in the doorway a few minutes later to report on his session with Magruder.

Nixon knew he had to act immediately if he was going to get any credit for carrying out his own investigation. He had to show that he had not been dragged "kicking and screaming into this thing." He ordered Ehrlichman to telephone Mitchell's successor as attorney general, Richard Kleindienst, to inform him of the latest developments. A lawyer from Arizona with impeccable Republican connections and a good old boy demeanor, Kleindienst had moved up from the number two position at Justice after Mitchell took over the Committee to Re-elect the President.

Ehrlichman made the call from a phone next to the couch as Nixon and Haldeman listened in from across the room. Kleindienst had just returned from his sacrosanct Saturday golf game and was dressing for the annual black-tie dinner thrown by the White House press corps.

"Hi, General," said Ehrlichman cheerfully. "How was the golf?"

"Half good and half bad."

Ehrlichman quickly got down to business. The president had asked him to get to the bottom of "this whole transaction," Ehrlichman's euphemism for Watergate, in place of Dean. He had been talking to "everybody but the milkman." He had just come from a meeting with Magruder, who had been "telling everything" to the prosecutors.

"He has decided to come clean."

There was a gasp of surprise from the other end of the line. Klein-dienst had been kept in the dark by his subordinates who feared that otherwise everything that happened in their office would be immediately reported back to the White House.

"No kidding."

"He had his informal conference ten minutes before he came in to see me."

"And would that be inconsistent with his testimony to the grand jury?"

"Dramatically inconsistent."

"Jesus Christ almighty."

The White House Correspondents' Association dinner was the kind of social event Nixon instinctively loathed. For an entire evening, he was forced to make polite chitchat with people who were out to get him the rest of the year. He had much more productive ways of spending his time than listening to jokes at his expense. At the beginning of January, he had instructed Haldeman to schedule "trips out of Washington" to coincide with the dates of the dinners. He did not plan to attend any such gatherings in the future.

In the end, he relented. In between crisis sessions on Watergate with Haldeman and Ehrlichman, he struggled with the text of his remarks later that evening. The conventions of the Washington game required him to include some mildly self-deprecatory comments to show that he had a sense of humor. He reviewed and rejected most of the suggestions of the presidential gag writers. (Sample: "I'd hoped to be home for the eleven o'clock news . . . I try to watch it every night to see what I've done wrong all day.") But he kept one about his press secretary. ("You have him well trained. This morning, I asked him what time it was, and he put me on background.") He wrote most of the speech himself on his legal pad, striving for a balance between the serious and the lighthearted.

Because he had no wish to eat the typical rubber-chicken dinner offered by the correspondents, he asked Manolo to bring him a plate of bacon and eggs. When he finished his meal, he dictated a diary entry about the events of the day, reflecting ruefully on his failure to put his house in order earlier:

> It's too bad we were unable to do something about it. I suppose during the election campaign there was a feeling we couldn't do anything for fear of risking the election. Yet that was a mistake, as it turned out, because we were just postponing the day that we would have to face up to it. Immediately after the election, of course, would have been the time to move on it frontally, and yet we did not move then for reasons that I probably will understand later. I just wasn't watching it that closely then and nobody was really minding the store. We were leaving too much to Dean, Mitchell, et al.

He arrived at the Washington Hilton just after nine, when the festivities were already in full swing. Arrayed in front of him, in tuxedos and formal dresses, were the pillars of Washington society: senators and judges, cabinet members and generals, along with their journalist hosts. Nixon had conveniently missed the mock introductions between senior members of his administration and Judge Sirica, "a man they may be getting to know better." Nevertheless, he was obliged to applaud politely as the men Ehrlichman had taken to calling "Bernstein and whatsis-

name" were given the association's top award for their dogged investigation into Watergate. When he was finally given the microphone, he
emphasized his own role in building a new, more stable world order.
He invented a conversation with a recently deceased conservative journalist friend whom he quoted as saying, "The only thing harder than
a president waging war is a president waging peace." No other nation
could provide the required leadership. "Others have the good intentions, but only America has the power."

Nixon spent just over an hour at the dinner before escaping back
to the White House. Soon he was on the phone to his aides from the
Lincoln Sitting Room, reviewing his performance. He was particularly
proud of the fake quotation. "It's not a bad line," he told Haldeman.
"Goddamn it, that's the mark of this administration. We're waging
peace like hell." The evening had gone off much better than expected.
The reporters had treated him respectfully and had even presented him
with a silver globe to honor his international achievements. His legacy
would be foreign policy, not some construction project in the middle
of America.

"It's a little melodramatic," he mused later that evening, "but it's
totally true that what happens in this office in these next four years will
probably determine whether there's a chance for some sort of uneasy
peace for the next twenty-five years."

After a few drinks, he began to forget his political problems, and
even think better of his enemies. He put some of his favorite classical
music on the tape player, turned the volume up loud, and sank back
into his favorite armchair. Shortly after one, he telephoned Ron Ziegler,
who had been making the rounds of the after-dinner media parties.
Both men were in a mellow mood.

"What do you think, it was worth going?"

"That was a great evening, Mr. President," the press secretary gushed,
giddy with free drink. Friends and enemies alike had been "very
complimentary."

"What did they like about it? The serious part or the humorous part?"

Ziegler knew how to please his boss. "Both," he said. He went on
to note that there had not been much applause when Woodward and
Bernstein accepted their awards.

"You noticed I congratulated them," said Nixon. As the music swelled from the speakers across the room, he became sentimental. "These guys are also human beings. They're touched by any sense of emotion. The poor bastards, they want peace as much as I do."

The president suddenly remembered the subject that had consumed his entire day.

"They're all worried about Watergate but what the hell. Seriously, these guys know that, goddamn it, Watergate will pass. They know I had nothing to do with it."

"There was very little discussion tonight about Watergate, Mr. President."

"Well, there will be later. When they indict Mitchell, all hell will break loose."

Ziegler retreated to safer ground.

"I appreciated the comments tonight, Mr. President."

Nixon immediately perked up.

"Ha. I was sticking it to them a little, you know. The bastards."

"Yes, sir. They deserve it."

"When I said, 'That will be on background.' Ha, ha, ha." He chortled at his own joke.

"That was very good."

"Okay, Ron, get a little rest."

The day had ended on an ambivalent note. The president had failed to get in front of events, as he had initially hoped, but remained confident that he could ride out the scandal. At the very least, Magruder's confession to the prosecutors had cleared the air. As Nixon remarked to Haldeman earlier, it was hard to imagine "what the hell else they could have that's any worse." He went to bed in the early hours of Sunday morning thinking, "We pretty much know what the worst is." By the time he woke up a few hours later, he was facing an entirely different state of affairs.

CATASTROPHE

καταστροφή—katastrophḗ

a disastrous event of great significance

———————

I'm never going to discuss the son-of-a-bitching
Watergate thing again. Never, never, never, never.

—RICHARD NIXON
April 30, 1973

The attorney general was at one of the receptions following the White House correspondents' dinner when he received word that there had been a big break in the Watergate case. The prosecutors needed to see him as soon as possible. They arrived at his home in McLean, Virginia, around one in the morning.

Richard Kleindienst had done everything he could to steer clear of the Watergate imbroglio. He thought back with horror to his bizarre encounter with Gordon Liddy on the Saturday afternoon following the break-in, ten months previously. He had been attorney general for exactly five days. He had just finished his regular round of golf at the Burning Tree Club in Bethesda and was eating lunch in the members' lounge. Across the room, he spotted an excited-looking man attempting to attract his attention with furtive hand gestures. Thinking that he better find out what the man wanted, he walked over to join him. The stranger claimed to be carrying an urgent message from Kleindienst's predecessor, John Mitchell.

When they were alone, Liddy explained that he was the leader of a group of five men arrested at the Watergate a few hours earlier. The break-in had been part of a CREEP "intelligence operation." The burglars were all "good men who would keep their mouths shut." They were all using aliases. Unfortunately, one of the men, James McCord, was on the committee payroll. It would not take long for the cops to find out his real name. Liddy claimed that Mitchell wanted McCord to be released immediately, before the police established "who he really is." Kleindienst could not believe that Mitchell would make such an outlandish request. For all he knew, Liddy might simply be protecting himself. It was "the goddamndest thing" he had ever experienced in more than two decades as an attorney. "What happens to the President if I try a fool thing like that?" he asked. He told Liddy he would handle Watergate "like any other case." He passed the same message on to the head of the Justice Department's criminal division, Henry Petersen.

In fact, Kleindienst was walking a political tightrope. Despite rejecting Liddy's overture, he did not report it to investigators. It took the FBI several more weeks to make the connection between Liddy and the burglars. Valuable clues about the planning of the break-in, and the involvement of higher-ups, went unexplored. Kleindienst delegated management of the case to Petersen. Petersen in turn kept the White House fully informed of every step in the investigation. He even shared top secret grand jury testimony, to the dismay of his subordinates. Watergate would never be a case "like any other."

Now, ten months after Kleindienst's strange encounter with Liddy, Petersen had shown up on his doorstep in the middle of the night. Accompanying him were the two lead prosecutors, Silbert and Glanzer. Over the next four hours, they gave the attorney general a detailed account of everything they had learned from Dean and Magruder. The government attorneys believed that they had finally cracked the case. They were ready to issue indictments against a long list of suspects, headed by John Mitchell. This news greatly upset Kleindienst, who regarded Mitchell as his political mentor. He told Senate investigators later he had not felt so churned up inside since his mother died when he was a young boy.

It occurred to Silbert that the former attorney general had a strange effect on people. Coldly analytical when discussing anyone else, John Dean had trouble talking about a man who was "like a father figure" to him. Fred LaRue cried when questioned about his longtime boss. Magruder reacted in similar fashion. "Old Stone Face" had the reputation of being a gruff, "almost heartless type of person," yet his equally hard-nosed associates teared up when they spoke about him. Even the prosecutors felt a little emotional.

Most troubling to Kleindienst were the allegations against Haldeman and Ehrlichman. Mitchell was no longer in office, but the twin pillars of Nixon's "Berlin Wall" continued to see the president on a daily basis. Haldeman, in particular, was Nixon's alter ego, closeted with him throughout the day. He was closer to the president than any chief of staff in living memory. If he and Ehrlichman were guilty of obstruction of justice, Nixon had to be informed immediately. The conspiracy might still be continuing. They could not sit on the information that Dean had shared with them in confidence any longer.

The prosecutors explained that the charges against Haldeman and Ehrlichman rested primarily on their off-the-record interviews with Dean. To get him to testify in court, they would have to strike a deal, probably in the form of a plea bargain. Through his attorney, Dean was demanding full immunity, but the prosecutors were resisting. It would look very bad if someone who was central to the criminal conspiracy was allowed to escape scot-free. Silbert and Glanzer believed that they would be able to confirm the key parts of Dean's testimony from other witnesses, including Magruder, who were now crawling out of the bureaucratic woodwork. There was certainly a circumstantial case to be made against Haldeman and Ehrlichman. Investigators did not have all the pieces of the jigsaw puzzle just yet, but a pattern was clearly discernible.

In some cases, assembling the puzzle was as simple as following the money. The $350,000 in campaign funds that had been used to pay the burglars and their lawyers was a good example. The money, most of it in crisp $100 bills, had made a remarkable journey. It had originally been raised from private donors who thought they were helping Nixon's reelection effort. Because it had been pledged prior to a new campaign finance law taking effect in April 1972, it did not have to be officially reported. Instead of being used for election expenses, the funds were sent over to the White House and reserved for private polling. Haldeman asked his aides Gordon Strachan and Alexander Butterfield to look after the money. One of Butterfield's friends agreed to keep the thick wads of cash in a safe-deposit box in a bank across the river in Arlington, Virginia, until Haldeman found a use for what they now called "the 350."

By the time the prosecutors met with Kleindienst in the early morning hours of April 15, they had succeeded in linking the 350 to the hush money trail. According to Dean, the funds had been used to pay off Howard Hunt, who was blackmailing the White House. By contrast, Strachan claimed to have "returned" the money to CREEP on Haldeman's behalf. This explanation made little sense to investigators. They noted that Strachan had actually transferred bundles of $100 bills to Fred LaRue, Mitchell's aide and trusted confidant, in several batches. Had Haldeman really wanted to return the 350 to the committee, he would have sent it to the finance department rather than the man who was paying off the Watergate burglars.

Kleindienst finished with the prosecutors around 5:00 a.m. After three hours' sleep, he phoned the White House and asked to speak to the president. Nixon was still in bed, having stayed up late the night before. He did not call back until after ten. Instead of seeing the attorney general immediately, Nixon invited him to join a special Palm Sunday worship service in the state rooms of the White House. They would talk afterward. Kleindienst was finally ushered into the president's hideaway office in EOB 175 at 1:21 p.m. He had never been there before. Nixon noticed that his voice "choked periodically" with emotion and "his eyes were red with fatigue and tears." Nixon, by contrast, was calm and in control.

It took Kleindienst some time to get to the point. Mitchell, Magruder, and Dean were all in serious trouble. That much Nixon knew already. But the shocker was that his two closest aides, Haldeman and Ehrlichman, also faced possible criminal prosecution. The evidence was not yet conclusive but was very disturbing. The story was likely to be "all over town" very soon. Kleindienst suggested that the two men take leaves of absence. That would limit the damage to the presidency if they were eventually indicted. Nixon bridled at this idea, which he saw as tantamount to an admission of guilt.

"The point is, Dick, I can't," he protested. "I can't let an innocent man down."

Kleindienst refused to involve himself further in the case. He was too close to the principal suspects, particularly Mitchell. His assistant, Henry Petersen, would be in charge from now on. It was nevertheless clear from his presentation that Nixon and his aides had been focusing on the wrong threat. They had been galvanized into action by rumors that Howard Hunt and Gordon Liddy had done deals with the prosecutors. This was misinformation, probably spread by the prosecutors themselves to put pressure on other witnesses. Far from "telling all," Liddy had not "said a word to anybody," Kleindienst informed Nixon. Hunt was not on the verge of breaking. The real threat to Nixon was coming from inside the White House.

John Dean was furious with the prosecutors for failing to keep his dealings with them confidential. Instead of consulting his attorney, they had simply phoned Charlie Shaffer after midnight to void their earlier agreement. They argued that they could no longer withhold potentially explosive information, portions of which had been confirmed by other witnesses, from the leadership of the Justice Department. From past experience, Dean knew exactly what would happen next. The White House, and therefore the president, would immediately be informed. Dean could no longer play his double game, with a foot in both camps.

The prosecutors were also frustrated with Dean. Guided by Shaffer, he had been very selective about his disclosures. Pressed to provide a detailed chronology, he instead described isolated incidents, like Ehrlichman's instruction to "deep six" the contents of Howard Hunt's safe. He refused to talk about his own conversations with the president on the grounds of executive privilege and national security. It had taken several sessions to extract from Dean the first incriminating details about Haldeman and Ehrlichman. Shaffer's strategy seemed obvious to Silbert. By dribbling the revelations out, he was attempting "to make Dean so valuable to us that we would grant him immunity from prosecution." It was like a card game in which the players were constantly raising the stakes.

For all the mistrust, each side needed the other. Dean wanted immunity. The prosecutors were seeking information only he could provide. Much as Dean was tempted to throw in his cards, he was drawn back inexorably to the gambling table. "We don't have any choice," Shaffer told him. "We've got to pump them full of the cover-up now. I've got to up the ante with them to have a shot at immunity. That's your only chance not to be the fall guy."

As Nixon was meeting the attorney general at the White House,

Dean was closeted once again with the prosecutors in Shaffer's office in Rockville. They circled each other warily for several hours. Seymour Glanzer played bad cop to Earl Silbert's good cop.

"I'm tired of hearing about this great obstruction case your client is supposed to have for us," Glanzer told Shaffer. "His story is jumbled and disjointed. We can't do anything with what he's told us."

The foxhunting attorney countered with one of his equestrian analogies.

"You guys remind me of a bunch of horses going to the starting gate. You want to run before the bell is sounded. We plan to take this thing one step at a time."

As everybody was preparing to leave, Shaffer signaled his client to play his trump card. Dean made a cryptic reference to "information already in Justice Department files" that would help explain the cover-up. The FBI had photographs of Liddy and Hunt outside the office of a Beverly Hills psychiatrist by the name of Lewis Fielding. The photographs would incriminate the two Watergate principals in an earlier conspiracy to steal the mental health records of the leaker of the Pentagon Papers, Daniel Ellsberg.

The prosecutors struggled to make the connection between Ellsberg, an obscure California psychiatrist, and Watergate. It was all very confusing. To complicate matters even further, Ellsberg was currently on trial in Los Angeles for espionage. If there was evidence relevant to his case in Justice Department files that had not been disclosed, that could become grounds for a mistrial. The judge would have to be informed immediately.

"Quit playing games with us," Glanzer demanded. "What's this all about? And what the hell's it doing in our files?"

Dean explained that Hunt and Liddy had used camera equipment on loan from the CIA to reconnoiter the Fielding office prior to the bungled September 1971 burglary. They had given the film to the CIA for processing. The agency had subsequently provided the FBI with copies of the photographs, along with other Watergate-related evidence, without revealing their significance. The photos had remained a puzzle to investigators who failed to connect the dots.

It gradually dawned on the two prosecutors that their obstreperous witness had produced a plausible motivation for the Watergate cover-up.

The obstruction of justice had been necessary to conceal other felonies. They were no longer investigating "a third-rate burglary," in Ziegler's dismissive phrase. They were uncovering an entire web of "high crimes and misdemeanors" that could be used to impeach a president.

Always leery of embarrassing situations, Nixon recoiled from directly confronting Haldeman and Ehrlichman. He summoned Ehrlichman to EOB 175 for an hour-long meeting after Kleindienst left at 2:22 p.m. but avoided the subject that was now uppermost on his mind. As soon as he was through with Ehrlichman, he telephoned Haldeman at his home in Georgetown. The chief of staff had spent the afternoon mired in the messy details of the forthcoming Senate hearings. As he had with Ehrlichman, Nixon adopted a tone of contrived joviality that was the opposite of his true feelings.

"Hope you're enjoying this lovely day?"

"'Fraid not," was the clipped response. "Got to get out and take a look."

As he pondered the charges against his two top aides, Nixon met with the man who was now effectively in charge of the Watergate investigation. By now it was 4:00 p.m. Assistant Attorney General Henry Petersen had spent the weekend working on his boat. Summoned urgently to the White House, he appeared in Nixon's office in jeans, sneakers, and a grimy, oil-stained T-shirt. He had never been there before and felt completely out of place. He was more accustomed to prosecuting Mafia bosses and other racketeers than meeting with presidents. Although he was a registered Democrat, Petersen supported Nixon's tough law-and-order policies. He had served in the Marine Corps in the South Pacific during World War II: his craggy face looked as if it had taken a few knocks. "Petersen is a soldier," Dean had told the president on March 21. "He kept me informed. He told me when we had problems, where we had problems. He believes in you. He believes in this administration. This administration has made him."

Nixon would later claim that meetings in his EOB hideaway went unrecorded that Sunday afternoon and evening because the Secret Service technicians responsible for changing the tape did not work on weekends. As Nixon subsequently told the story, Petersen urged him to dismiss both Haldeman and Ehrlichman immediately. The two men were likely to become "a source of vast embarrassment to the presidency." According to Nixon, the following exchange then took place:

> Nixon: "I can't fire men simply because of the appearance of guilt. I have to have proof of their guilt."
> Petersen: "What you have just said, Mr. President, speaks very well of you as a man. It does not speak well of you as a president."

It was the first truly beautiful spring weekend in Washington, with temperatures in the high sixties. Nixon had been trapped inside all day and was desperate to get out. He had invited Bebe Rebozo for a cruise on the Potomac on the presidential yacht. A 104-foot houseboat with polished mahogany fittings, the *Sequoia* had originally been put into service by Herbert Hoover. FDR and Truman had used the yacht for summit meetings and fishing trips. A few months before his assassination, Kennedy had celebrated his forty-sixth and final birthday with a lavish party on board. But no president had sailed on the elegant old tub as often as Nixon. The elaborate navy ritual transformed him into the commander in chief of a miniature realm, like a boy playing with toy soldiers. He particularly loved sailing past George Washington's estate at Mount Vernon, where the founder of the nation lay buried. When they came abeam of Washington's tomb, Nixon and his guests would stand at attention to the mournful strains of taps echoing across the water and a solemn salute from the crew.

The president and his friend were piped aboard the USS *Sequoia* at 5:32 p.m. after driving to the Washington Navy Yard from the White House. As the sun began to set over the blue-gray hills of Virginia, Nixon sat with Bebe on deck, describing the latest charges against Haldeman and Ehrlichman. He worried that they would be unable to cope financially if they became targets of an extensive criminal investigation. The two men had served him "loyally and selflessly" for many years. Whatever happened, he wanted to help them with their legal fees.

"How much money do I have in your bank?" Nixon asked, referring to the financial institution in Key Biscayne that Rebozo had founded decades before.

The Nixon family stands at attention on the USS Sequoia *as the crew salutes the grave of George Washington at Mount Vernon, June 1972.*

Bebe would not allow Nixon to dip into his own savings. He said that he and Bob Abplanalp would be able to raise a couple of hundred thousand dollars for Haldeman and Ehrlichman. He insisted, however, that donations be made in cash and kept entirely secret. He would not be able to perform the same favor for other, equally deserving Nixon associates.

It was dark by the time the *Sequoia* returned to the navy yard. In the depths of Nixon's soul, it was even darker. He had sent word to his two top aides that he wanted to meet with them after his boat ride with Bebe. He would write later in his memoirs, "I dreaded having to go back to the White House and face the bleak choices I knew were waiting there."

The president masked his inner turmoil with cheerful remarks about the gorgeous weather as he greeted Haldeman and Ehrlichman in his EOB hideaway. He sensed dangers from all sides—from the prosecutors, from Congress, from Judge Sirica, from the press, from men like Dean and Mitchell and even Colson, whom he had trusted with his innermost secrets. He knew he would have to find a way to "prick the boil" of Watergate, however painful the procedure. He now realized that Dean had been right when he talked about a cancer threatening his presidency.

"Petersen wants you both out," Nixon announced abruptly, after some awkward preliminaries. "Says the evidence that Dean and Magruder are giving the prosecutors implicates you both so much you're an embarrassment to the president."

Haldeman was stunned. He had given the best years of his life to Nixon. His wife, Jo, and four children had paid a high price for his single-minded devotion. Connected to the president by buzzers and pagers that required him to come whenever summoned, he had neglected his family. That very week, he had learned that his second son, Peter, had been expelled from an elite Washington secondary school for smoking dope and cutting class. Agonized discussions with his wife on what to do with Peter had been interrupted by yet another call from the White House. Now, it seemed, he might be shown the door.

The dazed chief of staff found it difficult to concentrate on what the president was saying. Gradually, however, his mind returned to its normal focus. Ever the loyal soldier, he was ready to sacrifice himself "to save the man who had brought me here." He told Nixon he was prepared to resign if it became politically necessary.

Ehrlichman was much more antagonistic, according to Haldeman's later account. He referred angrily to "brother Dean" who was "grabbing every document in sight by day and talking to the prosecutors by night." Surely the traitor should be punished before the two men closest to the president. Nixon had a different opinion.

"I can't fire Dean. I can't risk his going after the president."

"Well, you certainly can't risk his bouncing around here, playing his little game, tiptoeing through the files gathering ammunition," Ehrlichman protested. He volunteered to draft "a little resignation note" for Dean to sign.

In the middle of this discussion, Nixon received a telephone message from Dean. It consisted of three numbered points:

1. I hope you understand my actions are motivated totally out of loyalty to you. If it's not clear now, it will become clear.
2. Ehrlichman requested to meet tonight but I feel inappropriate at this time. I am ready and willing to meet with you any time to discuss these matters.
3. I think you should take your counsel from Henry Petersen, who I assure you does not want the presidency hurt.

Nixon replied by inviting his nemesis to meet with him alone in EOB 175. Dean arrived at 9:17 p.m. as Haldeman and Ehrlichman scuttled out the side entrance. As Dean later recalled, the president was sitting in the comfortable lounge chair in the far corner of the room next to his desk. His feet were propped up on the ottoman. Dean pulled up one of the hard-back chairs from the conference table and sat down opposite him. He noticed that the president looked both exhausted and disheveled. He was wearing a smoking jacket that resembled a dressing gown. "His usually neatly creased trousers looked as if he had slept in them, and his necktie was stained. This was not the well-manicured Richard Nixon I was used to."

Nixon was at pains to appear friendly. "Would you like something to drink?" he asked. "Scotch? Martini? Anything?" Dean declined. This was the first time the president had offered him a drink, alcoholic or otherwise. He felt awkward. When Nixon insisted, he requested a Coke. Nixon ordered Manolo to bring a Coke for Dean and a coffee for himself. He understood very well that Dean had betrayed him but was obliged to pretend that their relationship was unchanged. He did not want to precipitate an open war with the man who was still his legal counsel. Dean had turned against Haldeman and Ehrlichman; he could turn against the president at any moment. Better to hold him close to the chest—"an asp at your bosom," as Colson put it—than push him away. Dean, meanwhile, was desperate to avoid being made to take the blame for Watergate. As long as he remained on the White House staff, he knew he would enjoy a measure of protection.

Nixon asked whether Haldeman and Ehrlichman had been part of the cover-up. Dean explained that the two men had guided him "every inch of the way." He had kept them fully informed about the burglars' demands for hush money. They had approved the raising of funds. They could both be charged with "obstruction of justice," a section of the legal code "as broad as the imagination of man." Dean also mentioned Ehrlichman's instruction to "deep six" documents found in Hunt's safe. Nixon noticed that Dean's voice took on a "vindictive edge" whenever he talked about Ehrlichman, his predecessor as White House counsel and direct superior.

Nixon was most concerned about the confidentiality of their private conversations. Discussions between the president and his lawyer were covered by "executive privilege," he insisted. Some involved matters of "national security." There was a risk that some of his remarks would be misunderstood if they ever became public. The March 21 "cancer on the presidency" meeting was a case in point. Nixon wanted Dean to know he had been "joking" when he discussed the possibility of raising a million dollars for the burglars. That was not how Dean remembered the conversation, but he sought to strike a reassuring tone.

"Well, Mr. President, I'm not even going into those areas. You can be assured of that."

Dean was struck by the way Nixon asked a series of leading questions that appeared designed to get him to acknowledge the president's lack of involvement in Watergate. He wondered if he was being taped. Nixon also made a show of instructing Dean to "tell the truth" to the prosecutors. Toward the end of the meeting, he got out of his chair and retreated to a corner of his office, well away from any microphones. The lights of the White House on the other side of the road shone through the curtains behind him. In a barely audible voice, Nixon referred hesitantly to another conversation, also in March, when he had acknowledged discussing a presidential pardon for Hunt with Colson.

"I guess it was foolish of me to talk to Colson about clemency, wasn't it?"

Dean merely nodded. The president had just mentioned their two most problematic conversations. "He knew they were his biggest mistakes, but he was telling me that he considered them small ones," Dean wrote later. "Jokes, little errors."

Dean sensed that Nixon was on the brink of a momentous decision that could determine his fate. If he acted swiftly, it was still possible he could cut out the cancer that imperiled his presidency. As Nixon led him to the door to say goodbye, Dean impulsively raised a subject he had never had the courage to mention before.

"You know, uh, Mr. President," he stammered. "I would hate to have anything I have started here by talking to the prosecutors and getting these facts out . . . uh, I would hate to have any of that ever result in the impeachment of the president."

Dean's mention of the ultimate constitutional sanction seemed to take Nixon by surprise. He thought a moment before vigorously shaking his head.

"Oh, no, John, don't you worry about that. We're going to handle everything right."

After his evening session with Nixon and Haldeman, John Ehrlichman left the White House "heartsick." He felt he was being unjustly blamed for Watergate. True, he had performed some dirty tricks for Nixon in the past, including his involvement in the Ellsberg psychiatrist affair. But he had done his best to minimize his exposure and had urged the president to make a clean break with Mitchell and Magruder. He now risked being dragged down with men he regarded as much more culpable. He had barely reached home when he received a call from the White House. For the third time that Sunday, his ostensible day off, the president wanted to see him urgently.

Haldeman was already with Nixon in his hideaway office by the time Ehrlichman arrived at 10:16 p.m. Nixon wanted to brief his two aides on his talk with Dean. It had clearly disturbed him. He was particularly troubled by the story of Hunt's safe. There had evidently been material in the safe documenting dirty tricks by Colson, including his investigations into the Kennedy clan, that could be extremely damaging to Nixon himself. Ehrlichman denied ordering Dean to "deep six" the files but acknowledged approving his alternative proposal to transfer the "political dynamite" to Patrick Gray.

Nixon instructed Ehrlichman to phone the acting FBI director and find out what had happened to the documents. An early riser, Gray was already in bed when his special FBI phone rang. The conversation began awkwardly. Ehrlichman informed Gray that the Watergate prosecutors had questioned Dean about the transfer of a folder of files from Hunt's safe.

"He'd better deny that," said Gray, who had told Justice Department investigators he had no knowledge of the documents.

"He's apparently pretty much on the record on that. I thought I'd better alert you."

"What the hell am I going to do about that?"

"I don't know. Is it still in being?"

"No. I was told that was purely political and I destroyed it."

Nixon could not hear Gray's end of the conversation, but he could see the blood draining from Ehrlichman's face. There was a pause as Ehrlichman processed this information.

"I see," he finally managed to say. "Well, it probably was."

"Is there any way you can turn him off?"

There was another long pause. Aware that whatever he said might become part of a court record one day, Ehrlichman became the epitome of bureaucratic correctness.

"No. Not in any orbit that we cognize around here."

Resorting to a gambling circumlocution, Ehrlichman advised Gray to examine his "hole card." This was an old poker expression meaning that he should calculate the strength of his hand before placing his next bet. The allusion was lost on the naive Gray, who was under the impression that he had been executing the wishes of his masters.

"The only thing I can do with this is deny it," said Gray, who had burned the documents in an incinerator in his yard, along with discarded Christmas wrapping paper. A dark thought occurred to him. Ehrlichman might corroborate Dean's testimony, in which case Gray would be hung out to dry. "You're not going to back him up, are you?"

Ehrlichman mumbled something unintelligible and quickly hung up. He stared blankly at the wall. He imagined the newspaper headline: *Head of FBI Destroyed Evidence at Behest of President's Aides.* Nixon and Haldeman tried to cheer him up. Maybe it was not so bad. The idea of hand delivering the documents to Gray had come from Dean, not Ehrlichman. He could not therefore be blamed for their disappearance. None of this was of any comfort.

"It was done in my office. I'm implicated," he said bitterly. "There goes my license to practice law."

W
ith suspicion falling on his closest aides, Nixon now took personal charge of the Watergate cover-up, which had become a
battle for his own survival. It was akin to a military campaign
in which he was the commanding general, director of operations, and
chief intelligence officer, all rolled into one. To plan his counteroffensive, he needed accurate intelligence about the intentions of the enemy
and state of the terrain. He was obliged to conduct his own scouting forays into hostile territory. While he relied on others to supply him with
information, there was no one else he could completely trust. Once
loyal associates like Mitchell, Ehrlichman, and Dean were openly feud-
ing. The pissing contest that Nixon had warned about back in March
had become a reality. The president was alone.

He was determined to claim credit for cracking Watergate before
the press learned about the latest developments. That meant getting
out ahead of the Justice Department and the Senate, where that Bible-
quoting charlatan, Sam Ervin of North Carolina, was preparing to hold
open hearings. Judge Sirica was another wild card who could spring
a surprise at any moment. The White House was awash with rumors
about bombshell news stories about to break in *The Washington Post*
or *The New York Times*. "Ziegler has just left my office," Ehrlichman
informed Nixon at 9:50 on Monday morning. "He's got some input
from the *Post*. It's his estimate that unless we take the initiative by nine
o'clock tonight, it will be too late."

Ten minutes later, Nixon welcomed Dean to the Oval Office as the "two Germans" left by the side entrance, laughing conspiratorially. He directed Dean to the chair just vacated by Haldeman. "Sit down, sit down." The president came to the point very quickly. He presented his legal counsel with two letters, both drafted by Ehrlichman. One letter offered Dean's immediate resignation "as a result of my involvement in the Watergate matter." The other requested an "indefinite leave of absence" from the White House staff. Nixon wanted Dean to sign both letters so he could have them "in hand." He would have the option of releasing one or the other or neither, depending on how events developed.

The canny Dean immediately suspected a plot to blame him, and him alone, for the obstruction of justice. His legal strategy hinged on demonstrating that he had been carrying out orders from superiors, particularly Haldeman and Ehrlichman. His defense was that he had been a simple errand boy, or "conduit" in legal terminology. Signing these letters would be tantamount to signing a confession that could be used against him in court. His suspicions were confirmed when he asked the president if he had requested similar letters from the others.

"Are we talking Dean, or are we talking Dean, Ehrlichman, and Haldeman?"

"Dean at this moment," Nixon acknowledged.

"You have problems with the others too."

Fumbling nervously on his desk, the president absentmindedly pressed a button by mistake. An aide entered the Oval Office seconds later in response to the summons. Dean was unable to suppress a laugh as Nixon waved the intruder away impatiently.

Nixon claimed that Haldeman and Ehrlichman were ready to submit their resignations anytime he asked. This gave Dean an idea. He would link his departure to the departure of his two main antagonists. He suggested writing his own version of the letters that Nixon had shown him. He promised to make them "short and sweet."

"Fine," said the president, realizing he had to keep the viper close to his chest.

Reminding Dean that he was "still the counsel round here," Nixon asked for his help on "the PR side" of Watergate. He sure as hell was not going to allow the Justice Department or anyone else to grab the headlines for solving the crime. By Nixon's account, he had exposed the cover-up himself, with perhaps a minor assist from his legal counsel. Dean had come to him on March 21, warning of a cancer on the presidency. This was the first time Nixon had any inkling of wrongdoing. Shocked, he had launched his own investigation, which had finally established the truth.

"We triggered this whole thing. You know what I mean?"

"That's right."

"You helped the trigger."

Once again, Dean remembered events differently. In his version, he was the hero, with the president little more than a spectator. He minimized his own role in coaching Magruder to commit perjury and managing the cover-up over a period of eight months.

"I put everybody's feet to the fire because it just had to stop."

As often happened, Nixon saw a parallel with the Alger Hiss case, one of the proudest moments in his political career. "That son of a bitch Hiss would be free today if he hadn't lied about his espionage." The disgraced State Department official had gone to jail for "the lie rather than the crime." When it came to dealing with federal investigators, Nixon's advice was this: "Believe me, don't ever lie with these bastards."

"The truth always emerges," said Dean.

Nixon told Dean he would "like to take the credit" for persuading Magruder to talk to investigators. Dean should make the point that the case had been broken "as a result of the president's action." By now, Nixon was in full fantasy mode, inventing a starring role for himself. He had told his subordinates, "I want to get to the bottom of this thing, period."

"Believe me, I put a little bit of pressure on Magruder and a few of these clowns," he boasted. "Also I put pressure on the Justice Department. I told Kleindienst, 'Goddamn it!'"

Dean lacked the heart to contradict him. He left the Oval Office without signing the resignation letters, torn between a residual sense of loyalty to the president and a feeling that Nixon was a "devious bastard" who was out to get him. "The voices canceled each other out," he wrote later. "I was just strong enough to resist the president, not strong enough to defy him."

Nixon resumed his spin control efforts with Haldeman and Ehrlichman as soon as Dean was safely out of the way. After considering various "scenarios" that highlighted bold action by the president, they came up with one that turned Dean into the villain. According to this version of events, Dean's failure to produce his long-promised report on White House involvement in Watergate had brought the crisis to a head. He obviously had something to hide.

"Remember you had John Dean go to Camp David and write it up," Ehrlichman reminded Nixon. "He came down and said, 'I can't.'"

"Right."

"That is the tip-off. Right then you started to move."

"That's right." Nixon agreed enthusiastically. "He said he could not write it."

"Then you realized that there was much more to this than you had been led to believe."

This made sense to Nixon. He moved on to the question he had previously asked Dean. "How do I get the credit for getting Magruder to the stand?"

"Very simple," replied Ehrlichman. He explained that the president had taken Dean "off the case" after losing confidence in him. He had then assigned his Watergate responsibilities to Ehrlichman with a mandate to establish all the facts. That was the crucial turning point.

"Why did I take Dean off?" Nixon asked.

"Because he was involved."

"The scenario is that he told you he couldn't write a report," said Haldeman. "Obviously you had to take him off."

"Right, right."

"Then we started digging into it," said Ehrlichman. "I talked to a lot of people on the phone, I talked to several witnesses in person, kept feeding information to you."

"Right."

"You began to move."

What was emerging as the official White House narrative had numerous holes in it, beginning with the fact that Nixon had been aware of

Magruder's perjured testimony all along. Buried in the piles of tapes in the EOB safes were recorded conversations showing that Ehrlichman and Haldeman had discussed the matter with him as far back as July 1972, a month after the Watergate break-in. Rather than putting a stop to Magruder's lies, Nixon had emphasized the need to cut the investigation off "at the Liddy level if possible." Dean reported on his cover-up efforts to Haldeman and Ehrlichman, who in turn briefed Nixon. The "scenario" of a deceived president moving to clean house when he finally discovered the truth was pure political spin. But it would serve its purpose for now.

Nixon had the usual ceremonial duties to perform in addition to managing the gravest crisis of his presidency. After his session with Haldeman and Ehrlichman, he was whisked by motorcade to the Washington Hilton for a trade union conference. Then it was back to the Oval Office for a presentation of the millionth copy of the Alcoholics Anonymous "Big Book" and receipt of an honorary award from Rotary International. There was no time for lunch or his normally sacrosanct afternoon "thinking time." He had arranged to receive yet another Watergate briefing from Assistant Attorney General Henry Petersen in his private study.

He jogged up the twenty-six stone steps that adorned the entrance to the Executive Office Building, on the other side of the closed-off avenue. By the time he reached the top, he was out of breath. Petersen was waiting for him in the anteroom of EOB 175, next to the wall of framed political cartoons. This was the second time in less than twenty-four hours that he had been called to a face-to-face meeting with the president. In addition, they had spoken by phone four times, most recently just before midnight on Sunday evening.

"Always come here in the afternoons," the president told his new consigliere as he led him into his private office. "I always run upstairs. That's why I'm a little panting. I get my exercise."

Petersen expressed his admiration. He was overworked and out of shape. He had difficulty running up steps.

"What's your age?"

"Fifty-two, sir."

"My, you've got some great years ahead of you," said the sixty-year-old president.

Nixon was eager to put Petersen at his ease and establish a friendly relationship. He knew he would need his help if he was ever going to find a way out of the morass of Watergate. Petersen had provided invaluable assistance to Dean in keeping track of the investigation. With Dean out of the picture, Nixon had to rely on Petersen directly as his primary source of intelligence on the activities of the Justice Department and grand jury. To wheedle information out of Petersen, he presented himself as the investigator in chief. They would crack the case together. "You know I am in charge of this thing—you are and I am," he told Petersen. "You understand now, you're talking only to me. There's not going to be anybody else on the White House staff. In other words, I am acting counsel and everything else."

Petersen was awed by his sudden elevation to the president's inner circle after twenty-six years laboring in the anonymity of the federal bureaucracy. He was amazed by Nixon's ability to remain "calm and collected" amid the chaos all around. The president had displayed a "complete lack of shock" when informed about Dean's allegations against Haldeman and Ehrlichman. "Here I was recommending that two people whom he had known and worked with for years be dismissed," he recalled later. "I would have been cussing and fuming." Petersen accepted the president's assurances that he genuinely wanted to get to the bottom of the Watergate conspiracy.

The assistant attorney general willingly shared the innermost secrets of the grand jury proceedings with the man who would eventually become an "unindicted co-conspirator." He reasoned that the president had a right to direct the investigation as head of the executive branch. Loyal to his superior, he did not question Nixon's motives. From Petersen, Nixon gained a detailed understanding of the case against his closest associates and the potential threats to himself. Petersen explained the way in which the prosecutors were methodically interviewing people lower down the totem pole before going after Haldeman and Ehrlichman. He outlined the timetable for calling various witnesses to testify and provided highlights of the interviews with Magruder and Dean. In response to Nixon's probing questions, he also described the tortuous negotiations with Dean's attorney, Charlie Shaffer, over immunity.

Shaffer was refusing to plea-bargain, Petersen reported. Instead, he wanted "a deal" that would afford his client full protection. Petersen was inclined to grant Dean immunity if it would clinch the case against Haldeman and Ehrlichman. This put Dean in a different category from Magruder, who had agreed to plead guilty to one charge of conspiracy. Shaffer's argument was that Dean was not guilty of anything. As far as the cover-up was concerned, he had simply been acting as "an agent" on behalf of White House superiors. If the Justice Department put Dean on trial, Shaffer would level the same charges against "Ehrlichman, Haldeman, Nixon, and this administration."

"The president too?" asked Nixon, suddenly alarmed.

"It's a goddamned poker game. Yes, sir."

Nixon demanded clarification. Dean "told you that unless you grant him immunity, he's going to attack everybody, including the president. Is that right?"

That had come not from Dean but from his lawyer, Petersen explained. It was framed in terms of Dean's defense strategy in the event of a trial rather than as a direct threat. So far at least, Dean had implicated only Haldeman and Ehrlichman, not the president himself. But Nixon was still concerned.

"He hasn't testified that he's an agent for the president in any of this, has he?"

"No, sir."

"If he has, I need to know."

"Yes, sir. I know."

"I didn't see Dean until a month ago. Never saw him."

Thanks to Petersen, Nixon understood that Dean had a winning card he was prepared to use if he was ever put on trial. In the meantime, Dean had another card up his sleeve that he played later that afternoon. Summoned back to EOB 175, he produced his rewrite of the resignation letters prepared by Ehrlichman. As promised, his version was pithy and to the point:

Dear Mr. President,

You have informed me that Bob Haldeman and John Ehrlichman have verbally tendered their request to be given an immediate and indefinite leave of absence from your staff. By this letter I wish to confirm my similar request that I be given such a leave of absence from the staff.

Sincerely, John Dean

"You don't want to go if they stay?" Nixon asked.

Dean mentioned his fear of being turned into "the scapegoat."

"Like Magruder's been a scapegoat for Mitchell?"

"Right."

By linking his fate to those of Haldeman and Ehrlichman, Dean had made it much more difficult for Nixon to single him out for blame. His letter avoided any mention of Watergate. Beyond complaining that "you" was not "a polite word" to use in addressing a president, Nixon did not argue the merits of the rival drafts. He would later acknowledge that Dean's latest ploy was "very cute." If he sacked Dean alone, he would risk the accusation that he was "covering up for Haldeman and Ehrlichman." He knew when he had been outmaneuvered.

A sense of impending doom enveloped the White House on Tuesday morning. The *Los Angeles Times* had published a story overnight claiming that the president would soon acknowledge the involvement of one or more of his high-level aides in the Watergate affair. The newspaper's list of potential "sacrificial lambs" included Mitchell, Dean, Magruder, and even Haldeman. Every hour seemed to bring fresh press speculation about "dramatic developments."

"I think we have to move today," Nixon informed Haldeman at their regular morning meeting in the Oval Office at 9:47. "It's breaking so fast."

In addition to dealing with the gravest political crisis of his career, Nixon was obliged to simultaneously play host to the prime minister of Italy, Giulio Andreotti. He barely had time to share the latest news from the grand jury—"LaRue has talked very freely, he's a broken man"—before being rushed off to greet his visitor on the South Lawn. For the rest of the morning, he was occupied with "the Italian." It was not until 12:35 that he was able to resume his Watergate discussions with Haldeman and Ehrlichman.

They sat on either side of his desk, like schoolboys summoned to meet the principal, Haldeman to his left, Ehrlichman to his right. They had been there together, in the same positions, on countless previous occasions, but this time was different. Earlier that morning, Nixon had hinted they would have to go, not because they were guilty, but to avoid

Nixon in the Oval Office with Haldeman and Ehrlichman, December 1969.
The photograph of Earth on the wall was taken
by the Apollo 8 astronauts as they orbited the moon in December 1968.

being slowly "nibbled to death" and the torture of endless scandal. Nixon wanted the two men to know how much he depended on them and how much he would regret losing them. They were the "two most valuable members" of his staff, in addition to being "the two most loyal and the two most honest."

Ehrlichman was determined to prevent the granting of immunity to Dean. He had just been meeting with Colson, who argued that Dean would be obliged to deliver a "quid pro quo" to the prosecutors in return for immunity. This would most likely come in the form of public testimony against Colson, Haldeman, and Ehrlichman. The president would be dragged down by association. Nixon only half agreed with this analysis. As he knew from Petersen, Dean had not directly accused him of anything. Not yet, anyway. He wanted to make sure he kept his mouth shut. That meant handling him "very gingerly." There was a potential for "blackmail."

"There's no sense aggravating Dean," said Nixon. "He'll do anything to save his own ass. He's pissing as high as he can get now. We can't let him piss any higher, which would be on the president."

Yet another fault line was opening up at the very top of the White House. Nixon's top aides were no longer automatically aligned with him, or each other. Rival factions formed, broke apart, and re-formed on a daily basis. Some of his advisers were urging him to get rid of his German guard dogs and focus on saving himself. Leonard Garment, who had taken over many of Dean's duties as legal counsel, advocated a "clean sweep" of the top White House staff. Nixon agonized over the decision. "I was selfish enough about my own survival to want them to leave," he later wrote of his two top aides, "but I was not so ruthless to be able to confront easily the idea of hurting people I cared about so deeply. I worried about the impact on them if they were forced to leave; and I worried about the impact on me if they didn't."

Ehrlichman was particularly aggressive in demanding the immediate dismissal of Dean. He reacted scornfully to Dean's attempt to link his resignation to the departure of his superiors. The president should reject such "I'll go if they go" tactics. Everybody should be treated on the merits. He, Ehrlichman, was in an entirely different category from Dean, who had admitted his involvement in the cover-up.

"Supposing I said, 'I won't go unless Henry Kissinger goes,'" said Ehrlichman. "It's ridiculous."

Nixon feared he had played into Dean's hands by telling him that Haldeman and Ehrlichman were ready to resign if necessary.

"Maybe I've trapped myself," he said with a sigh.

Ehrlichman was also furious with Henry Petersen, who, he was convinced, was preparing to indict him. If he was pushed out of the White House, he would expose Petersen's dealings with Dean, particularly the leaking of secret grand jury testimony. It was intolerable that a man who had contributed to the cover-up was making prosecutorial decisions. Haldeman agreed that "Petersen was up to his ass with Dean in violation of the law."

"One of the first things I am going to do is to sink Petersen," Ehrlichman warned. "I'll do it by fair means or foul."

"I hope so," said Nixon softly. He was unprepared for such hostility and sounded momentarily stunned. He was relying on Petersen as his eyes and ears into the investigation. Now he had a new problem on his hands.

Ehrlichman was still not done describing his plan to "very vigorously" defend himself in the event of his forced resignation. As he saw it, Dean was the "sole proprietor" of the cover-up project and had been actively involved in the payment of hush money as recently as March. The record would show that "he reported to the president" and only "incidentally" to Ehrlichman. This new "scenario" alarmed Nixon greatly. Ehrlichman was attempting to pass the poisoned chalice to his boss.

"Reported to the president?" Nixon protested.

"Yes, sir. I would have to say that because . . ."

"When?"

For Nixon, this was the crucial question. His defense hung on the assertion that he had very limited personal dealings with Dean during the most crucial stages of the cover-up. Dean's reports had been channeled through Haldeman and Ehrlichman. He could blame them for failing to keep him fully informed.

"I don't know when," conceded Ehrlichman, "but, uh, the point is . . ."

"He didn't see me when he came out to California [in mid-February]. He didn't see me until the day you said, 'I think you ought to talk to John Dean.' I think that was in March."

In fact, Nixon and Dean had their first Watergate-related discussion on September 15. Their next meeting was on March 1, three weeks before the fateful "cancer on the presidency" conversation. But the precise timing of the meetings had little bearing on the point Ehrlichman was trying to make. Ehrlichman explained that he and Haldeman served as "agents" of the president. A jury was entitled to assume that they relayed to the president any information they received from Dean. Lawyers referred to this as the "imputed knowledge" rule. Ehrlichman gave an example. If Dean testified, "I told Ehrlichman that Liddy did it," he was in effect saying, "I told the president, through Ehrlichman, that Liddy did it." As far as Ehrlichman was concerned, Nixon was as exposed as his two top aides.

"I get into a very funny defensive position vis-à-vis you and vis-à-vis him," Ehrlichman summed up. "It's very damned awkward."

Nixon reverted to his original contention.

"Basically, of course, he didn't report to me. I was a little busy, and all of you said, 'Let's let Dean handle that and keep him out of the president's office.'"

Ehrlichman countered that he had been busy too. He had a lot of other things on his plate, besides Watergate.

Then "who the hell" did Dean report to? Nixon wanted to know.

"In many cases to no one," replied Ehrlichman, conveniently forgetting his own meetings with Dean. "He just went ahead and did things."

The immunity issue was a tricky one for Nixon. Although the decision ultimately rested with the Justice Department, he could probably prevail on Petersen to follow his recommendation. There were huge risks either way. Denial of immunity might provoke an angry Dean to escalate his attacks on the administration. Alternatively, he might be emboldened by the granting of immunity. Nixon was swayed by Ehrlichman's argument that giving his top aides a free pass would look bad from a public relations perspective. But the key factor was Nixon's calculation that his own position would be strengthened by rejecting Dean's pleas for immunity. In this event, his best option would be to refuse to invoke his Fifth Amendment right against self-incrimination and refuse to testify in the hope that Nixon would "grant him an eventual pardon." After thinking about the pros and cons, Nixon instructed Ehrlichman to put his opposition to immunity in writing.

The curtains at the end of the White House briefing room had been drawn back to reveal a podium emblazoned with the presidential seal on top of a platform encased in plush beige carpeting. A hundred or so reporters had gathered on short notice to hear "an important statement" from the president. He was running late. They engaged in competitive humor as they waited for him to arrive. "He's out getting a cocker spaniel and a cloth coat for Pat," joked one, a reference to the 1952 Checkers speech. "He's going to waive executive privilege for Manolo and finally throw him to the wolves," cracked another.

The briefing room was another Nixon innovation. Prior to his presidency, reporters had hung out in a cramped West Wing corner office. They slung their coats and hats over a large round table in the lobby,

Nixon meeting with reporters in the new press room that he had built over the FDR-era swimming pool, January 1973.

where they could waylay visitors to the Oval Office. Intent on gaining some privacy from his tormentors, Nixon had sacrificed the swimming pool and massage rooms built by FDR to relieve the effects of polio. In return for vacating their old press room, which was turned over to Kissinger, the reporters were given much fancier facilities adjoining the colonnade between the mansion and the West Wing. The new space resembled "the lobby of a fake Elizabethan steak house," wrote one White House correspondent when it was first unveiled in April 1970. A variety of suede-covered chesterfield sofas, captain's chairs, and other imitation antique furnishings were scattered around the room. Muzak was piped in over speakers. "Put in a washer and dryer and we could live here," enthused another member of the fourth estate.

Due to the lack of chairs, some reporters were squatting on the floor when the president finally appeared in the briefing room, while others perched on coffee tables. Nixon was dressed in a dark blue suit and held a typewritten statement in his hand, which he proceeded to read out loud. Carl Bernstein of *The Washington Post* noticed that his hands were shaking as he announced "intensive new inquiries" into the Watergate matter stemming from "serious charges" that had first come to his attention on March 21. This was an allusion to Dean's "cancer on the presidency" warning. Nixon went on,

> I can report today that there have been major developments in the case concerning which it would be improper to be more specific now, except to say that real progress has been made in finding the truth. If any person in the executive branch or in the government is indicted by the grand jury, my policy will be to immediately suspend him. If he is convicted, he will, of course, be automatically discharged. I have expressed to the appropriate authorities my view that no individual holding, in the past or at present, a position of major importance in the administration should be given immunity from prosecution.

After condemning "any attempts to cover up in this case, no matter who is involved," he left the room.

In the space of just three minutes, Nixon had effectively abandoned his long-standing position that no senior member of his administration had been involved in Watergate. He left the cleanup operation to his press secretary. Nicknamed Zig-Zag by reporters, Ron Ziegler was known for his frequently incomprehensible pronouncements, which were termed "ziggeratti." He had become the youngest White House press secretary in history at the age of twenty-nine, after several years in advertising and a stint as a tour guide at Disneyland, where he drove a Jungle Cruise boat thirty-three times a day. As pressure from Watergate mounted, he had frequently berated reporters for "shabby journalism" and "character assassination." After months of being abused, misled, and sometimes lied to, the press now resembled a pack of angry sports fans baying for blood. The faux English club had become a coliseum.

For the next half hour, reporters bombarded Ziegler with questions he was unable, or unwilling, to answer. *What happened on March 21? Who conducted the investigation on behalf of the president? Was John Dean still on the president's team? What about the broader allegations of espionage and sabotage? Were indictments expected? Was anyone planning to resign? What was the purpose of Mitchell's visit to the White House the previous weekend? What happened to the Dean report? Have anyone's duties been curtailed? Did Nixon stand by his earlier statement that no one on the White House staff had knowledge of the Watergate matter?*

By prior agreement with Nixon, Ziegler kept referring to the president's latest remarks as the "operative statement" on Watergate. He repeated the word "operative" six times, like a mantra. This gave R. W. Apple Jr. of *The New York Times* an opening. Known as Johnny to his friends, he had honed his verbal sparring skills as one of the "boys on the bus" covering the 1972 presidential campaign.

"Ron, could I follow up on your comment about the operative statement?" he asked innocently, before delivering a hammer blow. "Would it be fair for us to infer, since what the president said today is now considered the operative statement, that the other statement is no longer operative, that it is now inoperative?"

Ziegler owed his advance to an aura of Boy Scout eagerness combined with a talent for obfuscation, but now, entangled in his own circumlocutions, he momentarily dropped his guard. "The president refers to the fact that there is new material. Therefore, this is the operative statement. The others are inoperative."

"*Kallump,*" recorded one of the ringside observers. "Ziegler was down, and his wavy black hair was no longer parted. The life had gone out of his muscular legs, and his vacant stare never looked so empty. Many in the crowd cried for the kill, and others mercifully asked that the fight be stopped. While there never had been a presidential press secretary saddled with a Watergate, neither had there been one who declared that all his previous declarations were so much horse manure." In vain did Ziegler insist that he was merely relaying fresh information. It was his embrace of the euphemistic term "inoperative," with its Orwellian connotation of rewriting history, that did him in. The word "inoperative" would be associated with the name Ziegler forevermore.

Nixon's big announcement had not worked out the way he had planned. He had hoped to receive credit for "breaking the case" but instead had opened the floodgates to new lines of inquiry for investigative reporters, more mistrustful of government than ever. Following his appearance in the press room, he retreated to EOB 175 to commiserate with

Haldeman and Ehrlichman. He still had a big evening ahead of him—a state dinner for 110 guests in honor of "the Italian," with Frank Sinatra providing the entertainment. The conversation soon turned to anticipating John Dean's next move.

"I have no intention to see Dean again, unless it's useful," said Nixon as Manolo Sanchez served everybody Cokes. "I don't think you can control him. He's fanatic." He would not talk to Henry Petersen either "except to suck all the information I can get from him, you know what I mean."

Ehrlichman thought Dean could be provoked into making a "slanderous" public statement that the president's men could exploit. Nixon eagerly looked forward to the day when they could hammer their enemies with libel suits.

"I'd use the most vicious libel lawyer there is. I'd sue every son of a bitch . . . Sue, sue, right down the line."

This was only partially comforting to Ehrlichman. He feared that he and Haldeman had both become "damaged goods" even if they managed to "beat the rap." He had just bumped into a mournful-looking Henry Kissinger in the hallway. "I could have sworn I had a spot of leprosy," said Ehrlichman. "He greeted me like my wife had just died."

Nixon tried to cheer up his aides by suggesting they work for the foundation he was planning to establish out in California to promote his presidential legacy. It was going to be "a hell of a big thing." Ehrlichman refused to be consoled. He feared he would be unable to practice law even if he was cleared of criminal offenses.

"You can be my partner," offered Nixon.

"Yeah, and we can try traffic cases out in San Clemente," said Ehrlichman sourly.

"To hell with the traffic cases," said Nixon, to general laughter.

Nixon went off to the residence to dress for dinner, carefully adjusting his black bow tie before greeting his guests at the North Portico. Henry Kissinger would remember the occasion as the "last normal dinner" of the Nixon presidency. The atmosphere was "festive and relaxed." The White House was "like the *Titanic:* one part of the ship was flooding but no one else was aware, or affected to be aware, of the danger. The band played on."

The band, on this occasion, was again the President's Own, decked out in glittering red dress uniforms. They dined on duckling, wild rice, and artichokes. Nixon acted the suave and gracious host, hiding his inner turmoil. He compared Sinatra to the Washington Monument, a man who rose to the very top of his profession from humble beginnings as the son of an Italian immigrant. The singer, who had come out of retirement to perform at the White House, responded by serenading the audience with his most popular numbers, including "Fly Me to the Moon," "Ol' Man River," and "I've Got the World on a String." There was a standing ovation at the end.

"Did you stay for the entertainment?" Nixon asked Kissinger toward midnight, when they connected by phone. He had retired to the Lincoln Sitting Room for a nightcap and wanted to talk about the events of the day. They had barely spoken since their morning meeting with "the Italian."

"Yes, it was moving," the national security adviser replied. "One of the most moving things I've heard."

"You know, Frank's voice is gone, as he told me before he came. But by gosh, you know, the emotion in the room was just unbelievable. I think some of the people were crying."

Nixon could no longer keep up the pretense. Were people crying for "Ol' Man River" or for the old man in the Oval Office? His upbeat voice finally cracked.

"Well, rather a hard day, wasn't it?"

"It was hard for you," said Kissinger, his Germanic gravitas wrapped in the consoling tones of a professional undertaker. "When I think of the discipline with which you conducted the meeting in the morning."

Nixon sighed deeply. "And then going through the evening."

His thoughts turned to the agony of the people close to him.

"The problem I have is that I can't look at it in the detached way I really should: *these people, they're guilty, throw them out, and go on.* Just the personal things are . . . Goddamn, I think of these good men . . ."

". . . who wanted to do the right thing."

"Yeah, it's going to splash on a lot of them." Faithful Haldeman would probably have to go. "They're going to rip him up good."

Nixon had avoided speaking to Kissinger about his Watergate troubles until now. If he alluded to the subject at all, it was only to repeat his

public denials that he had known about the misdeeds of his subordinates. For his part, Kissinger kept his distance from the scandals cours-
ing through the White House. He prided himself on being a substance
person, not a process person. Furthermore, his expertise was foreign
policy, the one area of government where even the critics were willing
to credit the president with significant achievements.

Over the last few days, however, Kissinger's complacency had turned
to alarm. His chief informant was Leonard Garment, a former law partner of Nixon's who had been brought into the White House as the in-
house liberal, to counterbalance conservatives like the speechwriter
Patrick Buchanan. On April 14, the day of the futile confrontation with
Mitchell, Garment had visited Kissinger's corner office to tell him that
Watergate was "about to blow up." It was not just the break-in at Democratic Party headquarters; it was a long series of other burglaries and
conspiracies implicating the highest levels of the administration. In
Garment's view, "only radical surgery and the fullest admission of error
could avert catastrophe." Haldeman and Ehrlichman would definitely
have to go. Even the president was threatened unless he acted to "brutally eradicate the rot."

Discussing Garment's recommendations with Nixon, Kissinger said
the two men should "resign on the grounds that their usefulness is
impaired." A White House staffer needed to be above suspicion, "like
Caesar's wife."

"The major thing now, Mr. President, if I may say so, is to protect the
presidency and your authority."

"Well, if we can." For a few seconds, Nixon sounded like a defeated
man, on the verge of tears. "If we can, we will, and if we don't, then what
the hell . . . I've even considered the possibility of, frankly, just throwing
myself on the sword . . ."

"No, no!"

". . . and letting Agnew take over. What the hell!"

"That is out of the question, with all due respect, Mr. President. That
cannot be considered. The personality, what it would do to the presidency, and the historical injustice of it. Why should you do it? What
good would it do? Whom would it help? It wouldn't help the country. It
wouldn't help any of the individuals involved . . . and of course it would
be personally unjust."

The conversation wore on after midnight, with each man attempting to bolster the other.

"Don't you get discouraged," Nixon told Kissinger.

"Mr. President, I'm not discouraged."

"You do your job. Two or three of us have got to stick around to hold the goddamn fort."

Kissinger tried flattery and an appeal to posterity, tools that had served him so well in the past.

"You saved this country, Mr. President. The history books will show that, when no one will know what Watergate means."

"Nobody really will know what they put a president through on a thing like this," said Nixon.

"It's inhuman, Mr. President. These bastards know damn well that you couldn't have known about it. If one considers all the things you had to go through, you couldn't be a police judge, too. You're running the government, you're doing all the negotiating, you're carrying a bigger load than any president has."

Nixon was momentarily revived.

"God, we were going to Russia and China, and ending the war, and negotiating. I wasn't even thinking about the goddamn campaign . . . If I had been spending time on the campaign, maybe I wouldn't have pulled off Vietnam."

After ruminating about the "fun evening," Nixon reverted to Watergate. "Well, it will be a great day on the other side for all of our enemies, won't it? The *Times,* the *Post,* the rest. Shit."

Kissinger urged him to "gather the wagons and pull it through, as you've done so often." The priority now was "to get the pus out of the system. Let it be squeezed out a little at a time."

"That's right, that's right."

The president had reached his national security adviser at an after-dinner party for Sinatra. The guests included Vice President Spiro Agnew, who came into the room just as Kissinger was finishing his telephone call with Nixon. They began chatting about Watergate.

"The president is kidding himself if he thinks he can avoid firing

Haldeman and Ehrlichman," said Agnew. "He will be lucky if he can save himself."

Kissinger was shocked by such unsentimental brutality on the part of Agnew. The vice president had assumed the role of Nixon's most outspoken acolyte, lashing out at his enemies with unmatched zest. He had dismissed reporters as "nattering nabobs of negativism" and attacked critics of the Vietnam War as "pusillanimous pussyfooters." He out-Nixoned Nixon in presenting himself as the voice of the "silent majority." If the president's chief defender denigrated him in such a cynical fashion, things must be even worse than Kissinger imagined. Agnew's "icy detachment" from Nixon's political tribulations "brought a premonition of imminent disaster."

What Kissinger did not know at the time was that Agnew had troubles of his own that were at least equal to those of the president. The previous week he had confessed to Haldeman that he was being investigated by a federal grand jury for taking bribes from consultants while serving as governor of Maryland. He had sought Haldeman's assistance in shutting down the investigation, but the chief of staff had refused to lift a finger. Agnew felt abandoned. He was angry with both Haldeman and Nixon for declining to come to his aid. If they refused to help him, why should he help them?

The Agnew investigation, which was still under wraps, contained a hidden plus for Nixon. In the event of his death or removal from office, the Constitution mandated that he would be succeeded by the vice president. It had already occurred to Nixon that people might think twice about replacing him with an obviously unworthy successor. As he once joked to Kissinger, only half facetiously, "Agnew is my insurance policy against assassination."

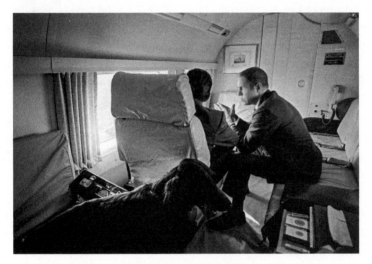

*Nixon flies to Camp David on Marine One with Haldeman
and King Timahoe, February 1971.*

The tension of the last few days had left Nixon exhausted and even more sleep deprived than usual. He was planning a trip to Key Biscayne for Easter weekend but felt the need to get away earlier, if only for a night, to "try to see if I can break my sleeping pattern." On Wednesday morning, he suggested to Haldeman and Ehrlichman that they chopper up to Camp David for a change of scenery. A little rest had become as "necessary as hell." Nixon thought about inviting Kissinger as well, but quickly dismissed the idea. Henry would just be "a pain in the ass."

The helicopter ride to Catoctin Mountain in Maryland took half an hour. They arrived at six as the sun was going down. The president settled into his suite in Aspen Lodge, while Haldeman and Ehrlichman went to a staff cabin a few minutes' walk away. From the entranceway Nixon walked through a large living room with a fireplace, vaulted cathedral ceiling, and assortment of chintzy furniture. Behind the living room was a sunroom overlooking a wide terrace and banks of tulips just beginning to bloom. Another lower terrace led down some stone steps to a peanut-shaped swimming pool heated throughout the year, one of several improvements that Nixon had made to the comfortable but far from luxurious lodge. Along a corridor in a separate wing of the cabin were the bedrooms and a wood-paneled den Nixon used as a study. It too boasted a cozy fireplace, like the one in the Lincoln Sitting Room back at the White House.

The evening was the opposite of relaxing. Nixon was fretting about the threat from Dean, who had reacted angrily to the president's "no immunity" announcement. Aides reported that Dean was "charging around the White House like a wild animal" and spreading word that he would not be intimidated. Nixon understood that it would be exceptionally damaging, and potentially fatal to his presidency, if Dean broke ranks completely. As the man who had managed the cover-up from the very beginning, Dean was privy to the administration's most embarrassing secrets, including the most recent blackmail attempt by Howard Hunt. As Nixon explained to Haldeman, the renegade White House counsel effectively had "a gun to our head."

Nixon now suspected that the Justice Department might have secretly immunized Dean. To test this theory, he phoned Henry Petersen, claiming he had heard the news from Dean himself. This was a gross misinterpretation of an offhand remark by Dean three days earlier, but Nixon made a good show of his indignation.

"That simply isn't so," Petersen protested. As the Justice Department official in charge of criminal prosecutions, he would have had to approve such a step.

"I have it on tape," said Nixon. "Do you want to hear it?"

No need, said Petersen. He would find out from the prosecutors directly. Nixon's talk about a tape made little impression on him. He assumed that presidents routinely recorded their important conversations. He called back a little later to report that Dean's lawyers had denied the story. They had been negotiating for immunity, but no immunity had been conferred, "either formally or informally." This seemed to reassure the president.

"What else is new?" Nixon asked.

Petersen had a bombshell to report. While he had been meeting with Nixon on Sunday afternoon, the prosecutors had learned about the raid on the office of Daniel Ellsberg's psychiatrist in California. Acting on a tip from Dean, the FBI had discovered the photographs of Dr. Fielding's office and parking spot taken by Liddy and Hunt. Investigators had finally made the connection between the photographs and the subsequent burglary. This was yet more evidence of illegal activity by the White House Plumbers, in addition to Watergate.

"I know about that," the president snapped. "It's involved with national security. I don't want it opened up. Keep the hell out of it! Your mandate is to investigate Watergate."

Hanging up the phone, Nixon turned to Haldeman and Ehrlichman who had joined him for dinner. "There's no reason for them to get into it," he told them, referring to the FBI. "What those fellas did was no crime. They ought to get a medal for going after Ellsberg."

As Haldeman recorded in his diary later that evening, the dinner conversation was "rather painful because the President got into the whole problem of whether John and I should go." He envisaged three possibilities. They might be "nailed in open court by Magruder which we can't let happen"; they could resign of their own accord, which might at least forestall indictments; or they could hang on, in which case they would be destroyed "by constant nibbling."

"We don't want to be destroyed, so therefore we have to move," Nixon concluded. "We have to figure out another strategy: get out and fight like hell."

Even though Nixon insisted he had not made up his mind, he seemed to be preparing the two men for their inevitable departure. He tried to boost their spirits by promising that they could continue to visit Camp David, "regardless of what happens," as long as he was president. Haldeman had the feeling that Nixon saw "no real way out except for us to pull out and fight." It seemed like a "farewell dinner."

Reporters had been camped outside John Dean's town house on Quay Street in Old Town Alexandria since Tuesday evening. He felt like a prisoner in his own home, which overlooked a park and the river beyond. To leave the house without being ambushed, he had to walk across a back alleyway, enter the home of a friend, and exit onto the next street.

Dean learned about Nixon's exchange with Petersen about immunity from his lawyer Charlie Shaffer. He was indignant. The president was obviously playing some kind of game when he claimed to have Dean "on tape" stating that he already had immunity. Dean asked Shaffer to send word back to Petersen that he should request the tape from the White House. "I guarantee you he'll never get it," he scoffed.

Dean's suspicion that he was being set up as a scapegoat was heightened by a story in the *Post* under the joint byline of Bob Woodward and Carl Bernstein. The article was splashed across the front page, along with mug shots of Dean, Mitchell, and Magruder. The opening paragraphs read:

Former Attorney General John N. Mitchell and White House counsel John W. Dean III approved and helped plan the Watergate bugging operation, according to President Nixon's former special assistant, Jeb Stuart Magruder.

Mitchell and Dean later arranged to buy the silence of the seven convicted Watergate conspirators, Magruder has also said.

There was a big mistake in the lead paragraph. Dean had participated in some of the early conversations about Liddy's Gemstone plan but had not approved the Watergate operation. Quite the opposite: he had dismissed it as crazy and assumed it had been turned off. The story was attributed to sources in the White House and reelection committee. His resignation as counsel to the president was reported to be "imminent." This was all confirmation to Dean that his enemies in the administration were out to get him. He decided to fight back through the press.

Dean had recently hired another lawyer by the name of Robert McCandless to handle his contacts with reporters. The gregarious, well-connected McCandless also happened to be his brother-in-law through a former marriage. (They had both married daughters of a prominent U.S. senator, Tom Hennings of Missouri.) Together, they worked on a statement calling for release of all the facts in the Watergate scandal. The sting came in the final paragraph: "Some may hope or think that I will become a scapegoat in the Watergate case. Anyone who believes this does not know me, know the true facts, nor understand our system of justice." He had his secretary read the statement to the wire services and a couple of newspapers, including the *Post*.

Ripping the story from the wires, an alarmed Ron Ziegler rushed to brief the president, who had returned to Washington from Camp David immediately after breakfast. Nixon ordered Ziegler to telephone Dean to find out what was going on. He should say he was calling from his own office, not the Oval Office. The White House operator connected them.

"Hi, John," Ziegler began. "Saw your statement."

"Got a problem with it?" Dean's voice had a sharp edge.

Ziegler said he would need to make clear to reporters that the president was not looking for "a scapegoat." He was searching for "the truth." Assuming that Dean was no longer showing up for work, Ziegler asked if he had reached him at home.

"No, I'm here in the office," Dean said calmly. Ziegler quickly hung up.

Dean was not engaged in White House business, however. He had come to his office, down the corridor from Nixon's EOB hideaway, to work on his Watergate testimony. At the urging of his lawyers, he was assembling "a detailed chronology of everything I knew—dates and statements that I could swear to." That afternoon, he filed a request with the White House archivist for "more specific information" about his meetings with the president, including the duration of each session and who else was present. As a bargaining chip with the Justice Department, he also made a list of all his telephone calls with Henry Petersen. If the prosecutors refused to grant him immunity, he had a backup plan. He would testify in open Senate hearings, due to get under way on May 17.

In the meantime, the McCandless press operation was producing results. *The New York Times* had run an article that morning describing Dean as "alone but confident," ready to "guide investigators to other members of the President's inner circle." The story cited "close friends" of the White House counsel. In a conversation with Carl Bernstein of *The Washington Post,* a Dean "associate" named Haldeman and Ehrlichman as the masterminds of the cover-up. Dean, the associate insisted, had never done anything, including making arrangements for the payment of hush money, without the approval of his superiors. The "Dean report" exonerating White House officials for involvement in Watergate was a fiction. The associate told Bernstein that Dean wanted to be able to swear under oath that he had not talked to the press. Interviews with the White House counsel were out for now, "but that doesn't mean that you and I can't do a little visiting with each other."

After pooling his information with Woodward, Bernstein hammered out a story for the next day's newspaper. He called Ziegler for comment around 9:30 p.m. The *Post* would report that Dean was preparing to tell the grand jury everything he knew about Watergate, implicating people both "above and below himself." He would also allege "a coverup by White House officials, including H. R. Haldeman, President Nixon's principal assistant," who wanted to make Dean "a sacrificial lamb." Ziegler called Dean again to see if he knew anything.

"Oh fuck," said Dean, when Ziegler outlined what "a Dean associate" had been telling the *Post.* "I have a pretty good suspicion who that is. He's got things scrambled. I never mentioned Haldeman. I just said 'higher-ups.'"

Ziegler wanted Dean to call the *Post* to deny the story. Dean refused. There was "some fact and some fiction" in the report, and he did not want to get involved. Ziegler called Bernstein himself. It was getting very late for the White House to play defense. The story ran with only minor modifications.

Haldeman briefed Nixon on the *Post*'s story in a late-night phone call. The president had retired to the Lincoln Sitting Room. The chief of staff speculated that Dean now had "other people playing his game" who were using tougher language than Dean intended.

"His lawyer probably?" asked Nixon.

"I would say his lawyer, yes."

"We just batten down the hatches and take it," said Nixon.

They veered off into a discussion about the coming Easter weekend. Haldeman explained that he and Ehrlichman could not accompany the president to Key Biscayne as planned because they had to meet with their lawyers. "We can just say you're going down to spend Easter with your family and we're spending Easter with our families." This seemed like a plausible excuse to Nixon. "That's right. It's a family deal." The two men then returned to the subject of the traitors in their midst.

"The difficult one to figure out here is Dean," said Nixon.

"Yes, sir."

"Goddamn him."

"He's totally distorted in his own mind now and consequently, I guess, very dangerous," said Haldeman. "Sort of pathetic at the same time."

"Trying to save himself," said the president.

"Lost his moorings."

"Saying anything."

"Swinging out in all kinds of ways."

"That's right."

Wearily, Nixon hung up the phone.

J ulie Nixon was worried about her father. He had always kept his
political life separate from his private life but was now "withdrawing into his own world." He was excusing himself from family
dinners, pleading his heavy workload. He had even stopped using the
new bowling alley underneath the North Portico that had given him so
much pleasure just a short time before. On Thursday evening, he had
gone for a river cruise by himself on the *Sequoia*, past George Washington's grave. During previous moments of crisis, including the darkest
days in the Vietnam War, the family had come together, but "this time
he was on his own." Always close to her father, Julie had never really
experienced the "Gloomy Gus" side of his personality that others talked
about. She considered him a naturally "upbeat person, no matter how
tense a situation gets." There was obviously something "terribly wrong."

She did what she could to revive his spirits. She phoned him regularly with nuggets of uplifting news. She tried to take his mind off
Watergate by talking enthusiastically about other matters. She sent him
handwritten "Dear Daddy" letters, passing on praise from people she
met, which he read with obvious pride to Haldeman. When he arrived
in Key Biscayne on Friday evening, he received a note from Julie that
said simply, "We love you, we stand with you." None of it seemed to
help. They had come to Florida to relax, but the tension in the air was
"so thick that it was almost unbearable."

The Nixons had been spending holidays in Key Biscayne since the early 1950s, when life on the island revolved around a single hotel, a lone gas station, and a small shopping center. The rest was half-wild mango groves and a few modest beachfront houses. They bought their vacation home on Bay Lane in 1968 for $125,000 from Senator George Smathers, who had introduced Nixon to Bebe Rebozo back in 1951. Bebe owned the house next door. A property farther along the street belonged to another Nixon friend, the aerosol magnate Bob Abplanalp, who rented it out to White House support staff. The military had built a helicopter pad jutting out into the bay to make it easy for the president to fly in and out. The Nixon house was a typical 1950s ranch-style bungalow with three bedrooms, plus a partially enclosed front entrance adjoining a circular driveway. Built out of whitewashed concrete blocks and surrounded by a few scraggly palm trees, the house was not nearly as luxurious as the hilltop villa in San Clemente. But the location was ideal. Sitting on his lounge chair, books and papers by his side, Nixon looked out onto a private beach and the serene waters of Biscayne Bay. The Miami skyscrapers five miles away looked like abstract boxes on the horizon.

Nixon stuck to his typical Key Biscayne routine, but his thoughts were elsewhere. He would return from his late afternoon swim not saying anything. He joined the family for dinner and the traditional private movie afterward but was morose and uncommunicative. He ignored Pat, who was doing her best to be supportive. On Friday, they watched a Frank Sinatra movie, *Some Came Running,* to celebrate the singer who had entertained Nixon's guests three nights earlier. The Saturday night movie was *The Seven Year Itch* with Marilyn Monroe and Tom Ewell, a romantic comedy about a publishing executive caught in a midlife crisis. On one of these occasions, Julie later recalled, she made sure to sit next to her father.

"Mother's trying so hard to make things right, and you don't realize it," she told him. "It's hard for her too."

"I guess so," said Nixon.

Julie felt terrible throughout the movie for adding to her father's burdens at a time when he was obviously under great stress. But he turned to her at the end and said, "You're right. It's hard for her too. I'll try."

Nixon's career was defined by crisis. He had been tested time and time again, from the Hiss case in the late 1940s to his Checkers speech to failed runs for the presidency and the governorship of California. In every single case, he had eventually emerged stronger and more resilient. He studied political crises the way others study the stock market or the racetrack or nineteenth-century Russian literature. After losing to Jack Kennedy in 1960, he had prepared for his second presidential campaign by writing a book called *Six Crises*. "The easiest period in a crisis situation is actually the battle itself," he wrote. "The most difficult is the period of indecision—whether to fight or run away. And the most dangerous period is the aftermath. It is then, with all his resources spent and his guard down, that an individual must watch out for dulled reactions and faulty judgment." This was a good description of the last few months, when, lulled into overconfidence by his smashing reelection victory, he had failed to pay sufficient attention to the crisis around the corner.

He had been battling others for so long that political confrontation had become part of his very identity. He relished being the underdog. "Once you learn that you've got to work harder than everybody else it becomes a way of life," he explained to a friend. "In your own mind you have nothing to lose so you take plenty of chances and if you do your homework many of them pay off. It is then you understand, for the first time, that you have the advantage because your competitors can't risk what they have already. It's a piece of cake until you get to the top. You find you can't stop playing the game the way you've always played it because it is part of you and you need it as much as an arm and a leg . . . You continue to walk on the edge of the precipice because over the years you have become fascinated by how close to the edge you can walk without losing your balance."

In the past, he had taken the view that crises were good for the soul. As he wrote in *Six Crises*, they enabled a man to "discover all the latent strengths that he never knew he had." In more stable times, these qualities remained dormant. "Crisis can indeed be agony. But it is the exquisite agony which a man might not want to experience again—yet would not for the world have missed."

Nevertheless, this crisis was different from the previous ones. One difference was that he was now president, and therefore had much more to lose than when he was still on the rise, challenging people above him. Another was that there was no obvious escape route, however obsessively he studied the problem and however much he was willing to risk. Under attack for his campaign funding practices while running for the vice presidency in 1952, he had staked everything on a bold appeal to the American people. When he lost to JFK, he knew that he was still a young man who could run for the presidency again in a few years. On this occasion, he was hemmed in on all sides: by a judicial system that proved impossible to manipulate and obstruct, a Congress under the control of the opposition party, a vengeful press, and subordinates like Dean and Magruder bent on protecting themselves. The usual levers of power and political influence had ceased to respond to his command. After months of inaction, he had finally become aware of the danger and had struggled mightily to find a solution, to no effect.

Even worse, the crisis Nixon now faced was largely of his own making. He had created the culture that allowed the cancer to spread. He had failed to cut the tumor out while there was still time. He had encouraged his aides to perjure themselves, even though he knew from his experience in the Hiss case that lying under oath was a potentially fatal trap. He had approved the payment of hush money. Even his latest gambit—denying Dean immunity from prosecution in the hope of bringing him to heel—had backfired. Dean had become a bigger threat than ever. Nixon had contributed to each stage of the unfolding tragedy. He had given his enemies a sword that they had "twisted with relish" into his open wounds. If he had been in their position, he reflected later, he would probably have done the same thing.

In the short term, there appeared to be only one way forward. For the past twenty-four hours, he had been pondering a memo written by his favorite "bomb thrower," Patrick Buchanan. Along with Colson, Buchanan was one of the architects of the "silent majority" strategy designed to cleave off large segments of the Democratic coalition. Still only thirty-four, he had honed his writing skills as a conservative editorial writer on a St. Louis newspaper before being hired by Nixon in 1964. Drawing on his own experiences as a working-class Irish Catholic, Buchanan had helped articulate the politics of grievance that propelled Nixon to the presidency in 1968. Within the White House, he had developed a reputation as a scourge of the liberal establishment and conservative true believer. Nixon prized him for both his speechwriting skills and his mischievous streak. "Buchanan," he once told him, "you're the only extremist I know with a sense of humor." And now this 100 percent Nixon loyalist was urging the president to clean house before it was too late. As he put it in his memo,

> We have used up all our capital with the public on [Watergate]; any game plan or scape-goating, or sophistry or attempts to pro- tect one person or another will only force others to conclude that the President is involved, and that the cover-up continues. The credibility of the President and the Presidency will then become suspect. We have to come clean on this one: there is no margin for error left, no more credibility in the account on this issue.

On Easter morning, the Filipino stewards laid out the Sunday newspa- pers as usual on the glass-topped dining room table in the Nixon house on Bay Lane. When Nixon came down to breakfast at 7:35, he was greeted by the sight of four Watergate-related stories on the front page of *The Washington Post*. The lead story, splashed across the top of the page, was headlined "Watergate: A Crisis of Authority for President Nixon." The political writer David S. Broder speculated that Watergate was about to become "the seventh crisis" of Nixon's career. "Under unrelenting pres- sure, the carefully constructed facade of cool White House control has begun to crack," Broder reported. "A rush of events that came almost too fast for comprehension" had dragged the president deeper into the Watergate mire than anyone ever imagined. According to a Gallup opin- ion poll, four in ten Americans now believed that Nixon had known about the Watergate break-in in advance. Another story reported that the grand jury was investigating an alleged link between Haldeman and a $350,000 campaign fund used to pay off the Watergate conspirators.

After breakfast, Nixon began making morale-boosting calls to his staff, his regular practice at Easter. He reached out first to Chuck Col- son, whose role in Watergate had become the subject of growing press speculation. Colson wanted to explain his telephone call to Magruder in early 1972 urging him to "make a decision" on Liddy's intelligence- gathering proposals. According to Magruder, this call had helped precipitate the chain of events that led to the break-in. Colson wanted the president to know it had been entirely "innocent." He had been unaware of the bugging plan.

"I believe you completely," Nixon assured his former aide. They wished each other "Happy Easter."

Next, he called John Dean. "Good morning, John," he began. "I'm just calling to wish you and your wife a happy Easter. It's a lovely day here in Florida."

Dean was at home in Alexandria, Virginia. He had been up until four that morning, working on his statement to the Senate Watergate Committee. He had drunk even more than his "usual generous quantity" of scotch, figuring that he could sleep off the hangover on Sunday morning. He had rolled out of bed naked at 8:24 a.m. to pick up the ringing phone. This seemed like a bad dream.

"Uh, fine," he replied, still half-asleep. "Happy Easter to you." He wondered to himself if anyone had ever told Nixon that he was "full of shit."

"I want to wish you well, we'll make it through," said the deep voice at the other end of the line. "You said this is a cancer that must be cut out. I want you to know that I am following that advice."

Nixon reminded Dean that he was still his counsel. He probed for information about his intentions with regard to the grand jury and sought his "advice" on legal questions. They talked about the immunity laws and the destruction of documents from Howard Hunt's safe. After fifteen minutes, Nixon said he needed to get ready to go to church. As he hung up the phone, Dean felt momentarily ashamed for doubting the president. Perhaps he really was determined to cut out the cancer. It had been kind of him to call. It was the last time they would ever talk.

Next up were Haldeman and Ehrlichman, who were both at Camp David, piecing together their legal defense strategy. Nixon's Easter message to them, and perhaps to himself, was that they had survived even tougher times before. The previous Easter, they had been fighting off criticism over the bombing of North Vietnam. "Just remember you're doing the right thing," Nixon told Haldeman. "That's what I used to think when I killed some innocent children in Hanoi."

After getting off the phone with his aides, Nixon joined his family for

The Nixon family after posing for an Easter portrait at Key Biscayne.
According to Julie Nixon, the tension was "so thick that it was almost unbearable."

a long-planned photo shoot outside. They lined up stiffly on the lawn overlooking the bay in their Easter finery beside a pair of pink Easter bunnies. When the formal shoot was over, Pat moved away from the group and stared off into the distance. Her daughters—Tricia in a Little Bo Peep outfit with bonnet and Julie in bright blue and yellow—looked at her concerned, their husbands by their sides. Nixon had his head down, momentarily estranged from the rest of the family. After a few seconds of awkwardness and private agony, they trooped back dutifully inside the house.

A few minutes before eleven, the Nixons made the two-minute drive to the Presbyterian church at the northern end of the island for the Easter service. They were joined by Bebe Rebozo. The pastor described the cycle of sin and redemption, urging his parishioners "to fish or cut bait." It was never too late to repent. On the way out, Nixon noticed a protester with a crudely written sign that read, "Is the president honest?" During his first four years in office, he reflected, he had been greeted by antiwar slogans. The national conversation now was all about Watergate.

Nixon returned to his residence for lunch. At 1:50, he walked to the Key Biscayne helipad. The presidential helicopter lifted off four minutes later, heading in a northeasterly direction across the sparkling blue expanse of the Atlantic Ocean, far beyond American territorial waters. He was accompanied by Bebe, his military aide, and two Secret Service agents. At 3:10, the chopper landed on a remote island in the Bahamas. This was Grand Cay, the private playground of Nixon's aerosol magnate buddy, Robert Abplanalp. A golf cart carried Nixon to a two-story villa high on a hill on the southern side of the island, with magnificent views of the pristine blue-green waters of a sheltered archipelago. The master bedroom and private study set aside for the president looked out over the ocean, small terrace, and private swimming pool.

The Bronx-born son of a Swiss-immigrant truck mechanic, Abplanalp (German for "from the mountain plain") was popularly known as "the president's other friend." Like Rebozo and Nixon himself, he personified the Nixonian ideal of the self-made man who lifted himself out of poverty through grit and perseverance. A college dropout, he had even won a Horatio Alger award for his incessant tinkering with faulty aerosol valves until he finally came up with a reliable product at low cost. "He had to bust his hump to do it," an admiring business acquaintance told *The New York Times*. "There's nothing like an aerosol can sitting on the shelf and starting to leak." As his reward for fixing that problem, he now got to indulge his passion for sportfishing and fast boats. The burly, six-foot Abplanalp had known Nixon for much less time than Rebozo had, only since 1961. Their friendship was cemented by Abplanalp's campaign contributions to Nixon, assistance with real estate transactions, and invitations to his island paradise. Even more than Key Biscayne and San Clemente, the solitude and watery splendor of Grand Cay was the ideal antidote for presidential stress. Nixon had made seventeen trips there since becoming president, landing on a helipad constructed specially for him.

A little over a mile long and three hundred yards wide, Grand Cay resembled the island fortress of an evil mastermind in a James Bond movie when the president came to visit. Bright lights illuminated the island at night. Frogmen inspected every square inch of the hull of Abplanalp's fifty-five-foot marlin-hunting racing boat, *Sea Lion II*. Secret Service men patrolled the beachfront in speedboats. A warship

*Nixon enjoys the sunset on Grand Cay with his friends Robert Abplanalp
(owner of the property) and Bebe Rebozo, May 1973.*

lingered offshore, turning away any vessel that got too close. A network of shortwave radio towers on Grand Cay and the neighboring island of Walker's Cay provided voice circuits direct to Washington reliable enough to handle a presidential order for Armageddon. Emergency generators made the island self-sufficient in power.

Within ten minutes of arriving on Grand Cay, Nixon was in the ocean, swimming in the surf with his two rich friends. That evening, after a fresh fish dinner, they went out for a two-hour cruise, beneath an almost full moon. The president's favorite spot on *Sea Lion* was in the lookout chair, perched precariously on stilts twenty-five feet above the deck. "That's where Nixon likes to ride, up in the 'tuna tower,'" Abplanalp would tell a reporter a few months later. "It scares the hell out of me every time." Nixon, however, was adamant. An hour or two on a boat with the wind in his face restored him to life in a way that nothing else did. High above the waves that stretched to the horizon, and beyond the reach of aides and reporters and even his own family, he could finally be alone with his demons.

Nixon had been staying on Grand Cay with Rebozo and Abplanalp, watching the movie *The Notorious Landlady,* on the night of June 17, 1972, when burglars on the payroll of his reelection committee broke in to the Watergate. For ten months, he had failed to recognize the scope of the scandal and deal with it effectively. Back on the island on Easter Day, he made a painful decision.

Nixon flew back to Key Biscayne in the morning with Bebe. Prior to leaving for Grand Cay, he had selected, in great secrecy, three men for advice on what to do next. One was Ron Ziegler, his press secretary, who was filling in for Haldeman as his loyal confidant. The second was Pat Buchanan, the author of the "clean house" memo. The third was a prominent lawyer, Chapman "Chappy" Rose, a friend from the Eisenhower days. Buchanan and Rose (traveling as Mr. X) had flown down to Florida from Washington on a presidential jet. Ziegler had briefed them on the latest legal developments, and the tortuous history of Watergate, while Nixon was enjoying his moonlight cruise with Abplanalp and Rebozo. The three of them had argued back and forth but, by midnight, were agreed that Haldeman, Ehrlichman, and Dean would all have to go. "Get out in front of it, get it over with," was Buchanan's position, accepted with reluctance by the other two.

At noon on Easter Monday, the three men joined Nixon in the living room of his home on Bay Lane. "It was an emotional session," Buchanan later recorded. "Chappy's eyes were wet; RN was deeply moved by what had to be done." They considered all the options, with Ziegler playing devil's advocate, forcing Buchanan and Rose to justify their positions. Nixon complained that he was unable to function as president effectively as long as his top aides were under constant attack. As the meeting dragged on, it became clear that he agreed with Buchanan. He was validating a decision he had made in private on Grand Cay. Rose supplied the clinching argument, invoking a historical parallel that was sure to resonate with Nixon.

"The first essential for a prime minister is to be a good butcher," he told Nixon, quoting the nineteenth-century English statesman William Gladstone.

By the end of the three-hour session, Nixon also had tears in his eyes. The truth was he had never been "a good butcher." He did not want to order Haldeman and Ehrlichman to resign. The initiative had to come from them. Nixon suggested that Buchanan make the call to Haldeman. Buchanan passed the buck to Ziegler. The press secretary had been a Haldeman protégé from their time together at the J. Walter Thompson advertising agency. Ziegler stared out the window and said nothing.

"There are no good choices," said Nixon.

Nixon joined Bebe for another boat ride, leaving Ziegler to phone Haldeman. Ziegler reached the chief of staff at his home in Georgetown in the early evening. Haldeman had just got back from Camp David.

"His mind is made up," said Ziegler. "It was made up at Grand Cay last night." Reading from his notes, he relayed Nixon's somewhat disjointed thoughts:

> There's no way this will not go down in history as a very bad chapter. The Presidency is seriously hurt. I must accept responsibility. Haldeman and Ehrlichman are strong men, probably the strongest men who have ever served the Presidency. But as we look at the political forces against the President, the country must have a President moving in a direction. I know there will be a clamor. This will not pass. I'm still involved. Charges and claims are made that I knew about it and was aware of it. But I must make a decision and move ahead . . . I believe in these two men, I love these two men. The White House can't respond and can't operate with this force against us, however.

Ziegler told Haldeman that he would have to resign, along with Ehrlichman. Leaves of absence would only prolong the agony. Haldeman seemed to accept his fate with his usual stoicism and agreed to inform the domestic policy czar. It quickly became apparent that Ehrlichman had no intention of going meekly. He denied any involvement in the planning of Watergate or the cover-up effort. Swayed by these objections, Haldeman himself began to waver. He talked to the lawyers he and Ehrlichman had hired. They argued that resignations would amount to "confessions of guilt" and would not solve anything. Haldeman called Ziegler back to urge the president to reconsider.

"This would be the first real victory of the establishment against Nixon," he argued. "This is what the media wants. Sooner or later, they will see it as phony. It won't help."

The president had made his decision. Persuading his aides to accept it was another matter.

Henry Kissinger was stunned by the speed with which everything had fallen apart. In the days following his second inaugural, Nixon had been on top of the world. He had achieved three overriding goals: "to win by the biggest electoral landslide in history; to be remembered as a peacemaker; and to be accepted by the 'Establishment' as an equal." And then it had all come crashing down. Kissinger was reminded of the plot of a Greek tragedy in which the hero fulfills his destiny but destroys himself in the process. Afflicted by chronic insecurity, Nixon had sought to remake himself entirely. The gods were exacting "a fearful price" for such hubris. Nixon was learning what the Greeks had already known: "that the worst punishment can be having one's wishes fulfilled too completely."

The disintegration of the government was shocking to observe. Kissinger thought back to his conversation with Len Garment, just a few days before. Other White House aides had dismissed the lawyer's premonition of catastrophe as exaggerated, but Kissinger took him seriously enough to ponder the consequences for U.S. foreign policy. "If Garment was right, political and moral authority inexorably would start draining away from the Presidency. The dream of a new era of creativity would in all probability evaporate. Even preserving what we had achieved—the Indochina settlement, for example—would become precarious. There was real peril. Without the impression of American authority, aggressors would be tempted." The international system, with the United States as the cornerstone of the free world, could unravel.

"Everything you predicted is unfortunately coming true," Kissinger told Garment when they spoke again on Easter Saturday by phone. "If this goes much further we won't have a foreign policy left."

In the short term, Kissinger was worried that the president was not retaliating against North Vietnam for violations of the peace agreement. Infiltration of Communist troops into the South along the Ho Chi Minh trail was increasing by the day. The administration's Vietnam strategy was "in tatters." Preoccupied by Watergate, Nixon had repeatedly postponed a punitive bombing campaign against the North. In a telephone call to the president in Key Biscayne on April 21, Kissinger complained that the "goddamn domestic situation" was undermining his efforts to deter Hanoi. The only silver lining to Watergate was that it was pushing all other bad news, including the latest setbacks in Vietnam and spiraling inflation, to "page 20" of the newspapers. On Easter Monday, he shared his concerns with Al Haig, his former deputy, who moved over to the Pentagon.

"I don't see how we can get anything done in this climate. I mean, supposing we start bombing. This will crystalize all the congressional opposition."

Haig lamented that the Democrats were attempting "to screw the president on this Watergate thing." Kissinger was more concerned about the Vietcong.

"I have no doubt that if it weren't for this mess, we'd back them off."

"I'm worried about the Middle East for the same reason," said Haig.

From Kissinger's perspective, the once vaunted White House machine had come to resemble "a vehicle careening out of control in a fog." Part of the problem lay with the man Nixon had selected as the driver. Kissinger knew that he could rely on Bob Haldeman to relay his views accurately to the president, without filtering them through the prism of Haldeman's own biases. The chief of staff was a ruthlessly efficient manager, seemingly devoid of personal ambition or ideology. The problem was that he lacked independent judgment. He was a California advertising executive "with no political past," a serious failing in the eyes of a world-weary Jewish refugee who had fled Nazi Germany at the age of fifteen. To make matters worse, he had packed the White House with "miniature versions of himself." Many of these people had followed Haldeman out of the marketing world, where their focus was on fulfilling the demands of their temperamental clients rather than guiding a country through a turbulent period. Their loyalty was determined by shifting circumstances.

"They were expediters, not balance wheels," Kissinger would later observe. "And once the machine started skidding, they accelerated its descent over the precipice rather than braking it in time."

The president returned to Washington from Key Biscayne late on Tuesday evening. On Wednesday morning, following a visit to the White House barber, he met with Ron Ziegler in the Oval Office. The press secretary had supplanted Haldeman as Lord High Executioner. Nixon now wanted Ziegler to step up the pressure on the twin pillars of his Berlin Wall.

"Let's just see if we can get them to resign today," he mused. "What would you do, tell them to resign? Or would you say, 'Alright, fellows, you've got a week'?"

Ziegler passed the message on to Haldeman and Ehrlichman, explaining that the presidency could no longer function "in this atmosphere." But the two men were still resisting. They enlisted their lawyers to plead with Nixon. Ushered into the Oval Office after Ziegler's departure, the lawyers argued that amputations would not "get the gangrene out of the White House." Nixon disagreed. "If the patient survives, then maybe it's worthwhile."

The president walked over to his EOB hideaway around eleven to meet with the two Germans. For the next three hours, they argued back and forth, but mostly round in circles, about what should happen next. Haldeman allowed his angrier, more forceful partner to lead the conversation. Boiling inside at the injustice of being put into the same category as the turncoat Dean, Ehrlichman insisted on being brutally candid.

"Let me just spin something out for you," he began, as if outlining another "scenario" for leading the press on a merry ride, before dropping the hammer. "It's entirely conceivable that if Dean is totally out of control, and if matters are not handled adroitly, that you could get a resolution of impeachment."

Nixon looked stunned. Dean had made a passing reference to impeachment ten days earlier, but this was the first time the topic had been broached by men he still trusted. The great unmentionable had finally been spoken out loud. Ehrlichman pressed ahead.

"I got to thinking about it last night. On the ground that you committed a crime and there is no other legal process available to the United States people other than impeachment. Otherwise, you have immunity from prosecution."

Ehrlichman had another startling suggestion. From an offhand remark by Haldeman, he had learned that Nixon might have tapes of some of his conversations with Dean. Ehrlichman used the Dictaphone on his desk to clandestinely record some of the meetings in his White House office, such as his session with John Mitchell on April 14. He assumed that Nixon was doing the same, even though he had no idea of the scale of the practice. He now recommended that Nixon deploy his secret weapon.

"You've got John Dean prancing in there saying, 'The president said this, the president said that,'" he explained. "The only way I know to make a judgment on this is for you to listen to your tapes and see what was actually said, or maybe for Bob to do it, or somebody. See what was said there. And then analyze how big a threat it is."

"Right," said Nixon.

"You'd better damn sure know what your hole card is," said Ehrlichman, using his favorite poker expression.

"I agree."

The suggestion that he examine his hole card filled Nixon with a mixture of hope and dread. This was certainly one way that he could gain an advantage over his enemies. He instructed Haldeman to "go back and get the tapes of everything we had with Dean—see what the hell has been discussed." But what if he found material on the tapes that undermined Nixon's own position? He was particularly worried about the March 21 conversation when Dean warned of a cancer on the presidency and had also mentioned the blackmail threat from Howard Hunt.

"Remember my saying to Dean, 'Well, look, for Christ's sake, take care of him'?" he asked Haldeman, who had attended the latter part of the meeting. "'Be sure the son of a bitch doesn't talk.'"

The three men dredged their memories for potentially compromising snippets of conversation with Dean. They agreed that destroying Dean's credibility had become a top priority. By this time Nixon had a new concern. He had been taping Dean. Perhaps Dean had been taping him.

"Is it possible he carries a tape? Does he do that?" he asked. He worried that Dean might have smuggled a recording device into the Oval Office.

Ehrlichman sought to soothe the president's fears. From his own experience, he knew that secret wires "almost always go haywire." Haldeman pointed out that such recordings would involve "privileged conversations" that could not be disclosed to anyone. This produced a rueful laugh from Nixon.

"Privileged conversation is going all out the window."

Ehrlichman steered the conversation back to his own situation. He pleaded with Nixon to treat him differently to Haldeman, and Haldeman differently to Dean. They all had varying degrees of guilt. Dean should be fired. Haldeman should be allowed to take a leave of absence pending a full investigation of his links to the secret "350 fund" used to pay off the burglars. He, Ehrlichman, should remain in place but be ready to take a leave if credible charges surfaced. To underscore his point that dismissals were a slippery slope, Ehrlichman produced his own list of Nixon aides with some kind of "Watergate problem." There were seventeen names on the Ehrlichman list, including Colson and Ziegler.

Nixon did not want to get into an argument. Instead, he repeated his earlier offer to help his two assistants with their legal fees, using Bebe Rebozo's money.

"Is there any way you can use cash?" he asked the two men.

It seemed a strange suggestion, given that they had spent many hours agonizing over the payment of hush money to the Watergate defendants.

"I don't think so," said Ehrlichman.

"That compounds the problem," said Haldeman. "It really does."

After Haldeman and Ehrlichman left, the president received an urgent call from his attorney general, asking to see him immediately. Dick Kleindienst showed up in EOB 175 at 3:35 p.m. in a frantic state. He had concluded he had a duty to inform the judge in the Ellsberg trial, out in Los Angeles, about the attempt to steal Ellsberg's psychiatric records. If he withheld this information from the court, Kleindienst himself could be charged with obstruction of justice. Nixon made a halfhearted attempt to dissuade him. As he had previously told Petersen, it was a national security matter, involving the White House Plumbers. Besides, said Nixon, "they got nothing. It was a dry hole."

"We can't have another cover-up, Mr. President," the attorney general said firmly. He had privately decided that he would have to resign if overruled.

Nixon feared that Dean was using the Ellsberg break-in to "point a gun" at Ehrlichman, who had authorized the Plumbers to travel to California. Nevertheless, he understood the limits of his power. He authorized Kleindienst to proceed, thinking to himself "how everything was about to become even bleaker for John Ehrlichman."

"Let me say, I want no cover-up. Good God almighty."

From the Oval Office, Haldeman had telephoned Nixon's assistant Steve Bull, who was now responsible for the secret taping system. Speaking in thinly disguised code, Haldeman told Bull to retrieve any recordings for the period March 10 to 23 from the Secret Service storage room on the ground floor of EOB. "Have them put it in some sort of bag so it isn't obvious," he ordered. "Also have them get a machine that is technically capable of listening to it, the smallest and simplest such machine. Do it as quickly as possible."

Instead of returning to his own grand office, Haldeman went to a smaller, windowless room next door where he would not be disturbed. A pile of twenty-two tapes was waiting for his review, along with a portable Sony tape machine. He locked the door. He then selected a tape

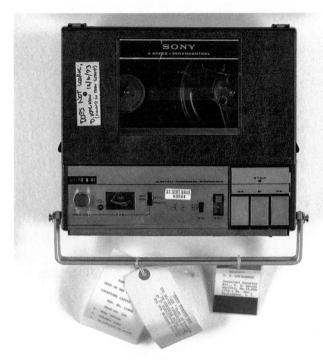

Bob Haldeman used this Sony tape recorder to review the "cancer on the presidency" conversation between Nixon and Dean.

marked March 21, 1973, the day of the "cancer on the presidency" conversation, which he inserted into the tape machine. Aware that nobody had ever listened to this tape before, he pressed the play button. It was difficult to locate the right place. There were many different items on the reel, ranging from top secret intelligence briefings to a meet and greet with the Soviet gymnastic sensation, Olga Korbut. He had to fast-forward and rewind a lot but finally found what he was looking for. He heard John Dean telling the president in his almost expressionless voice, "Good morning, good morning." And Nixon welcoming him into the Oval Office. "Sit down, sit down."

For the next two and a half hours, Haldeman sat hunched over the Sony, jotting down the highlights of the conversation. He covered twenty pages of his legal pad with densely scrawled notes. It was a slow, sometimes agonizing process. Dean's voice was reasonably clear. He was evidently sitting in the chair to the left of the president where Haldeman normally sat. There were two microphones embedded in the desk on either side of the chair. But Nixon's voice was muffled, more distant. Occasionally he would sit back and put his feet on the desk, producing a sound akin to a roll of thunder. Cups and saucers screeched like loud rattles; the knocking of a knee or an elbow against the desk drowned out normal conversation.

At 4:40, Haldeman was back in the Oval Office, informing an impatient president of his findings. "Well, that's hard work. Good God! It's amazing." He explained that the system had picked up Dean "awfully well" but it was "hard as hell to hear you, so you gotta keep looking back and reworking." He then read from his notes, with Nixon making only minor interjections. The point that most troubled the president was whether he had authorized the payment of hush money to Howard Hunt following Hunt's threat to to bring Ehrlichman "to his knees and put him in jail." Haldeman ran through the most incriminating parts of the conversation.

"You said, 'How much money is involved in this?' Dean said, 'Probably a million dollars over the next few years.' And you said, 'If we need the money, we can get the money. We can get it in cash.'"

"Hmmm," said Nixon.

"Then you said, 'Your major one to control is Hunt because he knows so much.' He said, 'Right' . . . And you said, 'Looking at the immediate problem, don't you have to handle Hunt's financial situation?' And Dean said, 'I talked to Mitchell about that last night.'"

While listening to the tape, Haldeman had also noted down a potentially useful remark from Nixon concerning a possible pardon for Hunt. "Then you said, 'Suppose you got the money and had a way to handle it. It would seem to me that would be worthwhile, but we'd still have the problem of Hunt's clemency.' Dean said, 'Right . . . I'm not sure you can deliver on clemency.' And you said, 'Not before the '74 election for sure.' He said, 'It may further involve you.' And you said, 'Yes, and it's wrong.'"

"That's not bad," Nixon said, suddenly more upbeat.

As Haldeman later recalled, Nixon clung to the word "wrong" "like a drowning man in a hurricane." For both of them, it would become evidence that the president had rejected the blackmail attempt. In fact, Nixon had used the word to describe a potential pardon for Hunt prior to the midterm elections, not the payment of hush money. There was a twenty-minute gap between the two topics on the tape, but they became conflated in Haldeman's compressed narrative. Determined to find something exculpating to share with his boss, the chief of staff put the best spin he could on the conversation.

"You're smoking him out on what he thinks the alternatives are."

"Yeah," said Nixon, spotting a possible line of defense.

"You're pumping him."

"Yeah."

After several hours of listening to tapes in a locked room, Haldeman's normally sharp mind had ceased to function clearly. The more Nixon pushed him for answers and explanations, the more befuddled he became. Soon, they were telling each other what they wanted to hear and believing what they wanted to believe.

Nixon tried one more time. "When we discussed raising the money," he summed up, "I said, 'That's wrong.' Didn't I? Or 'wrong' on clemency?"

"Trying to get the money," said Haldeman. "I don't think that you felt that clemency was wrong. I think you felt that you had some justification for clemency on Hunt."

By convincing each other that the president had said the opposite of what he had actually said, Nixon and Haldeman had finally come up with their best-case "scenario." If it was ever tested in public, it would be the word of the president against the word of a disgruntled aide. Nixon now reverted to his other big worry. What if that "son of a bitch" Dean had also managed to record the conversation? It was a thought that troubled him for the rest of the day. By dinnertime, it had become an obsession.

He phoned Haldeman at home at 6:57 and again at 7:46. "Is there any way, that even surreptitiously or discreetly or otherwise, I mean, any way you could determine whether, uh, Dean might have walked in there with a recorder on him?" he asked Haldeman on the second call.

"I don't think there is any way," said Haldeman, tired of hearing about Dean's mythical tape recorder. "It's so remote as to be almost beyond a possibility."

But Nixon would not let up. "That may be his bomb. He puts that on the desk with Henry Petersen and says, 'I got a recording of the president of the United States, and here's what he said.'"

"That would be very hard."

Nixon began wondering where a recorder could be concealed, perhaps in a hip or breast pocket.

"Or under your arm, you know, where they carry a pistol holster," said Haldeman, humoring the president for a moment. But he quickly added this was "almost beyond the realm of possibility."

"In this matter, nothing is beyond the realm of possibility," said Nixon grimly. He drew comfort from a trip he was scheduled to make to Mississippi on Friday to dedicate a U.S. Navy facility and inspect flood damage. His opinion poll ratings had been dropping everywhere else, but he was still popular in the Deep South. Surely, there were at least "half a dozen people" in the state who would remain "for the president," whatever happened.

"A lot more than that," said Haldeman, laughing.

Nixon decided to call it a night. Later that evening, he went bowling, alone.

The newspaper headlines that greeted Nixon on Friday morning were brutal. "Gray Says He Destroyed Files from Hunt Given Him as He Met Ehrlichman and Dean," declared the front-page banner headline in *The New York Times*. The story reported that Dean had told the acting FBI director, "These papers should never see the light of day." Earlier, Ehrlichman was "understood" to have urged Dean to throw the incriminating documents into the Potomac on his way home from work. Anyone who read between the lines could see that the *Times* was getting information from the Gray and Dean camps, Senate investigators, and inside the White House itself. Other newspapers carried similar stories, citing a variety of "confidential sources." The *Washington Post* report was based in part on a leak that Bob Woodward had received from the source he knew as Deep Throat, the deputy FBI director, Mark Felt. The longtime J. Edgar Hoover protégé was scheming to succeed Gray as head of the bureau.

The entire town had become a gigantic information faucet. New allegations engulfed the White House every hour. Amid the general confusion, it was difficult to distinguish the true from the false. The faithful Ziegler was doing his best to hold back the rising floodwaters, a task akin to throwing himself against a dam that had already burst. As the deluge swept in from all directions, officials high and low were calling their favorite reporters. Motives varied. Some were outraged by the abuse of power; some were settling scores; some wanted to get their version of the story on record; some yearned to share the excitement of the moment. And some were driven by a complex mixture of reasons they had difficulty explaining even to themselves.

Nixon pondered the newspaper stories as he flew down to Mississippi on Friday morning on the *Spirit of '76*. Five minutes after takeoff, he called Haldeman to his private office in the forecabin of the brand-new Boeing. It had been obvious since the evening before, when the press calls started to flood in, that Gray would have to be thrown overboard. There was no way of defending an acting FBI director who had admitted to destroying evidence. The appalling headlines also threatened Ehrlichman, who had been fighting to distance himself from Haldeman. Nixon had concluded that the two men were no longer "seperable." He had "to clear the goddamn air." His "right hand" and "left hand" would both have to go. The only possible concession was to disguise their departure as "a leave of absence," pending the grand jury investigation. Under the most optimistic scenario, they might be able to return to the White House someday in different positions.

"It's obvious the president expects us to leave," Haldeman noted gloomily in his diary. "Wants me to talk to Ehrlichman in very direct terms. Says there are no good options. We can't wait until next week."

After Haldeman went back to his work desk in the center of the plane, the White House operator put through a ground-to-air radio call from Gray. The former submarine captain was "filled with shame" for allowing his ship "to run onto the rocks." He wanted to tender his resignation to his commander in chief, but Nixon refused to speak with him. He still could not get over Gray's "unbelievable stupidity" in destroying documents. Such a contrast with the late J. Edgar Hoover, who kept "every doodle that anybody ever had around right there in his files." The operator switched the call to Larry Higby, the junior aide known as Haldeman's Haldeman, back in Washington. Gray left the bunker-like J. Edgar Hoover Building on Pennsylvania Avenue for the last time early that afternoon, heading back to his home in Connecticut. After six weeks of agony, his corpse had finally stopped "twisting slowly in the wind."

In the meantime, Haldeman informed Ehrlichman of their now joint fate. The domestic policy chief was overwhelmed by bitterness and despair. As Air Force One flew over Mississippi, he was invited up to

Ehrlichman and Haldeman sitting together on Air Force One prior to landing in Mississippi on April 27, 1973. Ehrlichman fantasized about crashing the plane.

the flight deck to get a better sense of the floods devastating large parts of the state. The pilot brought the plane down to thirty-five hundred feet to allow the presidential party to inspect the rain-soaked cotton farms around the Mississippi delta. Standing directly behind the pilot as they flew over the muddy fields, Ehrlichman fantasized about a mass murder-suicide. "I could end everybody's troubles by throwing myself against the controls, wedging myself between the pilot's yoke control and the pilot. We'd all be gone in about a minute and a half. I stood there chatting with the navigator, measuring my chances for a moment; then turned and went back to my seat."

The big blue plane with "United States of America" plastered along its fuselage landed safely at Naval Air Station Meridian at 11:46 East Coast time. The enthusiastic crowd included hundreds of schoolchildren waving American flags. Everyone seemed happy to see the president. The only person who even alluded to Watergate during the ceremonies at the naval base was the state's longtime senior senator, John C. Stennis. He told Nixon, "You do not panic when the going gets tough. I believe you have what it takes to tough it through. We admire that." A few minutes earlier, in a private conversation aboard Air Force One, Stennis had urged Nixon to act decisively before it was too late. "We say down in our country that the rain falls on the just and the unjust. Time is running out."

Nixon was back at the White House by 3:30, in time for a reception in honor of National Secretaries Week, hosted by his own longtime secretary, Rose Mary Woods. He then returned to the Oval Office. His most pressing order of business was choosing a new FBI chief to succeed the disgraced Pat Gray. Both Gray and Kleindienst were pushing for the appointment of Felt. The man known in the bureau as the White Rat was ruthlessly ambitious, but at least he knew how to run the place. Nixon would not countenance the idea. While he did not have the proof, he suspected Felt of disloyalty. He was almost certainly a leaker. "I don't want him, I can't have him," he told Kleindienst in a 4:14 p.m. telephone call. "I want a fellow in there that is not part of the old guard and that is not part of the infighting in there."

While Nixon was dealing with the fallout from the Gray fiasco, a separate but related drama was unfolding on the other side of the country. For the past three months, Daniel Ellsberg had been on trial on charges of espionage, conspiracy, and theft of government property arising from his unauthorized disclosure of the Pentagon Papers. He had worked on the multivolume history of the Vietnam War as a Defense Department consultant for the Rand Corporation, a strategic think tank in Santa Monica. He admitted leaking the documents to *The New York Times* but claimed a higher, moral justification. In tearful testimony to the court, he explained that his experiences in Vietnam had turned him against the war. He had been overwhelmed by the sight of burning villages, children killed by American bombs, and corrupt South Vietnamese officials living in luxury while peasants starved. The contrast between the reality on the ground and what Americans were being told by their government was stark. He hoped that publication of the secret papers would encourage Congress to end the war.

It had been a dull, routine kind of trial, hinging on the transfer of classified information to unauthorized persons. Ellsberg fully expected to go to jail for twenty to thirty years. The evidence against him was overwhelming. But on April 26 a miracle intervened. The prosecutors informed Judge Matthew Byrne that evidence had surfaced that "at a date unspecified, Gordon Liddy and Howard Hunt burglarized the offices of a psychiatrist of Daniel Ellsberg to obtain the psychiatrist's files relating to Ellsberg." The government lawyers argued against disclosing the Justice Department memorandum to the defense since it had no bearing on Ellsberg's guilt or innocence. Judge Byrne disagreed. By law, the prosecution was required to share any information relating to "a possible taint or impropriety" in the case. On Friday, April 27, day 80 of the trial, he ordered all parties to approach the bench.

Byrne was in a tricky position. At the time he received the government memorandum, he was himself under consideration for the post of FBI director. Three weeks earlier, he had been invited to San Clemente for an informal conversation with John Ehrlichman. While walking along the cliff overlooking the beach, Ehrlichman asked the judge whether he would like to head the FBI. Byrne was intrigued by the proposal but said he would have to wait until the end of the Ellsberg trial to give a firm answer. Heading America's foremost law enforcement agency would cap a distinguished career. Right on cue, Nixon emerged from his villa to shake hands with the presumptive nominee and chat briefly. Haldeman filmed the two men strolling in the garden with his home movie camera. The offer of the FBI directorship was still dangling in front of Judge Byrne as he weighed whether to release information that would be highly damaging to the president.

With Ellsberg standing in front of him, and the attorneys huddled around, Judge Byrne lowered his voice as he read from the government memorandum. Reporters and spectators were out of earshot. The jury had not yet been admitted to the courtroom. There was still a chance that Ellsberg might be reluctant to disclose that he had been seeing a psychiatrist. The judge addressed him directly.

"Mr. Ellsberg, I don't need to put this out."

"Are you kidding?" Ellsberg replied. "Put it out!" His co-defendant, Anthony Russo, flashed a V sign behind his back.

After everyone returned to their seats, Judge Byrne read the memorandum in open court. He then ordered the government to make a "thorough investigation" of the facts behind the burglary and report back "forthwith." He also insisted on being told "at whose direction" Liddy and Hunt had been operating. While the trial would continue pending the results of the investigation, the entire case was now in jeopardy. Reporters dashed for the pay phones, just as they had a few weeks earlier during the Watergate trial in Washington, after Judge Sirica read out the letter from James McCord.

Talking to reporters outside the courtroom, a stunned but happy Ellsberg said he was unsurprised by the new developments. "The message of the Watergate, as I read it, is the same as the message of the Pentagon Papers: that in the eyes of the people who work for the president, all law stops at the White House fence, and they are above the law."

While there had been much speculation about a connection between the Pentagon Papers and Watergate, nothing had been proven. It was now clear that the two cases were inextricably linked. They had involved the same players. If the allegations against Liddy and Hunt were true, they had broken in to the psychiatrist's office nine months *before* the break-in at the Watergate. What was not yet publicly known was the nature of cause and effect. History would show that Nixon authorized the creation of a "special investigations unit," more popularly known as the White House Plumbers, within a month of the publication of the Pentagon Papers on June 13, 1971. The first order of business of the new unit was the discrediting of Daniel Ellsberg, to be achieved in part by the theft of his medical records. The long-forgotten burglary in Beverly Hills, which was never properly investigated, turned out to be a precursor of the crime that had grabbed the nation's attention at the Watergate.

In both cases, Nixon's thirst for political intelligence had spawned a "whatever it takes" culture that led to massive lawbreaking by his administration. With his encouragement, his subordinates resorted to illegal covert action to gather dirt on his enemies and settle scores with "leakers" and "traitors." Nixon claimed a U.S. national security justification for such activity at a time when he was fighting a war on two fronts, abroad and at home. He had the right to determine for himself what was permissible. As he later told the British TV interviewer David Frost, "When the president does it, that means that it is *not* illegal." Because the other branches of government took a different view, he felt the need to hide his actions from public scrutiny. Had Watergate been an isolated incident, it would have been relatively simple for Nixon to shift the blame to overzealous subordinates. But the fact that crimes traceable back to the president had previously been committed by the same gang made it imperative to prevent a full investigation. His reelection was on the line.

Dean's disclosures about the earlier antics of Liddy and Hunt, and the attorney general's decision to relay that information to the Ellsberg trial judge, dealt a deathblow to the Watergate cover-up. The link between the two cases became apparent for all to see. Ellsberg's leaking of the classified history of the Vietnam War had triggered a cycle of illegal activity by the Nixon White House that led to Watergate that in turn led back to Ellsberg. The wheel had turned full circle.

Unbeknownst to Judge Byrne, Nixon had ruled him out for the FBI position the previous evening because of his involvement in "the Ellsberg thing." Appointing the Ellsberg judge to head the FBI would only complicate matters. Instead, Nixon decided to offer the job to the administrator of the Environmental Protection Agency, William Ruckelshaus, whom he viewed as "Mr. Clean." He summoned Ruckelshaus to the Oval Office at 3:48 to secure his agreement. They were joined by Ehrlichman. As they were talking, a pair of FBI agents waited outside the door to interview Ehrlichman about his role in the Ellsberg affair.

The choice of Ruckelshaus as acting FBI director was a bitter blow to Mark Felt, who had set his heart on climbing to the top of "the FBI pyramid." He would use this phrase in the title of his 1979 memoir, noting proudly that he had achieved his ambition for precisely two hours and fifty minutes, the interregnum between the resignation of Gray and the appointment of Ruckelshaus. The political tornado sweeping through Washington was turning everything upside down, destroying some people, elevating others.

At 4:31, Nixon received a call from Henry Petersen with an update on the Ellsberg case. Everything seemed to be falling apart at once. "Just pray to God we live through this thing," Nixon told Haldeman tearfully, when they were alone a short time later. "We'll live through it," the chief of staff assured him. "And we'll come out damn well."

More bad news soon arrived via Ziegler. Reporters were seeking reaction to a story that Dean had directly "implicated the president." Bob Woodward was telling people at the White House that Watergate was about to be taken to a whole "new dimension, a new plateau."

"Jesus Christ," said Nixon. He demanded a full explanation from Henry Petersen, who was ushered into the Oval Office later that afternoon. "You heard anything like that?"

"No, sir," said Petersen.

"You're certain?"

"Absolutely."

"You swear to God?"

The president was displaying signs of panic. Petersen tried to allay his fears by saying the prosecutors had "no mandate to investigate the presidency." Their job was to "investigate Watergate." Still he promised to check. He made a few calls and reported back that there was "some substance, some falsity" to the story. Dean's aggressive lawyer, Charlie Shaffer, was threatening to unearth dirt about the president, "not in this case, but in other things." For the moment, it was all bombast. This was another reason why it had been essential to disclose the Ellsberg psychiatrist break-in information to the trial judge. Withholding those details would have given Dean a blackmail weapon he could have used against everybody.

"That shows you what a prick he is," said Nixon, referring to Dean. He complained that he had called to wish his wayward legal counsel "Happy Easter" the previous Sunday and "it was all over the press" the following day.

After cursing Woodward and the other reporters ("they better watch their damned cotton-picking faces"), Nixon ordered Ziegler to deny the latest news stories. "You've got to knock that crap down." The press secretary left to carry out the order while the president bared his soul to Petersen.

"I sometimes feel like I'd like to resign. Let Agnew be the president for a while. He'd love it."

"I don't even know why you want the job," said Petersen.

After loyally sticking by the president, and feeding him secret information from the grand jury, Petersen was beginning to have doubts. He shared with Nixon a conversation he had had with his wife—a "charming" but politically unsophisticated woman—over the breakfast table. She had asked him whether he was upset by the latest revelations in the press. "Of course," he had replied. "You think the president knows?" was her next question. To this he had responded, "If I thought the president knew, I would have to resign."

"You know, that's my own family, Mr. President," said Petersen. "Whatever confidence she has in you, her confidence in me ought to be unquestioned. When that type of question comes through in my house, we've got a problem."

Petersen left at 6:47, to be replaced immediately at Nixon's side by Haldeman. The chief of staff could not understand why Nixon was continuing to treat Dean with kid gloves, avoiding an outright rupture. Nixon explained that he needed "to avoid at all costs getting into any position where John Dean tries to barf on me." He had to handle Dean his own way. Haldeman conceded that there was a possibility that Dean would "totally flip" and perhaps become "a John Wilkes Booth or something." That was an exaggeration, of course, but Dean was "a vicious and evil enough guy to be willing to use everything in his command any way he feels is the most effective way of using it."

"The son of a bitch is finished in my view," said Nixon.

"There seems to be a place in the world for people like that," said Haldeman.

The conversation meandered around in circles for more than an hour until 8:00 p.m., when Nixon dismissed Haldeman on a note of renewed determination: "Today we start fighting." Nixon announced that he would go to Camp David for the weekend to think about his options.

At 8:22 p.m., Nixon moved over to EOB 175 with Ron Ziegler. They were joined by the president's Irish setter, King Timahoe, named after a beloved dog that had belonged to his parents. Even though he had always considered himself a dog person, Nixon was as ill at ease around animals as he was around people. When he tried to play with King, he often got tangled up in the leash. To gain the dog's affections, he stashed dog biscuits in strategic locations, including the drawer to his office desk. King had grown accustomed to constant treats, and Nixon now had difficulty keeping him away.

"*Rrrr-ruff,*" barked King as Nixon launched another diatribe against

Manolo Sanchez escorts Nixon to Marine One on the White House lawn followed by a military aide carrying the nuclear codes, November 1970.

Dean for going to Camp David to write his report and deciding instead that "he better save his own ass."

"King!" said Nixon as the dog jumped up on him. And then a more irritated "goddamn, get off of me!"

"Ruff," said King.

Manolo entered the room to remove the protesting dog. After bottling his anger inside him all day, the president let loose. It was inconceivable to him that his enemies wanted to replace him with Spiro Agnew.

"Good God almighty, they've got to want this country to succeed." He hammered violently on his desk. "The hopes of the whole goddamn world of peace, Ron, you know, where do they rest? They rest right here. In this goddamn chair. They can't allow this shitting, frickass thing . . ."

"That's right."

"The press has got to realize that . . . Whatever they think of me, they've got to realize that I'm the only one at the present time in this whole wide blinking world that can do a goddamn thing. You know, keep it from blowing up."

"Yes, sir."

Nixon complained that Haldeman and Ehrlichman were making it difficult for him to do what needed to be done.

"Bob made the point to me today. He said, 'Look, half of me is worth one of anybody else,' and he's exactly right."

"But that isn't the point," said Ziegler.

"Half of him is damaged goods. That's what he doesn't realize, you see. He's damaged goods. Right?"

"That's right."

"You can't have damaged goods in the White House."

It had been another long day. At 9:31 p.m., the president walked from his EOB hideaway to the South Lawn of the White House. Marine One was waiting to take him to Camp David, accompanied only by Manolo Sanchez, King Timahoe, his doctor, and a military aide carrying the nuclear launch codes.

Nixon rose early on Saturday morning. He had breakfast alone in the sunporch of Aspen Lodge, overlooking the terrace and steep rock garden, now wreathed in fog. Manolo had laid out the morning newspapers on the table for his perusal. At 8:21, Nixon was in his study at the other end of the cabin, on the phone with Ziegler in Washington. He made a determined effort to sound cheerful.

"What time did you go to bed?"

"About 12:30, one o'clock."

"Ha, ha, ha. Well, you're a young fellow. You can take it, I guess. Fine, fine. That's quite a collection of headlines this morning, isn't it?"

"Oh, boy!"

The Washington Post had bannered its main Watergate story across the top of the front page, with rogues' gallery mug shots of Gray, Hunt, and Liddy:

> Gray Resigns; Ruckelshaus Heads FBI;
> Hunt, Liddy Linked to Ellsberg Case

The New York Times featured a photograph of Haldeman and Ehrlichman getting off Air Force One at Andrews Air Force Base following their trip to Mississippi with Nixon. Both men looked grim, their eyes fixed on the ground. Above the photograph was another eight-column banner headline:

Gray Quits the F.B.I., Ruckelshaus Named;
A Justice Dept. Memo Says Liddy and Hunt
Raided Office of Ellsberg's Psychiatrist

After completing his morning round of calls, the president walked down the corridor to the living room, in search of Manolo and a cup of coffee. He was surprised to see his older daughter, Tricia, sitting in front of the blazing fire. She had been up all night in the White House with Julie and Julie's husband, David Eisenhower, discussing the family crisis. They agreed there was no alternative: Haldeman and Ehrlichman would have to resign. The family had never much cared for the "Berlin Wall" that separated Nixon from the rest of the world. But that was no longer the point. Driven to the fogged-in camp by the Secret Service, Tricia told her father that the attacks on the two men had destroyed their ability to serve him effectively.

"That is our opinion. But we also want you to know that we have complete confidence in you. If you decide not to take our advice, we will understand. Whatever you do, just remember we will support you, and we love you very much."

Unlike her younger sister, Tricia rarely showed any emotion. A *Post* society columnist had angered Nixon by calling her "a vanilla ice cream cone" at the time of her Rose Garden wedding in June 1971. Now her eyes were filled with tears. Nixon asked if she would like to stay, but she preferred to leave her father alone with his decision. She hugged him and was gone.

Ehrlichman called that evening. He was still angling for "separation" from Haldeman, but Nixon did not see how this would be possible. On top of everything else, Ehrlichman was now implicated in the Ellsberg psychiatrist operation, even though he claimed to have later "turned it off." Reporters were also asking questions about fake State Department cables purporting to show Kennedy administration involvement in the 1963 assassination of the South Vietnamese prime minister, Ngo Dinh Diem. The cables were in the package of documents Gray had burned in his backyard.

"Have you ever heard of such a goddamn thing?" Nixon asked Ehrlichman.

"Yes, sir," said Ehrlichman. "I believe it leads directly to your friend Colson."

"Had you heard of it before?"

"Yes."

"Goddamn it, I never heard of it, John," said Nixon. "A fake letter? From John F. Kennedy? My God, I just can't believe that."

Ehrlichman had a distinct memory of briefing the president about the fake Diem cable during a walk along the beach at San Clemente a couple of weeks after the Watergate break-in. They had been discussing various dirty tricks carried out by Howard Hunt on behalf of the White House. Ehrlichman had also mentioned Hunt's involvement in the Ellsberg affair. Now that he was fighting for his own survival, Ehrlichman was in no mood to let the president off the hook.

"I don't know where Colson got this inspiration, but he was very busy at it," he told Nixon.

"And he told you there was a *fake* letter or a *fake* cable?"

"Yes."

"I should have been told about that, shouldn't I?" said Nixon.

"I'm not so sure you weren't," said Ehrlichman. "I'd have to go back and check my notes. But my recollection is that this was discussed with you."

There was a long, tortured silence on Nixon's end of the phone line. It was not just Dean and Magruder. Ehrlichman was now a threat as well. God only knew what else he had squirreled away in his notes and recordings. The president insisted that he had been unaware of Hunt's existence prior to Watergate.

"Is that right?" said Ehrlichman sarcastically.

"I never heard of E. Howard Hunt, no, sir, no," said Nixon. "No, sir." This was untrue. His own tapes would later prove that Colson had enthusiastically recommended the former CIA agent to the president on July 1, 1971, the day after the Supreme Court ruled against the White House in the Pentagon Papers case. Colson had described Hunt as ideologically reliable and "kind of a tiger," precisely the type of person Nixon needed to plug government leaks.

Nixon was shaken by Ehrlichman's telephone call. His embattled aide was claiming that responsibility for the crimes and abuses of power that led to Watergate rested ultimately with the president. "He implied that I was the inspiration behind them," Nixon wrote later in his memoirs. The man who should resign, Ehrlichman seemed to be saying, was Nixon himself.

The president slept late on Sunday morning. He had been up much of the night, thinking about what Ehrlichman had told him and his own responsibility for Watergate. He took breakfast alone on the sunporch at 10:05. The newspaper headlines were as dark and relentless as the day before. According to *The Washington Post*, Dean had accused Haldeman and Ehrlichman of supervising the cover-up. The latest opinion poll showed that fewer than one in ten Americans believed the White House was being "frank and honest" on Watergate.

Retreating down the corridor to his study, Nixon steeled himself for the torture of the day ahead. His mind was now made up. Leaves of absence would no longer suffice for Haldeman and Ehrlichman. That would only prolong the agony. Both men would have to "voluntarily" resign. Dean would be fired. He also needed to find a new attorney general to replace Richard Kleindienst, who was damaged by his association with John Mitchell. He was leaning toward Elliot Richardson, a pillar of establishment rectitude who had been serving as defense secretary. A D-day veteran who had participated in the assault over Utah Beach, Richardson had a reputation for independence. "He's sort of Mr. Integrity," Nixon told aides. "A little tortuous at it [but] smart as hell."

The president continued to blame many of his problems on the Justice Department and the FBI. Returning a telephone call from Henry Kissinger soon after breakfast, Nixon said he planned "to get the most mean son of a bitch I can find and put him in the FBI, and let all hell break loose." The bureau had failed to investigate Ellsberg, which was why "some of that crap was done in the White House."

"I just wanted you to know when that comes out, don't back off," said Nixon. "Anything that's national security, we're going to fight like hell for."

"Absolutely," Kissinger agreed. "I will certainly not back off."

Nixon wanted his friend William Rogers to be with him when he delivered the bad news to Haldeman and Ehrlichman, but the secretary of state declined. He would have trouble answering questions from federal investigators if either aide started lashing out at the president. There were some things it was better not to know. "Men get shaken and desperate, particularly ones that have been dictatorial in their conduct with others, they get pretty goddamn nasty," Rogers warned. He advised Nixon to take a hard line with both men. "Just say, 'I've thought it over, I know how tough it is, you told me that you'd do whatever I decided on, and this is what I decided on, and this is my judgment.' Period."

At 12:18 p.m., Nixon called Haldeman at his home in Georgetown. The chief of staff had just got back from church and was drinking coffee with his wife. Nixon sounded nervous as he repeated the lines fed to him by Rogers. "We have to make a decision on this. I've thought it through all the way. It's got to be a resignation." He asked Haldeman to inform Ehrlichman. They should fly to Camp David together, but he would meet with them separately, at Ehrlichman's request.

"I hope Ehrlichman is as big a man as you are when I talk with him," said Nixon.

Determined not to leave anything to chance, Nixon dictated drafts of the two men's resignation letters to Ziegler, who had already joined him at Camp David. His voice was hoarse. The more distraught he became, the more difficult it was for him to talk.

"What the hell do you do for money for them, Ron, during this period? What the hell do you do about that?"

Ziegler mumbled something about "friends" coming to their aid. There was a long silence at the other end of the phone as the president muffled his sobs.

"Okay, thank you," said Nixon, in a barely audible whisper, before putting down the phone.

As Nixon rehearsed his lines for later that afternoon, Haldeman drove to the Pentagon helipad. Ehrlichman showed up a few minutes later. The presidential chopper flew low up the Potomac, offering the passengers spectacular views of the Capitol, the Washington Monument, and the White House. Soon they were flying over the Watergate complex and the redbrick row houses of Georgetown, before heading north across Maryland, toward the grayish-green blur of Catoctin Mountain.

"It's resignation, John, not leave of absence," Haldeman told his companion.

"Both of us?" asked Ehrlichman angrily.

"That's right."

They barely spoke for the rest of the thirty-minute flight. A naval officer met them at the Camp David helipad and drove them to Laurel Lodge, a couple hundred yards from Aspen. Ron Ziegler was standing outside, a shadow of his usual perky self. Ehrlichman despised the onetime Disneyland tour guide. He had already concluded that Nixon's magic kingdom was in a lot of trouble if Ziegler was now Lord Chamberlain. Sensing he would get little cooperation from the beetle-browed Ehrlichman, Ziegler invited Haldeman to take a stroll. As they walked through the woods, he reported that Nixon had decided to resign himself.

"He's deadly serious and absolutely firm," said Ziegler. "The president's taking it so hard. He's just totally broken, Bob."

Haldeman doubted that Nixon really intended to resign. Rather, he thought, he was steeling himself to demand the resignations of his two top aides. He was "creating a big crisis that he knew he couldn't meet in order to be able to meet the lesser crisis that he has to meet."

Soon afterward, Haldeman received the summons to meet the president in Aspen Lodge. He took a bicycle from the stand outside Laurel and pedaled over to Aspen. It was, he reflected later, "rather an unusual way to ride to political doom."

He arrived at 2:20 p.m. Nixon was waiting for him, wearing a checkered sports jacket, his notion of rustic simplicity. He looked in "terrible shape." He extended his hand in greeting, the first time Haldeman could recall such a gesture during their many years of association. The president led his chief of staff through the sunroom to the terrace to admire the tulips which were now in full bloom. The fog and clouds had cleared

Nixon in the sunroom of Aspen Lodge with Bob Haldeman,
photographed through a window.

to reveal a sea of light green leaves covering the mountainside. They made small talk about the beauty of Camp David in the springtime.

"I have to enjoy it because I may not be alive much longer," said Nixon, before guiding Haldeman into the living room. Back inside, he talked about his religious beliefs, a subject he rarely discussed with others. Every night since becoming president, he told Haldeman, he got down on his knees next to his bed and prayed to God for guidance.

"Last night, before I went to bed, I knelt down and this time I prayed I wouldn't wake up in the morning. I just couldn't face going on."

As Haldeman had predicted, Nixon was highlighting his own personal crisis to deflect from the political crisis he had finally forced himself to confront. Telling Haldeman he felt "enormous guilt," he rattled off a list of reasons why he was responsible for all that had happened.

He had "started Colson out on his projects," "told Dean to cover up," and delegated enormous power to a distracted Mitchell. Now it was Haldeman's turn to feel sorry for the older man. He told Nixon that he disagreed with his decision on resignations as opposed to leaves of absence but would carry out his wishes. Whatever happened, Nixon should not himself resign.

"Mr. President, you can't indulge yourself in that kind of feeling. You've got to go on. If there are any other problems, they have to be dealt with. That's all."

The interview lasted twenty-two minutes, although it seemed much longer at the time. It was difficult for Haldeman to tell with Nixon where human empathy ended and political calculation began. His talk about "praying not to wake up" might have reflected his true emotions. Alternatively, it could have been a ploy, designed to steer the conversation in the direction Nixon wanted. Or perhaps, most plausibly, it was both at the same time. The thirty-seventh president of the United States was an unfathomable mixture of idealism and cynicism, greatness and pettiness. After seventeen years working with Nixon, Haldeman still did not have his measure.

Ehrlichman arrived seven minutes later, at 2:49. Nixon shook hands with him as well, before taking him out onto the terrace to admire the view. "His eyes were red-rimmed and he looked small and drawn," Ehrlichman later recalled. Nixon "began crying uncontrollably" as he talked about cutting off his arms, meaning Ehrlichman and Haldeman. He repeated his line about praying for death to come during the night. Instinctively, Ehrlichman put his arm around the president's shoulder to console him.

"Don't talk that way. Don't *think* that way."

Back in the living room, Nixon again offered his assistant financial support through the difficult days ahead, not only for his family, but also to pay his mounting legal bills. Ehrlichman suddenly rediscovered his boiling, inner anger.

"That would only make things worse," he told Nixon. "You can do one thing for me, though, sometime. Just explain all this to my kids, will you? Tell them why you had to do this." Wiping his eyes with his handkerchief, he turned and walked out the door. Manolo, hovering in the kitchen, recorded his departure at 3:25. Ehrlichman had been with the president for thirty-six minutes.

After securing the resignations of Haldeman and Ehrlichman, Nixon met with his lawyer, Len Garment. He was physically and psychologically drained by the experiences of the last few hours. Garment later compared the loss of Nixon's two top aides to the loss of his two brothers, Arthur and Harold, during his adolescence. "Whereas the early deaths were not of his doing, Haldeman and Ehrlichman had to be cut down by Nixon's own hand for faithfully serving his political needs. No wonder it was terrible to contemplate."

Later that evening, Nixon met with Ziegler.

"It's all over, Ron," he said. "Do you know that?"

"No, sir," replied the faithful press spokesman. Ziegler thought his boss was referring to the turmoil in the White House, which would continue at least through Monday night, when Nixon addressed the nation from the Oval Office. In fact, Nixon was talking about his presidency.

"Well, it is," he repeated. "It's all over."

E xactly one hundred days had passed since Richard Nixon's triumphant second coronation, the same amount of time it had taken FDR to launch his New Deal, putting a devastated American economy on the road to recovery. But the wounded monarch was in no mood to celebrate. His odyssey more resembled the hundred-day journey of Napoleon from Paris to Waterloo after his daring escape from Elba, another second act that ended in catastrophe.

He remained at Camp David for much of the day, haunted by premonitions of his abdication. The amputation of his two arms, he wrote later, "may have been necessary for even a chance at survival, but what I had to do left me so anguished and saddened that from that day on the presidency lost all joy for me." He stopped scrawling comments on the daily White House news summaries and even ceased recording his nightly audio diary. Events had become "so cheerless that I no longer had the time or the desire to dictate daily reflections." Places like Camp David and even the White House that were once a source of enjoyment and pride turned into gilded prisons. Along with an intense desire to relieve himself of his burden, he felt a compulsion to press ahead. He would address the nation in the evening. His first call that morning was to Bebe Rebozo, who had come to Washington to show his support.

"I had a very hard day yesterday," Nixon told his friend, his voice raw with fatigue. "I had to bite the bullet on a few things, and now I'm trying to work out a damn speech. If I survive it, I don't know. I was thinking

*Nixon gazes through the window of Aspen Lodge at Camp David
on November 22, 1972, two weeks after his reelection landslide.*

that maybe the one who should resign should be me. I should just check out, what the hell! Go down and sit around in Florida in that nice sun."

Bebe tried to raise his spirits, as a brother might. "You've hit the very bottom, and you've done it before." The only way out now was up.

Nixon would not be consoled. "It's torn me up," he confessed. "When you've got a problem like that, you've just got to rip it all out. It tears them up. It tears me up. It won't do much good what I say, but what the hell! The assholes will still keep attacking, and that's that."

He spent the next ten hours working on his television address with his chief speechwriter, Ray Price. It would be his first ever speech devoted exclusively to Watergate. Price worked on the text in a nearby cabin, incorporating the numerous contributions and corrections of his demanding boss. They exchanged ideas and telephoned back and forth all day. Rose Mary Woods typed up the successive drafts in a third cabin. Nixon told Price that the speech should be "a talk rather than a sermon," but he had difficulty establishing the proper tone. He wanted to bare his soul to the nation but was wary of being "too emotional." He planned to accept responsibility for Watergate but not to "sackcloth" himself too much. He wanted to emphasize that Haldeman and Ehr-lichman had done nothing wrong, but why then were they resigning? It occurred to Nixon that Americans might want to know why "this poor, damn, dumb president" was not resigning himself, if he was truly accepting the blame.

"Which might not be a bad idea," he told Price at 10:42 a.m. "The only problem is you get Agnew. You want Agnew?"

"No," said Price.

It was not until late afternoon that Nixon finally summoned the speechwriter to his side. They met in his study in Aspen Lodge, over-looking a well-tended stretch of lawn sloping down to the forest beyond. The president was in a corner chair, facing the blazing fireplace, his back to the windows. Price had never seen him "so distraught." He looked "emotionally ravaged, his hands unsteady, anguish written in every one of the deepened lines of his face." Pages of the draft lay scattered on the floor as Nixon again raised the issue of his own resignation.

"If you think I should resign, just write it into the next draft, and I'll do it."

Price had no way of gauging how close the president was to quitting. He was clearly seeking reassurance but was also "deeply tormented." Reflecting on the scene years later, he felt that Nixon had reached the "emotional nadir of his presidency" and could "very easily have been pushed over the brink into resignation." Like Kissinger and Haldeman before him, Price told Nixon he had a duty to remain in office to protect "the structure of peace" he had put in place. This seemed to snap the president out of the worst of his depression.

To prepare himself physically and mentally for his television appear-ance, Nixon decided to go for a swim. Fearing that the president would stumble and bang his head on the concrete, Price insisted on escorting him to the pool on the lower terrace. As Nixon descended the steps, he stopped to talk about the challenges confronting America from the Soviet Union, China, the Middle East. The more he talked about the state of the world, the more animated he became. He agreed with Price that he, not Agnew, was the right man to "navigate those treach-erous shoals." The immediate crisis was over. At 7:21 p.m., Nixon went to the Camp David helipad and flew to Washington on Marine One, landing on the White House lawn at 7:58. It was dark by the time he arrived.

At 9:00 p.m., following a touch-up by the White House barber, he went before the cameras in the Oval Office. A portrait of his wife and daughters was carefully positioned by his right elbow next to the American flag; a bust of Abraham Lincoln was visible to his left. He sounded hoarse but in control of himself as he announced the resignations of Haldeman and Ehrlichman ("two of the finest public servants it has been my privilege to know") and Kleindienst, as well as the firing of Dean. He acknowledged that people he had once trusted had been involved in Watergate but did not name them. Suppressing his true feelings, he paid tribute to "a determined grand jury, honest prosecutors, a courageous judge—John Sirica—and a vigorous free press" for exposing wrongdoing. The new attorney general, Elliot Richardson ("a man of unimpeachable integrity"), would have "absolute authority" to pursue "this case, wherever it leads."

"There can be no whitewash at the White House," Nixon declared. At the end of the twenty-four-minute speech, he pushed his pile of papers slowly aside, lowered his eyes in silent prayer, stared back into the camera, and added his own impromptu peroration. "God bless *America* and God bless *each* and every one of you."

He left the Oval Office through the French doors and walked along the colonnade adjoining the Rose Garden, past the Cabinet Room. But instead of turning right, back to the residence, he went straight ahead toward the press office. His unexpected appearance in the briefing room caught a dozen or so reporters and photographers by surprise. The lights around the lectern were out, so he stood in the semidarkness. His voice was barely audible. "Ladies and gentlemen of the press, in the last several years, we've had our differences and we'll have some more. Continue to give me hell every time you think I'm wrong." He then left abruptly, putting his arm around the shoulders of Rose Mary Woods, who put her arm around him. Together, they headed upstairs to the Lincoln Sitting Room. The act of reaching out to people he despised had left Nixon badly in need of a drink. As Ron Ziegler later put it, he had "to kill the pain" of his separation from Haldeman and Ehrlichman.

He had been disciplining himself for days, knowing that he would need all his focus and energy to survive perhaps the greatest trial of his life. He had limited his intake of alcohol. Along with sleeping pills and other medications, it had never taken many drinks before he felt light-headed and woozy. Now he let go and was soon slurring his words. Sitting in his armchair facing the soapstone fireplace, he was disappointed no one had called to congratulate him, as was routine after a big speech. At 10:16 p.m., he finally made his own call to Haldeman. His voice choked with emotion.

"I hope I didn't let you down," he began.

"No, sir, you got your points over, and now you've got it set right and move on. You're right where you ought to be."

"Weeell, it's a tough thing, Baawb, for you and for John and the rest," said Nixon, dragging out the syllables like an old-time southern pol, "but, goddamn it, I'm never going to discuss the son-of-a-bitching Watergate thing again. *Never, never, never, never.* Don't you agree?"

"Yes, sir."

"Keep the faith. You're going to win this son of a bitch."

They reviewed the speech together, as they had so often in the past. Nixon was proud of the "God bless America" touch at the end, even though sentimentality of that sort drove his advisers "up the wall." He then asked Haldeman "to call around and get any reactions and call me back—like in the old style, would you mind?"

"I don't think I can," said the ousted chief of staff. "I'm in kind of an odd spot to do that."

"Don't call a goddamned soul," said Nixon, abruptly reversing course. "The hell with it."

Haldeman cleared up the mystery of the president's silent phone. The switchboard had been ordered not to put through any calls.

"All right, I'll change it," said Nixon. "God bless you, boy."

"Okay."

"I love you, as you know." There was an agonized pause. "Like my brother."

The president was joined in the Lincoln Sitting Room by Pat, Tricia, Bebe Rebozo, Rose Mary Woods, and his son-in-law David Eisenhower. (Julie was away in Florida.) They operated like a team of seconds during the rest period in a boxing match, seeking to revive a groggy fighter. Bebe was in charge of morale. Rose Mary ran back and forth with messages. Tricia kept her father supplied with drink and answered the telephone. David helped screen the callers. Billy Graham praised Nixon for his "humility"; Henry Kissinger again invoked the favorable judgment of history; Chuck Colson wanted the president to know that "the country is with you." Even Bob Abplanalp made a cameo phone-in, exchanging a few jokes with Bebe.

"Don't cut anyone off, unless it's an asshole," Nixon instructed his staff. And to Tricia, who was keeping watch by his side, "Honey, put some more of that in here." The tinkle of ice cubes in his glass was recorded for posterity on the tapes as the calls continued.

Nixon often turned mean when he had been drinking, but on this occasion he was a happy drunk, addressing White House staff and cabinet secretaries alike as "boy" and complimenting them on their choice of wives. "How did you ever get to marry such a pretty girl?" he asked the governor of California. *"My God!"*

"Well, I'm lucky," drawled Ronald Reagan.

"Damned nice of you to call," said Nixon, emulating the Gipper himself, with his folksy, aw-shucks courtesy.

"This, too, shall pass," said Reagan.

At 10:34, Elliot Richardson called to congratulate Nixon on his "finest hour." The attorney general designate had been attending a dinner party and sounded fairly well lubricated himself, or perhaps it was just his upper-class Brahmin manner. "I won't let you down," he promised the president.

"Do your job, boy, and it may take you all the way," said Nixon. "Get to the bottom of this son of a bitch."

Richardson did not tell the president of his decision, made earlier in the evening with Bill Ruckelshaus and Len Garment, to send FBI agents to the White House to make sure that none of the dismissed staff members removed any documents. Nixon only found out the following day. Walking through the West Wing on his way back from his EOB hideaway, he came across a man in a dark suit, blocking his path to the Oval Office.

"Who the hell are you?" he demanded.

"FBI," replied the agent. He explained that he had been ordered to guard Haldeman's office.

The president grabbed the man by his jacket and shoved him against the wall.

"Get out of here," he ordered, telling the agent to wait inside the chief of staff's office rather than loiter outside. At a cabinet meeting shortly afterward, he exploded with anger. The sight of G-men patrolling the hallowed White House corridors was "the most shocking thing" he had ever seen; Haldeman and Ehrlichman were "honest men" who could be trusted with their files; the president had "nothing but contempt" for whoever ordered such a "terribly arrogant move."

"Whoever did this should have his ass fired," Nixon declared. "This is a cheap publicity stunt."

Richardson did his best to avoid the president's accusing gaze. The Watergate investigation had reached the corridor leading to the Oval Office, the heart of the White House. It seemed only a matter of time before Nixon himself would be dragged down by the scandal. Downstairs from the Cabinet Room, in a closet hidden in the West Wing basement, the tape machines continued to roll, bearing witness to the humiliation of their creator.

ACT IV

CATHARSIS

κάθαρσις—katharsis

release of emotional tension after overwhelming experience

———————————

A man is not finished when he's defeated.
He's finished when he quits.

—RICHARD NIXON

A few days after his television address on Watergate, Richard Nixon received a note from his old friend Clare Boothe Luce that was calculated to appeal to his fighting spirit. The society wit and former ambassador quoted from an old English ballad about a sailor named Sir Andrew Barton who rallied his men against their Portuguese enemies even after his leg was blown off by musket shot:

> *I am hurt, but I am not slain;*
> *I'll lay me down and bleed a-while,*
> *And then I'll rise and fight again!*

Although Nixon had sworn never to talk about Watergate again, the subject refused to go away. The prosecutors, media, and opposition-controlled Congress were all relentless in exploring inconsistencies in the official White House position and raising new questions. On May 10, the grand jury issued its first obstruction of justice indictments against John Mitchell and three other CREEP officials. The Senate Watergate hearings opened on May 17 beneath the crystal chandeliers of the marble-pillared Caucus Room of the Old Senate Office Building. "A very dull show," Nixon commented that evening. "They're going to lose their audience with that stuff. People will be looking for late, late shows."

Nixon could not have been more wrong. The hearings quickly

attracted millions of television viewers who followed the multiple twists in the drama with the avidity of soap opera fans. One of the first witnesses was James McCord, who used a dismantled telephone to explain how he bugged the Democratic Party offices. Every day brought a startling development in the plot or colorful new character. Some of the witnesses who paraded through the committee room became minor celebrities, like the saggy-jowled former New York policeman Tony Ulasewicz, who entertained everyone with his tales of the undercover life. "Who thought you up?" asked Senator Howard Baker of Tennessee as the CREEP "bagman" described the world of secret code names and stashes of $100 bills left in mailboxes and airport lockers. "My parents, maybe," replied Ulasewicz, to general laughter.

Pushed onto the defensive, the president was forced to admit he had approved a secret wiretap program to investigate the national security leaks that had led to publication of the Pentagon Papers. On May 22, he issued a four-thousand-word statement acknowledging the existence of a "special investigative unit," known as the Plumbers, to stop the leaks. He conceded for the first time that some of his top aides "may have gone beyond my directives" in covering up aspects of the Watergate case for fear of disclosing other, supposedly legitimate, covert intelligence operations. The attempt to distance himself from the actions of overzealous subordinates triggered a fresh wave of press invective. *The Washington Post* dubbed his latest explanations "pathetic, unconvincing, confused." *The New York Times* accused the White House of "criminal behavior which has brought the office of the President into grave disrepute."

Nixon sought relief from his woes by wrapping himself in the flag. He had long been planning a patriotic homecoming for the 591 released Vietnam POWs and their families. It would be the largest sit-down dinner in White House history, with multiple bands and Hollywood-style entertainment provided by America's finest performers. Because it was impossible to accommodate 1,300 dinner guests in the White House state rooms, a giant circus tent was erected on the South Lawn, larger than the entire first floor of the mansion. Pat Nixon spent weeks supervising the arrangements, which included creating floral centerpieces for 126 tables, chilling hundreds of bottles of champagne in aluminum canoes, and running crates of strawberries through military-grade Pentagon blenders for the mousse dessert. Remembering that he had presented Pat with her first orchid corsage on their wedding day, Nixon had earlier sent every POW wife and mother a bouquet of white orchids as his personal gift.

The great day was set for Thursday, May 24, in the middle of the Senate hearings. The Nixons opened up the White House, allowing their guests access to the usually off-limits private residence on the second floor. Men who a few weeks before were sleeping on straw pallets in the Hanoi Hilton posed for pictures in the Lincoln Bedroom. Downstairs, in the East Room, Jimmy Stewart and John Wayne chatted about their roles in old war movies with B-52 pilots who had been shot down over North Vietnam. Although it rained all afternoon and into the evening, spirits remained high. Women gathered their long gowns up to their knees as they splashed through muddy puddles to their tables in the rain-soaked marquee on the lawn. Chandeliers hung from the canvas ceiling, matching the chandeliers in the hearing room at the other end of Pennsylvania Avenue.

Nixon was the uncontested hero of the evening, followed at a distance by Kissinger, basking in his reputation as America's most eligible bachelor. ("The biggest thrill for anyone in show business is to be introduced by the president," joked Bob Hope as master of ceremonies. "The second biggest thrill is a date with Henry Kissinger.") Almost to a man, the former prisoners credited Nixon for bringing them home. "We knew you were in a very lonely position," said Brigadier General John Flynn, the senior POW, referring to Nixon's decision to launch massive bombing raids against the North the previous December. "When we heard heavy bombs impacting in Hanoi, we started to go and pack our bags, because we knew we were going home, and we were going home with honor." Nixon received one of several thunderous standing ovations when he was presented with a plaque inscribed to "Our leader— our comrade, Richard the Lion-Hearted."

It was left to John Wayne to sum up the mood of the evening. "You hung in there while the going was rough, and so did he," he told the former POWs. "You stuck by your guns, and so did he. You love this blessed country, and so does he. You're the best we have, and I'll ride off into the sunset with you any time."

Shortly after midnight, Nixon introduced the eighty-five-year-old Irving Berlin to lead the crowd in his most famous song, "God Bless

*Nixon singing "God Bless America" with Irving Berlin, Sammy Davis Jr.,
and Pat Nixon at the POW reception. The miniature American flag was made
by a POW while in captivity in Hanoi.*

America." They sang it once, and then they sang it again. By the time
they sang it a third time, even louder than before, Nixon imagined that
"the words could be heard all the way to Hanoi." *God bless America, my
home sweet home.*

The party was still going on when Nixon retired to the Lincoln Sitting Room. The sounds of music and laughter and people dancing in
the state rooms below floated up to him as he stared into the fire. He
considered the evening he had just experienced "one of the greatest
nights of my life." He basked in the plaudits of the men on the soggy
lawn, praise that seemed to validate some of the toughest decisions of
his presidency. One of the former POWs had given him a personal note
that he had stuffed into the pocket of his dinner jacket, intending to
read it later. The note described a message that Americans in solitary
confinement at the Hanoi Hilton had tapped through the prison walls
to each other. The man wanted to pass the message on to the president:
"Don't let the bastards get you down."

Suddenly Nixon was drawn back to his political troubles. The contrast between "the splendid lift" of the POW dinner and "the dreary

daily drain of Watergate" struck him "with almost physical force." Not wanting to be alone, he picked up the phone and asked his daughters to join him. They found him smoking his pipe in the darkened room, lit only by the blazing logs in the fireplace. "My father seemed drained, as if the emotion of the evening had been too much for him," Julie recalled later. They sat with him as he ruminated on his predicament in telephone calls to his aides. Tricia wrote in her diary that it was "almost more than I could bear to stay there and see his sadness on what should have been a night of jubilant triumph."

One of the calls was to Al Haig, who had succeeded Haldeman as chief of staff. Haig did his best to boost his spirits, laughing off his renewed talk of resignation, but it was tough going. The president's mood cycled between elation and despair, resolve to continue the fight and a sense that it was all over. As was often the case, much of his anger was aimed at the press. He was convinced that the media jackals would simply ignore the good news from the dinner and feast forever on scandal. He fantasized about destroying the bastards once and for all.

"It'll be a fight to the death and it'll probably kill me," he told the four-star general. "But, by God, if I do, I am going to *kick their ass* around the block. I really am. Because we cannot allow this *crap* about Water-*bate*, Water-*gate*, trying to cover up and the rest, destroy the greatest foreign policy this country's ever had. Good God, wasn't Jimmy Stewart nice and old John Wayne?"

Haig could only agree. "I tell you, I was so proud tonight, it made all the fighting we've done worthwhile. By God, sir, it makes you want to stand up and take the monkeys on. We're going to wipe 'em out."

"The White House has never seen a party like this, believe me," said Nixon. "We stuck it to 'em on that December bombing. Hah?"

"The whole place was just oozing with patriotism," said Haig.

Nixon's mood suddenly turned bleak.

"They're all saying they're going to try the president, and all that horseshit. It's going to be *rough*."

He described how he had gone table-hopping and was "almost torn apart" by the expressions of support from "all these kids and their wives, crying and kissing." If only all Americans were like the men who had endured the horrors of the Hanoi Hilton.

"They're just so few, so few," he lamented. "Too bad the POWs aren't the country."

"They *are* the country, Mr. President. They are the country."

When Nixon finally put down the phone, he sank into a long silence. Eventually, he looked at Tricia and Julie and said, "Do you think I should resign?"

They were horrified not just by the sentiment but by the agony etched on his face and the tone of his voice, which seemed much graver than before.

"What can you be thinking?"

"Don't you dare."

"The country needs you."

Nixon smiled sadly. He thanked his daughters for joining him and said good night.

've got to listen to a lot of crap, and I want to get it over with as fast as I can," Nixon told his personal aide Steve Bull, shortly after nine on the morning of June 4. He had cleared an entire day from his schedule to listen to tapes of his conversations with John Dean and wanted to get started as soon as possible. But the sole Secret Service technician authorized to check out the tapes from the storage room was having trouble sorting through the uncataloged racks of materials. It took another hour for the first batch of tapes to be delivered to Nixon's EOB hideaway.

Bull showed him how to operate the Sony tape machine. Aware of Nixon's unease with mechanical devices, he proceeded step by step. "Push the play button when you are ready to listen, sir. Depress the stop button when you are done." He explained the purpose of the rewind button and the digital counter. "Got that, sir?"

Although he dreaded the task ahead, Nixon did not trust anyone else with listening to hours and hours of personal recordings. He feared what he might discover. "Get lost, Steve," he ordered.

He put on a pair of headphones and pushed play. For the next nine hours, he waded through stacks of tapes, breaking only for his usual hurried lunch of cottage cheese and pineapple. Soon his head began to spin from the effort of making sense of the meandering conversation. It was often impossible to figure out who was speaking and what exactly they were saying. "Sounds drifted in and out; voices overrode each other. Gradually, as my ears became accustomed, I could pick up more and more." He pressed the stop button frequently to make extensive notes on his yellow legal pads. As he worked on one tape, Bull would queue up another on a second machine next door. After listening to a few tapes, Nixon felt drained. This was the toughest job he had ever had.

By six o'clock, he had reviewed half a dozen tapes. Although he still had a few more to go, he was feeling much better about his conversations with Dean. As far as he could tell, there had been little discussion of the Watergate cover-up prior to the "cancer on the presidency" conversation of March 21. He saw no need to listen to the March 21 tape itself, because Haldeman had already been through that one. There were some troubling passages on the tapes, but Nixon was confident he could explain them away. He and Dean had focused primarily on how to contain the political damage from the upcoming Senate select committee hearings. In Nixon's mind, this was quite different from obstruction of justice. He rewarded himself with a relaxing drink with Ron Ziegler.

"Working my butt off here, whew," said Nixon. "Damn, it's hard work."

"It's so worthwhile," said the press secretary.

As he sipped his scotch and soda, Nixon shared his notes with Ziegler. He acknowledged there might be a problem with the March 17 conversation, when Dean told him that he had been all over Watergate, "like a blanket."

"But I said, 'John, you didn't know about it.' He said, 'That's right, I have no knowledge. No prior knowledge.'" Could that be construed as awareness of a cover-up?

"Not at all," said Ziegler.

Nixon found another passage on the tape where he had stressed the need to wind up the Watergate investigation before anyone "starts pissing on Haldeman." He wondered if Dean could point to that exchange as a cover-up instruction.

"I suppose he could say that in the context of the time," Ziegler conceded, but quickly added, "But still, there's nothing, Mr. President, there's nothing."

On balance, Nixon felt good about the tapes. They could disprove some of Dean's wilder charges if exploited skillfully enough, perhaps even trap him in perjury. Nixon's defenders would have to be careful not to reveal the secret of the taping system. But they could use bits and pieces here and there, in legal memoranda and targeted press leaks, to put the most favorable spin possible on the president's actions. Nixon comforted himself with the thought that the "goddamn record" was not so bad after all.

"Makes me feel very good," said Ziegler. Any differences in interpretation could be explained away by the "Rashomon theory," after the celebrated Japanese movie. "Five men sit in a room. What occurs in that room, or what is said in that room, means something different to each man, based upon his perception of the events that preceded it. That's exactly what this is."

Nixon listened to a few more tapes before finally giving up. "I've just spent nine hours on this crap and, boy, I got to go to bed," he told Haig at 9:39 p.m. He had concluded that "the whole damned Dean thing is a fraud."

"That's what I thought," said Haig.

"Looking back, I can see where he may have been involved, but I wasn't involved. I've listened to stuff until I'm sick."

Exhausted, he walked back to the residence and put in a call to Bob Haldeman from the Lincoln Sitting Room. His former chief of staff was at home in Georgetown, preparing to return to California with his wife, four children, and "assorted birds, dogs, fish etc." He was expecting the call. Despite his exile from the White House, the president still depended on his unrivaled knowledge of how the place worked. If anyone could be relied upon to lend a sympathetic ear to his travails with the tapes, it was Haldeman, the first person to ever attempt to make sense of them. They had shared a similar agony. Nixon wanted to let his longtime associate know that the Dean threat had been much exaggerated.

"Got a minute?" the president asked.

"Sure."

"I thought you should know that starting at, uh, 9:30 this morning, I have been working until just now. I listened to every tape."

"Good Lord!" said Haldeman, deeply impressed.

"I listened to every damn thing and, Bob, this son of a bitch is bluffing," said Nixon. "He didn't ever mention the cover-up. Never."

For months, John Dean had stopped short of directly implicating the president in the crimes of Watergate. He had begun his journey into apostasy by refusing to support the lies of Jeb Magruder, the man he had coached to commit perjury. During his meetings with Justice Department prosecutors, he had leveled accusations against Bob Haldeman and John Ehrlichman but had avoided answering questions about Nixon's culpability. His restraint finally vanished with his own dismissal as White House counsel on April 30. When he learned that FBI agents had been sent to his office to seal his files, he immediately blamed the president. "This is like something out of the Third Reich," he told his lawyer. Nixon, he concluded, was "capable of anything."

His dance with the prosecutors continued a few more days, until it became clear that they would refuse his demand for immunity. They felt it would be unfair to allow someone so central to the cover-up to escape punishment while other, more peripheral people were sent to jail. Charlie Shaffer reminded them that they were not "the only game in town." The Senate select committee also had authority to grant witnesses immunity—not the complete "transactional immunity" in the power of the Justice Department, but a more limited "use immunity." Testimony that Dean gave to the committee could not be used against him in court. If the prosecutors wanted to bring charges against him, they would have to find independent witnesses. This route would give Dean the opportunity to speak directly to the American people. In return, however, he would have to be completely honest. He could hold nothing back.

A deal was quickly struck. Accompanied by Maureen, Dean retired to a beach house on the Maryland shore to compile a narrative history of Watergate, both before and after the break-in. He dredged through piles of old newspaper clippings to assemble a detailed chronology. He inserted the complete list of all his meetings and telephone conversations with the president that he had obtained from the White House archivist. He then combined all these materials with documents he had succeeded in smuggling out of the office. He drew on his own extensive but occasionally faulty memory to fill in the details. By the time he finished, six weeks later, he had written sixty thousand words, the length of a short novel. He also repaired some of the damage to his marriage caused by the strains of Watergate. The relaxed atmosphere of the oceanfront house and deserted beach—with no television and no reporters hammering at the door—provided a much-needed break for both him and Maureen. While she had not yet fully recovered, she "looked happier" than she had for many weeks.

Dean's account of his inside knowledge of Watergate still fell short of the standard set by the select committee for granting immunity. The committee's chief counsel, Samuel Dash, complained that he had failed to "tell all." He would not make a credible witness if he shifted all the blame onto others, minimizing the significance of his own actions. As an example, Dash pointed to a passage about helping Magruder prepare for his grand jury appearance while avoiding any mention of his own role in suborning perjury.

"Did you know, in advance, that Magruder was going to lie to the grand jury?" Dash asked.

"Sure," said Dean.

"That's what I want you to put in the statement," said Dash.

Dean was stung by the criticism, but Shaffer supported Dash. He told his client to delete the "self-serving crap" in his statement. If Dean was going to cooperate with the committee, he would have to tell them "every last fucking thing" he did, "no matter how bad or lousy it sounds."

He agreed to rework the draft. Fortunately, there was still time to make improvements. The committee postponed its public hearings by a week to avoid upstaging a U.S.-Soviet summit meeting. While Nixon played host to Leonid Brezhnev in San Clemente, Dean put the finishing touches to his statement. Press speculation about what he might say mounted by the day, along with incoming hate mail. A few days before he was due to testify, the committee received an anonymous note that read, "JOHN DEAN WILL NEVER BE A WITNESS. HE WILL BE DEAD." The committee requested round-the-clock protection for their star witness. A team of U.S. marshals moved into Dean's house and accompanied him whenever he appeared in public.

At 10:00 a.m. on June 25, Dean rose to take the oath beneath the chandeliers and klieg lights of the packed Caucus Room. Police guarded the entrance doors. Every seat was taken; scores of spectators stood at the back, jammed between the Corinthian columns. Facing the witness behind a wide green baize table were the seven members of the select committee led by the Democrat Sam Ervin of North Carolina, a grandfatherly figure with white hair and bushy eyebrows. Dean and his attorneys had thought through every detail of his television appearance. He sat at the witness table alone to emphasize the confidence with which he was telling his story. He kept his voice as neutral as possible so as not to

John Dean testifies before the Senate Watergate Committee
with his wife Maureen in the background.

sound melodramatic. To assume a gravitas beyond his thirty-four years, he dispensed with his contact lenses and put on a pair of horn-rimmed glasses. He had his hair trimmed "nice and clean" before the hearing to avoid the shaggy look that had marred some of his television appearances. The most memorable touch was to position Maureen directly behind his right shoulder. An ice-cold beauty with a pained expression on her perfectly groomed face, her golden hair pulled back severely, she would become the eternal symbol of the loyal, long-suffering Washington spouse. "Exhibit number one," Shaffer called her.

Heeding his lawyer's plea to sound humble and contrite, Dean began by saying it was difficult for him "to testify about other people." It would be "far easier" to describe the way he had obstructed justice, "assisted another in perjured testimony," and "made personal use of funds that were in my custody." This was a reference to a story in *The New York Times*, a few days before, that he had "borrowed" $4,850 from a Nixon campaign fund to pay for his honeymoon the previous year. The apologies out of the way, he launched into a lengthy account of Nixon administration misdeeds, from wiretaps of reporters and the plot to bomb the Brookings Institution to the destruction of forged State Department documents and the payment of hush money to the Watergate conspirators. In a flat, emotionless tone, he described the moment when Nixon had asked "how much it would cost" to keep the Watergate defendants happy. "I told him I could only make an estimate, that it might be as high as a million dollars or more. He told me that that was no problem." His narrative culminated with his Oval Office meeting with Nixon on March 21.

"I began by telling the president that there was a cancer growing on the presidency and if the cancer was not removed that the president himself would be killed by it," he recalled.

To counter Dean's testimony, which continued all week, the White House released a long memorandum that put a totally different interpretation on the same set of facts. According to this version, it was Dean who initiated the cover-up, Dean who proposed destroying politically sensitive documents, Dean who dragged his feet on informing Nixon about the mortal threat to his presidency. When Dean finally gave the president "a more complete but still laundered version of the facts" on March 21, Nixon was "so surprised" that he jumped out of his chair.

The charges and countercharges caused the senior Republican on the committee, Howard Baker, to reduce everything he had heard to a central issue: "What did the president know, and when did he know it?" For the moment, there was no definitive answer to this deceptively simple question. It all depended on whom to believe: John Dean or Richard Nixon.

A lexander Butterfield had been wrestling with his conscience for weeks. The White House aide responsible for installing Nixon's taping system was one of only a handful of people aware of its existence. As he watched Dean testify before the Senate, his thoughts had repeatedly turned to the tapes. Having observed Nixon closely, he was sure the recordings would demonstrate the essential veracity of Dean's charges. The president was "the choreographer of the cover-up." In the recesses of his mind, Butterfield kept murmuring to the television set, "God, if they only knew, if they only knew."

An old college friend of Bob Haldeman's, Butterfield had supervised the paper flow in and out of the Oval Office. Despite his closeness to both Haldeman and Nixon, the retired air force colonel had avoided being tarred with Watergate. His strength lay in his administrative skills, not political skulduggery. He had left the White House in good standing in March, following his appointment to head the Federal Aviation Administration. His sense of duty told him that he had to protect the secrets of his commander in chief, but his sense of honor and respect for the rule of law obliged him to tell the truth if questioned by Senate investigators.

It took the staff of the Watergate select committee several months to even bother with him. When they invited him for an interview on the afternoon of Friday, July 13, they had no expectation of learning anything substantive. It was a routine background session, designed to add to their understanding of how the White House operated. No senators were present, just a few bored staff members. Room G-334 in the new Senate office building stank of stale cigarette butts, unfinished fast-food meals, and a filthy, grease-stained carpet that had not been cleaned in weeks. Janitors were prohibited from carrying out their usual duties for fear they might plant an eavesdropping device. The swelteringly hot Washington air seeped through the walls of the poorly air-conditioned committee room, contributing to the general listlessness.

A twenty-seven-year-old Harvard Law School dropout by the name of Scott Armstrong conducted the questioning of Butterfield on behalf of the Democratic majority. He fished for information about the relationship between Nixon and Dean, but the witness had little useful to contribute. Disappointed, Armstrong began questioning Butterfield about Nixon's office routine and the records of his meetings. He invited Butterfield to inspect a document, provided to Republican staffers by the White House as part of their defense strategy, describing Nixon's meetings with Dean.

The document included a direct quotation from the March 21 meeting, describing Nixon's reaction to Howard Hunt's demands for blackmail. "How could it possibly be paid?" the president had purportedly asked Dean. "What makes you think he would be satisfied with that?"

"Where did you get this?" asked Butterfield.

Armstrong explained that a Nixon attorney had shared the information with the committee. He asked if the quotation could have been drawn from someone's notes.

"No, it seems too detailed," said Butterfield. Privately, he had decided he would not volunteer information but would answer truthfully if asked a direct question about the existence of a taping system.

How often did the president dictate memoranda about meetings in the Oval Office? Armstrong wanted to know.

"Very rarely," said Butterfield.

"Were his memos this detailed?"

"I don't think so."

"Where else could this have come from?"

Butterfield made a show of studying the document some more. He saw no reason to speculate. His interrogator was getting close to his imaginary red line but had not quite reached it.

"I don't know. Let me think about this for a while." He pushed the document back across the table.

As Armstrong moved on to other topics, Butterfield breathed a sigh of relief. After three hours of questions from the Democratic side, it was time for the Republican minority to have a shot. The lead Republican staffer in the room was Donald Sanders, a former FBI agent trained in tying up loose ends. Sanders recalled that Dean had talked about an incident in which Nixon pulled him into a corner of his EOB hideaway to whisper a confidence in his ear. This had led Dean to suspect that the office might be bugged, and the president was trying to avoid being recorded.

His heart pounding as he posed the all-important question, Sanders asked Butterfield whether Dean might be right. Was there any "voice recording system" in the president's office other than the Dictabelt machine he used to dictate his personal diary?

"I hoped you fellows wouldn't ask me that," Butterfield replied. "I'm concerned about the effect my answer will have on national security and international affairs. But I suppose I have to assume that this is a formal, official interview in the same vein as if I was being questioned by the committee under oath."

"That's right," said Sanders.

"Well, yes," said Butterfield. "There is a recording system at the White House."

Three days later, on the afternoon of Monday, July 16, the Senate select committee summoned a reluctant Butterfield to testify in public. Hesitantly but methodically, he described how recording devices had been installed in the Oval Office, the president's private study in the Executive Office Building, the Cabinet Room, various White House telephones, and the presidential retreat at Camp David. With the exception of the Cabinet Room, the devices were all voice activated, switching on automatically. There was likely a comprehensive electronic record of the president's disputed conversations with John Dean and others.

"Wonders of Watergate do not cease," *The Washington Post* reported the following day. The "ultimate witness" had emerged from the shadows—"not John Dean or John Mitchell, not Haldeman or Ehrlichman, not even President Nixon himself. In the search for truth, they have all been upstaged, appropriately enough, by an electronic gizmo—a tape recorder that faithfully eavesdropped on all presidential conversations."

Nixon learned of the disclosure of his most closely guarded secret as he lay in a hospital bed recovering from pneumonia. He had woken up four days earlier with "a stabbing pain" in his chest that reminded him of cracking a rib playing football at Whittier College. He stuck to a crowded schedule of meetings and telephone calls but soon found it difficult to breathe. By Thursday afternoon, he had a hacking cough and a 102-degree temperature. X-rays showed that he had viral pneumonia. That evening, he was driven to Bethesda Naval Hospital, in the Maryland suburbs just outside Washington, and checked in to the third-floor presidential suite. It was the first time he had been hospitalized since the 1960 election campaign when he injured his knee on a car door.

Except for the tubes, breathing equipment, and monitoring devices that surrounded his bed, his quarters resembled a suite in a luxury hotel. There was a bedroom, a living room, and a kitchen, where Manolo puttered about as usual. Lingering chest pains prevented Nixon from getting much sleep. He lay awake at night counting the minutes. According to his daughter Julie, there were times when he "seemed almost delirious with fever and worry." He was in "no condition to make important decisions." Meetings with advisers and cabinet members were sandwiched between rounds of inhalation therapy. To cheer him up, Pat Nixon dropped by on Monday afternoon with Tricia, Bebe Rebozo, King Timahoe, and the other family dogs, a French poodle named

Vicky and a Yorkshire terrier named Pasha. She replaced the drab government artwork on the walls with some personal paintings from their New York apartment that had been in storage at the White House.

Nixon spoke with his new chief of staff several times that afternoon and evening. General Haig summed up the dilemma he faced with military clarity: "You have two options: you can either keep the tapes or you can destroy them."

It was a ghastly choice. If Nixon kept the tapes, he would likely spend the rest of his presidency battling demands from the prosecutors, Congress, and news media for their release. "In the end, you may very well have to give them up," warned Haig. If he destroyed the tapes, he would be "violently attacked." The critics would see his action as "an admission of guilt"; his supporters would applaud his common sense. There was certain to be another huge battle, perhaps even an attempt at impeachment. On the plus side, the ordeal would probably be over fairly quickly.

While Haig had been informed about the existence of the tapes soon after his appointment as chief of staff, he had only a vague idea how the system operated. He was appalled to discover that the recording devices were triggered automatically, whenever the president walked into a room. As he later wrote, "It never occurred to me that anyone in his right mind would install anything so Orwellian as a system that never shut off, that preserved every word, every joke, every curse, every tantrum, every flight of presidential paranoia, every bit of flattery and bad advice and tattling by his advisors." As he waited for Nixon to make up his mind about the fate of the 950 reels of tape locked away in EOB safes, Haig ordered the removal of the entire taping system.

On Tuesday morning, Haig drove out to the hospital with Ziegler and members of Nixon's legal team. They pulled up a row of chairs to face the president's bed and the array of medical gadgets. The president's legal counsel, Len Garment, made the strongest argument for preserving the evidence. Even though the White House had not received a formal subpoena for the tapes, congressional leaders were known to be on the verge of issuing one. Destruction of the tapes could be viewed as obstruction of justice under federal law. At the same time, Garment believed Nixon had the right to reject a congressional subpoena on grounds of executive privilege. The tapes were, and should remain, his personal property. They should never be released publicly. Another lawyer, Fred Buzhardt, urged Nixon to burn the tapes. The president still had the political strength to ride out the inevitable storm.

Haig was ambivalent. His instinct told him that the tapes should be destroyed. On the other hand, such a step would "forever seal an impression of guilt in the public mind." There was also a practical problem: Who would carry out a presidential order to dispose of the tapes? Haig was not prepared to risk his own future career by personally putting a torch to materials that would answer the question posed so insistently by Senator Baker: *What did the president know, and when did he know it?*

"I can't do that," Haig replied bluntly, when Nixon asked him, hypothetically, if he would be willing to destroy the tapes. "I can't put my family in that position." Perhaps Manolo or someone "completely outside his inner circle, such as a member of the Secret Service," could be persuaded to do the deed. They, at least, would have much less to lose.

Later that afternoon, Nixon was visited by Vice President Spiro Agnew, who was facing his own criminal investigation into bribes he had accepted from contractors as a politician in Maryland. Agnew's advice was unambiguous. "Boss, you gotta have a bonfire," he told the president. "Get rid of those tapes while they're yours."

The only person who had actually listened to any of the tapes, apart from Nixon himself, was Bob Haldeman, now back in California. Asked by Haig to give his opinion, he advised against destruction. He continued to feel that there was exonerating material on the tapes. Nixon could claim he first heard about the cover-up from Dean on March 21 and had then launched his own investigation. Haldeman believed that the recordings were Nixon's "best defense" and important for writing his memoirs. He was convinced that the executive privilege argument invoked by previous presidents would apply to the Nixon tapes as well.

"We've got total control of them," Haldeman told Haig. "If there's executive privilege applying to anything, it sure as hell applies to that."

"Is there anything on them that's going to be harmful to the president?" Haig wanted to know.

Haldeman conceded that there was "a lot of stuff" that could prove extremely embarrassing. But because the White House would control release of the recordings, it could spin their content to its own advantage. Overall the tapes were likely to be "very helpful" to Nixon.

Torn between conflicting sets of advice, Nixon told Haig he would
"sleep on it."

After a brush with political and even physical death during the dark
days of April, Nixon's thoughts had turned to resurrection. He no longer talked about resignation. Prior to being admitted to the hospital
on July 12, he had been looking forward to fighting his way out of the
Watergate mess. He now applied his restless but medicated mind to
analyzing the problem created by the revelation of his taping system.

Nixon was impressed by Haig's argument that destruction of the
tapes would create "an indelible impression of guilt." He felt that the
recordings would give him "at least some protection" if men like Ehrlichman, perhaps even Haldeman, turned against him, as Dean already
had. Having spent many exhausting hours listening to his conversations
with Dean, he believed the tapes would clear him of the charge that they
had conspired together to obstruct justice.

He made his decision overnight. His fever had broken thanks to the
drugs, and he was able to think more clearly now. When Haig came into
his bedroom at 11:35 a.m., he announced he would keep the tapes. They
were his "best insurance against perjury."

"Al, I've thought about this all night long," said Nixon. "Those tapes
are going to defend me."

The battle for control of the tapes began immediately. Later that same
day, Archibald Cox, the special prosecutor appointed by Elliot Richardson, formally requested access to eight presidential recordings, including the "cancer on the presidency" briefing from Dean. That night
Nixon wrote a note to himself on the legal pad he kept on his bedside
table: "Should have destroyed the tapes after April 30, 1973." But it was
too late now to change his mind.

Nixon treated Cox's subpoena as simply one more stage in the never-
ending war of politics. His enemies had put stakes through his body
and left him for dead many times, but he had never succumbed to his
wounds. Like the ancient mariner, he was hurt but was not slain. He
would lie down and bleed awhile before rising to fight again. Picking
himself up from the ground was the quality that defined him, both as

a politician and as a person. It was an instinct he had relied upon his entire life, summed up in a note he had written to himself a few years previously: "Defeat-doesn't finish a man-Quit-does- A man is not finished when he's defeated. He's finished when he quits."

The alchemy of virtues and defects that propelled Richard Nixon to high office—smoldering hatreds and resentments, a determination to get even with his enemies, a sense of destiny, a willingness to take huge risks, an obsession with detail—led also to his downfall. Those same qualities would surely lift him up one more time. It was a cycle of disgrace and redemption he had experienced many times before. Each disgrace turned into a motivation to resume the fight.

As he lay in his hospital bed, the path ahead was very clear to the boy from the dirt-poor farm settlement in California named after an English Crusader king by his Quaker mother. He would fight back, as he had always fought back. He would fight for control of his tapes and fight to remain president. When he ceased being president, he would fight for his place in history. After making himself and then destroying himself, he would make himself anew. The tapes, witnesses to his dreams and nightmares, light side and dark side, triumphs and defeats, would be his partner in a campaign that would last until his death, and even beyond.

EXODUS

ἔξοδος—exodus

departure, conclusion to a story

I have sought [God's] guidance and searched my own conscience with special diligence to determine the right thing for me to do with respect to my predecessor in this place, Richard Nixon, and his loyal wife and family.

Theirs is an American tragedy in which we all have played a part. It could go on and on and on, or someone must write the end to it. I have concluded that only I can do that, and if I can, I must.

—GERALD FORD
on pardoning Richard Nixon, September 8, 1974

The idea for this book originated with a conversation I had with the dean of Watergate historians, Stanley Kutler, shortly before his death in 2015. I was working for *The Washington Post* at the time. I had telephoned Kutler to discuss the release of the Nixon tapes by the National Archives. As the leader of a team of scholars who had waged a series of legal battles for control of the tapes, Kutler had arguably done more than anyone else to shine light on the inner workings of the Nixon presidency. His book *The Wars of Watergate,* first published in 1990, remains the authoritative account of every twist and every character in the scandal. I expected to engage Kutler in a discussion about the latest Watergate revelations, but he surprised me with a much larger observation: "In twenty years, all the Watergate characters will be forgotten. The only one anyone will remember will be Nixon himself—and he will endure forever."

How to explain our fascination with the nation's thirty-seventh president long after we have ceased to think about the likes of Gordon Liddy, John Dean, and Jeb Magruder? Part of the answer lies, of course, in the historic nature of his presidency. Nixon changed the world, and changed America, in ways that have taken decades to reveal themselves. We are still experiencing the aftershocks of his opening to China and remaking of the Republican Party as a voice for a "silent majority" of Americans who felt threatened by the upheavals of the 1960s. But another part of the explanation lies in the story of Nixon himself— a man who "climbed to the top of the greasy pole," in the phrase of one of his heroes, Benjamin Disraeli, and then slid all the way down. As a self-made man with a loner's disposition and few true friends, he was personally responsible for both his rise and his fall. His strengths, notably his propensity for turning everything into a fight, were also his fatal flaws. Everything he gained, and subsequently lost, was the result of his own actions.

Together with Harry Truman, he was one of the most ordinary of American presidents, a common man distinguished mainly by his restlessness and awkwardness. He lacked the pedigree of the Roosevelts, the glamour of the Kennedys, the privilege of the Bushes, the star power of Ronald Reagan, the eloquence of Barack Obama, the showmanship of Donald Trump. What he possessed instead were the virtues and defects of regular Americans, the difference being that he displayed these qualities in outsize quantities. He worked harder than anyone else, hated his enemies more intently, took bigger risks, and dreamed bigger dreams. He never accepted defeat and was constantly remaking himself. To cite the slogan from his first political campaign, Nixon was, ultimately, "one of us."

And then there are his tapes. It is a paradox that this most private and secretive of presidents should have left behind the most detailed and revealing of historical records. During the twenty-nine-month period in which the tape recorders were running, until July 1973, we can follow Nixon as he moves from room to room around the White House, deals with crises, harangues aides, exchanges loving telephone calls with his daughters, and rages at people who have crossed him. By eavesdropping on his intimate conversations, we can share his private torments and visit places normally out of bounds to ordinary mortals. It is not just the great affairs of state that command our attention but the personal details as well. We know what Nixon had for breakfast, when he took a nap, how he fumbled with gadgets of all kinds, the music he listened to alone in the Lincoln Sitting Room. The treasure trove of archival riches poses a challenge for historians and biographers who must be ruthlessly selective in order to make sense of the material.

In *King Richard*, I have attempted to meet this challenge by focusing on the extraordinary unraveling of Nixon's presidency during the hundred days that followed his second inaugural. It is safe to say that no pivotal moment in American history has ever been documented more comprehensively. In addition to the Nixon tapes, we have the detailed nightly diaries of Bob Haldeman, the clandestine recordings of John Ehrlichman and other aides, countless pages of contempora-

neous notes and memos by White House staffers, thousands of photographs, the files of multiple congressional and FBI investigations,
and dozens of memoirs and oral histories. One of the by-products
of the Watergate scandal is that no future U.S. president will ever
keep the kind of record that Nixon left to posterity, against his every
intention.

In structuring the story like a classical tragedy, I have echoed the sentiment of many witnesses to Nixon's downfall beginning with Gerald
Ford and Henry Kissinger. Greek and Shakespearean tragedies unfold
according to a fixed pattern. A ruler who wants to do good commits a
fatal error of judgment stemming from pride or *hubris* that leads to a
personal *crisis*. This is followed by a *catastrophe* of some kind in which
he is publicly disgraced. The hero's suffering evokes feelings of awe and
pity from the audience, who learn lessons from the way in which the
crisis is resolved (*catharsis*). I leave it to readers to judge what lessons
we have learned from the torment Nixon inflicted on the country and
himself. As Chou En-lai remarked about the French Revolution, it is
perhaps "too early" to reach definitive conclusions about Nixon's place
in history, which will depend on the future course of events on both
sides of the Pacific Ocean. Nevertheless, I believe that only the most
hard-hearted of critics will fail to feel any empathy for the pain of a man
whose dreams turned to nightmares as a result of his own mistakes.
Half a century after the Watergate break-in, the grandeur of Nixon's
ambitions and the suddenness of his fall still inspire awe. Fittingly, it
was Nixon himself who captured the essence of the tragedy best on
the eve of his resignation as president when he told his staff, "Always
remember, others may hate you, but those who hate you don't win
unless you hate them. And then you destroy yourself."

There is one way in which *King Richard* differs significantly from the
standard format. In classical tragedy, the hero typically dies at the end of
the play. In this story, the catastrophe we witness onstage does not lead
directly to the death of the hero. Instead of dying, the hero reinvents
himself, like the nation that elected him. As "new Nixons" emerge from
the ashes of the old, we do not know whether to feel hope or despair,
to laugh or to cry. Which just goes to show that the story of Richard
Nixon's fall is neither a Greek tragedy nor a Shakespearean tragedy but

a uniquely American drama that we continue to live through today. It is a story without end because it is the story of us all.

Richard Nixon resigned the presidency of the United States on August 9, 1974, sixteen days after the Supreme Court ordered him to turn over tapes requested by the special prosecutor. The so-called smoking gun conversation of June 23, 1972, showed that he ordered a cover-up of Watergate within a few days of the break-in. He was pardoned by his successor, Gerald Ford, for any crimes he might have committed while president. Following his death on April 22, 1994, he was given a full state funeral, attended by all five surviving U.S. presidents. Around thirty-seven hundred hours of his secretly recorded tapes finally became available to the public in 2013 following a forty-year legal battle involving historians, the government, Nixon, and his heirs.

Spiro Agnew resigned as vice president in October 1973 after agreeing to plead no contest to a single charge of tax evasion.

John Mitchell served nineteen months in prison for Watergate-related offenses. He separated from his wife, *Martha,* in 1974. He never admitted to ordering the Watergate break-in.

H. R. "Bob" Haldeman spent eighteen months in prison for his role in Watergate. His White House diaries are an indispensable source for chronicling the Nixon presidency.

John Ehrlichman served eighteen months in prison for Watergate-related offenses. He later became an accomplished novelist and sketch artist.

Charles "Chuck" Colson spent seven months in prison after pleading guilty to obstruction of justice. He became an evangelical Christian and founded Prison Fellowship International.

Jeb Magruder served seven months in prison following a plea bargain with federal prosecutors. He was ordained a Presbyterian minister in 1984.

John Dean pleaded guilty to obstruction of justice in a plea deal with prosecutors in October 1973. He spent four months in a safe house while testifying against other Watergate defendants.

Gordon Liddy spent four and a half years in prison for Watergate-related offenses, the longest of any of the defendants. For many years, the personalized license plate on his vintage Rolls-Royce read "H2oGATE."

Manolo Sanchez and his wife, *Fina,* retired to their native Spain after serving the Nixon family in New York, the White House, and California.

ACKNOWLEDGMENTS

I have long been interested in hinge moments in history. My book on the Cuban missile crisis, *One Minute to Midnight,* described our closest ever brush with nuclear apocalypse. Another book, *Down with Big Brother,* told the astonishing story of the collapse of communism and the fall of the Soviet empire. The hundred days that followed Richard Nixon's second inaugural in 1973 is replete with similar drama. A president who had been re-elected in one of the largest landslides in American history found himself in the middle of a constitutional crisis as his past crimes returned to haunt him. The journalist-historian Theodore White wrote a series of acclaimed books titled *The Making of the President,* but how often does one get to witness the "unmaking" of the president and the sudden unraveling of presidential authority?

My goal with this book, as with previous books, has been to tell the story the way a novelist or playwright might, through a narrative arc that builds toward a climactic moment that changes our world forever. I imagine myself sitting unnoticed in the corner of a room, the reader by my side, as we witness a series of extraordinary events that pit the characters against each other, revealing their inner strengths, weaknesses, and torments. The difference with fiction, of course, is that the historian is not allowed to invent anything. He relies instead on a mine of archival material that takes many forms—documents, oral histories, photographs, home movies, letters, newspaper articles, memoirs, and, most famously in Richard Nixon's case, tapes. Gaining access to such material depends in turn on a multitude of archivists, donors, librarians, scholars, and lawyers who have labored for years behind the scenes preserving and protecting the historical record. Like other Nixon biographers, I owe a huge thank you to these largely unsung archival heroes.

In a 1972 essay for *Esquire* magazine, Tom Wolfe cited "scene-by-scene construction" as the basic novelistic technique that can be employed by non-fiction writers to bring this archival material alive. So-called "realistic" writers like Dickens and Balzac and Chekhov told a story "by moving from scene to scene . . . resorting as little as possible to sheer historical narrative." The goal was to immerse their readers in the lives of their characters without subjecting them to didactic lectures, what modern-day writing coaches would call "show, don't tell." In general, readers should be left free to decide which characters they find admirable or detestable based on the evidence presented to them. According to Wolfe, the creation of a convincing scene depends in turn on three other literary devices, all of which I made use of in researching and writing *King Richard:*

- *Realistic dialogue.* Carefully chosen dialogue is both a great revealer of character and a primary means of engaging the reader. In the hands of a master like Dickens, dialogue can largely substitute for physical description in breathing life into a character. It is hard to imagine a richer repository of authentic dialogue available to a historian than the thirty-seven hundred hours of Nixon tape recordings that were finally released to the public in 2013. Organizing and cataloguing this material involved a multi-decade effort on the part of the National Archives and the Richard Nixon Library in Yorba Linda, California. Before releasing anything, archivists had to listen to every inch of tape to determine what should be withheld on national security or privacy grounds. They also compiled detailed finding aids without which researchers would find it impossible to navigate their way through the morass of meandering and sometimes unintelligible conversations. While I have drawn extensively on these tapes to give a flavor of the debates between Nixon and his advisors, there is no substitute for listening directly to the original recordings. I have posted extracts from some of these tapes on my website at www.michaeldobbsbooks.com/nixontapes, as well as links to the full conversations on the Nixon library website.

• *Descriptive detail.* Like any good reporter, a historian should have an eye for the tiny details that create a sense of being present in the room when great events are unfolding. One of my literary role models, Barbara Tuchman, was an advocate of "history by the ounce," as opposed to "history in gallon jugs": she valued "corroborative detail" over grand theories and sweeping generalizations. Following her example, I believe that the photograph on page 53 of Nixon's customary lunch of canned pineapple and cottage cheese illustrates the grim self-discipline of our thirty-seventh president in pithier, more accessible form than any psychological study. As both a writer and a reader, I want to visualize Nixon in action, not just hear him courtesy of his tapes. This meant assembling the kind of detail about the Nixon White House—floor plans, placement of furniture, pictures on the walls—that would permit me to find my way around the place without a guide. Fortunately, I was able to tap into the research of others, for example the meticulous notes of a tour of the White House by the former Watergate investigator Scott Armstrong, which are now part of the Woodward and Bernstein archives at the University of Texas. I also relied on an exhaustive study by an architectural historian, Patrick Phillips-Schrock, *The Nixon White House Redecoration and Acquisition Program.* Outtakes for the NBC News program "A Day in the Life of Richard Nixon," filmed on December 6, 1971, accessible through the Nixon library, were also helpful. These sources were supplemented by the wonderful collection of White House photographs in the Nixon Library, many of which feature in this book.

• *Third-person point of view.* To understand someone, it is important to imagine events from their point of view. Reporters traditionally do this by interviewing their subjects at length and asking about their thoughts and emotions. Almost fifty years after the Watergate break-in, most of the key players in *King Richard* were no longer available for interview. Fortunately, they left behind numerous memoirs and oral histories that enabled me to describe what was going through their minds at critical junctures. Nixon's own memoir, *RN*, includes extracts from his personal audio diary that he dictated every evening until April 14, 1973, when events became "so cheerless" that he could no longer bear to continue. The other memoirs range in quality from the pedestrian (Jeb Magruder) to the revealing (John Dean) to the ponderous yet often insightful (Henry Kissinger) to the outrageously frank (Gordon Liddy). Bob Haldeman's nightly audio entries are an invaluable resource that offer an exceptionally rich eyewitness narrative from the perspective of the president's closest aide. While I have favored contemporaneous accounts over post-facto reconstructions of events, I also made use of the in-depth oral histories compiled by the Nixon library and its former director, Timothy Naftali.

Among the joys of writing non-fiction books is the opportunity to follow in the footsteps of your subjects. As a longtime resident of Washington and reporter for *The Washington Post,* I was already familiar with many of the places featured in *King Richard,* including the Watergate complex itself. I visited the West Wing of the White House on numerous occasions from the presidencies of Ronald Reagan onward, as well as the hulking Executive Office Building next door. I would like to thank Lea Berman, White House social secretary under George W. Bush, for sharing historical details about the private residence. I am grateful to Judge David Tatel of the U.S. Court of Appeals for the District of Columbia for arranging a memorable visit to the chambers and courtroom of Judge John Sirica, courtesy of the present occupant, Trevor N. McFadden. A two-week research trip to "Nixon country" in California took me to the president's birthplace in Yorba Linda (now preserved as part of the Nixon Museum and Library), Whittier College, and the beach at San Clemente, where Nixon dreamed of his opening to China.

While in California, I had the great good fortune of having long conversations with Frank Gannon, a former White House aide to Nixon who helped him later with several of his books. An entertaining dinner companion, Frank was generous in sharing insights and anecdotes about his former boss which helped shape my own thinking. Other Nixon aides whom I consulted during the early stages of researching this book included Chuck Colson (prior to his death in 2012) and John Dean, while he was undertaking his own in-depth study of the Nixon tapes. I would like to thank all the archivists at the Nixon Library, but particularly Ryan Pettigrew, who had the foresight to assemble a huge electronic database of the Nixon photo archive several years ago. This database proved invaluable when the library, along with other branches of the National Archives, was compelled to close its doors to researchers during the coronavirus pandemic. Without this electronic treasure trove and Ryan's assistance, I would been unable to obtain many of the photographs that appear in this book in time for publication.

My interest in Nixon and Watergate was sparked in part by my work for *The Washington Post* over more than two decades, as both a foreign correspondent and a member of the investigative staff. I benefited over the years from many conversations about Watergate with Bob Woodward and Carl Bernstein who inspired a generation of reporters like me with their ground-breaking investigative journalism. the *Post* assigned me to write several in-depth stories about the Mark Felt case after the former FBI deputy director was identified as Deep Throat in 2006. I cooperated with George Lardner on a series of stories about revelations from Nixon tapes as a result of the 1992 lawsuit by a group of historians led by Stanley Kutler. (We had the dubious distinction of reporting that Nixon had called our publisher, Katharine Graham, "a terrible old bag.") I am grateful for the assistance of Scott Armstrong and Max Holland, author of *Leak: Why Mark Felt became Deep Throat,* on several Watergate-related stories.

This book could not have been completed without the assistance of numerous friends and fellow Watergate junkies. I am particularly indebted to Tom Blanton, director of the indispensable National Security Archive, which played a key role in securing public access to the papers of Henry Kissinger. After filing an initial Freedom of Information request in 2001, the Archive went to court in 2015 to win the release of hundreds of Kissinger memcons that had been withheld on spurious national security grounds. Tom critiqued an early draft of this book with his customary blend of enthusiasm, incisiveness, and historical knowledge. Other friends who read the manuscript, pointed out mistakes, and suggested improvements included Paul Taylor, David Ensor, Adam Tanner, and Doyle McManus. Needless to say, I am responsible for any remaining errors.

My publishing home for nearly three decades, Knopf has rightly been celebrated for its superb editorial judgment and beautifully produced books. Among its many virtues (from the point of view of a grateful beneficiary) has been an almost legendary patience with authors who miss contractual deadlines. When I finally turned in the first draft, I relied greatly on the wisdom of my editor, Andrew Miller, to make it much more readable by suggesting cuts and restructuring of various sections. Andrew and his assistant, Maris Dyer, were a constant source of valuable feedback and encouragement as the book went through a long series of revisions and factchecks. I would like to thank production editor Maria Massey, text designer Maggie Hinders, jacket designer Tyler Comrie, and copy editor Ingrid Sterner for their meticulous attention to detail and enforcement of the exacting standards we have come to expect from Knopf, and Erinn Hartman for her promotional flair. I am also indebted to my far-seeing agent, Rafe Sagalyn, now a partner at ICM, for doing so much to shape this and other projects by asking the right questions and pointing me in directions I had not previously considered.

As with my earlier books, my closest reader has been my wife Lisa, who was a constant source of encouragement and advice. My daughter, Olivia, caught many inconsistencies and errors. I am dedicating this book to my three brothers, Geoffrey, Peter, and Christopher, in memory of our wonderful parents and our years growing up in Russia, India, Poland, Italy, and the former Yugoslavia, among other exotic locales. Each of them has distinguished himself in his own unique field. Even though we are now scattered across the globe, I continue to benefit from their generous hospitality in places like Sri Lanka, the French Alps, and Ireland. After a year in which we kept in touch largely through Zoom calls and WhatsApp chats, I am looking forward to many more years of skiing, hiking, eating, reminiscing, and yes, fraternal arguments.

NOTES

AP	Associated Press
DNSA	Digital National Security Archive (ProQuest database)
FOIA	Document released under Freedom of Information Act
HAK	Henry A. Kissinger
HJC	House Judiciary Committee
HJC SI	HJC Statement of Information
HJC SRPC	HJC Submission of Recorded Presidential Conversations
HJC TW	HJC Testimony of Witnesses
HRH	H. R. "Bob" Haldeman
LAT	*Los Angeles Times*
LBJL	Lyndon B. Johnson Library, Austin, Tex.
NA	National Archives
NA-SSC	SSC records in NA, Washington, D.C. (RG 46)
NA-USDC	U.S. District Court records in NA, College Park, Md. (RG 21)
NA-WSPF	WSPF records in NA, College Park, Md. (RG 460)
NYT	*New York Times*
OH	Oral History
PDD	Presidential Daily Diary, RNL
RN	Richard Nixon
RNL	Richard Nixon Library, Yorba Linda, Calif.
RNL-POF	President's Office Files, RNL
RNL-PPF	President's Personal File, RNL
RNL-SMOF	Staff Member and Office Files, RNL
SSC	Senate Select Committee
SSC FR	SSC Final Report
WHT	White House Tape, RNL
WP	*Washington Post*
WSPF	Watergate Special Prosecution Force

PROLOGUE

3   "one helluva show": WHT 036-016, January 20, 1973, RNL.

3   "ruffles and flourishes": HRH Action Memo, January 11, 1973, Tapes, memos, and notes, Haldeman RNL-SMOF.

4   "As I stand": Inaugural address drafts, President's Speech File, RNL-PPF; Haynes Johnson, "Inaugural Smooth, President Clearly in Good Spirits," *WP,* January 21, 1973.

4   "a word over 1200": RN to Ray Price, December 28, 1972, Memoranda from the President, RNL-PPF.

6   "the son I never": Charles Colson OH, August 17, 2007, RNL.

7   "Yes, sir, Mr. President": WHT 036-018, January 20, 1973, RNL. Unless otherwise indicated, all quotations in this section are taken from this conversation.

7   A few months earlier: Colson OH, August 17, 2007, RNL. White House diaries indicate that the conversation took place in the early morning of June 7, 1972. The National Archives withheld the tape recording (133-003) of this conversation for privacy reasons.

10 "Mr. Can-Do": Lukas, *Nightmare,* 11; Aitken, *Charles W. Colson* , 126; Haldeman, *Ends of Power,* 60.

11 "a complete change": Charles W. Colson, "Eyes Only Memorandum for the File," January 15, 1973, P Memos 1973, Haldeman RNL-SMOF.

12 The tape recorders in room WT-1: James Zumwalt and Randolph Nelson testimony, November 1, 1973, Subpoena issued to President Nixon for production of tapes, U.S. District Court for the District of Columbia, NA-USDC.

13 "scribbling intruders": H. R. Haldeman, "The Nixon White House Tapes," *Prologue: The Journal of the National Archives* (Summer 1988), NA.

13 "far too inept": Ibid.; Haldeman, *Ends of Power,* 207.

14 "suede-shoe operators-hucksters": Alfred Wong testimony, November 1, 1973, U.S. District Court for the District of Columbia, NA-USDC.

15 "It doesn't have": WHT 450-001, February 16, 1971, RNL.

15 "continuous film recording": John Powers, "The History of Presidential Audio Recordings and Archival Issues Surrounding Their Use," July 1996, unpublished paper, NA.

15 "Mum's the whole word": WHT 450-010, February 16, 1971, RNL.

16 At times, he even forgot: Nixon, *RN,* 502; Haldeman, "Nixon White House Tapes."

ACT I: HUBRIS

19 his "brainwork": Reeves, *President Nixon,* 29.

21 Hidden behind the bathroom: U.S. Secret Service memorandum, "Secret Service Participation in Tapings," March 1, 1974, FBI FOIA.

21 "a big comfortable chair": RN memo to Patricia Nixon, February 5, 1969, cited by Phillips-Schrock, *Nixon White House Redecoration and Acquisition Program*, 41.

21 For relaxation: Saul Pett, "Nixon on Nixon," *WP,* January 14, 1973.

22 After ten years in Nixon's: Jody Jacobs, "Nixon's Valet Talks About His Boss," *LAT,* November 6, 1972; Marie Smith, "How Nixon Lives, What He Likes," *WP,* January 17, 1969. See also PDD, January 22, 1973. In addition to the published diaries available online from the Nixon Library, I consulted the underlying source materials, which can be found in the Daily Diary files, Office of Presidential Papers and Archives, in RNL-SMOF.

22 The voice-activated Sony: WHT 398-016, January 22, 1973, RNL.

23 "All set for your trip?": WHT 399-002, January 22, 1973, RNL.

23 "peace with honor": Colson, *Born Again,* 88.

23 "It must be a typing thing": HAK-RN telephone conversation transcript (hereafter cited as telcon), January 22, 1973, accessed via DNSA.

23 "They will, of course": WHT 036-037, January 22, 1973, RNL.

24 This was the signal: HRH OH, April 11, 1988, RNL.

24 "From now on, Haldeman": HRH diary, June 29, 1971, RNL. Complete diary entries, as well as corresponding audio recordings by Haldeman, are available online from the Nixon Library. See also Haldeman, *Haldeman Diaries,* 309.

25 "hard to tell": Ehrlichman, *Witness to Power,* 78; Colson OH, September 21, 1988, RNL.

25 "nameless and faceless": Ehrlichman, *Witness to Power,* 24.

26 "circling like the dog": HRH OH, August 13, 1987, RNL.

26 "Colson—he'll do": Colson, *Born Again,* 54, 77.

26 "the strangest man": Strober and Strober, *Nixon Presidency,* 40.

26 "add hours to the day": HRH OH, April 11, 1988, RNL; Safire, *Before the Fall,* 287.

27 "head and shoulders": HRH OH, August 13, 1988, RNL.

27 There had been only one: Haldeman, *Ends of Power,* 65.

27 The first order: HRH handwritten notes, January 22, 1973, Haldeman RNL-SMOF.

28 He called for Manolo: WHT 400-002, January 22, 1973, RNL.

28 "It's important to live": Pett, "Nixon on Nixon"; Farrell, *Richard Nixon,* 399.

28 He claimed he was following: Sidey, *White House Remembered,* 37.

29 "Great men of action": Reeves, *President Nixon,* 29.

29 "Thinking about schedule": HRH diary, May 18, 1979, RNL.

29 "Read de Gaulle": Safire, *Before the Fall,* 688.

29 "an introvert": Wills, *Nixon Agonistes,* 32.

30 "All of those things": HRH diary, April 13, 1971, RNL.

30 "Lincoln was the great": HRH diary, December 30, 1970, RNL.

30 "at a loss to explain": Nixon, *RN,* 717.

31 "We must avoid": Donald Rumsfeld notes on cabinet meeting, November 8, 1972, Rumsfeld private archive.

31 "Presidents noted for": RN note, October 10, 1972, "Materials Removed from President's Desk," RNL-PPF.

31 "No one is finished": RN note, January 9, 1973, RNL-PPF; Safire, *Before the Fall*, 693.

32 "I protect the people": "The Spy in the Cold," *Time*, January 29, 1973.

33 "the dark side": Colson OH, August 17, 2007, RNL.

33 "In view of *Time*": WHT 036-044, January 22, 1973, RNL.

34 "Of course, it's particularly": WHT 036-046, January 22, 1973, RNL.

34 "awful, mindless chant": Nixon, *RN*, 755.

34 Nixon regarded the dean: WHT 829-009, January 1, 1973, RNL; Robenalt, *January 1973*, 4.

35 "Regardless of what": WHT 036-055, January 22, 1973, RNL.

35 "This is the first time": WHT 036-061, January 22, 1973, RNL.

37 "this hulking, imperious": Kissinger, *White House Years*, 1472.

38 "Very narrow space": Horne, *Kissinger*, 48.

38 "I changed a few pages": Memorandum of conversation (hereafter cited as memcon) between HAK and Le Duc Tho, January 23, 1973, DNSA.

39 "If the government is": HAK–Zhou En-lai memcon, July 9, 1971, DNSA.

39 Determined to flatter his boss: Nixon, *RN*, 691; HRH diary, October 12, 1972, RNL.

39 "Have you ever seen": Dallek, *Nixon and Kissinger*, 435.

40 "We believe peace": HAK press conference, *NYT*, October 27, 1972.

40 "tawdry, filthy shits": Dallek, *Nixon and Kissinger*, 444–47; Isaacson, *Kissinger*, 467.

40 "total brutality": WHT 827-010, December 20, 1972, RNL; Brinkley and Nichter, *Nixon Tapes*, 707; Farrell, *Richard Nixon*, 499.

41 "Call it cosmetics": WHT 371-019, October 23, 1972; Hughes, *Fatal Politics*, 120.

41 Nixon had repeatedly: HRH diary, November 22, 1972, RNL; WHT 160-008, January 5, 1973, RNL. See also Isaacson, *Kissinger*, 467.

42 "a glittering Potomac Titanic": Philip D. Carter, "Watergate: Potomac Titanic," *WP*, May 3, 1970.

42 "media-age Marie Antoinette": Rosen, *Strong Man*, 119.

43 In Watergate social terms: Rodota, *Watergate*, 92–94; Marie Smith, "A Wealth of Talent," *WP*, November 1, 1968.

44 "Five of the easiest": Emery, *Watergate*, 135–36.

45 Judge Sirica did not accept: Sirica, *To Set the Record Straight*, 64.

45 "I'm sorry": Ibid., 71; Bernstein and Woodward, *All the President's Men*, 233–34.

46 "political overtones": Sirica, *To Set the Record Straight*, 49.

46 "the smart-alecky, cocky": Ibid., 71.

46 "Gordon Liddy doesn't bail": "Flamboyant Watergate Defendant: George Gordon Liddy," *NYT*, February 1, 1973.

47 "Some people got caught": Liddy, *Will*, 245–46.

48 "every tree in the forest": McCord to Jack Caulfield, December 28, 1972, Select

Committee of the U.S. Senate on Presidential Campaign Activities, Book 3 (hereafter cited as SSC 1, 2, 3, and so on), 1235.

48 "was as smooth": Sirica, *To Set the Record Straight,* 74; Bernstein and Woodward, *All the President's Men,* 239.

49 "any assignment concerning": Transcript 1400-1423, CR 1827-72, *United States v. Liddy,* U.S. District Court for the District of Columbia, NA-USDC.

50 "the Game Plan Man": Safire, *Before the Fall,* 634.

50 "a cocky little bantam": Magruder, *American Life,* 173.

50 "Jeb," he growled: Liddy, *Will,* 212; Hunt, *American Spy,* 184.

50 "To permit the thought": Liddy, *Will,* 193–94.

51 "Liddy's a Hitler": Emery, *Watergate,* 99; Magruder, *American Life,* 171–73; Dean, *Blind Ambition,* 76–77.

51 "Why don't you get": Colson testimony in *United States v. John Mitchell,* December 5, 1974, cited in Robenalt, *January 1973,* 328. See also Magruder, *American Life,* 195; Emery, *Watergate,* 103.

52 "James Bond had been exposed": Magruder, *American Life,* 223.

52 When they crossed paths: Bernstein and Woodward, *All the President's Men,* 239.

52 Sensing his discomfort: Magruder, *American Life,* 281; McCord testimony, SSC 1, 241–42; McCord witness file, NA-WSPF.

52 "tougher and stronger": Colson, *Born Again,* 83, 89.

53 "How rough it's been": Ibid., 88–89.

53 "talented debauchery": "Self Portrait of an Angel and Monster," *Time,* January 22, 1973.

54 "the bastards at *Time*": WHT 036-086, January 23, 1973, RNL.

54 "When you have": WHT 407-018, January 23, 1973, RNL; Brinkley and Nichter, *Nixon Tapes: 1973,* 17–18.

55 "The more I think": WHT 036-089, January 23, 1973, RNL.

55 "to wear the flag": Nixon, *RN,* 763.

56 "really stuck 'em": WHT 036-091, January 23, 1973, RNL.

56 "I just hope": WHT 036-094, January 23, 1973, RNL.

56 "a real gem": WHT 036-099, January 23, 1973, RNL.

56 "solitary and withdrawn": Kissinger, *White House Years,* 1475.

58 "If there was a Lone Ranger": Ehrlichman, *Witness to Power,* 313.

58 "Make the point": HRH diary, November 19, 1972, RNL.

58 "white-lipped in anger": Haldeman, *Ends of Power,* 84; HRH diary, December 15, 1972, RNL.

58 "write the whole story": James Reston, "Nixon and Kissinger," *NYT,* December 31, 1972.

58 "I will not tolerate": Colson, *Born Again,* 86.

59 "Dr. Kissinger remains": Joseph Kraft, "Twelve Days of Bombing," *WP,* January 4, 1973.

59 "I'll be goddamned": WHT 160-002, January 5, 1973, RNL.

59 "It's not good": Colson, *Born Again,* 87; Horne, *Kissinger,* 6.

60 "physically move": HRH diary, November 20, 1972, and January 7, 1973, RNL.

60 "inner aggression": Arnold A. Hutschnecker, "The Lessons of Eagleton," *NYT,*
    October 30, 1972.

60 "wants to be sure": HRH diary, December 7 and 8, 1972, RNL; Gellman, *The Presi-
    dent and the Apprentice,* 274.

61 As they agonized over: HRH diary, March 11, 1971, RNL.

61 "Never forget": WHT 823-001, December 14, 1972, RNL; Brinkley and Nichter,
    Nixon Tapes, 703.

62 "vulnerability of a man": Kissinger, *Years of Upheaval,* 103.

62 "Henry got Nixon cranked up": Isaacson, *Kissinger,* 329–30.

63 "Us against Them": Hunt, *American Spy,* 321.

63 "the hottest property": HRH diary, January 14, 1973, RNL; RN to HRH, January 25,
    1973, Memoranda from the President, RNL-PPF.

64 "Henry kept saying": HRH diary, January 27, 1973, RNL.

64 Three out of four Americans: George Gallup, "Ceasefire Gives Nixon 68% Again,"
    WP, February 6, 1973.

65 All this documentation: FBI memorandum, January 16, 1973, FBI file 139-4089-
    1871, FOIA.

66 "Morale outstanding": Michael Dobbs, "Watergate and the Two Lives of Mark
    Felt," *WP,* June 20, 2005.

66 "ring of homosexuals": Gentry, *J. Edgar Hoover,* 624; Woodward, *Secret Man,*
    17–23.

67 "on deep background": Woodward, *Secret Man,* 63–67.

67 "FBI Finds Nixon": Carl Bernstein and Bob Woodward, "FBI Finds Nixon Aides
    Sabotaged Democrats," *WP,* October 10, 1972; Woodward, *Secret Man,* 74–80. See
    also Woodward notes of meeting with Mark Felt, October 9, 1972, Harry Ransom
    Center, University of Texas, Austin.

67 Felt was frustrated: Felt and O'Connor, *G-Man's Life,* 206; Woodward, *Secret
    Man,* 74.

67 "apply public pressure": Felt and O'Connor, *G-Man's Life,* 202.

68 "Three-day Gray": Ibid., 188.

68 "Shit, what a royal": Bernstein and Woodward, *All the President's Men,* 195–96;
    Woodward, *Secret Man,* 91.

69 "If the FBI couldn't prove": Bernstein and Woodward, *All the President's Men,*
    243–46; Woodward notes of meeting with Mark Felt, January 24, 1973, Ransom
    Center.

71 "Plead guilty": McCord testimony, SSC 1, 135.

71 "Jeb Stuart Magruder": Myra MacPherson, "Jeb Magruder: Input and Flow," *WP,*
    January 14, 1973.

72 "all who are involved": Caulfield testimony, SSC 1, 255. According to Caulfield, this conversation took place on January 12. It more likely occurred on January 14, given that he clearly refers to the January 14 *WP* article mentioned above.

72 "The president's ability": McCord testimony, SSC 1, 139–40.

72 "Jim, I have worked": Caulfield testimony, SSC 1, 266.

72 "I have had a good life": McCord testimony, SSC 1, 141.

73 "mastermind, the boss": Lawrence Meyer, "Ex-aides of Nixon to Appeal," *WP*, January 31, 1973.

74 "Arms up": Liddy, *Will*, 286.

74 "outstanding performance": Lukas, *Nightmare*, 171.

74 "a courtyard befouled": Liddy, *Will*, 287.

75 "This is an act": William Claiborne, "They Led Me into a Hall, Saying 'Don't Hurt Him,'" *WP*, October 12, 1972.

75 "cruel and unusual": William Claiborne, "Suit Asks End of 'Cruel, Unusual' Jail Conditions," *WP*, October 21, 1972.

75 "You Watergate?": Liddy, *Will*, 289.

76 "Is it always": Ibid., 290–94.

76 "I am still not satisfied": Lawrence Meyer, "Watergate Judge Scolds Prosecutor," *WP*, February 3, 1973.

77 "reconsider their defiant": Sirica, *To Set the Record Straight*, 89.

78 "She carried herself": Safire, *Before the Fall*, 686–87; HRH diary, February 8, 1973, RNL.

79 That evening, Nixon flew: Eisenhower, *Pat Nixon*, 362–63; AP, "President Flies West in New Spirit of '76," *LAT*, February 9, 1973.

79 "illegal, improper, and unethical": Senate Resolution 60, February 7, 1973.

79 He had purchased: Lukas, *Nightmare*, 345–47; see also General Accounting Office, "Protection of the President at Key Biscayne and San Clemente," December 18, 1973.

81 "In San Clemente": WHT 036-033, January 21, 1973, RNL.

81 "a man who had spent": Safire, *Before the Fall*, 617.

81 During his first presidential term: HJC SI X, 172–74; Nixon, *RN*, 769.

81 "Infinitely more effective": HRH diary, February 9, 1973, RNL.

83 "Two more temperamentally": Farrell, *Richard Nixon*, 47.

84 "a religious environment": Nixon, *RN*, 13–14.

85 "For the first time": Ibid., 10.

85 "He didn't want anybody": Morris, *Richard Milhous Nixon*, 99.

85 "he sank into a deep": Ambrose, *Education of a Politician*, 57.

86 "Put Nixon in!": Morris, *Richard Milhous Nixon*, 134–35.

86 "To be a good debater": Ibid., 132.

86 "They were the haves": Ibid., 119–21.

‹356› NOTES

87 "His face would cloud": Ibid., 141–45; Nixon, *RN,* 23–25.

87 "What starts the process": Ken Clawson, "A Loyalist's Memoir," *WP,* August 9, 1979.

89 "Four to five hours": RN to Rose Mary Woods, March 31, 1971, Higby Chron, Higby RNL-SMOF.

90 He maintained the tan: Dwight Chapin OH, April 2, 2007, RNL.

90 "He doesn't drink": Farrell, *Richard Nixon,* 162; "The Florida of Richard Nixon," *Newsday,* October 13, 1971; Safire, *Before the Fall,* 613.

91 "brooded well": Safire, *Before the Fall,* 614.

91 "Old Bebe is a great guy": WHT 035-067, January 2, 1973, RNL.

92 "The weirdest day": HRH diary, May 9, 1970, RNL; Jacobs, "Nixon's Valet Talks About His Boss."

92 "Wait, it'll get better": Safire, *Before the Fall,* 621; Eisenhower, *Pat Nixon,* 320.

92 "He who would be great": Lou Cannon, "Nixon Urges Privacy for Returned POWs," *WP,* February 12, 1973; PDD, February 11, 1973.

93 "At times the rain": Bull to HRH, "Bebe Rebozo's Driving," February 13, 1973, Higby Chron, Haldeman RNL-SMOF.

94 Complete with health spa: Lukas, *Nightmare,* 278.

94 "Dean's doing a hell": WHT 231-016, November 28, 1972, RNL; Kutler, *Abuse of Power,* 178–79.

95 "A behind-the-scenes media effort": SSC FR, 76; HRH diary, February 11, 1973, RNL.

95 Nixon had originally heard: Haldeman, *Ends of Power,* 80; HRH diary, January 8, 1973, RNL.

95 "Hold on, we are": Walt Rostow to LBJ, November 2, 1968, doc. 30, "Chennault Affair" collection, LBJL. Chennault called the embassy at 11:44 a.m. prior to leaving her Watergate apartment at 1:45 p.m. See LBJ telephone call with Cartha "Deke" DeLoach, November 13, 1968, LBJL, transcribed by the Miller Center, University of Virginia.

96 "This is treason": LBJ call to Senator Everett Dirksen, November 2, 1968, telcon 13706, LBJL.

97 He warned the White House: HRH diary, January 12, 1973, RNL.

97 "Any other way": Farrell, *Richard Nixon,* 343.

97 "FBI investigation against": HRH to Dean, February 10, 1973, HRH Chron, Haldeman RNL-SMOF. See also WHT 852-007, February 7, 1973, RNL, cited by Hughes, *Chasing Shadows,* 157. For background on the "Chennault Affair," see online media kit released by LBJ Library.

97 "We need to get": HRH to Dean, February 10, 1973.

98 At the end of the La Costa meeting: SSC FR, 77.

98 "What we've been getting": Hunt conversation with Colson, exhibit 152, SSC 9, 3888–91; SSC FR, 57.

99 "Tell them to get lost": SSC FR, 77.

100 "If Liddy decides": WHT 831-006, January 3, 1973, RNL; Robenalt, *January 1973*, 73.

101 "the machismo cult": Colson, *Born Again*, 90–92.

102 "Johns Hopkins and Harvard": Farrell, *Richard Nixon*, 115.

102 "The administration was doubly guilty": WHT 855-010, February 14, 1973, RNL; WSPF transcript, RNL; Brinkley and Nichter, *Nixon Tapes: 1973*, 54–63.

103 "There is a limit": Hunt to Colson, December 31, 1972, 146A-Dean Documents, NA-WSPF, reprinted in Hunt, *American Spy*, 271–72.

105 "pull down the temple": WHT 601-033, October 25, 1971, RNL; WSPF transcript, RNL.

105 "a little bit on the stupid side": Lukas, *Nightmare*, 228–29.

106 "I've been wiping": WHT 858-003, February 16, 1973, RNL; WSPF transcript, RNL.

108 "the desk officer": Dean, *Nixon Defense*, 240.

109 "neat and spotless": Dean, *Blind Ambition*, 185–86.

109 "I'm convinced we're going": WHT 865-014, February 28, 1973, RNL; WSPF transcript, RNL.

109 "The talk with John": Nixon, *RN*, 779–80.

109 In a subsequent conversation: WHT 867-016, March 2, 1973, RNL; Dean, *Nixon Defense*, 255–56.

110 Appearances were deceiving: Dean, *Blind Ambition*, 161, 241.

110 "I redecorated for the sake": Ibid., 29–30, 171.

112 "a public Watergate target": Ibid., 183–84; David Rosenbaum, "Reluctant F.B.I. Gave Aide of Nixon Watergate Files," *NYT*, March 1, 1973. See also Dean, *Nixon Defense*, 331.

112 "I know the type": WHT 871-004, March 7, 1973, RNL; Kutler, *Abuse of Power*, 223–25.

112 "Let him twist slowly": Ehrlichman, *Witness to Power*, 374.

113 "looked magnificent": Interviewed for *The Vietnam War*, PBS, by Ken Burns and Lynn Novick.

114 "This is Colonel Risner": Nixon, *RN*, 861.

114 "Compare these fine men": Ambrose, *Ruin and Recovery*, 65.

114 "The Unemployed": *Atlanta Journal*, March 13, 1979, Annotated News Summaries, RNL-POF.

115 He pored happily over: U.S. POW returnee statements, March 1973, President's Handwriting, RNL-POF.

115 "It insults the POWs' intelligence": Ambrose, *Ruin and Recovery*, 65.

117 "We have to take them on": WHT 037-130, March 16, 1973, RNL.

117 "simply unable to concentrate": Kissinger, *Years of Upheaval*, 318.

119 "a trifle ridiculous": HRH diary, March 17, 1973, RNL; PDD, March 17, 1973.

120 "And I'd say Dean": WHT 882-012, March 17, 1973, RNL; WSPF transcript, RNL; Dean, *Blind Ambition*, 187–90.

120 "the hangout road": WHT 878-014, March 13, 1973, RNL.

120 The CIA had retained: See SSC 9, 3870–71, for photographs of Dr. Fielding's office. Ehrlichman initialed an August 11, 1971, memorandum approving "a covert operation" to examine Ellsberg's medical files on condition that "it is not traceable" (exhibit 90, SSC 6, 2643–45). For Dean's account of pressure from Ehrlichman for the CIA to retrieve the photographs, see Dean, *Blind Ambition*, 198.

122 "a magical moment": White, *In Search of History*, 524–25. See also Theodore H. White, "For President Kennedy: An Epilogue," *Life*, December 6, 1963.

122 "Z[iegler] note!": Henry Fairlie, "Camelot Revisited," *Harper's Magazine*, January 1973, as annotated by RN, President's Handwriting, RNL-POF.

123 "spoken to a President": White, *Breach of Faith*, 250–51; White, *Making of the President, 1972*, 353. See also WHT 416-050, March 17, 1973, RNL.

123 "My judgment": White, *Making of the President, 1972*, 360, 371.

ACT II: CRISIS

127 "We become lawless": Tim Weiner, "E. Howard Hunt, Agent Who Organized Botched Watergate Break-In, Dies at 88," *NYT*, January 24, 2007.

127 "The way you have it": Hunt, *American Spy*, 264.

128 "All of us": Hunt, *Berlin Ending*, 309.

128 "the sort of spy": Thomas, *Being Nixon*, 332; Patricia Sullivan, "Ex-spy Crafted Watergate, Other Schemes," *WP*, January 24, 2007.

128 "debonair, smooth-talking, unobtrusive": Colson, *Born Again*, 62.

129 "Hard as nails": WHT 534-005, July 1, 1971, RNL; Kutler, *Abuse of Power*, 10–14; Hughes, *Chasing Shadows*, 128.

129 "Got any ideas?": Hunt, *American Spy*, 192–93, 270.

129 Prior to leaving: Ibid., 189.

130 "self-executing arrangements": Memo from Colson lawyer David Shapiro, March 16, 1973, HJC TW III, 326–28; Liddy, *Will*, 276.

130 "Why me?": Dean, *Blind Ambition*, 192–93; see also O'Brien account in HJC TW I, 124–28.

132 "Well, sit down": WHT 886-008, March 21, 1973, RNL; WSPF transcript, RNL; Brinkley and Nichter, *Nixon Tapes: 1973*, 275–323. See also Dean OH, July 30, 2007, RNL.

132 "an actor on stage": Dean, *Blind Ambition*, 201.

132 "where all the bodies": WHT 037-176, March 20, 1973, RNL; WSPF transcript, RNL; Brinkley and Nichter, *Nixon Tapes: 1973*, 267–75.

135 "It will be each man": Nixon, *RN*, 800.

136 "squeezed in a vise": Dean, *Blind Ambition*, 210.

136 "I suggest you call Mitchell": LaRue testimony, SSC 6, 2297–98.

137 "He was homely": Magruder, *American Life*, 183.

137 "We don't need this": Extracts from LaRue testimony, HJC SI I, 116–40.

138 "an illegal activity": Ulasewicz testimony, SSC 6, 2237; Witness Files—Ulasewicz, NA-WSPF; Lukas, *Nightmare,* 255. Different investigations recorded minor discrepancies in the distribution of hush money to the Watergate defendants. I have relied primarily on the reconstruction by Watergate prosecutors.

138 Recipients included: Witness Files—LaRue, NA-WSPF; see also LaRue testimony, SSC 6, 2294–97.

138 "Will you be at home": Bittman testimony, HJC SI III-2, 1227.

139 "Somehow this payment": Hunt, *American Spy,* 283.

140 "I've found the heavyweight": Safire, *Before the Fall,* 263.

140 "I've made more money": Rosen, *Strong Man,* 34–35.

141 It was the attraction of opposites: Ibid., 24, 405.

142 "short cocktail things": Eye Too, *Women's Wear Daily,* March 20, 1970.

142 "the soothsayer": WHT 394-021, January 8, 1973; Brinkley and Nichter, *Nixon Tapes: 1973,* 11.

142 "This could land": Rosen, *Strong Man,* 304.

143 "That little sweetheart": Helen Thomas, "Martha's Ultimatum," *WP,* June 24, 1972; Rosen, *Strong Man,* 304–7.

143 "If you could see me": Helen Thomas, "Martha Is 'Leaving' Mitchell," *WP,* June 26, 1972.

143 "the Watergate thing": Nixon, *RN,* 649.

143 "Very subtle": WHT 744-024, June 30, 1972, RNL; Kutler, *Abuse of Power,* 78–81; Emery, *Watergate,* 202.

144 "Don't tell me about it": WHT 739-004, June 21, 1972, RNL; Kutler, *Abuse of Power,* 55.

144 "What's it all about?": Stans testimony, SSC 2, 697.

144 "putting the wagons": WHT 422-020, March 22, 1973, RNL; WSPF transcript, RNL.

145 "strength as a counselor": Nixon, *RN,* 648.

145 "What words of wisdom": WHT 422-033, March 22, 1973, RNL; WSPF transcript, RNL; Brinkley and Nichter, *Nixon Tapes: 1973,* 338–71. See also Dean, *Blind Ambition,* 212.

146 "oblique way": Nixon, *RN,* 802.

147 "I do not believe": HRH OH, April 12, 1988, RNL.

147 "I had the wisdom": Nixon, *RN,* 226.

148 "We wanted to make": Magruder OH, March 23, 2007, RNL. For Henry II comparison, see also Farrell, *Richard Nixon,* 434.

148 "I want, Bob": WHT 505-018, May 28, 1971, RNL.

148 "We're up against an enemy": WHT 534-002, July 1, 1971, RNL; Hughes, *Chasing Shadows,* 126.

148 "Never strike a king": WHT 525-001, June 17, 1971, RNL.

149 "Convict the son of a bitch": WHT 534-005, July 1, 1971, RNL; Hughes, *Chasing Shadows,* 126.

149   "Most Jews are disloyal": WHT 536-016, July 3, 1971, RNL; Hughes, *Chasing Shad-ows,* 139.

149   "I want it implemented": WHT 525-001, June 17, 1971, RNL; Hughes, *Chasing Shadows,* 1–2.

149   "a used but late-model": Liddy, *Will,* 171–72.

150   "a little nuts": WHT 741-002, June 23, 1972, RNL; WSPF transcript, RNL; Kutler, *Abuse of Power,* 67–69.

150   "The problem is": WHT 739-004; Kutler, *Abuse of Power,* 50–61.

150   "Play it tough": WHT 741-002.

151   "We'll just basically": WHT 348-010, July 19, 1972, RNL; Dean, *Nixon Defense,* 111.

151   "We are whistling": WHT 748-007, July 20, 1972, RNL; Kutler, *Abuse of Power,* 99–101.

151   "Hunt's happy": WHT 758-011, August 1, 1972, RNL; Kutler, *Abuse of Power,* 109–12. For payments to Bittman and Hunt, see Ulasewicz testimony, SSC 6, 2226–31.

152   "a preliminary matter": Transcript, CR 1827-72, *United States v. Liddy et al.,* March 23, 1973, NA-USDC.

152   "break this case": Sirica, *To Set the Record Straight,* 97–107.

153   "a massive injustice": McCord statement to investigators, May 18, 1973, McCord Security File, NA-SSC.

153   "There was political pressure": Transcript, *United States v. Liddy et al.,* March 23, 1973.

154   "no one was breathing": McCord, *Piece of Tape,* 61.

154   "It was nearly more": Sirica, *To Set the Record Straight,* 108.

154   "an unintended but welcome": Liddy, *Will,* 301.

155   "stench of urine": Hunt, *American Spy,* 288–92.

155   "breach of the most": Liddy, *Will,* 301–4.

155   "knowledgeable of": McCord note to investigators, March 24, 1973, McCord Security File, NA-SSC.

157   "McCord Says Dean": Robert L. Jackson and Ronald J. Ostrow, "McCord Says Dean, Magruder Knew in Advance of Bugging," *LAT,* March 26, 1973.

157   "Sir, I can give": WHT 886-008.

158   "The Dean Investigation": SSC exhibit no. 34–43, reprinted in HJC SI IV-1, 285–310.

158   "I'm thinking of getting": Dean, *Blind Ambition,* 213, 216.

158   He remembered that Colson: Telephone call from Hunt to Colson, late November, 1972, HJC SI III-1, 407–10. See also Dean, *Blind Ambition,* 152–53.

159   "Hi, Jeb": SSC exhibit no. 33–40, reprinted in HJC SI IV-1, 333.

159   "a basket case": Magruder, *American Life,* 286.

160   "We were not covering": Ibid., 229–30; Witness Files—Magruder, NA-WSPF.

161   "We've been protecting": Dean, *Blind Ambition,* 220. According to Dean, this

conversation took place before his taped conversation with Magruder. However, an examination of Haldeman's contemporaneous diary entry and notes suggests that it took place immediately afterward. See HRH diary, March 26, 1973, RNL.

161 "any prior knowledge": AP report, March 26, 1973, HJC SI IV-1, 327.

162 The stunning developments: Joseph Kraft, "The Watergate and the White House," *WP,* March 27, 1973; James Reston, "The Nixon Dilemma," *NYT,* March 25, 1973.

162 He invented a mythical: Art Buchwald, "Wages of Sin," *WP,* March 29, 1973.

163 "She is like her father": Safire, *Before the Fall,* 622.

164 "Going to jail": WHT 888-004, March 27, 1973, RNL; Dean, *Nixon Defense,* 346–51.

164 "We don't give a damn": WHT 044-027, March 27, 1973, RNL; HRH diary, March 27, 1973, RNL.

164 "Daddy!" she said: WHT 044-028, March 27, 1973, RNL.

165 The following evening: PDD, March 27–28, 1973.

165 "Let's face it": WHT 044-058, March 28, 1973, RNL.

165 "a Hollywood set": MacPherson, "Jeb Magruder: Input and Flow," *WP,* January 14, 1973.

166 "Those bastards": Magruder, *American Life,* 247.

166 "Don't worry, Jeb": Ibid., 287.

167 "Keeping Jeb happy": "Options for Jeb Magruder," February 28, 1973, White House memo, copied in Witness File—Magruder, NA-WSPF; see also Higby-Kehrli, March 7, 1973, and other memos in Higby Chron, Haldeman RNL-SMOF.

167 "The president and I": Magruder, *American Life,* 287–88.

168 "This could be the little thing": HRH diary, March 28, 1973; see also HRH note same day, Haldeman RNL-SMOF.

169 "True, I had helped": Dean, *Blind Ambition,* 223–24.

169 "on the verge of breaking": HRH diary, March 28, 1973.

169 "I fear for my husband": "Mrs. Mitchell Fears Plot to Tie Watergate to Husband," *NYT,* March 28, 1973.

169 "I ain't going to jail": HRH diary, March 27, 1973.

170 "Your theory is not": Dean testimony to SSC, June 25, 1973, reprinted in HJC SI IV-1, 384–85. Dean provides a slightly different and more graphic account of this conversation in *Blind Ambition,* 224–25. A week before his death in November 1988, Mitchell described the *Blind Ambition* version of the conversation as "ridiculous." See Rosen, *Strong Man,* 362–63. I have relied on the more restrained version from Dean's earlier sworn testimony.

170 "Good idea": HRH diary, March 28, 1973.

170 "Christ, I wouldn't think": WHT 044-061, March 28, 1973, RNL.

172 "He feels there will": Higby to HRH, "Phone Call from Bill Carruthers," March 28, 1973, Higby Chron, Haldeman RNL-SMOF.

172 "I discussed his sleeping pills": Thomas, *Being Nixon,* 443, citing Riland diary; Gellman, *The President and the Apprentice,* 277.

172 Nixon also experimented: WHT 837-003, January 10, 1973, RNL; WHT 868-013, March 3, 1973, RNL; Dreyfus interview for the 2000 BBC documentary *The Secret World of Richard Nixon.*

173 "That's not good": WHT 044-058, March 28, 1973, RNL.

173 The technical details: Alvin Snyder to Higby, "President's Oval Office Address," May 2, 1973, Higby Chron, Haldeman RNL-SMOF; WHT 044-085, March 29, 1973, RNL.

174 "Tricia told me": WHT 044-090, March 29, 1973, RNL.

175 "Fantastic, beautiful": WHT 044-088, March 29, 1973, RNL.

175 "A very strong speech": WHT 044-086, March 29, 1973, RNL.

175 "Scarcely anyone in the media": Nixon, *RN,* 812.

176 "an open war pissing match": WHT 044-080, March 29, 1973, RNL.

177 "John, you're in big trouble": Dean, *Blind Ambition,* 227–29; HJC TW II, 254.

178 "I'm an equestrian": Interviews with Shaffer and Glanzer, 1994 BBC documentary *Watergate.*

178 "everything he knows": Haldeman note, April 7, 1973, based on Dean telcon, Haldeman RNL-SMOF.

179 "I could smoke this guy out": Dean, *Blind Ambition,* 231–33.

180 "We can't have a situation": HRH diary, April 2, 1973, RNL.

180 "ultimate solution": WHT 044-080, March 29, 1973, RNL.

181 "he will unravel": HRH diary, April 2, 1973.

181 Nixon instructed Haldeman: HRH diary, April 5, 1973, RNL; Colson testimony to SSC, HJC TW III, 434.

181 Dean lulled Nixon: HRH diary, April 2, 1973.

182 "Dean feels we're at the moment": HRH diary, April 7, 1973, RNL.

182 "Just remember that once the toothpaste": Dean, *Blind Ambition,* 234.

182 "meeting with Mr. Dean": Silbert memo, "John Dean," April 11, 1973, Silbert Chron File, NA-WSPF.

183 "Liddy's been talking to us": Dean, *Blind Ambition,* 235–36.

183 The examiners had concluded: Christopher Lydon, "Colson Reported Passing a Lie Test on Watergate," *NYT,* April 8, 1973.

184 "Chuck's more than a match": WHT 044-103, April 8, 1973, RNL.

184 "You bastard": Dean, *Blind Ambition,* 237–38.

184 "His feeling is that Liddy": WHT 044-103, April 8, 1973, RNL.

185 "an invasion of privacy": William Doherty, "Washington's Wounded Knee," *WP,* April 9, 1973.

185 "You know, I was thinking": WHT 891-001, April 9, 1973, RNL; Dean, *Nixon Defense,* 364–66.

187 An alarm on the door: James Baker, interview by FBI, January 21, 1974, NA-WSPF.

187 "months and months": Nixon, *RN,* 900; George Lardner Jr., "Nixon to Get Day in Court on Tapes Compensation," *WP,* March 29, 1998.

188 "That's the honest": WHT 891-001; Kutler, *Abuse of Power,* 292.

188 "We had a long discussion": HRH diary, April 9, 1973, RNL; WHT 425-044, April 9, 1973, RNL.

188 "We survived": WHT 891-007, April 9, 1973, RNL; Brinkley and Nichter, *Nixon Tapes: 1973,* 400–403.

189 "A lot of fun": WHT 044-141, April 10, 1973, RNL; PDD, April 9, 1973.

189 "I hope we have tapes": Nixon, *RN,* 900.

189 "keep the damn machine": WHT 900-004, April 18, 1973, RNL. Nixon instructed Haldeman to review the tapes as "a service" to his future library.

190 "That's enough, John": Dean, *Blind Ambition,* 239–41.

192 "Forget about the easel": Magruder, *American Life,* 289, 292–93.

193 "a position of weakness": Silbert memo, "Negotiations Concerning Jeb Magruder," April 16, 1973, Silbert Chron File, NA-WSPF.

193 "whose interests I'd ignored": Magruder, *American Life,* 294.

193 "Bullshit": Transcript of Magruder-Higby conversation, April 13, 1973, HJC SI IV-2, 612–55.

194 "truthful, candid, and cooperative": Silbert memo, April 16, 1973; Magruder, *American Life,* 295.

195 "fall apart": Nixon, *RN,* 819.

195 "The damnable part": WHT 044-158, April 12, 1972, RNL; WSPF transcript, RNL.

195 "I've really got to tend": WHT 038-012, April 13, 1973, RNL; Kutler, *Abuse of Power,* 311–14.

196 "Once Hunt goes on": WHT 428-019, April 14, 1973, RNL; WSPF transcript, RNL.

199 "I won't even comment": WHT 428-019. According to Ehrlichman, Dean relayed the suggestion shortly after midnight on April 14, contradicting Dean's later account in *Blind Ambition* (248–49).

200 He placed asterisks: SSC exhibit no. 34–37, reprinted in HJC SI IV-2, 701.

200 "a gunslinger practicing": Dean, *Blind Ambition,* 249–52; Dean testimony, HJC SI IV-2, 699–702. Dean later remembered meeting with Ehrlichman and Halde- man *after* Ehrlichman had met with Mitchell. However, Ehrlichman's contem- poraneous diary shows that the Ehrlichman-Haldeman-Dean meeting began at 12:15 p.m., preceding the Ehrlichman-Mitchell meeting, which ran from 1:40 to 2:10 p.m.

201 "You drive across": HJC SI II, 416–18; Emery, *Watergate,* 197; Lukas, *Nightmare,* 226–28.

202 "I'm going to plead": Haldeman-Magruder telephone call, April 14, 1973, HJC SI IV-2, 707–15; Magruder, *American Life,* 296–97.

202 The change in seating: Mitchell testimony, HJC SI IV-2, 722–23.

203 "a very, very bad": WHT 896-005, April 14, 1973, RNL; WSPF transcript, RNL.

203 "Obviously you're in a situation": Transcript of Mitchell-Ehrlichman meeting, April 14, 1973, HJC SI IV-2, 725–68.

205 "I think everybody": UPI, "Mitchell Expects Nixon Aides to Talk to Watergate Panel," *NYT,* April 15, 1973.

205 "Who would have thought": Safire, *Before the Fall,* 635.

206 The garden tour: Anthony Ripley, "Nixons Lead White House Garden Tour," *NYT,* April 15, 1973; AP, "11,474 Stream in to See White House Gardens," *NYT,* April 16, 1973; Eisenhower, *Pat Nixon,* 390–91; Sidey, *White House Remembered,* 43; Bob Bostock, "The White House Garden Tours," White House Historical Association, April 9, 2019.

206 "All finished?": WHT 896-005.

207 "They're still piling through": WHT 038-029, April 14, 1973, RNL.

208 "Hi, General": WHT 038-031, April 14, 1973, RNL.

208 He did not plan: HRH Action Memo, "Master Schedule," January 4, 1973, Tapes, memos, and notes, Haldeman RNL-SMOF.

209 "I'd hoped to be home": President's Speech file, RNL-PPF.

209 "It's too bad": Nixon, *RN,* 822.

210 "Others have the good intentions": AP, "Nixon Says America Must Build Peace," *NYT,* April 15, 1973; Emery, *Watergate,* 316.

210 "It's not a bad line": WHT 038-034, April 14, 1973, RNL. Nixon had attributed the quotation to the conservative publisher David Lawrence, who died in February. "He never told me that, but I knew he felt that," he told Haldeman.

210 "It's a little melodramatic": Conversation 038-037, April 14, 1973, WHT.

210 "What do you think": WHT 038-039, April 15, 1973, RNL.

ACT III: CATASTROPHE

215 "good men who would keep": Liddy, *Will,* 251–53; Kleindienst, *Justice,* 145–46.

216 Over the next four hours: HJC SI IV-2, 868; Kleindienst, *Justice,* 160–61.

216 It occurred to Silbert: Silbert OH, March 7, 1992, Historical Society for the D.C. Circuit; Kleindienst testimony, HJC SI IV-2, 869.

218 This explanation made little sense: WHT 038-048, April 15, 1973, RNL; Kutler, *Abuse of Power,* 315–16; Brinkley and Nichter, *Nixon Tapes: 1973,* 475–76.

218 "choked periodically": Nixon, *RN,* 826; Kleindienst, *Justice,* 162.

218 "The point is, Dick": WHT 428-036, April 15, 1973, RNL; HJC SRPC, 696–746.

219 "to make Dean so valuable": Silbert OH, March 7, 1992.

219 "We don't have any choice": Dean, *Blind Ambition,* 253.

220 "I'm tired of hearing": Ibid., 256–57.

220 If there was evidence: Silbert memo, April 16, 1973, HJC SI IV-2, 1016.

221 "Hope you're enjoying": WHT 038-043, April 15, 1973, RNL.

221 "Petersen is a soldier": WHT 886-008, March 21, 1973, RNL.

221 Nixon would later claim: Approximately six hours of conversation are missing.

While Watergate prosecutors were suspicious of the official White House explanation, they were unable to prove malfeasance. In his book *The Nixon Defense* (pages 412–13, 698), John Dean speculates that Haldeman had both the motive and opportunity to destroy the "missing" tape.

222   "I can't fire men": Nixon, *RN,* 827.

222   The president and his friend: PDD, April 15, 1973; Staff Secretary Memoranda Files—*Sequoia,* RNL-SMOF.

222   "How much money": Nixon, *RN,* 827.

224   "Petersen wants you both": Haldeman, *Ends of Power,* 258–59.

224   That very week: Peter Haldeman, "Growing Up a Haldeman," *NYT Magazine,* April 3, 1994.

225   "I hope you understand": WHT 038-053, April 15, 1973, RNL. Recording devices attached to phones were operating normally; they were on a different system from the microphones in EOB 175.

225   Dean arrived at 9:17 p.m.: PDD, April 15, 1973.

225   "His usually neatly creased": Dean, *Blind Ambition,* 258. Dean adds that he noticed a "smell of liquor" on the president's breath during this meeting. I have omitted this detail because there is no evidence—for example, slurring of words— from Nixon's recorded telephone conversations on the evening of April 15 that he had been drinking excessively.

225   "an asp at your bosom": WHT 898-012, April 17, 1973, RNL; WSPF transcript, RNL; Brinkley and Nichter, *Nixon Tapes: 1973,* 511–32.

226   "I guess it was foolish": Dean, *Blind Ambition,* 260–63. See also Dean testimony, SSC 3, 1016–17; HRH diary, April 15, 1973; Nixon, *RN,* 828.

227   After his evening session: Ehrlichman, *Witness to Power,* 382.

228   An early riser: Gray testimony, HJC SI IV-2, 1073–74.

228   "He'd better deny that": WHT 038-060, April 15, 1973, RNL; Kutler, *Abuse of Power,* 318–19; Gray, *In Nixon's Web,* 138–39.

229   "It was done": Haldeman, *Ends of Power,* 260; Nixon, *RN,* 829.

230   "Ziegler has just left": WHT 897-003, April 16, 1973, RNL.

231   One letter offered: SSC exhibit no. 34–49, reprinted in HJC SI IV-3, 1146–47.

231   "Are we talking Dean": WHT 897-004, April 16, 1973, RNL; WSPF transcript, RNL; Brinkley and Nichter, *Nixon Tapes: 1973,* 486–507.

232   "The voices canceled": Dean, *Blind Ambition,* 264–67.

233   "Remember you had": WHT, 897-009, April 16, 1973, RNL; WSPF transcript, RNL.

234   "at the Liddy level": WHT 747-014, July 19, 1972, RNL; Dean, *Nixon Defense,* 105–7.

234   "Always come here in the afternoons": WHT 427-002, April 16, 1973, RNL; HJC SRPC, 842.

235   "You know I am": WHT 038-064, April 15, 1973, RNL; HJC SRPC, 773; WHT 427-002, April 16, 1973, RNL; HJC SRPC, 847.

235 "Here I was recommending": Petersen testimony, SSC 9, 3628; see also Lukas, *Nightmare*, 323.

236 "The president too?": WHT 427-002, April 16, 1973, RNL; HJC SRPC, 879–87.

237 "Dear Mr. President": WHT 427-010, April 16, 1973, RNL; WSPF transcript, RNL; Dean, *Nixon Defense*, 426–27.

237 "very cute": WHT 898-012, April 17, 1973, RNL.

238 "sacrificial lambs": Robert L. Jackson and Ronald J. Ostrow, "White House Likely to Admit Some Watergate Responsibility," *LAT*, April 17, 1973.

238 "I think we have to move": WHT 898-006, April 17, 1973, RNL; WSPF transcript, RNL; Brinkley and Nichter, *Nixon Tapes: 1973*, 507–11.

239 "two most valuable": WHT 898-012.

239 "very gingerly": Nixon, *RN*, 833.

239 "There's no sense": HRH diary, April 17, 1973, RNL.

240 "I was selfish": Nixon, *RN*, 832; Kutler, *Wars of Watergate*, 306.

240 "Maybe I've trapped": HRH diary, April 17, 1973.

240 "One of the first things": WHT 898-012.

242 But the key factor: Nixon, *RN*, 831.

242 "He's out getting": Bernstein and Woodward, *All the President's Men*, 290.

243 "the lobby of a fake": Don Oberdorfer, "Plushier Place for White House Press," *WP*, April 3, 1970; Robert Semple, "For White House Press, Currier & Ives with Muzak," *NYT*, April 3, 1970.

245 "operative statement": Transcript, News conference no. 1719, April 17, 1973, RNL.

245 "Ziegler was down": Nick Thimmesch, "The Ron Ziegler Behind Ron Ziegler," *WP*, February 24, 1974.

246 "I have no intention": WHT 429-003, April 17, 1973, RNL; WSPF transcript, RNL; HRH diary, April 17, 1973.

246 "last normal dinner": Kissinger, *Years of Upheaval*, 90.

247 "Did you stay": WHT 038-092, April 17, 1973, RNL; Kutler, *Abuse of Power*, 320–24.

248 "about to blow up": Kissinger, *Years of Upheaval*, 75–76.

249 "The president is kidding himself": Ibid., 90–92.

251 "try to see if": WHT 900-026.

252 "charging around the White House": Nixon, *RN*, 831; HRH diary, April 18, 1973, RNL.

252 "That simply isn't so": Petersen testimony, HJC SI IV-3, 1476.

253 "I know about that": Ehrlichman, *Witness to Power*, 405–6.

253 "rather painful": HRH diary, April 18–19, 1973, RNL.

254 "I guarantee you": Dean, *Blind Ambition*, 269.

254 The article was splashed: Bob Woodward and Carl Bernstein, "Mitchell, Dean Approved Watergate, Payoffs, Magruder Reportedly Says," *WP*, April 19, 1973.

255 "Some may hope": Bob Bernstein and Carl Woodward, "Dean Vows He Won't Be Scapegoat," *WP*, April 20, 1973.

255 "Hi, John": WHT 038-107, April 19, 1973, RNL.

256 "a detailed chronology": Dean, *Blind Ambition,* 268; see also Dean to John Nesbitt, April 19, 1973, Tapes, memos, and notes, Haldeman RNL-SMOF; Silbert memos, April 24–25, 1973, Silbert Chron file, NA-WSPF.

256 "alone but confident": Christopher Lydon, "Key Figures in Watergate Are Silent or Unavailable," *NYT,* April 19, 1973.

256 "but that doesn't mean": Bernstein and Woodward, *All the President's Men,* 296.

256 "Oh fuck": WHT 038-126, April 19, 1973, RNL; Brinkley and Nichter, *Nixon Tapes: 1973,* 565–73.

257 "His lawyer probably?": WHT 038-126.

258 "withdrawing into his own world": Eisenhower, *Pat Nixon,* 366–67; Safire, *Before the Fall,* 626–27.

258 "We love you": Nixon, *RN,* 838.

259 "Mother's trying so hard": Eisenhower, *Pat Nixon,* 367.

260 "The easiest period": Nixon, *Six Crises,* xv–xvi.

260 "Once you learn": Ken Clawson, "A Loyalist's Memoir," *WP,* August 9, 1979.

261 "twisted with relish": RN, interview with David Frost, May 4, 1977; see *NYT,* May 5, 1977, for transcript.

262 "We have used up": Buchanan to RN, April 20, 1973, cited in Buchanan, *Nixon's White House Wars,* 313–14.

262 "Under unrelenting pressure": David Broder, "Watergate: A Crisis of Authority for President Nixon," *WP,* April 22, 1973.

263 "I believe you completely": Nixon, *RN,* 837.

263 "Good morning, John": Ibid., 837–38; Dean, *Blind Ambition,* 271–73.

263 "Just remember": HRH diary, April 22, 1973, RNL.

264 "Is the president honest?": Nixon, *RN,* 838; Lou Cannon, "Nixon Hears an Easter Admonition," *WP,* April 23, 1973.

265 "He had to bust": Robert J. Cole, "The Aerosol World of Robert Abplanalp," *NYT,* August 12, 1973. For background on Abplanalp and Grand Cay, see Robert G. Hummerstone, "The President's 'Other Friend,'" *Life,* March 5, 1971. For Nixon's stays on Grand Cay, see PDD. Most trips were overnight, but some lasted two or three days.

266 "That's where Nixon likes": Washington Star-News, "Abplanalp Says He Has Spent $1 Million to Make His Island Secure for President," *NYT,* August 14, 1973.

268 "Get out in front": Buchanan, *Nixon's White House Wars,* 314–15.

269 "The first essential": Nixon, *RN,* 839.

269 "There's no way": HRH diary, April 23, 1973, RNL. I have made minor changes of punctuation and grammar for clarity.

270 "This would be the first": Nixon, *RN,* 840.

270 "to win by the biggest": Kissinger, *Years of Upheaval,* 1186–87.

270 "If Garment was right": Ibid., 76.

271 "Everything you predicted": HAK-Garment telcon, April 21, 1973, DNSA.

271 "goddamn domestic situation": HAK-RN telcon, April 21, 1973, DNSA.

271 "I don't see how": HAK-Haig telcon, April 23, 1973, DNSA.

271 "a vehicle careening": Kissinger, *Years of Upheaval*, 96–100.

273 "Let's just see": WHT 904-006, April 25, 1973, RNL; Dean, *Nixon Defense*, 485.

273 "If the patient survives": HRH diary, April 25, 1973, RNL.

274 "Let me just spin": WHT 430-004, April 25, 1973; RNL; WSPF transcript, RNL; Brinkley and Nichter, *Nixon Tapes: 1973*, 591–638; Dean, *Nixon Defense*, 489–95.

274 He assumed that Nixon: Ehrlichman, *Witness to Power*, 344.

276 "We can't have another": WHT 430-016, April 25, 1973, RNL; Kutler, *Abuse of Power*, 330–34; Dean, *Nixon Defense*, 496; Nixon, *RN*, 842; Kleindienst, *Justice*, 164–66.

276 "Have them put it in": WHT 038-141, April 25, 1973, RNL.

276 Instead of returning: HRH OH, August 13, 1987, RNL; Raymond Zumwalt, interview by FBI, January 24, 1974, NA-WSPF; HJC SI IV-3, 1571; HJC SI IX-1, 109–24.

278 "Well, that's hard work": WHT 430-022, April 25, 1973, RNL; WSPF transcript, RNL.

278 "like a drowning man": Haldeman, *Ends of Power*, 272; for copy of HRH notes, see HJC SI IV-3, 1575–605.

279 "Is there any way": WHT 038-157, April 25, 1973, RNL; WSPF transcript, RNL; Haldeman, *Ends of Power*, 275–81; PDD, April 25, 1973.

281 "Gray Says He": Walter Rugaber, "Gray Says He Destroyed Files from Hunt Given Him as He Met Ehrlichman and Dean," *NYT*, April 27, 1973; Bernstein and Woodward, *All the President's Men*, 306–7.

282 "It's obvious the president": HRH diary, April 27, 1973, RNL.

282 "filled with shame": Gray, *In Nixon's Web*, 244; PDD, April 27, 1973; Haldeman, *Ends of Power*, 285; Kutler, *Abuse of Power*, 345.

283 "I could end": Ehrlichman, *Witness to Power*, 389.

283 "You do not panic": Adam Clymer, "Flood Aid Is Widened by Nixon," *Baltimore Sun*, April 28, 1973; Nixon, *RN*, 844.

284 "I don't want him": WHT 045-034, April 27, 1973, RNL.

285 "at a date unspecified": Silbert memo, HJC SI IV-2, 1016. For Ellsberg trial transcript and exhibits, see HJC SI VII-4, 1930, 1996–2008.

285 "Are you kidding?": Ellsberg OH, May 20, 2008, RNL.

286 "The message of the Watergate": Sanford J. Unger, "Conspirators Said to Burglarize Ellsberg Analyst, Trial Told," *WP*, April 28, 1973.

286 "When the president does it": RN, interview with Frost, May 19, 1977.

287 "the Ellsberg thing": HRH diary, April 26, 1973, RNL.

287 "the FBI pyramid": Felt, *FBI Pyramid from the Inside*, 295.

287 "Just pray to God": WHT 906-012, April 27, 1973, RNL; Dean, *Nixon Defense*, 516–17.

288 "implicated the president": WHT 906-016, April 27, 1973, RNL; Dean, *Nixon Defense*, 519.

288 "You heard anything": WHT 906-017, April 27, 1973, RNL; Dean, *Nixon Defense*, 519–24.

288 "That shows you": WHT 906-023, April 27, 1973, RNL.

289 "to avoid at all costs": WHT 906-024, April 27, 1973, RNL; Dean, *Nixon Defense*, 525–26.

290 "he better save his own ass": WHT 432-001, April 27, 1973, RNL; Kutler, *Abuse of Power*, 349–52; Dean, *Nixon Defense*, 526–27.

292 "What time did you go": WHT 164-002, April 28, 1973, RNL.

293 "That is our opinion": Nixon, *RN*, 845–46; Eisenhower, *Pat Nixon*, 367–68.

293 "Have you ever heard": WHT 164-021, April 28, 1973, RNL; Kutler, *Abuse of Power*, 368–72.

294 "kind of a tiger": WHT 534-005, July 1, 1971, RNL; Kutler, *Abuse of Power*, 13–14.

295 "He implied that I was": Nixon, *RN*, 846.

296 The latest opinion poll: Louis Harris, "Nixon Credibility, Popularity Drop as Watergate Presses," *WP*, April 29, 1973.

296 "He's sort of Mr. Integrity": WHT 164-048, April 30, 1973, RNL; Kutler, *Abuse of Power*, 379–80; Ambrose, *Ruin and Recovery*, 134.

296 "to get the most mean": WHT 164-028, April 29, 1973, RNL.

297 "Men get shaken": WHT 164-032, April 29, 1973, RNL.

297 "I hope Ehrlichman": Haldeman, *Ends of Power*, 287–88; HRH diary, April 29, 1973, RNL.

297 "What the hell do you do": WHT 164-039, April 29, 1973, RNL.

298 "It's resignation, John": Haldeman, *Ends of Power*, 289–92; HRH diary, April 29, 1973; Ehrlichman, *Witness to Power*, 386, 389.

298 "He's deadly serious": HRH diary, April 29, 1973; Haldeman, *Ends of Power*, 292–94; Nixon, *RN*, 847–48; PDD, April 29, 1973. The meetings with Haldeman and Ehrlichman were not recorded. While there are some minor discrepancies between these accounts, they agree on the essential details. In resolving the discrepancies, I have given greater weight to the contemporaneous materials, for example, the extremely detailed Haldeman diary, which he dictated every night, over the later memoir accounts.

300 "His eyes were red-rimmed": Ehrlichman, *Witness to Power*, 390.

301 "Whereas the early deaths": Garment, *Crazy Rhythm*, 260. Although Garment writes that he met with Nixon in the morning, the PDD shows that they met in the late afternoon, *after* the meetings with Haldeman and Ehrlichman.

301 "It's all over, Ron": Nixon, *RN*, 848.

302 The amputation of his two arms: Ibid., 824, 849.

302 "I had a very hard day": WHT 164-040, April 30, 1973, RNL.

304 "Which might not be a bad idea": WHT 164-048.

304 "If you think I should resign": Price, *With Nixon*, 100–103.

305 He left the Oval Office: Memo to Ron Ziegler, April 30, 1973, Ziegler RNL-SMOF; "Nixon Asks Press for 'Hell' When Wrong," *NYT*, May 1, 1973;

Carroll Kilpatrick, "Nixon Pledges No Whitewash on Watergate," *WP*, May 1, 1973; Ziegler interview for 2000 BBC documentary *The Secret World of Richard Nixon.*

306   "I hope I didn't": WHT 045-041, April 30, 1973, RNL; Kutler, *Abuse of Power,* 381–82.

307   "Don't cut anyone off": WHT 045-045/046/051/065/070, April 30, 1973, RNL; Eisenhower, *Pat Nixon,* 369.

307   "How did you ever get to marry": WHT 045-053, April 30, 1973, RNL.

307   "Do your job, boy": WHT 045-048, April 30, 1973, RNL.

307   "Who the hell are you?": WHT 908-024, May 1, 1973, RNL; Haldeman, *Ends of Power,* 296; Dean, *Nixon Defense,* 543–44; Higby to HRH, "Rough Notes from Cabinet Meeting," May 1, 1973, Higby Chron, Haldeman RNL-SMOF.

ACT IV: CATHARSIS

311   "I am hurt": Nixon, *RN,* 858.

311   "A very dull show": WHT 046-098, May 17, 1973, RNL; Kutler, *Abuse of Power,* 523–24.

312   "may have gone beyond": Cross and Witt, *Watergate,* 79–81.

313   The Nixons opened: "Their Cheers, Their Tears, Their Day," *WP,* May 25, 1973.

314   "the words could be heard": Nixon, *RN,* 865–67; ABC News coverage of dinner.

315   "My father seemed drained": Eisenhower, *Pat Nixon,* 371–73; Nixon, *RN,* 867–69.

315   "It'll be a fight": WHT 039-016, May 25, 1973, RNL; Kutler, *Abuse of Power,* 553–57.

317   "I've got to listen": WHT 039-057, June 4, 1973, RNL.

317   "Get lost, Steve": WHT 442-001, June 4, 1973, RNL; WSPF transcript, RNL; Woodward and Bernstein, *Final Days,* 44.

317   "Sounds drifted in and out": Nixon, *RN,* 874–75.

318   "Working my butt off here": WHT 442-049, June 4, 1973, RNL; WSPF transcript, RNL.

319   "I've just spent nine hours": WHT 039-079, June 4, 1973, RNL.

319   "Got a minute?": WHT 039-081, June 4, 1973, RNL; WSPF transcript, RNL; Brinkley and Nichter, *Nixon Tapes: 1973,* 744–52; Haldeman, *Ends of Power,* 303.

320   "This is like something": Dean, *Blind Ambition,* 276.

321   "looked happier": Dean, *Blind Ambition,* 284-5.

321   "Did you know": Dash, *Chief Counsel,* 148–49; Dean, *Blind Ambition,* 301.

322   The committee requested: Dash, *Chief Counsel,* 161–62.

323   "Exhibit number one": Interview with Shaffer, 1994 BBC documentary *Watergate;* Dean, *Blind Ambition,* 304-5.

323   "made personal use of funds": Seymour M. Hersh, "Dean Said to Keep $14,000 Fund," *NYT,* June 19, 1973.

323 "I began by telling": Dean testimony, SSC 3, 995, 998. The "how much would it cost" exchange took place on March 21, not March 13, as stated by Dean. This is one of several errors in Dean's reconstruction of events, relying on his sometimes faulty memory.

323 "a more complete": Cross and Witt, *Watergate*, 162–63.

325 "God, if they only knew": Woodward, *Last of the President's Men*, 148.

326 "Where did you get this?": Scott Armstrong, "Friday the Thirteenth," *Journal of American History* (March 1989), 1234–44; Woodward and Bernstein, *Final Days*, 54–57; Woodward, *Last of the President's Men*, 153–56.

327 "I hoped you fellows": Donald Sanders, "Watergate Reminiscences," *Journal of American History* (March 1989), 1228–33; Alexander Butterfield, interview by David Thelen, *Journal of American History* (March 1989), 1245–62.

327 "Wonders of Watergate": William Greider, "Wonders of Watergate," *WP*, July 17, 1973.

329 "seemed almost delirious": Eisenhower, *Pat Nixon*, 380; PDD, July 16, 1973; Nixon, *RN*, 899.

330 "You have two options": Haig, *Inner Circles*, 374–75. Some details in Haig's ghost-written account, particularly on timing, conflict with the PDD. In such cases, I have relied on the PDD, a near-contemporaneous record of Nixon's meetings, supplemented by the original diary source materials in RNL-SMOF.

330 The president's legal counsel: Garment, *Crazy Rhythm*, 281–82; Nixon, *RN*, 901.

331 "I can't do that": Haig OH, November 30, 2007, RNL; Haig, *Inner Circles*, 380.

331 "We've got total control": HRH OH, August 13, 1987, RNL; Nixon, *RN*, 901.

332 "an indelible impression of guilt": Nixon, *RN*, 902–3.

332 "Al, I've thought about this": Haig, *Inner Circles*, 379; Haig OH. In *Inner Circles*, Haig suggests that this conversation took place on July 17, but the PDD, combined with his later oral history, indicates July 18.

332 "Should have destroyed the tapes": Nixon, *RN*, 901; Archibald Cox to Fred Buzhardt, July 18, 1973, HJC SI IX-1, 390–92.

333 "Defeat-doesn't finish a man": Safire, *Before the Fall*, 154–55.

SELECTED BIBLIOGRAPHY

Aitken, Jonathan. *Charles W. Colson: A Life Redeemed*. New York: Doubleday, 2005.

Ambrose, Stephen E. *The Education of a Politician*. Vol. 1 of *Nixon*. New York: Simon & Schuster, 1987.

———. *Ruin and Recovery, 1973–1990*. Vol. 3 of *Nixon*. New York: Simon & Schuster, 1991.

———. *The Triumph of a Politician, 1962–1972*. Vol. 2 of *Nixon*. New York: Simon & Schuster, 1989.

Bernstein, Carl, and Bob Woodward. *All the President's Men*. New York: Simon & Schuster, 1974.

Brinkley, Douglas, and Luke Nichter. *The Nixon Tapes*. Boston: Houghton, Mifflin, Harcourt, 2014.

———. *The Nixon Tapes: 1973*. Boston: Houghton, Mifflin, Harcourt, 2015.

Buchanan, Patrick J. *Nixon's White House Wars: The Battles That Made and Broke a President and Divided America Forever*. New York: Crown, 2017.

Colson, Charles W. *Born Again*. Old Tappan, N.J.: Chosen Books, 1976.

Cross, Mercer, and Elder Witt, eds. *Watergate: Chronology of a Crisis*. Washington, D.C.: Congressional Quarterly, 1975.

Crowley, Monica. *Nixon in Winter: Off the Record Reflections on the State of the World, the Scandals of Washington, and Life in and out of the Political Arena*. New York: Random House, 1998.

Dallek, Robert. *Nixon and Kissinger: Partners in Power*. New York: HarperCollins, 2007.

Dash, Samuel. *Chief Counsel: Inside the Ervin Committee: The Untold Story of Watergate*. New York: Random House, 1976.

Dean, John W. *Blind Ambition: The White House Years*. New York: Simon & Schuster, 1976.

———. *The Nixon Defense: What He Knew and When He Knew It*. New York: Viking, 2014.

Ehrlichman, John. *Witness to Power: The Nixon Years*. New York: Simon & Schuster, 1982.

Eisenhower, Julie Nixon. *Pat Nixon: The Untold Story*. New York: Simon & Schuster, 1986.

Emery, Fred. *Watergate: The Corruption of American Politics and the Fall of Richard Nixon.* New York: Touchstone, 1995.

Farrell, John A. *Richard Nixon: The Life.* New York: Doubleday, 2017.

Felt, W. Mark. *The FBI Pyramid from the Inside.* New York: Putnam, 1979.

Felt, W. Mark, and John O'Connor. *A G-Man's Life: The FBI, Being "Deep Throat," and the Struggle for Honor in Washington.* New York: Public Affairs, 2006.

Garment, Leonard. *Crazy Rhythm: My Journey from Brooklyn, Jazz, and Wall Street to Nixon's White House, Watergate, and Beyond.* Cambridge, Mass.: Da Capo Press, 2001.

Garza, Hedda. *The Watergate Investigation Index: House Judiciary Committee Hearings and Report on Impeachment.* Wilmington, Del.: Scholarly Resources, 1985.

———. *The Watergate Investigation Index: Senate Select Committee Hearings and Reports on Presidential Campaign Activities.* Wilmington, Del.: Scholarly Resources, 1982.

Gellman, Irwin F. *The President and the Apprentice: Eisenhower and Nixon, 1952–1961.* New Haven, Conn.: Yale University Press, 2015.

Gentry, Curt. *J. Edgar Hoover: The Man and the Secrets.* New York: Plume, 1992.

Gray, L. Patrick, III. *In Nixon's Web: A Year in the Crosshairs of Watergate.* New York: Times Books, 2008.

Haig, Alexander M. *Inner Circles: How America Changed the World: A Memoir.* New York: Warner Books, 1992.

Haldeman, H. R. *The Ends of Power.* New York: Times Books, 1978.

———. *The Haldeman Diaries: Inside the Nixon White House.* New York: Putnam, 1994.

Holland, Max. *Leak: Why Mark Felt Became Deep Throat.* Lawrence: University Press of Kansas, 2012.

Horne, Alistair. *Kissinger: 1973, the Crucial Year.* New York: Simon & Schuster, 2009.

Hughes, Ken. *Chasing Shadows: The Nixon Tapes, the Chennault Affair, and the Origins of Watergate.* Charlottesville: The University of Virginia Press, 2014.

Hughes, Ken. *Fatal Politics: The Nixon Tapes, the Vietnam War, and the Casualties of Reelection.* Charlottesville: The University of Virginia Press, 2015.

Hunt, E. Howard. *American Spy: My Secret History in the CIA, Watergate, and Beyond.* Hoboken, N.J.: John Wiley & Sons, 2007.

———. *The Berlin Ending: A Novel of Discovery.* New York: Putnam, 1973.

Isaacson, Walter. *Kissinger: A Biography.* New York: Simon & Schuster, 1992.

Kissinger, Henry. *White House Years.* Boston: Little, Brown, 1979.

———. *Years of Upheaval.* Boston: Little, Brown, 1982.

Kleindienst, Richard G. *Justice: The Memoirs of Attorney General Richard Kleindienst.* Ottawa, Ill.: Jameson Books, 1985.

Kutler, Stanley I. *Abuse of Power: The New Nixon Tapes.* New York: Touchstone, 1998.

———. *The Wars of Watergate: The Last Crisis of Richard Nixon.* New York: Alfred A. Knopf, 1990.

Liddy, G. Gordon. *Will: The Autobiography of G. Gordon Liddy.* New York: St. Martin's Press, 1996.

Lukas, J. Anthony. *Nightmare: The Underside of the Nixon Years.* New York: Viking Press, 1976.

Magruder, Jeb Stuart. *An American Life: One Man's Road to Watergate.* New York: Atheneum, 1974.

McCord, James W. *A Piece of Tape: The Watergate Story: Fact and Fiction.* Rockville, Md.: Washington Media Services, 1974.

Morris, Roger. *Richard Milhous Nixon: The Rise of an American Politician.* New York: Holt, 1990.

Nixon, Richard M. *RN: The Memoirs of Richard Nixon.* New York: Grosset & Dunlap, 1978.

———. *Six Crises.* Garden City, N.Y.: Doubleday, 1962.

Perlstein, Rick. *Nixonland: The Rise of a President and the Fracturing of America.* New York: Scribner, 2008.

Phillips-Schrock, Patrick. *The Nixon White House Redecoration and Acquisition Program: An Illustrated History.* Jefferson, N.C.: McFarland, 2016.

Price, Raymond. *With Nixon.* New York: Viking Press, 1977.

Reeves, Richard. *President Nixon: Alone in the White House.* New York: Simon & Schuster, 2001.

Robenalt, James D. *January 1973: Watergate, Roe v. Wade, Vietnam, and the Month That Changed America Forever.* Chicago: Chicago Review Press, 2017.

Rodota, Joseph. *The Watergate: Inside America's Most Infamous Address.* New York: William Morrow, 2018.

Rosen, James. *The Strong Man: John Mitchell and the Secrets of Watergate.* New York: Doubleday, 2008.

Safire, William. *Before the Fall: An Inside View of the Pre-Watergate White House.* Garden City, N.Y.: Doubleday, 1975.

Sidey, Hugh, ed. *The White House Remembered.* Washington, D.C.: White House Historical Association, 2005.

Sirica, John J. *To Set the Record Straight: The Break-In, the Tapes, the Conspirators, the Pardon.* New York: Norton, 1979.

Strober, Deborah H., and Gerald S. Strober. *The Nixon Presidency: An Oral History of the Era.* Washington, D.C.: Brassey's, 2003.

Thomas, Evan. *Being Nixon: A Man Divided.* New York: Random House, 2015.

White, Theodore H. *Breach of Faith: The Fall of Richard Nixon.* New York: Dell, 1978.

———. *In Search of History: A Personal Adventure.* New York: Harper & Row, 1978.

———. *The Making of the President, 1972.* New York: Atheneum, 1973.

Wills, Garry. *Nixon Agonistes: The Crisis of the Self-Made Man.* Boston: Houghton Mifflin, 1970.

Woodward, Bob. *The Last of the President's Men.* New York: Simon & Schuster, 2015.

———. *The Secret Man: The Story of Watergate's Deep Throat.* New York: Simon & Schuster, 2005.

Woodward, Bob, and Carl Bernstein. *The Final Days.* New York: Simon & Schuster, 1976.

INDEX

ILLUSTRATION CREDITS

A NOTE ON THE TYPE

This book was set in Minion, a typeface produced by the Adobe Corporation specifically for the Macintosh personal computer, and released in 1990. Designed by Robert Slimbach, Minion combines the classic characteristics of old-style faces with the full complement of weights required for modern typesetting.

Composed by North Market Street Graphics, Lancaster, Pennsylvania
Printed and bound by Berryville Graphics, Berryville, Virginia
Designed by Maggie Hinders